Allen Construction Company
1302 Lovers Lane   P O. Box 716
Bowling Green, Ky. 42101

How to Sell Your Home
without a Real Estate Broker

CARL J. KOSNAR
President, Realcor, Ltd., Chicago, Illinois

McGRAW-HILL BOOK COMPANY

*New York   St. Louis   San Francisco   Auckland   Düsseldorf
Johannesburg   Kuala Lumpur   London   Mexico   Montreal
New Delhi   Panama   Paris   São Paulo
Singapore   Sydney   Toronto   Tokyo*

Library of Congress Cataloging in Publication Data

Kosnar, Carl J   1938-
    How to sell your home without a real estate broker.

    Includes index.
    1. House selling. I. Title.
HD1379.K67   658.89'3333'3   74-28033
ISBN 0-07-035364-6

1234567890 BPBP 7987655

*The editors for this book were W. Hodson Mogan and Patricia A. Allen,
the designer was Naomi Auerbach, and the production supervisor was
Teresa F. Leaden. It was set in Times Roman by John C. Meyer & Son, Inc.*

It was printed and bound by The Book Press.

Contents

iv

To Andi

Preface

There is nothing wrong with expecting to earn a nice profit on the sale of your real estate. However, do not make the mistake of thinking that the inherent value of any property is increased simply because you are the owner. You make a similar error if you feel that you are assured of a high degree of sales success just because you are the seller. Selling real estate is akin to merchandising any other product—it takes imagination and a creative selling program.

Promoting the sale of your own real estate is what this book is all about. I am offering you a comprehensive sales promotion plan, guaranteed to find a buyer for your property quickly and at the highest possible price!

Read the following pages carefully and learn how to reap the benefits of selling a single-family detached house, a condominium, a cooperative, vacant land, or any kind of real estate you might own. This book is unique in that it is directed toward the real estate owner.

Carl J. Kosnar

Introduction

This book fills a gap in real estate literature. Numerous books have been written on the subject of "how to become wealthy in real estate." Most use sophisticated formulas for pyramiding equity and employ perilous financing techniques. Even more volumes have been printed for real estate brokers, giving them infinitely detailed instructions in how to convince a seller that a broker's services are indispensable.

How to Sell Your Home without a Real Estate Broker is the only book that gives you, the prospective real estate seller, a thorough, step-by-step guide to the basic fundamentals of real estate sales. The book is based on my actual experiences.

Obviously, many people have sold their own homes or other real estate without the benefit of this book. But surely it does not make any sense for you to learn the hard way, by trial and error, making unnecessary mistakes. A much better approach is to learn the principles presented in this book so that you will be able to plan your strategy before you put your home up for sale.

Since you have already decided to take the first step, here is what this book will do for you:

1. *Allow you to pocket the real estate commission.* The median sales price of an existing home in the United States now exceeds $27,000, and the commission charged the seller is usually 6 to 7 percent of the sales price. The commission paid by the seller on vacant land is usually 10 percent. So, using some simple arithmetic, you can see that the median-price home of $27,000, when sold at a 6 percent sales commission, costs the seller a $1,620 sales fee. The farmer or owner of vacant land who sells, let us say, 200 acres at a price of $1,000 per acre through a broker will pay a $20,000 sales fee. Today it is not uncommon to be confronted by a broker with a minimum sales fee. Many real estate brokerage houses word their listing agreements, which are the written contracts giving the broker the right to sell an owner's property for a certain price, so as to specify that the minimum commission paid by the seller, regardless of selling price, is $1,000.

2. *Help you obtain a higher sales price than you would if you worked through a broker.* Standard practice in most real estate offices is to get the seller to agree to a low price; then the property is considered half sold. Of course, many sellers are guilty of exactly the opposite in that they expect too much and place an unreasonably high value on their property. The important fact to remember is that when a middleman is talking you into accepting less money for your property, he is spending your dollars. Sure, he receives less commission if the selling price is less, but you are the one who really suffers. There is no question that a broker will sell more properties if they are priced low and, as a result, will earn more money; it is to his advantage to have you accept a low figure.

When you purchased your property, obviously there were

amenities that attracted you to this particular piece of real estate. In other chapters you will be instructed in how to exploit these amenities. But just think about this question for a few seconds: "Who knows your real estate better than you?" One of the basic rules of selling anything is to know the product, and you have the advantage in that respect. Knowing your community is also important because a buyer will want information about shopping, schools, public transportation, and neighborhood activities.

Besides the selling tools that you will get from this book, a very important element in the successful sale of your property is your proprietary interest—and, again, no one has more desire to obtain the best possible price than you, the seller. Combine that which you learn here with determination, and you will have little difficulty selling your property. So, before you put that "For Sale" sign up, read these pages with care and, if necessary, reread the book until you are familiar with each section. After you have thought about and digested this material, you will be prepared to reach, stimulate, and motivate the prospective buyer. The result? "Top dollar!"

3. *Allow you to sell in a shorter period of time.* With the skills learned here, you will be in a position to expose your property to the market as well as, or better than, most brokers. The difference is that you will be concentrating on one property, whereas the average full-time real estate salesman has a book full of listings and is trying to sell a number of properties. If your house or land is not one of his favorites, he is not going to push it. The chances are that if your property *is* one of his favorites, it is because he has talked you down to the "right price." A sincere effort on the part of the seller, coupled with the proper exposure of the property, is bound to produce a fast sale.

4. *Teach you negotiating skills.* This book includes a chapter devoted to negotiating, and the pointers given there can be

used extensively in other areas of sales, such as automobiles, boats, trailers, or any other assets. The negotiating techniques discussed can also be very helpful if you subsequently become a purchaser of real estate.

Although it is not my intent to provide the reader with any get-rich-quick schemes, it is quite conceivable that if you apply the merchandising and other techniques presented in this book, you will be able to build a respectable personal real estate portfolio.

1

Pricing Your Home

"How much can I get for this place?" is usually the first question that comes to mind when the seller subconsciously or consciously thinks of selling his property.

Residential real estate, which includes single-family detached dwellings, condominiums, co-ops, and owner-occupied two- to four-family buildings, presents a special kind of problem when trying to determine a selling price. One reason for this is a very nebulous set of factors called "amenities." Amenities are those subjective, intangible benefits which are agreeable to the owner of the real estate. They can include such things as a backyard view, a river, or trees, all of which have no value that can be measured precisely. However, even though the value of an amenity cannot be accurately measured, it can have a great influence on the selling price of a home. Consider your amenities very carefully when pricing your property.

Two other influences on the selling price are the character

of the neighborhood and the design and style of the house. Obviously, the proximity of a factory will have more influence on the price of a home than on the price of an office or commercial building. An architectural style that is out of place in a neighborhood also affects the selling price. Another factor to consider is that not all actual selling prices represent the fair market value. If the buyer is under pressure to buy because of a housing shortage or some such reason, he probably will pay more than the fair market value. If the opposite is true and the seller is under pressure to sell, he may take less than the fair market value. If either the buyer or the seller is not well informed, this too can lead to a price higher or lower than fair market value.

Important Elements in Appraising Your Home

The salient elements in determining the value of your real property are as follows:

1. Site elements:
   Shape and size of lot
   Landscape design
   Utilities
   Topography
   Soil
   Drainage
2. Area elements:
   Land covenants
   Zoning
   Character of neighborhood
   Detrimental influences
   Hazards
   Style and design of neighborhood buildings
   Community planning

Social characteristics
Schools and churches
Shopping
Transportation
Real estate taxes
Special assessments
Trends in neighborhood
3. Structural elements:
Style and architectural design
Functional use
Shape and size of building
Type and quality of construction
Floor plan
4. Cost elements:
Land cost
Building cost
5. Depreciation elements:
Physical deterioration
Obsolescence of building

Estimating the Sales Price

For many years now it has been the accepted practice of real estate appraisers to use three basic approaches in determining real estate value: the cost method, the income method, and the market method. These approaches, which are based on facts existing in the market, enable an owner to determine a selling price using separate indications of market value.

Cost Method This approach to pricing your home, or any other structure, tends to set the upper limits of price. To arrive at a fair market value using the cost method, add the following factors:

1. The estimated per square foot cost to reproduce the build-

ing, less the depreciation that has accrued each year after the house was built. Government charts tell us that most residences have a useful life of approximately forty years. Example: You check with local builders, architects, or lumberyards and find that comparable housing is being built and sold at approximately $35 per square foot for the building only; this does not include the land. The exterior measurements of your house indicate the square foot area to be 1,200. You also know that your house is ten years old. To calculate the cost to reproduce, multiply the per square foot cost times the total square feet. You get $42,000 ($35 per square foot × 1,200 square feet). Now, to determine how much depreciation occurs each year, divide the cost to reproduce $42,000 by forty years of useful life; you arrive at $1,050 of depreciation each year. Since your house is ten years old, subtract $10,500 (10 years × $1,050) from $42,000. You find that the cost to reproduce, less depreciation, is $31,500.

2. The cost of comparable land with the same utilities, walks, driveways, fences, retaining walls, etc. For example, let us say that a comparable lot with the same square foot area is selling for $10,000.

The total of the above two items gives you the fair market value of your property, using the cost method.

Reproduction cost, less depreciation	$31,500
Land cost	10,000
Fair market value by cost method	$41,500

Income Method The income approach to determining the fair market value of a residence really does not give a good measure of what sales price can be obtained. It is a much better indicator of value for two- to four-unit family dwellings. There are basically two approaches to the income method of determining value: (1) the gross annual income multiplier and (2) capitalization of net income.

The gross annual income multiplier is usually used most frequently with small-income properties. The computation is rather simple; it involves merely multiplying the annual rental times a predetermined multiplier. Example: The monthly rental on a residential unit is $200, which is an annual rental of $2,400. To arrive at the indicated property value, multiply $2,400 times the predetermined multiplier of 10. The result is a value of $24,000. The multiplier will vary from one location to another. Discuss this with a loan officer at your lending institution.

Capitalization of net income is a complicated approach to value and really does not adapt well to single-family detached housing.

Market Method   The market method compares similar properties that have been sold recently with the subject property. This is probably the best method of determining the value of residential property, if enough sales data are available to analyze. The market method is used by appraisers, owners, real estate brokers, mortgage lenders, and purchasers. This comparison method should be used only when properties are relatively similar. Care must be taken not to compare properties that vary greatly as to cost, size, design, type of construction, or location. However, seek out people who have recently purchased or sold similar property in your neighborhood and ask for their help. Many will surprise you and tell you exactly what they paid or received for their real estate.

You will find that a savings and loan association or bank will appraise your home for you in order that they might make the loan for the prospective purchaser. Your job is to collect as much reliable information as you can concerning the market, and then to make a value judgment.

Regardless of the method you use, you must be as objective as possible and recognize the undesirable features of your property as well as the amenities. Obviously, you will want to get as much money as you can for your property, but you must be reasonable when pricing, or you risk the possibility of not selling your real estate or of taking an unusually long time to sell it.

When to Sell

Many people do not have a great deal of flexibility in terms of timing their sale. Of the many reasons why people sell their homes, the most common are job transfers, divorce, sickness, an increase or decrease in family size, and financial problems. Often the real estate must be sold as soon as possible, and the seller must begin to act immediately.

On the other hand, if you can control the timing of the sale, it is usually best to sell your home in the spring, summer, or fall, in that order. Spring and early summer are the best times to put your home up for sale, and fall and winter are the least desirable. Traditionally, holiday seasons are not a good time to sell real estate since people generally have too many other things on their minds.

Also, economic conditions, either local or national, will affect sales. If at all possible, it is better to put off selling if unemployment figures and interest rates are unusually high. In most instances, however, the seller does not have the luxury of selecting the most suitable time to sell his property. On the contrary, he is usually under pressure to sell his home in a short period of time and to get a good price!

2

Preparing Your Property for the Sale

Give proper consideration to getting your property into top shape. Repairs and maintenance are to be done before showing your property to a prospective buyer. Use the Presale Inspection Report at the end of this chapter to determine what improvements should be made. It is remarkable how the appearance of a property can be enhanced by a little scrubbing, painting, and landscaping.

The exterior of your property creates the first impression. The lawn and shrubberies should be trimmed. Touch up and paint gutters and downspouts and under eaves, if necessary. Remove any litter that has accumulated.

The interior should shine brightly, so wash all dirt marks from the walls or, if necessary, paint the walls and woodwork. Be sure to wash windows on the inside and outside. Get rid of all trash in the basement, attic, and garage. Repair loose doorknobs, sticking doors, dripping faucets, and faulty plumbing. Closets should be neat and orderly, with clothes properly hung and shoes in order. The kitchen should be spotless. Wash all appliances and wipe the sink and all counter tops clean. The bathrooms always need special attention. See that the caulking is like new around the toilet and bath fixtures and that towels and washcloths are hung in an orderly fashion. Polish all metal fixtures. Keep your rooms bright; if you are showing the house in the late afternoon or evening, turn on all the lights just before the prospect arrives. Spending a few pennies on electricity pays off—dark and gloomy rooms will not sell. Of course, immediately after the prospect leaves, you should turn off some of the lights in order to conserve energy.

From a practical viewpoint, you should not make an improvement unless you can reasonably expect to receive $2 in additional sales price for every $1 in improvement costs. It would be financially unsound to invest $1 to enhance the appearance of your property in order to receive only $1 in additional sales price; you would merely be trading dollars.

Time is another element that determines the extent of repairs. If your home must be sold immediately, there is little or no time to spend getting the repairs finished. The seller is usually involved in making moving arrangements and has little time for major repair projects.

Normal home maintenance and repairs usually do not increase your real estate taxes and will hasten the sale. Good maintenance not only will preserve your investment and allow you to receive a higher sales price but also will upgrade the neighborhood. Generally, you can make many home improvements that will not increase your real estate taxes because they are considered to be normal upkeep. Although the following maintenance and repairs usually do not increase your taxes, it is wise to check with local authorities if there is a question. Also, some of the items might require a permit; these have been noted by an asterisk (*). Again, if you are in doubt, ask your local building department officials.

On the exterior you can:
Add a dormer or bay window*
Add or replace gutters or downspouts
Place new siding over existing siding*
Repair or replace sidewalks or drives
Repair porches or steps
Replace porches*
Insulate with weather stripping, storm doors, or storm windows
Repair or replace fence
Replace existing masonry*
Repair roof
Replace roof (if not tile or slate)*
Construct patios or paved parking area
Build a screened-in or totally open porch*
Add or improve lawns, trees, and landscaping
Paint
Install awnings or shades

On the interior you can:
Rewire electrical system* and modernize fixtures
Replace plumbing fixtures (if not part of complete modernization)*
Replace old furnace with a new one of the same type*
Add closets and built-in storage areas
Install automatic hot-water heaters*
Add partitions, new wall surfaces, and new ceilings (excluding conversions)*
Replace old flooring
Paint, plaster, or redecorate
Install exhaust fans*
Add a toilet (not a complete bath)*

Improvements requiring permits which may result in increased taxes:

The benefits you receive from these improvements far exceed the slightly higher taxes you may pay as you increase the value of your home.

Structural changes resulting in a larger building area (if zoning permits):

Adding a complete bathroom
Finishing off a room in the attic or basement
Enclosing and heating a porch
Complete modernization and conversion
Changing from single-family to multiple-family use (if zoning permits)
Adding a garage or breezeway
Replacing stove or hot-air gravity heat with forced hot-air heat
Replacing siding with masonry veneer or face brick

Again, it is quite possible that your property does not need any of the repairs mentioned above if you have taken care of it and maintained it reasonably well. Your Presale Inspection Report will be a good guide as to what work should be completed prior to offering your home for sale. Proper care and maintenance will help sell your home faster and produce a higher price. But remember the "1-for-2" formula! Do not invest $1 in repairs unless you feel this will reflect an additional $2 in the sales price.

PRESALE INSPECTION REPORT

Interior of House

Items	Condition	Needs	Estimated Expense Involved
Vestibule			
Door			
Hinges			

PRESALE INSPECTION REPORT (Continued)

Interior of House

Items	Condition	Needs	Estimated Expense Involved
Lock			
Floor			
Walls			
Ceiling			
Light fixtures			
Light switches			
Coat Closet			
Door			
Floor			
Interior walls			
Ceiling			
Shelves, rods, hooks			
Living Room			
Floor			
Baseboards			
Walls			
Ceiling			
Windows			
Doors			
Light fixtures			

PRESALE INSPECTION REPORT (Continued)

Interior of House

Items	Condition	Needs	Estimated Expense Involved
Electric outlets			
Electric switches			
Dining Room			
Floor			
Baseboards			
Walls			
Ceiling			
Doors			
Light fixtures			
Electric outlets			
Electric switches			
Buffets			
Kitchen			
Doors			
Locks			
Floor			
Baseboards			
Walls			
Ceiling			
Light fixtures			

PRESALE INSPECTION REPORT (Continued)

Interior of House

Items	Condition	Needs	Estimated Expense Involved
Electric outlets			
Electric switches			
Stove			
Sink			
Cupboards			
Refrigerator			
Pantry			
Doorbell			
Ventilating fan			
First Bedroom			
Doors			
Floor			
Baseboards			
Walls			
Ceiling			
Windows			
Light fixtures			
Electric outlets			
Electric switches			
Closets			
Second Bedroom			

PRESALE INSPECTION REPORT (Continued)

Interior of House

Items	Condition	Needs	Estimated Expense Involved
Doors			
Floor			
Baseboards			
Walls			
Ceiling			
Windows			
Light fixtures			
Electric outlets			
Electric switches			
Closets			
Third Bedroom			
Doors			
Baseboards			
Walls			
Ceiling			
Windows			
Light fixtures			
Electric outlets			
Electric switches			
Closets			
Family Room			
Doors			

PRESALE INSPECTION REPORT (Continued)

Interior of House

Items	Condition	Needs	Estimated Expense Involved
Floor			
Baseboards			
Walls			
Ceiling			
Windows			
Light fixtures			
Electric outlets			
Electric switches			
Closets			
First Bathroom			
Doors			
Floor			
Walls			
Ceiling			
Window			
Tub			
Shower			
Shower curtain			
Lavatory			
Toilet bowl			
Flush tank			
Faucets			

PRESALE INSPECTION REPORT (Continued)

Interior of House

Items	Condition	Needs	Estimated Expense Involved
Light fixtures			
Electric outlets			
Electric switches			
Towel racks, etc.			
Cabinets			
Second Bathroom			
Doors			
Floor			
Walls			
Ceiling			
Window			
Tub			
Shower			
Shower curtain			
Lavatory			
Toilet bowl			
Flush tank			
Light fixtures			
Electric outlets			
Electric switches			
Towel racks, etc.			
Cabinets			

PRESALE INSPECTION REPORT (Continued)

Interior of House

Items	Condition	Needs	Estimated Expense Involved
Windows and Shades			
Frames			
Sashes			
Sills			
Stops			
Weights			
Locks			
Glass			
Weather stripping			
Shades			
Blinds			
Curtain fixtures			
Linen Closet			
Door			
Floor			
Ceiling			
Walls			
Shelves			
Drawers			
Electric lights			
Basement			
Floor			

PRESALE INSPECTION REPORT (Continued)

Basement

Items	Condition	Needs	Estimated Expense Involved
Walls			
Ceiling			
Washer			
Dryer			
Tub			
Faucets			
Toilet bowl			
Lavatory			
Drains			
Windows			
Doors			
Shades			

Exterior of House

Yard			
Soil			
Grass			
Shrubs			
Flowers			
Trees			
Fences			
Urns			
Walks			
Cement flashings			

PRESALE INSPECTION REPORT (Continued)

Exterior of House

Items	Condition	Needs	Estimated Expense Involved
Driveway			
Brick			
Walls			
A. Base			
B. Top			
C. Coping			
D. Tuck pointing			
E. Cleanliness			
Gutters			
Wood trim			
Wood exterior			
Garage			
A. Gutters			
B. Brick			
C. Trim			
Mailbox			
Doors			

Care and Maintenance of Your Real Estate

The following list of maintenance suggestions will get sales results. Some of the sections may not apply to your property, but read them through and make a note of the maintenance items that will benefit you. A well-maintained building always brings a higher sales price.

Air Conditioners—Room

WARNING: Never clean your room air conditioner while it is running.

Cleaning the cabinet: It may be cleaned with a vacuum-cleaner brush attachment or with a cloth dampened in a mild detergent. It is best not to use any type of wax cleaner or polish.

Cleaning the filter: A clean filter means better and more economical cooling. Check the filter every thirty days during the cooling season. If you have a washable filter, it should be washed in hot, soapy water just like a sponge. Then rinse and squeeze dry. A nonwashable filter should be replaced when it gets dirty. A clean filter saves money on utilities.

Oiling: Today's room air conditioners have a compressor that is oiled for life. The fan motor has sufficient oil for five years of operation under normal conditions.

Condenser coils: These are in the back of your air conditioner and face the outside. For peak efficiency, they should be checked periodically and cleaned if clogged with grass, dirt, or leaves.

Before calling for service:
1. Is the cord plugged firmly into the wall outlet?
2. Is a fuse blown or a circuit breaker tripped?
3. Is the filter clogged?
4. Are the controls set properly?

Appliances

This section covers refrigerators, ranges, dishwashers, disposers, washing machines, and dryers.

Refrigerators

How to defrost: If your refrigerator is not of the automatically defrosting type (called "frost-proof" or "frost-free"), defrost it when the frost gets ¼ inch thick to keep operating costs low. Remove the contents of the freezer chest and chiller drawer.

Turn the temperature control to DEFROST. When all frost has melted, turn the control back to the original position. For faster defrosting, turn the control to OFF and put a pan of hot water in the freezer chest. *Do not remove frost with a sharp instrument!*

Cleaning:

CAUTION: Never use gritty soaps, abrasive cleaners, or heavy-duty cleaners on any part of your refrigerator.

Before you start cleaning, turn the temperature control to OFF.

Food compartment: Wash with a solution of warm water and baking soda (3 tablespoons baking soda to 1 quart of water) or with mild soap and water. Rinse and dry.

Ice trays: Wash with warm, sudsy water. Do not use hot water or abrasive cleaners.

Door seal: Clean with mild soap and water, mild detergent and water, or the soda solution described above.

Exterior: Wipe with a damp cloth.

Frost-proof Refrigerators: If you have this type of refrigerator, it will have a grille on the front at floor level. Check this grille periodically and clear of lint, using a brush or vacuum-cleaner attachment. At least twice a year, remove the grille and clean the area behind it with a vacuum-cleaner attachment. At the same time, remove and clean the evaporator pan.

Before calling for service:

1. Is the cord firmly plugged into the wall outlet?

2. Have you blown a fuse or tripped a circuit breaker?

3. If you have a frost-free model, check the front grille for heavy dirt accumulation and clean if necessary.

Ranges

General: Be sure to turn off all controls before cleaning. Do not use or spill oven cleaner on metal trim! Never use gritty soaps or abrasive cleaners on any surface. *Do not use a sharp instrument (such as a knife or razor blade) to clean any surface.*

Exterior: Wipe up spills at once with a paper towel. Clean with a damp, sudsy cloth when surface cools. Then rinse and dry with a cloth.

Control panel: Wash with a damp, sudsy cloth. Then rinse and dry with a cloth.

Oven capillary tube (temperature-sensing unit): This is not removable and is probably the most fragile part of your oven. Wipe it gently after using oven cleaner so that the cleaner does not build up and cause false temperature readings.

Electric ranges: CAUTION: If aluminum foil is used on the oven floor under the bake unit, be sure the foil does *not* touch the bake unit or receptacle. If foil touches either of these, it will fuse to the unit and damage it.

Gas ranges: Clean the cooking units with detergent and hot water. Rinse and dry. Scouring pads can be used to remove burned-on food. Check the holes in the cooking units occasionally. If they are clogged, clean with a wire. Turn the gas valve off when doing this.

Before calling for service:

Electric ranges:

1. Is the cord plugged firmly into the wall outlet?

2. Have you blown a fuse or tripped a circuit breaker?

3. Is the surface heating unit level? Was the unit replaced properly after cleaning? Is the burner perfectly flat? Is the range level?

4. If the oven does not heat, is the oven control turned to the BAKE or BROIL position and the temperature control turned to ON?

Gas ranges:

1. Is the valve in the gas supply pipe to the range turned on?

2. Is the pilot light on?

3. If the oven is not heating properly, is the heat-sensing capillary tube in the oven covered with grease or oven cleaner? This could cause false temperature readings.

4. Are the holes in the cooking tops clogged?

Dishwashers

Interior: Generally, the dishwasher tub is self-cleaning. However, after long usage in hard-water areas, a white film may develop. The tub should then be wiped with a damp cloth and a mild cleansing powder.

Exterior: To clean, wipe with a warm, damp, sudsy cloth; rinse and wipe dry. Do *not* use gritty or harsh cleaners.

Special tops: If you have a laminated plastic top (like Formica), it may be cleaned with soap and warm water or a mild cleaning powder. *Never* take cooking utensils directly from the range surface units or oven and place them on the dishwasher top.

If you have a wooden top, avoid allowing water to stand on it for long periods. If the top shows warpage after unusual exposure to moisture, wipe it dry and allow it to remain undisturbed for forty-eight hours; warpage should disappear. Avoid thawing out frozen foods on the top, even when placed on aluminum foil. To remove water stains, wipe with a cloth saturated with nontoxic mineral oil.

Before calling for service:
1. Is the control that starts your dishwasher in the ON position?
2. Is the door closed?
3. Have you blown a fuse or tripped a circuit breaker?
4. Is the water-supply shutoff valve turned on?

Disposers

A garbage disposer requires only a small amount of attention to give trouble-free service.

There are two basic types of disposers:

1. Continuous-feed
2. Batch-feed or lock-cover

To operate a continuous-feed disposer:
1. Turn on a strong stream of *cold* water.

2. Turn on the disposer switch.
3. Feed food waste into the disposer.

To operate a batch-feed disposer:
1. Drop food waste into the disposer (do not pack it in).
2. Turn on *cold* water.
3. Place the stopper in unit and twist to ON position.

Things you *should do*:

1. Do replace the drain cover while the disposer is not being used; this prevents silverware from accidentally getting into the disposer. For water drainage, you may have to tip the cover slightly.

2. Do flush the disposer for self-cleaning. Allow the disposer and cold water to run after grinding or draining the sink of dishwater. Some detergents are caustic; flushing will pass such material into the drain line without causing harm to the disposer.

3. Do grind food waste only with strong flow of *cold* water.

Things you *should not do*:

1. Do not turn off water until grinding is completed and only water and motor sounds are heard.

2. Do not use hot water when grinding food waste. However, hot water can be drained into the disposer between grinding periods.

3. Do not feed large quantities of fibrous food like celery and corn husks into the disposer. Mix this type of food waste with other food waste and feed into the disposer gradually.

4. Do not put big bones into the disposer. A big bone will jam it. Break large bones up into several smaller pieces. Chicken bones of any size have a tendency to jam disposers.

5. Do not stuff large, bulky food waste into the disposer opening. It should be broken or cut in pieces that will drop readily into the disposer opening.

6. Do not let dishcloths, bottle caps, glass, crockery, string,

hairpins, etc., get into the disposer. Such items can cause jamming or drain stoppage and may even damage the disposer.

7. *Do not put a drain cleaner into the disposer.* Drain cleaners can ruin a disposer. If you have a two-compartment sink, you can use a drain cleaner on the nondisposer side. But first check to make sure that it does not drain into the disposer.

If the disposer does not operate or stops while running, the cause is usually an overloaded or jammed condition.

First, turn disposer switch off. Then:

1. Remove the material in the disposer.

2. Wait about three minutes before pushing the reset button (usually red) on or near the bottom of the disposer.

3. Check to make sure you have not blown a fuse or tripped a circuit breaker.

4. Turn the disposer switch to ON.

If the disposer still will not run, the rotating plate at the bottom of the food-waste compartment may be stuck. Insert a long-handled object, such as a broom or mop handle, into the disposer. Pry against either side of the hammer until the rotating bottom turns freely. Push the reset button again and turn the disposer on. It is a good idea to unscrew the fuse or trip the circuit breaker when doing this.

Washing Machines

The smooth porcelain tub is practically self-cleaning. After each use, leave the lid open until all moisture has completely evaporated. Hard scrubbing or scouring should never be necessary. Do *not* use harsh soaps, lye, scouring powder, or acids on the porcelain and enameled surfaces in the washer.

You can keep the exterior of your washer clean and bright just by wiping it off with a damp cloth. The surface should be kept free of washing compound and suds, which may drip onto it during use.

Before calling for service:
1. Are all controls set correctly?
2. Is the cord plugged firmly into the outlet?
3. Are both faucets turned on?
4. Is a fuse blown or a circuit breaker tripped?
5. Is the drain hose stopped up or bent so that water cannot pass through it?

Dryers

To protect the finish, wipe with a damp cloth. Do *not* use abrasive cleaners.

Clean the lint trap before each use.

Wipe out the inside of the dryer about once a month to remove excess lint. For a thorough cleaning job, remove and clean the lint trap. Then insert a brush or vacuum-cleaner hose through the lint-trap opening. Wipe off the inside of the door and loading opening with a damp cloth.

Before calling for service:
1. Is the cord firmly plugged into the outlet?
2. Have you blown a fuse or tripped a circuit breaker?
3. Is the door firmly shut? The dryer will not operate if the door is ajar.

Asphalt

Asphalt driveways, parking areas, walks, and other surfaces can be seriously damaged if gasoline, oil, and other such materials are dropped or spilled on them. If you do spill such materials on blacktop, wash it off immediately with lots of water.

Burning leaves, trash, and other debris on asphalt will cause damage. Similarly, trash burners should not sit directly on asphalt. Never place sharp objects such as motorcycle stands or lawn furniture on asphalt or blacktop surfaces. These make holes in the surface.

Balconies

A balcony is for enjoyment. Storing items on the balcony not only makes your condominium look bad but also can create a safety hazard.

If your balcony floor is made of wood with space between the flooring, be careful when you clean it so that you do not drip or spill water on your neighbor below. It is best to use a damp mop which has had most of the water squeezed out of it.

If your condominium building allows grills on balconies, be sure you do not accidently spill live coals on the floor. It is a good idea to keep your grill away from walls to prevent grease splatters from getting on them. Your neighbors will appreciate it if you are careful not to let smoke drift onto their balcony.

Ceramic Tile

Very little maintenance is required for ceramic tile. It does not need waxing or polishing. Wash it with warm water and a mild detergent; then rinse and wipe clean and dry with a soft cloth. To clean the grouting between the tiles, use a brush and a mild scouring powder.

You can use a silicone sealer material that will leave a transparent film on the surface of the ceramic tile. It results in a high luster that reduces surface attraction of dust, dirt, staining, and water spotting. The silicone sealer will also deposit a waterproof seal on the grout between the tiles; this resists water and dirt penetration and helps to keep the grout looking new.

Concrete Driveways, Walks, and Steps

The very nature of concrete makes it impossible to prevent cracking, even though expansion and contraction joints were used to relieve the internal shrinking stresses that occur in all good concrete. While cracks are not pretty, they do not reduce the serviceability of the concrete.

The indiscriminate use of de-icing salts can cause rapid deterioration or flaking of concrete surfaces. Do not use de-icing material containing ammonium nitrate or ammonium sulphate. Check the contents on the de-icing package before you try it.

Electrical Systems

If the wiring in your house or condominium building meets code requirements and safety standards, it will accommodate an adequate number of electrical appliances. Portable appliances which require your personal attendance for their operation may be used without fear of overloading a circuit. However, larger appliances sometimes require separate circuits for their operation. If you plan to purchase a larger appliance, be sure to check first with an electrician.

Electrical system safety devices: Fuses or circuit breakers are located in a main electrical panel. They are the safety valves for your home's electrical system. Never use pennies or substitute larger fuses for those which have burned out. A fire could result.

To reset circuit breakers, follow the instructions on the panel.

Replacing fuses is a simple process. First, pull the handle on the main fuse panel, thus shutting off the current. Then locate the blown fuse. It will usually have a burned spot on its top surface. Unscrew it and replace it with one of the same ampere rating. Keep extra fuses on hand so that one will be available immediately when it is needed.

Power failure: In case of a complete power failure in your home, first check to see whether your neighbors have power. If they do, probably one of your main fuses has blown. Find out what caused the fuse to blow before you try to replace it! Your main fuses are located behind a pullout in your panel bearing the designation MAIN. If your neighbors do not have power, the difficulty is probably somewhere on the power lines outside your home. If you live in a condominium, report the problem to your manager. If you do not, call the power company and report it.

Electric heat: Use your vacuum cleaner occasionally to get any dirt out of baseboards.

Radiant electric heat units heat like sunshine. Thus for best results, they have to be able to "see" into the room. Convection units must have a constant supply of free-flowing air. Avoid placing large pieces of furniture, which will block radiation and restrict air flow, in front of heating units.

The National Electrical Manufacturers Association (NEMA) makes these recommendations concerning draperies for condominiums having NEMA-verified baseboard electric heating systems:

1. Hang draperies a minimum of ½ inch from the top of the rug or finished floor covering.

2. Allow a minimum of 1 inch of clearance between the maximum projection of the heater and the portion of the fold in the drape that is nearest to the heater.

3. Hang draperies a minimum of ½ inch from the ceiling.

4. If a drape is to be cut off above a heater, it should be cut off a minimum of 6 inches above the top of the heater, and preferably more.

Rugs and carpets also should not restrict air flow. If exhaust fans are controlled by humidistats, set them at 30 percent during very cold weather and 40 to 45 percent during the milder weather of the heating season.

Fans—Ventilating

Be sure to turn the fan off before cleaning or removing the filter.

Filters: The mesh filters in the hood fan of your kitchen range should be cleaned regularly to reduce fire hazard and keep the pulling power of your fan up to its maximum. This will also help keep the area walls, floors, and ceiling clean.

Clean the filter or filters by swishing them up and down in hot, sudsy water. Then rinse with hot water and let drip dry.

Fan blades and motor: Clean with a damp, sudsy cloth. Do *not* put the fan or motor in water.

Hood: Clean both the top and the underside of the hood with a damp, sudsy cloth. Cleaning the underside is very important since deposits, if not removed regularly, will form a hard residue that is very difficult to remove.

Floors

Wood floors: The first rule for proper care is: *Never use water on wood floors.* That is why self-polishing waxes which contain water should not be used. Rather, use a polishing-type wax, in liquid or paste form. The frequency of application depends on floor wear. For regular maintenance, a liquid "cleaning" wax that removes dirt, scuff marks, and grease and leaves a protective coat of wax is preferred.

If excessively soiled, hardwood floors may be cleaned with mineral spirits, benzene, or some of the brand-name cleaners designed for this purpose.

To protect the floor's finish and prevent indentations, it is wise to put furniture rests under the legs of furniture to distribute the weight.

Carpets: Carpets will give excellent service if they receive reasonable care and attention.

Day-to-day vacuuming: This has two purposes: to remove loose soil and to keep the pile erect. Vacuum daily in moderate and heavy traffic areas such as doorways and halls. Vacuum the entire carpet weekly. This prolongs the life of the carpet and delays the need for wet shampooing.

Be sure to keep your vacuum cleaner mechanically fit for best results. Brushes should be kept clean and replaced when worn out. Belts should be replaced from time to time because they stretch and slow the speed of the brushes. Dirt bags should not be allowed to fill more than halfway.

A light vacuuming consists of three individual strokes over a given area of carpet. A thorough vacuuming takes up to seven strokes.

Quick attention to spots: When anything is dropped or spilled, remove spots and stains quickly before they dry or become set. Always have the necessary cleaning equipment on hand. Try to identify what caused the spot or stain and remove it by following directions carefully.

There are two cleaning solutions that you may safely use. One is a teaspoonful of a neutral detergent (like Tide, Ajax, or Rinso) added to a quart of warm water and a teaspoonful of white vinegar. This is a weak acid and will serve to neutralize any alkaline materials. The other is a solvent type of cleaning fluid.

If you cannot identify a spot or stain on your carpet, use this cleaning procedure:

1. Remove excess materials. In the case of liquids, absorb with a clean white cloth or facial tissue. If the material is semi-solid, scrape with a knife or use a sponge.

2. Apply the detergent–vinegar-water solution. Use a clean white cloth and wipe gently from the edge of the solid area toward the center. At intervals blot with a dry, clean cloth to absorb excess solution.

3. Dry the carpet.

4. Apply the dry-cleaning fluid, wiping gently and working from the edges of a spot or stain toward the center.

When using the above procedure, you should exercise judgment as to whether both types of cleaning solutions are necessary and as to whether any application should be repeated. For example, if the detergent–vinegar-water solution seems to remove most of the stain, it would be wise to repeat the application.

Last, but not least, is the all-important walk-off mat. An inside doormat is an excellent way to help keep dirt off your floors. The soil normally falls off shoes when we take the first and second steps inside.

Tile floors (resilient or asbestos): Sweep daily with a soft brush, dry mop, or broom to remove surface dust and soil. When washing is necessary, a solution of cleaner and lukewarm water (approximately ½ cup of cleaner to 5 to 6 quarts of water) should be used. Avoid using strong cleaners. After washing the floor, rinse with clear, cold water to remove the cleaning residue. Allow the floor to dry thoroughly before waxing.

Vinyl floors, like other types of resilient floors, should receive regular applications of a protective floor polish to prevent excessive surface soiling.

Periodically, you should use a good wax remover on your tile floors. If you do not, the buildup from repeated waxing will yellow and ultimately ruin the floor.

Rubber heel marks can be removed by rubbing with a dry 000 grade steel-wool pad containing no soap. Food stains can be removed by rubbing with a 000 grade steel-wool pad moistened with a cleaner. A small amount of abrasive cleaner such as Ajax, Comet, or Bon-Ami, together with the steel-wool pad, should be used on very stubborn stains. In all cases, rinse, dry, and wax after scrubbing.

Special suggestions:

1. Do not use paste wax or waxes containing petroleum solvents. Use only self-polishing water wax or vinyl floor polish.

2. Do not use cleaning agents containing caustics, strong soaps or powders, or solvents such as gasoline, kerosene, turpentine, or benzene.

3. All resilient floors are subject to indentation from heavy loads. Nonstaining casters and glides must be used in order to provide adequate protection.

4. On new floors allow sufficient time for the tile to set before washing. This may take from a week to ten days. Daily sweeping with a soft broom is the only maintenance recommended for this period.

5. Never use sweeping compounds that contain free fats, oils, or chemicals on asphalt tile; they will soften the tile and muddy its appearance.

6. Coatings such as shellac, lacquer, varnish, or plastic finishes are not recommended for resilient floors. They may permanently injure the floor.

Kitchen Cabinets and Counter Tops

Kitchen cabinets: Wood cabinets should be treated just like good wood furniture. Clean with the same cleaners and polishes you use for your wood furniture.

Laminated plastic cabinets (like Formica) and metal cabinets should be washed with a mild soap and water, rinsed, and dried.

Counter tops: These are made of high-pressure laminated plastic and are not harmed by ordinary solvents, alcohol, boiling water, acids, or alkalies. They can withstand heat up to 275°F; however, do *not* place cooking utensils directly from your oven or range onto the counter top since they will be hotter than this. Do not cut anything directly on a counter top. Use a cutting board.

To clean, simply wash with mild soap and water; then rinse and dry. Waxing is not necessary.

Pest Control

Insects that invade a structure can be divided into three classifications: Some are destructive to the building, some are a menace to health, and some are a nuisance to have around.

Keep in mind that it is almost impossible to control all insects 100 percent of the time. A number of insects, like clover mites and flying ants, have a short life span. They originate outside and migrate into your home at certain times of the year—for a short period.

Most kinds of roaches can be controlled with insecticides available at your supermarket. You can keep an infestation from getting started by practicing good housekeeping and being very careful about things you bring into your home from the grocery and other stores.

In a condominium, if a situation is beyond your control, let your manager know so that professional help may be obtained.

Insects that are destructive to property are termites, powder-post beetles, and carpenter ants. If any of these are found, tell your condominium manager right away.

If a large quantity of insects is found, be sure to put a specimen in a bottle or envelope for later identification.

Walls

Although most walls are washable today, marks from ball-point pens, crayons, and felt-tip pens are almost impossible to remove.

When placing furniture in your rooms, keep it at least 3 inches from walls. Otherwise, the furniture causes a black line on the walls which is impossible to wash off.

General soil and dust on brick walls can be removed with a vacuum-cleaner brush attachment, but crayon marks, etc., can be cleaned only with special solutions designed for cleaning brick. Sometimes even these do not work when markings have been absorbed into the porous brick.

Preventive maintenance will pay off handsomely when you are ready to sell.

3
Advertising

Somewhere out there, someone wants to buy what you are selling, and advertising is the medium that brings buyer and seller together. Your property must be packaged and merchandised like any other product, and in this chapter you will learn how to get a prospective buyer to purchase your real estate instead of any of the other properties that are being offered for sale in your city or town.

After reading the opening statement in this chapter, you may be asking yourself, "Well, if someone wants to buy my property, who is he and how do I find him?" The answer to "Who will buy?" is that the property itself will determine this. If it is a house you are selling, then the number of bedrooms, the size of the kitchen, the type of heating, the number of bathrooms, and the garage are the type of things that will affect who will buy your home. The question "How do I find the buyer?" is discussed below.

Various methods of advertising will be discussed in this chapter. It is of paramount importance to plan and prepare your advertising so that your message will be directed to the right people with maximum effectiveness and economy.

Newspapers are certainly the favored medium for advertising real estate, especially residential property. When selling a house, classified advertising is the recognized marketplace in most communities. This chapter will help you prepare effective newspaper ads so that a prospective house buyer will immediately spot your copy when turning to the classified section.

Some form of direct-mail advertising should be undertaken, even if this consists only of mailing a Property Information Sheet to your neighbors informing them that your house is for sale. This allows them to help select their own new neighbor if they know of someone who is looking for a house.

"Cold-canvass" advertising involves very little cost. It requires that you get out of the house and talk to as many people in your community as possible, preferably those who are themselves in contact with groups of people, such as merchants, clergymen, public officials, and professional people.

Signs are one of the least expensive and most effective methods of advertising your real estate. When you decide to sell, put your sign up immediately; when the property is sold and after the buyer has obtained a mortgage, remove the sign so that people will not continue to telephone you.

The total cost of advertising, including classified newspaper ads, signs, and mailings, generally should not exceed ½ of 1 percent of the gross selling price of the property. However, if the property has a special problem, such as the age of the building or a bad location, the cost of advertising could exceed the ½ of 1 percent rule of thumb. For example, if your property has no special problem, the house is in reasonably good condition, and the location is not bad, with a gross selling price (total sales price without any expenses deducted) of $75,000 you should be able to advertise and promote the sale for approximately $375 or less. This amount does not include any monies necessary for repairs or maintenance.

Classified Newspaper Advertising

Newspaper ads can be a powerful sales tool, if used effectively. First, determine which publications will give you the best exposure and then advertise in the community publication with the greatest circulation in your area. Usually, the best policy is to place an ad once a week and continue it until the property is sold. It is generally better to limit your ads to one or two publications that will do the most for you.

The proper approach to writing a real estate ad is to decide what you want the ad to accomplish. If the ad contains few facts and has no "personality," it will not have any sales appeal. But if it is written correctly, it will attract attention, arouse interest, create desire, and get action. A good ad will follow this formula, and it costs no more to write a good classified ad than a poor one.

Here is the professional way to go about writing a real estate sales ad for a house. Write down all the selling points of your house, since these are the raw materials that must be included in the copy of your ad. A helpful list appears on page 46. To help you get started with this list, think about the reasons that induced you to buy your home. (Keep in mind that when reference is made to selling a house, the same ideas and principles can be adapted to other real estate, such as commercial, industrial, or four-flat buildings.) Chances are that what motivated you to buy your property will now help you to sell it.

Prospective home buyers are seeking more than just shelter. They are also concerned about the community in which they are going to live. You must be knowledgeable with regard to your city or village and, more specifically, your neighborhood. Be familiar with the facts concerning schools, shopping, and public transportation; these items are a part of any good ad.

Usually, very good sources for this type of demographic information are the community chamber of commerce, the local town hall, and the town industrial council.

The formula for a successful ad is

Attention — Interest — Desire — Action

Attract the Prospective Buyer's Attention A good headline will focus the buyer's attention on your ad. Before you write the headline or the first line of your ad, think about the unique benefits of owning your home. Use them in your headline to make the buyer say, "This sounds like the home we have been looking for!" Also, you will find that the headline "For Sale by Owner" or just "By Owner" in bold print will act as a magnet; it is a wonderful way to get attention.

Surveys indicate that home buyers are more concerned about location than about price and financing. Next, they want to know what the home is like — the number of bedrooms, the type and style of construction, and special features. Also important to home buyers is the convenience of the location — its proximity to transportation, schools, and shopping. Be sure to mention these features in your headlines or subheadlines. In preparing ads, remember that emotion plays a major role in home buying, so play up the home's amenities rather than the price. The following are two ads for the same property that illustrate the point.

This ad will attract attention:

By Owner
Red Brick Split-level
West Hillcrest

3 large bedrooms and bath upstairs. Formal dining room, living room with fireplace, and built-in kitchen. 4 blocks to Northshore R.R., 2 blocks to school and shopping. Price $35,000. FHA financing available.

Please phone today.   333-0008

This ad is a waste of space:

Great Buy—Owner Trans.
6 rm. brk. rch., 1½ baths, oil heat, basmt. See to appreciate.
Middle 30's.
By Owner   333-0008

Why does the first ad above do a better job of attracting attention? It is better for several reasons:

1. A "By Owner" ad gives prospective buyers the feeling that they will be able to negotiate a better price because they will not be dealing with a broker.
2. The headline in the first ad tells the buyer that the house is brick, which means it probably is well-constructed.
3. The buyer knows the style of the house at a glance.
4. The desirable location of the house is mentioned in the headline. The headline in the second ad does not catch the reader's attention.

Because the address is not included in the ad, those interested will have to telephone you; this gives you a chance to qualify the good prospects and arrange an appointment for them. To "qualify" prospects means to determine whether they are a good fit for your property. You can decide whether your property is right for a prospective buyer only if you find out his or her needs. Are there enough bedrooms or bathrooms? Does the buyer need a one- or a two-car garage? If your real estate is commercial property, will the present zoning accommodate the buyer's use? The buyer who is seeking space to set up a manufacturing facility does not qualify for a building situated on a parcel of land zoned for only commercial retail selling. Or, even if the building is zoned properly, does it have all the features the buyer needs, such as a loading dock or access to a railroad track? You must qualify buyers as to how much cash they have to invest also, but do not attempt to determine the availability of cash over the telephone. The discussion concerning a prospective buyer's financial strength should take place after you have met him in person and know that the property meets his most important needs. This does not mean that the prospect must approve of every single feature of your property; that would be an unrealistic expectation. Also, if you print the address in the ad, many people will drive by your home and, for any number of reasons, may keep on going without stopping to inspect it. It is extremely important to create enough desire over the telephone to get qualified prospects into your home so that you can make them aware of all the amenities that your property and community have to offer. Printing your address also means that prospective buyers may decide that everything about the exterior of your home and immediate area is perfect, without giving much thought to the inside. Do not forget that prospects have probably inspected several homes and may be thoroughly exhausted by the time they see yours; then something as minor as the color of your kitchen could trigger a negative response. That is why the things you say over the telephone must make prospects want to see the interior of your home. However, the telephone will not ring unless the newspaper ad attracts attention.

Hold the Prospective Buyer's Interest After you have made the prospect want to know more about your home, you must hold his interest. Advertising "By Owner" in the headline will gain your prospect's attention, but good copy is necessary to arouse real interest. Make your copy specific, appealing, and descriptive. Make it easy for your prospect to read and understand. Do not expect people to be decoders. An abbreviated ad produces abbreviated real estate sales. Again, once you have your prospect's attention, create interest by painting a mental picture of your home. Describe it in plain, straightforward language and do not skimp. A "rec room" sounds nice. A "fruitwood, family-sized recreation room" sounds even nicer. Sell your home by promising benefits. Spell out the features that will make a family want your home. This ad will develop interest:

> *By Owner*
> Yellow Brick Ranch
> In Westbrook
> Finest residential area, within walking distance to schools, shopping, transportation, and parks. 3 bedrooms, formal dining room, built-in kitchen. 1½ ceramic tile baths. 2-car garage with screened breezeway. Beautiful lawn with 4 elm trees. Price $47,000.
> Please phone today.   333-0008

The seller's name is another piece of information, in addition to the address, that should not appear in the newspaper ad. The reason for not including your name in the ad is that during the telephone reply, just before you ask the prospect his name, you should offer your own. By withholding your name until the telephone reply, you can, in effect, trade your name for the prospect's name. Simply say something like, "Incidentally, my name is Bud Johnson. What is yours?" Usually, you will catch the caller off guard, and he will not resist giving you his name. Also, not placing your name or address in the ad gives you an opportunity to screen callers over the telephone and eliminate those who are not really interested.

Promise the Prospective Buyer a Benefit and Create Desire
A good headline will stop a prospect, and good copy will create interest by promising a special benefit. Now, make the prospect want to buy *your* home, and describe what is so special about the house you are selling. Remember, the prospect is reading your ad because of a desire to buy a home. You must show that your property can satisfy his needs. Before you write

your ad, look at it from the buyer's point of view. Think of the specific features that will benefit the buyer. Talk about them, but keep your copy honest and believable. Nothing will kill a sale faster than an unbelievable ad. Try to prove your claims with facts. Describe as many benefits in the ad as possible. This is extremely important because what appeals to one family may not appeal to another, and by giving the prospect a selection, you improve your chances of creating desire. Obviously, a family with young children and one with students in high school look for different things. Here are just a few features you might mention in your ad:

Built-in appliances	Low down payment
Age of home	Schools
Type of neighborhood	Financing
Location (not address)	Landscaping
Price	Churches and synagogues
Patio	Family room
View	Garage
Fireplace	Kitchen size or view
Style and construction	Number of baths
Transportation	Shopping areas
Number of bedrooms	Gas grill
Storm windows	Type of heating and air
Low real estate taxes	conditioning

This ad creates desire:

By Owner
Cape Cod

Easy-to-maintain yellow brick 6-room home in High Ridge area. 2 large bedrooms up, 1 down. Efficient, bright built-in kitchen. Knotty-pine recreation room and large yard with 7 spruce trees. Ideal for young children. 3 blocks to schools and shopping. Price $48,000.
Please phone today.   333-0008

Now that you have created desire, you must get the prospective buyer to act.

Make the Prospective Buyer Take Action This is simple! Tell the prospect how to respond to your ad and to do it *now!* The ad that motivates a prospect to action will provide you with a buyer. So your newspaper ad must close with a call to action. If you are having an open-house viewing, extend a cordial invitation. "Open house" refers to a specific time during which you open your house for inspection. The length of time that you allow for viewing on an open-house day should be four to six hours, beginning at approximately 11 A.M. and ending at about 5 or 6 P.M. The open-house hours differ from the regular inspections because you do not require a prospective buyer to have an appointment. If people telephone in response to an ad, certainly set up a specific time for viewing, but on an open-house day you are inviting people passing by, who notice your sign, to come in without first telephoning for an appointment. An open house is well worth the inconvenience. Sunday is generally the best day to hold an open house, but do not begin your viewing before 11 A.M. since many people are attending church services until then, and the ones who are not just do not get out of the house earlier than that on a Sunday morning.

This ad will promote action:

> *Welcome—Open House*
> By Owner—Sunday, 1 to 5 P.M.
> Lovely wooded area with professionally landscaped lot. 4 bedrooms, 2 ceramic baths, and built-in appliances in kitchen. 28 × 15 foot family room with fireplace. Full basement. Price $69,900.
> Please phone today for directions.   333-0008

The interested prospect must telephone to get the address and directions for finding your home. If he or she qualifies over the phone, make the appointment and be sure to give explicit instructions on how to find your home. You want your prospect to arrive to inspect your home in the proper frame of mind. Nothing is more frustrating than driving around in circles because of faulty or vague directions.

An open-house ad should state the day and time of viewing. Be sure your ad discloses the price; this will save your time and a prospective buyer's time. Do not forget to put your phone number in the ad. As suggested previously, leave your address out so that the prospect must call you to find out where the property is located; this gives you the opportunity to qualify callers. You can also tell how effective your newspaper ad is and how well it is pulling.

You are now ready to write a classified newspaper ad that will sell your home. Try to determine which newspapers will obtain the best results. You can usually decide this by watching to see what publication contains the most real estate ads and at what time of the week. If the paper is a weekly publication, of course, you have no choice, but if the newspaper is a daily, usually the weekends are the best time to advertise. If you are not certain what day is best, telephone the classified ad department and ask a representative for assistance. It is far better to place a small ad more frequently than a large ad occasionally. Also, if you run ads in several newspapers, be sure to keep a count from your Prospective Buyer Qualification Sheets as to the source of the prospects. A sample sheet appears at the end of this chapter. One should be filled out after each initial contact with a qualified prospective buyer. These sheets should always be kept next to the telephone, and they are extremely helpful in your weekly sales analysis.

Direct-mail Advertising

Your direct-mail advertising campaign should be on a very select basis. Begin by making a supply of Property Information

Sheets. Samples of different types of sheets are given at the end of this chapter. Choose the one which applies to your property and fill it out accordingly. Sending a Property Information Sheet to local companies, for the attention of the personnel manager, can be very productive. Telephone the personnel manager prior to sending your Property Information Sheet and ask whether the company is transferring employees into the area in the near future and whether you may send him your sheet. Select names of the larger companies in your area from the local classified telephone book.

The company manager will usually post a sheet on a bulletin board or other conspicuous place. Post Property Information Sheets in food stores; many stores have a board to accommodate sale notices. Send sheets to churches, synagogues, and other houses of worship in the vicinity, as clergymen often know of new families who are moving into the area and need housing. Notify social and civic groups by mail also. Another excellent method of direct-mail coverage is to include your Property Information Sheet in the envelope when paying bills to local firms, since most people will take the time to read any material included in an envelope with a bill payment.

Cold-canvass Advertising

This approach to advertising is very economical and does not cost more than a little shoe leather. It requires only that you get out of the house and wander the neighborhood, talking to people on a day-to-day basis. Take a supply of Property Information Sheets with you whenever you go out of the house, since just about anyone you meet could lead you to a buyer. Keep a supply in the glove compartment of your car.

It is a statistical fact that the more people who know your property is for sale, the better your chances of selling it and selling it faster. The faculties of schools and universities in your area can be an excellent source of buyers, and do not neglect to contact parent-teacher associations. Tenants in nearby apartment buildings sometimes are excellent prospects, and motel or hotel managers can be a great source of prospective home buyers. To obtain the names of tenants living in nearby apartment buildings, it will be necessary to walk into the lobbies of the buildings and record the names from the nameplates on the mailboxes. If the apartment building is large and the list of names is lengthy, it is helpful to use a tape recorder. As you approach the building, record the address first; then when you are in the lobby, record the names of the tenants and their apartment numbers. Send your Property Information Sheet to these tenants with a short note or letter indicating that you are the owner of the real estate described on the sheet and saying that they should telephone you for an appointment to inspect the property if they are interested. I have used this technique successfully to sell all types of real estate, and at times it is worthwhile to follow up your letter with a telephone call. Your approach over the telephone should be very low-pressure. Merely introduce yourself and ask whether the tenant received the information that you sent him concerning the sale of your real estate. If he did, ask whether he is interested. If he did not, ask whether he would like to receive the material. If he says no, thank him politely for his time and hang up.

Use your imagination, and chances are good that you will think of sources not even mentioned here.

"For Sale" Signs

If using a "For Sale" sign does not violate any city or village ordinance, then by all means put one up. A "For Sale" sign can be your most effective sales tool. Make sure that it is large enough to be seen from a distance. The sign should measure at least 28 inches in width and 21 inches in height and should be high enough off the ground so that nothing is blocking it. Usually the best color combination is a white background and dark lettering, such as red or black. The sign should read as follows:

FOR SALE
BY OWNER
333-0008
APPOINTMENT ONLY

Place your sign in a conspicuous location on the property. If your property can be seen from two separate strategic locations, you may need two signs. If your real estate faces a road or street with fast traffic, your sign should be painted on both sides and positioned so that traffic going either way will have time to see it.

In addition to your "For Sale" sign, you will need another sign to use for the open-house viewings. This sign can be smaller and need say only "Open House" or "Open for Inspection." An "Open House" sign should be located on the nearest busy street, with arrows pointing in the direction of the property. The "Open House" sign is in addition to the "For Sale" sign and is usually posted only during the time you have the property open for inspection. Afterward, it is stored until the next weekend, or whenever you are holding the next open house. On the other hand, the "For Sale" sign is never removed until your property is sold.

Putting the Telephone to Work for You

The telephone is an extremely important tool to use when selling your real estate. The instant you begin to talk to someone over the phone, you begin to create an impression that can either hinder or benefit you. Your telephone personality is the key to creating interest on the part of prospective buyers sufficient to motivate them to come out and inspect your property. Have your Prospective Buyer Qualification Sheet, Property Information Sheet, and a copy of the most recently placed newspaper ad at hand next to the telephone, along with several pencils. Be prepared when your phone rings. All radios and television sets should be turned off, and background noises should be eliminated. Answer the telephone in a pleasant and cordial voice. Since prospective buyers cannot see the house over the telephone, your voice will influence them when you are describing your property.

Try to get the caller's name and telephone number as soon as possible, but do not ask at the very beginning of the conversation. It is not uncommon for prospective buyers to be hesitant about giving their names at first. After a short time, offer your name voluntarily and ask for the caller's name and phone number; this amounts to a trade of names. When discussing your property with callers, try to find out what their needs are. If you wrote your ad properly, callers will have a fairly good idea of what you are offering. However, not all replies will be in response to newspaper ads. Find out where callers learned that your property was for sale. Was it through a newspaper ad, your sign, or a neighbor? Qualify prospective buyers over the telephone so that if they come out to inspect your property, you already know most of their needs. The best way to accomplish this is by using your Prospective Buyer Qualification Sheet as a checklist for your questions.

Be very descriptive over the telephone and try to paint pleasant pictures: "The house is in a lovely, wooded setting," "The porch is open and sunny," or "The view of the yard from the kitchen window is so pretty," for example. Use descriptive phrases in your telephone conversation as well as your newspaper ads. After you have done a complete job of describing your home and qualifying the caller, set up an appointment: "I can show you our home this evening. Would six or seven o'clock be convenient?" If the buyer qualifies and you have made an appointment, be certain that you have noted all pertinent information on the Prospective Buyer Qualification Sheet so that you will be ready for the appointment.

Before your telephone rings, be certain that you are prepared:

1. Have your Prospective Buyer Qualification Sheet, Property Information Sheet, and a copy of the most recently placed newspaper ad at hand next to the telephone.

2. Be familiar with all the information listed on the Property Information Sheet so that you do not have to shuffle papers and waste time when answering questions.

3. Keep pencils near all phones and put all notes on the Prospective Buyer Qualification Sheet.

When your telephone rings, be certain to:

1. Answer it as soon as possible.
2. Have a positive attitude when answering.
3. Assume the caller is a good prospect.
4. Throw away gum or cigarette.
5. Speak clearly into the mouthpiece.
6. Smile when you talk; use a friendly voice.
7. Learn the caller's name and get the correct spelling; also get the address and phone number.

Before you hang up, check the following:

1. Have you been helpful?
2. Have you described your property vividly?
3. Have you learned all the needs of the caller's family?
4. Have you repeated points the caller seemed interested in?
5. Have you dealt with the caller's objections intelligently?
6. Have you asked for an appointment?

After the telephone call, be certain to complete all your notes on the Prospective Buyer Qualification Sheet and, of course. note the day and time of the appointment.

How to Handle Telephone Calls Understand that many prospective buyers are hesitant to disclose information about themselves over the telephone. In the following exchange, the caller is asking typical questions, and the owner is exchanging information and arousing the caller's interest in the property:

OWNER: Good morning. This is 333-0008. (Avoid giving your name immediately, since you can offer it a little later in the conversation in exchange for the caller's name. This seems spontaneous, and most callers will respond favorably. Most will be caught off guard and will divulge their names after you volunteer yours.)

PROSPECT: I read your ad and would like your address so that we can drive by and look at the house.

OWNER: I'd be most happy to give you our address. Are you familiar with Northbrook? Do you know the Meadowbrook area? (Avoid giving the address until you describe your home and get the information you are seeking to qualify the caller.)

PROSPECT: What is the address? I'd like to just drive by with my husband and see the area.

OWNER: Our home is on Whitehall Drive, a very quiet street with so many pretty trees. It is very nice for children. Do you have any? (Notice that part of the caller's question was answered, but the owner still has not given her the exact address. The owner answered her with another question in order to get more information.)

PROSPECT: We have two boys, seven and ten years old. (Now is the time to talk about features not mentioned in the newspaper ad.)

OWNER: Your children will be in School District 28, which is considered to be the finest in the area. And all of you can enjoy the family room. It's great for watching television or playing games. The lot is 50 by 197 and has many full-grown trees. Do you own a home now, or do you rent? (Again, the owner has answered the question about the address with another question.)

PROSPECT: We own a home in Antioch, but my husband has been transferred to his company's Northbrook office. (You now determine that this is a good prospect.)

OWNER: By the way, my name is Carl Kosnar. What is your name? (When you ask the caller's name, be firm; do not hesitate. That will make it difficult for the prospect to refuse to give you his or her name.)

PROSPECT: My name is Mrs. Fred Ballard. (You now have a possible buyer. Try to make an appointment. Often, by this time the prospect has asked for an appointment; if not, you take the initiative.)

OWNER: Mrs. Ballard, it sounds as if our home suits your needs. Would you and Mr. Ballard like to see it tonight or tomorrow night? Would six or seven o'clock be better? (Do not suggest only one time for an appointment; always offer an alternative. This makes it hard for the prospect to give you a "no" answer.)

PROSPECT: Mr. Kosnar, tonight at seven o'clock would be better, since my husband works tomorrow night. (Always try to arrange an appointment for both the husband and the wife to inspect together, or for anyone else who might be important to the decision, such as a parent who is loaning money for the purchase.)

OWNER: Good. We will be expecting you at seven o'clock. In case something comes up and I must reach you, Mrs. Ballard, what is your phone number? (You now have the prospect's name and telephone number, and should she and her husband not show up at the designated time, you can telephone them.)

The telephone conversation should have allowed you to gather much of the information you need for the Prospective Buyer Qualification Sheet. Review this information prior to the appointment.

When the Broker Calls Advertising, in addition to attracting buyers, will also attract real estate brokers. Brokers will telephone and tell you that they have a customer for your property. This is standard practice among real estate brokers, who want to talk sellers into using their services. A broker considers anyone who is trying to sell his own property to be a prime target for listing, since the owner has already made the decision to sell. Now, it is only a matter of convincing the owner to use the real estate broker's services. Be confident and firm. Let the broker know that you have no intention of using a brokerage firm. If you show the slightest indication of weakness, the broker will continue to call and try to create doubt in your mind about your ability to sell your own real estate. Generally, it is wise to include "Principals Only" or "No Brokers" in your newspaper ad. Keep a positive attitude and follow the instructions in this book, and you will be successful in selling your property. This system has worked for me, as it has for others I have taught—and it will work for you. It is a formula for selling real estate that just cannot miss!

PROSPECTIVE BUYER QUALIFICATION SHEET

1. Name_____Date_____

2. Telephone—Home_____Office_____

3. How did prospect learn about home? Newspaper_____

   Sign_____Neighbor_____Other_____

4. Prospect's approximate price range_____

5. How much cash does prospect have to invest in the down payment?

   _____

6. How large is prospect's family?_____

   Number of children and their ages_____

7. How many rooms does prospect need?_____

8. Where does prospect live now?_____

   If apartment, how many rooms?_____When does his lease

   expire?_____If in a home, must he sell his present

   home before he is able to buy?_____

9. How long has prospect been looking?_____

10. How many cars does prospect own?_____

    Does prospect need public transportation?_____

11. Are both husband and wife employed, and where?_____

    _____

12. Is prospect interested in the area because of a specific school, church, or

    synagogue or because of transportation facilities or proximity to husband's

    or wife's work?_____

    _____

PROPERTY INFORMATION SHEET

RESIDENTIAL

	DESCRIPTION
Address_____City_____Lot Size_____	
Style and Const._____Zoned_____Garage_____	
	ROOM SIZES
No. Rooms: 1st Fl._____Rms._____Baths	
2nd Fl._____Rms._____Baths	
Kitchen_____	L.R.
Range_____Refrig._____Screens_____Storm Sash_____	D.R.
Total Baths____Bathroom Walls____Kind of Tub____Showers...	Kit.
Bldg. Age_____Basement_____	Br.
Type Heat_____H.W. Heater_____Elect: 110V 220V	Br.
Taxes 197___Possession_____Mtge. Info._____	Br.
Schools_____Churches_____	
Other Information:	

Phone

Owner_____ PRICE

Address_____

PROPERTY INFORMATION SHEET

VACANT LAND

Size of Lot	Address	Zoning
	Faces	

Taxes

Assessments

DISTANCE TO	IMPROVEMENTS
School_____	Paving_____
Stores_____	Sidewalk_____
Transp._____	Sewer_____
Ctr. of City_____	Gas & Elec._____
	Water_____
	Switch Track_____

North

West   East

South

LEGAL DESCRIPTION

PRICE

Owner_____Phone_____ $

Address_____

PROPERTY INFORMATION SHEET

APARTMENTS

Zoned	Size of Lot	Address City	DESCRIPTION

Const. & Style_____

Apt. Description_____Garage_____

Room Sizes: L.R._____D.R._____Kit._____Br._____Br._____Br._____

No. Bathrooms_____Bath Walls_____Tubs_____Showers_____

Kitchens_____ Kitchen Walls_____ Ranges_____Refrigerators_____

Heat_____H.W. Heater_____Bldg. Age_____Elec. Serv. 110 220

Remarks: (Lease Possession) _____

_____

_____ Mtge. Info._____

MONTHLY INCOME	ESTIMATED ANNUAL EXPENSES

_____Apts.____Rooms @ _____   Taxes (   ) $_____Janitor $_____

_____Apts.____Rooms @ _____   Fuel $_____Insurance $_____

_____Apts.____Rooms @ _____   Gas $_____Refuse $_____

_____Apts.____Rooms @ _____   Electric $_____Decorating $_____

_____Apts.____Rooms @ _____   Water $_____ $_____

_____Garages_____ @ _____ $_____

Monthly Income $_____Annual Income $____Net Income $____Total $_____

Owner_____

Address_____

Phone_____

PRICE
$

PROPERTY INFORMATION SHEET

MANUFACTURING AND INDUSTRIAL BUILDING

Zoned	Size of Lot	Address	DESCRIPTION

Can be used for_____

_____

_____

		INCOME	EXPENSES

Bldg. Size _____Switch Track_____ _____   Taxes_____

No. of Floors___Loading___Heat____ _____   Fuel_____

Sq. Ft. per Fl.___Sprinkler___Bsmt.____ _____   Insurance_____

Construction___Ceiling Height_____ _____ _____

Floor Loads___Electric_____ _____ _____

Elevator_____ TOTAL EXPENSES $_____

Present   Mo.
Mtge. $_____Due_____Pmt._____(a)___% Annual Gross Inc. $_____

Indicated   Mo.
Mtge. $_____Term_____Pmt._____(a)___% Annual Net Inc. $_____

Lease Information_____

Owner_____

Address_____Phone_____

PRICE
Rental per month

PROPERTY INFORMATION SHEET

MISCELLANEOUS AND INVESTMENT PROPERTY

Zoned	Size of Lot	Address	DESCRIPTION
		City	

Taxes (   ) $_____   Janitor $_____

Fuel $_____   Insurance $_____

Gas $_____   Refuse $_____

Electric $_____   Decorating $_____

Water $_____ $_____

                                                $_____

Monthly   Annual   Net
Income $_____Income $_____Income $_____Total $_____

Owner_____

PRICE

Address_____Phone_____

$

4
Showing Your Home

In order to show your property to a purchaser, you obviously must attract a prospective buyer. Regardless of how you attracted the prospective buyer and whether the initial contact was by telephone or in person, the process of qualifying must start at once. As discreetly as possible, you must determine whether the price of your home is within the prospective buyer's ability to pay. If the prospect cannot afford your house, you had better determine this early in the negotiations. It matters very little that the prospective buyer loves your house and wants to buy it. If he does not have the financial means to do so, you will be wasting your time. The general rule in the housing industry is that a buyer should pay no more than 2½ to 3 times his gross annual income for a home. In addition to price, you must qualify the prospect with regard to family size, schools, public transportation, church affiliation, and civic activities.

If the prospect seems to be able to afford your property and appears to be a good fit for the house, you are now ready to show. Chances are that when a prospect arrives, he or she will be accompanied by one or more individuals. A husband and wife will sometimes bring the children or even the grandparents. You should, of course, be courteous to all members of the party, but try to determine who is the dominant figure and which one will make the final decision. When you discover which is the most influential member of the group, concentrate strongly on that person. Allow the key person to feel that he or she is inspecting a future home, not just bricks and mortar. Another important element in showing your house, or any other real estate, is to direct prospects to your property via the most scenic and attractive route. Do not direct them past unpleasant sights in the immediate area if you can possibly avoid it. You want prospects to be in a receptive frame of mind when they arrive at your front door.

When the prospect rings the doorbell, extend a cheerful greeting and introduce yourself to everyone in the party. You should have at least one person's full name already noted on your Prospective Buyer Qualification Sheet. Most people will telephone you before coming out, except when you are holding an open house. It is better to limit off-the-street inspections, without an appointment, to days designated and advertised as open-house days or as days when your house is open for inspection. An open house should be advertised in your newspaper ad and is best attended on weekends. However, as was previously pointed out, you should display an "Open House" sign on your property during the viewing hours in addition to your "For Sale" sign. At that time you will attract buyers who are out riding around looking at houses. Since some will not have read your newspaper ad or made an appointment, try to get the prospective buyer's name, address, and telephone number listed on your Prospective Buyer Qualification Sheet as soon as possible.

Before you begin showing prospective buyers through the house, hand them a Property Information Sheet so that they will have all the salient facts concerning the property in front of them as they inspect it.

Before the prospect appears on the scene, decide who will show your property. It is best to have either the husband or wife, not both, take the prospect through the house. Having more than one person show the property can cause confusion. Although my wife is not a real estate saleswoman or broker, she is especially good at showing a house, and she has been responsible for showing and selling two of our homes in the past four years. When we are selling any of our income property, I usually take the prospects through to inspect the building. Obviously, at busy times, we each might take a separate buyer through the property. After each showing, the husband and wife should discuss the prospect with each other and review the Prospective Buyer Qualification Sheet. This way, both will be fully briefed on every prospect.

When you are taking a prospective buyer through the property, there are a few simple rules to follow:

1. Do not take a caravan through your home; a group consisting of more than three people is difficult to handle.

2. Your pet should be out of the way. Keep your dog or cat outside while you are showing your property.

3. Turn all radios and television sets off; the noise is too distracting.

If, during the inspection, a prospect asks whether you will accept a lower price, try to avoid the question until you have had an opportunity to show the entire property; negotiating prematurely is a mistake.

As you take the prospect through the house, point out all the amenities—the dimensions of large rooms, the type of heating, special construction features like plastered walls, and appliances that stay with the house. Do not forget to point out closet space, special storage areas, and special features such as storm windows and screens. Mention carpeting in hallways or rooms if it will remain; however, if the carpeting is not in good condition, do not bring the subject up. Try not to overlook any feature that might help clinch the sale. Be quick to point out pleasant views, such as streams, trees, and other attractive homes in the neighborhood.

Certain people derive a high degree of satisfaction from living in a prestigious neighborhood. Snob appeal is a powerful motivating force, and it is worthwhile to mention the professional and social status of other owners in your immediate vicinity. Surprisingly enough, this social-esteem motivation is prevalent among lower- and medium-priced home buyers as well as those interested in buying high-priced homes.

When you have given a complete presentation and the prospective buyer has made a thorough inspection, stop talking. Give the prospect an opportunity to ask questions that have not yet been answered. Do a complete job of selling, but be cautious not to make any misleading statements. If you do not know the answer to a question, admit it, but tell the prospect that you will do your best to get the answer as soon as possible and will contact him or her later that day.

Be prepared to discuss the following neighborhood elements with the prospect:

Real estate taxes (high, low, or average)
Utility costs
Zoning (steady or changing)
Age of homes around you
Community planning
Police and fire protection
Recreation facilities—parks, beaches, playgrounds, and golf
    courses
Public sanitation or septic system
Schools

Transportation
Religious life
Shopping

Although the Property Information Sheet contains all this information, cover these points while the prospect is there in the house.

You should not be offended if a prospect mentions a deferred maintenance item. This is standard sales resistance, and you should try to anticipate questions concerning problem areas and be ready to answer them if they arise. Get cost estimates of work that should be done so that you can make positive statements about the cost of repairs. Generally, if the building is in good shape, the sales resistance will be at a minimum. The best policy is to do the maintenance and repair work prior to showing, since this usually will mean a better sales price. However, even if you disagree with the prospect, do not argue the point; if you cannot change a prospect's opinion tactfully, simply ignore the matter.

If two prospects should arrive at the same time, do not try to show both of them the house simultaneously. This could happen only during an open house, since any other inspections would be by appointment only. During an open house, it is a good idea for both the husband and wife to be at home. Even if you are fortunate enough to have several prospects come at once, do not rush; take enough time to show the house thoroughly and answer all questions. If the others are genuinely interested in the property, they will wait until you are finished. A prospect who wants to revisit a room or two, or even the entire house, should be allowed to do so alone, without the feeling of being pressured. Get the prospective buyer to relax.

Rarely will a prospect sign a contract immediately after seeing your property; to expect this would be a little unrealistic. However, after the inspection is completed and you have answered all questions, if the prospect is enthusiastic about the house, ask him to buy. If your prospect has been qualified properly and is very interested, let him know that you would like him to have your house. Asking a prospect to buy, if the house is a good fit and the prospect is truly interested, will usually move the negotiations along faster. Even though the prospective buyer will probably leave after the first viewing without signing a contract, be certain to part on a friendly note. By now, your Prospective Buyer Qualification Sheet should contain the prospect's name, address, and telephone number as well as all pertinent qualifying information. The more information you have, the more effectively you can negotiate. Arrange to talk to prospects soon after they have checked the details that concern them. Be sure that they have a Property Information Sheet when they leave.

5

Negotiating the Sale

Negotiation begins with the very first meeting between buyer and seller, regardless of whether this happens over the telephone or in a face-to-face situation.

All successful negotiators possess a quality called "empathy" —the ability to put themselves in the place of the other person and understand his thoughts. It is important for you to get to know the buyer and what is motivating him. Does he like to feel important? Does the buyer appear to make decisions quickly or to be a procrastinator? Get a reading on your buyer; working too fast with a slow-thinking buyer, or working too slowly with a buyer who decides quickly, can lose the sale for you. When you are dealing with a quick buyer, be thorough but concise. On the other hand, when you are working with a slow buyer, take the extra time and paint a convincing picture.

The consummation of your sale will be a direct result of your ability to negotiate. You will find that the time you spend reading and learning a few basic principles of negotiating will be converted into a higher selling price. Negotiating the sale of real property is a battle of wits between you and the buyer. Serious buyers have given a great deal of thought to their purchase strategy and will employ any number of techniques in order to buy for less money. A buyer's planned sales resistance can involve criticizing your property in order to discredit the value of your home, or the buyer may appear to have little or no interest in the property, employing time to his or her advantage in the hope that the price will be reduced.

Negotiating takes a cool head, and the experienced negotiator will immediately begin to question and draw out buyers in order to qualify them. A good negotiator also influences buyers in a subtle manner. A natural smile can be very effective because it indicates confidence in the property you are selling. You can be confident because you are selling a very fine product that no one knows better than you.

Buyers usually will not tell you what they are really thinking. They will tell you only what they believe will mislead you into thinking that they need your home far less than they actually do. Most buyers will try to disguise their true feelings. You must be confident and patient, and with the passing of time your qualifying procedure will begin to uncover the buyer's true attitude. Remember that your negotiating strategy should be mapped long before the prospect appears at your front door for an inspection.

Concessions are very much a part of negotiating. Most buyers like to dicker and haggle over price, and therefore it is often wise to put a "cushion" in your price. Estimate the fair market value of your property and then add some reasonable amount. In my estimation, this should be 2 to 3 percent of the selling price and should not exceed 5 percent. Buyers consider that paying the asking price is a bad reflection on their negotiating ability. Do not balloon your sales price unreasonably, or else you will find that you have discouraged sincere buyers in your price range. If buyers are discouraged before they see the property, you will be short on prospects.

An important fact to remember is that concessions do not necessarily have to be in the form of dollars. Maybe if you offer an earlier possession date to the buyer, he or she will be willing to pay your asking price. However, if the buyer is offering you all cash with no mortgage contingency in the contract, possibly you should consider an offer lower than your asking price. All cash in a tight mortgage market certainly is an attractive offer, if the price is not unreasonably low. There should be a compensating benefit for every concession. Do not reduce your asking price without requesting a compensating benefit because the prospect will then feel that he can do even better and will make endless demands.

No doubt, you will be confronted by the prospect who criticizes the price, ridicules your home, and tells you about all the excellent buys available down the street. If you determine that a prospect is not a bona fide buyer and is just trying to "steal" a house, do not spend any more time with him.

Sometimes in a last-ditch attempt to hold your price, you can offer to throw in a piece of furniture or an appliance that you really do not need. Mutual concessions by the buyer and seller do not necessarily have to match each other in monetary value. Even though you are not willing to reduce your price, the fact that you will give up a piece of furniture or some other item helps the buyer to feel that he is getting a bargain—that he is receiving a little extra for his money.

Even when an offer is low, try not to give the buyer a flat "no." The buyer might only be sending up a trial balloon and really be prepared to pay much more. If you have not had much action on your property and if the few offers you have had are all low, even after good exposure and sufficient time, you had better give some thought to accepting a lower price.

When you reject a written offer with an earnest-money check that is lower than your asking price, it is the same as buying your home back at the offered price. It is a good idea to remember that a smooth negotiator always tries another way to accomplish the objective—a different angle, a new twist.

As you get closer to negotiating a deal, you might wonder when the ideal time is to ask the buyer to sign the contract. There is no magic moment. If you have handled the buyer properly, his signing a contract and giving you an earnest-money check will be the natural culmination of the sequence of events. Do not let the signing hinge on a major "yes" or "no" decision; it might frighten the prospect away. Lead the prospect to sign the contract by an orderly, step-by-step procedure. This can be done by asking questions like, "How would you and Mrs. Ballard like to take title?" "When would you like to take possession?" Questions like these will prepare the buyer for the time when the contract must be signed. After the signature has been placed on the contract, there will be a sigh of relief because the buyer "never really knew when it happened."

How to Cope with Unusual Prospects

In dealing with prospective buyers, you will see that most of them act and behave in a rational and logical fashion. A few, however, will not react to your presentation the way they are supposed to.

Even though you may consider them strange or odd, most of these characters can be sold. It is simply a matter of knowing how to negotiate when you run into them. Your main concern is to recognize them early in the negotiations in order to handle them properly.

Buck Passers These prospects usually offer little or no sales resistance. They will not criticize, and quite often they have very little to say about the property. They cannot bring themselves to stand up to the seller in direct negotiations, and so they defer to someone else. Their usual pattern is to require consultation with a parent, a brother, or almost anyone they can think of just to avoid making a decision themselves. Be aggressive at this point and offer to show your property and speak to whomever is introduced into the deal. If the prospect says it is not feasible for you to meet the person who is being consulted, try another approach. Make the reluctant prospect see that he or she must make this decision, and ask very directly what special insight the consultant possesses. An important fact to remember is that this type finds it hard to say "no," so keep pushing in logical steps for a positive conclusion and finally a signature.

Mechanical Prospects   These prospective buyers will ask very specific question about construction, such as "What grade of lumber was used?" "What kind of roof shingle and insulation does the house have?" It may appear at first that they are trying to make you look stupid, but actually they are not. These prospects are usually genuinely interested in the technical and constructional aspects of the property. Attempt to answer their questions to be best of your ability, but if you do not know the answers, do not be ashamed to say so and to offer to get the information. Under no circumstances try to bluff such prospects because if they catch you in even a minor falsehood, you will have negated any credence established up to that point. After all questions are answered, press for a signature on the contract.

Quiet Prospects   Subdued prospects will walk through your home and listen to your sales talk while saying hardly a word to you. Actually, such prospects may have low sales resistance and use silence as a defense. Draw them out and make them talk. Keep shooting questions—questions about some feature of your home, about themselves and their families, or about anything that will help you qualify them.

"Me Too" Prospects Logic or reasoning will never sell this "keep up with the Joneses" type. Your best approach is to name-drop. Mention the important people who live near you. Scatter their names throughout your sales talk, and chances are that such a prospect will be impressed and will end up buying your home.

Egocentric Prospects These insufferable bores know everything and everybody; just ask them. You must make them feel important. Ask for their advice or opinion and, of course, be grateful for it. This approach is a lethal weapon against this type. Play up to them, and they will recognize your intelligence and—you hope—reward your patience by purchasing your property.

Self-conscious Prospects Typically, these prospects place an abnormal value on what others think. Their greatest fear is that they may not be doing the right thing and, what is worse, that they will be held up to ridicule by their friends. You can detect these prospects by their repeated references to what others might say. They rarely advance arguments of their own. Tell such a prospect how pleased other people who have purchased property in the area are. Point out how impressed the prospect's friends will be with your home. Oddly enough, you are not selling self-conscious prospects on the benefits of your home, although benefits should not be neglected; rather, you are selling them on what their friends and family will think of the property.

Sign on the Dotted Line

There is no mystery about getting a buyer's signature on a contract; it is purely a matter of motivating him sufficiently to make a decision. A buyer who has thoroughly inspected the house and has returned for a second visit has had enough time to consider, so press for a signature. There are no secret formulas for obtaining a buyer's signature, just as there is no specific time to sign a contract. The time to get a signature is when you feel that the buyer's willingness to purchase is high. If you have prepared for the sale and qualified the buyer, the signing will not be a problem. As a matter of fact, it will seem quite natural.

If your attorney has provided you with a contract that requires merely inserting the buyer's name and address, have the buyer sign this document and simultaneously provide you with an earnest-money check. If your attorney prefers to draft the contract after the buyer is known, be sure to receive a check immediately.

Tell the buyer that your attorney will contact him in a few days to arrange for his signature.

My personal preference is to have an attorney review a standard title insurance company contract form, which can be purchased at a store selling legal forms, in advance so that I will be in a position to ask the buyer to sign the contract at the property and write me an earnest-money check at the same time. There is no better time to get a signature and an earnest-money check than when you are sitting across from the buyer, watching his excitement. However, if your attorney instructs you to provide him with the buyer information and wishes to draft the contract after he reviews this information, do not argue the point. He is protecting your interest, and to argue would defeat the purpose of retaining an attorney. Allow me to give you a little sound advice about attorneys. Most good attorneys have a very busy schedule, but no matter how capable an attorney is, he is of no value to you unless he is on top of your deal. As a matter of fact, if he neglects your transaction, he can cause you unnecessary problems. If you feel that you are not receiving all the attention you should, contact him periodically to find out the status of your transaction. Remember, "The wheel that squeaks the loudest gets the oil." That might sound trite, but staying on top of a deal is the surest method of completing a transaction successfully and on time.

Always request a substantial deposit from the buyer, regardless of whether the contract is signed simultaneously or later. Asking for, and receiving, an earnest-money check will prevent the buyer from changing his mind the next day. He might otherwise reconsider because he thinks the price is too high or because he saw a better deal down the street. On the sale of a home, I usually request a deposit of $1,000, which is to be raised to 10 percent of the selling price within five days. The check should be made payable to you, your attorney's escrow account, or a mutually agreeable title company, to be held in their escrow account until the closing.

There still remains a large void between sincere interest on the part of the prospective buyer and getting a signature on the contract and receiving an earnest-money check. An alert seller will pick up warning signals that will tell him when the buyer is ready to sign a contract. For example, a prospective **buyer** is probably hooked when he and his wife start to visually place their furniture in your living room. If they go off to the side by themselves and whisper, "Well, honey, what do you think?" or "I think it fits the budget, don't you?" chances are good that they are ready to sign the contract.

Sooner or later, the buyer will want to discuss the price. Try not to talk about the price until you have sold the buyer on all the benefits of the home. If price enters in too soon, that becomes the main issue instead of the amenities and whether the house is a good fit for the buyer. Of course price is important, but many times a buyer will pay the asking price if certain terms can be arranged satisfactorily. It was previously mentioned that if you help the buyer out by carrying a second mortgage, if you allow the buyer to take possession earlier, or if you accommodate the buyer in some way, it is possible that the asking price will be paid and not become an issue.

When an offer is made that is less than your asking price, do not be offended; also, as was mentioned before, unless the price offered is ridiculously low, never give the buyer a flat "no" reply. You should attempt to negotiate the price upward. The buyer will point out drawbacks to your property in an attempt to substantiate the offer. Do not argue these points; merely reiterate the amenities of your property by way of review and refer to comparable sales in the area that support your price.

Here is another good bargaining tool to use when you are attempting to raise the buyer's price: Determine the additional price in terms of dollars per month and point out that even several thousand dollars more in price, when amortized over twenty-five years, depending on the prevailing interest rate, will amount to only a few dollars more per month when making mortgage payments.

However, before you reject an offer lower than your asking price, think about how long your property has been on the market. If, after three to four weeks, a number of people have inspected your home and no one has made an offer, this tells you something. Let us analyze your situation. If your property is in a generally good location, is in reasonably good repair, has had the proper exposure to the market, and is not subject to a tight mortgage market, there is only one other factor that could be affecting the response, and that is the price—it is too high!

There really is no generally accepted time schedule for selling a house or any other real property. In a hot market for house sales, a house might sell in a few days. Four years ago my wife and I sold our three-bedroom ranch home, and it took approximately four weeks from the time we put the "For Sale" sign up until we had a signed contract. Just recently, we sold our four-bedroom split-level home in exactly one week. At the end of each week, a review of that week's activity should be made to see what improvements can be instituted. Review your

Prospective Buyer Qualification Sheets. If you have used these sheets properly, they will hold a wealth of information for you.

Too high a price may or may not be the reason your property is not selling. After reviewing the prospect sheets, you might observe that the newspaper ads produced very few, if any, telephone calls. Either revise the ad or change newspapers. Have you held an open house at least once a week? Are your signs placed in conspicuous locations? Have you done any direct mailing? An honest and objective review of your entire sales presentation will usually uncover the problem.

Buyer's Monthly Payments

Some prospective buyers do not know how to calculate their monthly principal and interest payments for the mortgage repayment. Many times the buyer will raise this point just before signing the contract. The tables given in Chapter 9 will enable you to figure the buyer's monthly principal and interest payments.

Should the question of the buyer's closing costs come up, you had better instruct the buyer to discuss this matter with his attorney or lending institution. The seller's closing costs are discussed elsewhere in this book.

Once again, when all the buyer's questions are answered and he has been qualified, ask him to sign the contract. Obviously, you will be nervous, but unless you take positive action and ask him to sign (hand him the pen!), you will not have a deal. After both of you have signed the contract, do not allow your excitement to prevent you from asking for an earnest-money check.

Remember, too, that the buyer did not necessarily get a bad deal just because you received a price that was acceptable to you. The reverse is also true; the fact that you did not receive your asking price does not always indicate that you negotiated poorly or made a bad deal.

6
Financing

Assisting the buyer with financing is a critical step in selling your property. Approximately 80 percent of all homes sold require financing. The percentage for first-user homes is even higher. If your buyer does not have the knowledge to arrange his own financing, you can be of assistance. Even though this is an area about which most buyers and sellers know very little, you can obtain financing for the buyer if you know how and where to go for money. Granted, there are times when home mortgage money is more easily obtainable than it is at other times, and it is certainly easier to sell your home during a period when mortgage funds are readily available. However, my wife and I personally have sold two homes during two of the tightest home mortgage markets in recent times, and we helped both buyers to arrange financing successfully. When mortgage money is in short supply, everyone including real estate brokers will have difficulty finding mortgage money; but it is available.

Now, who will lend your buyer money to buy a house? The answer is that any number of lending institutions might. These include savings and loan associations, commercial banks, mutual savings banks, insurance companies, and mortgage companies. There are other sources, such as private investors, business people, professional people, and wealthy individuals. It is more likely, however, that a lending institution will be able to serve your buyer's needs best.

Kinds of Home Loans

The most common home loan made today is the conventional loan made by an institution such as a savings and loan association or a commercial bank, which assumes the risk of lending the funds. An FHA loan is insured by a federal government agency which actually insures the repayment of the principal amount of the loan to the approved lending institution. A VA loan is guaranteed by the Veterans Administration, which assures the lending institution repayment of the principal amount of the loan. Another kind of mortgage that is becoming more prevalent is the loan guaranteed by a private mortgage insurance company. This is a private insurer, and not a government agency, which assures the conventional lender that the principal amount of the loan will be repaid.

Conventional Home Loans Lending institutions are regulated as to the proportionate amount of the appraised value of a building that they can lend and the length of time the loan can be outstanding. For instance, commercial banks can lend 70 to 75 percent of appraised value for a period of twenty years. Savings and loan associations can loan up to 90 percent of appraised value for a twenty-five-year period. In both the above cases, the regulations can be relaxed, and more lenient terms can be offered by the same two lenders, if the loans are FHA-insured or VA-guaranteed loans. A loan insured by the FHA or guaranteed by the VA can, at times, provide 100 percent financing for a term of thirty years.

FHA-insured Home Loans The FHA is not a lending institution for single-family homes, but rather a federal agency that insures mortgages on homes, multifamily rental projects, cooperative and condominium housing, housing for members of the armed services, and housing designed for the elderly. The FHA protects the lender against loss by insuring the mortgage, which allows the buyer to invest a smaller down payment and to take a longer time to repay the loan. Limits are set by the FHA as to the interest rate and other charges, and it must conclude that the transaction is economically viable and that the mortgage applicant is credit-worthy. Interest rate ceilings will be adjusted from time to time according to market conditions. To qualify for participation in an FHA program, an applicant must meet certain standards and criteria. The real estate must also be examined to determine whether it meets a certain standard.

If your buyer plans to apply for an FHA-insured loan, he will avoid unnecessary delay if his application is completed accurately as follows: (1) Be sure that all required signatures are placed on the documents, (2) be sure that all exhibits have the necessary signatures, (3) place the correct address and legal description on all documents requiring them, and (4) be sure the lot dimensions are correct. Be exceptionally careful when completing FHA forms since a careless mistake will waste precious time. Accuracy on your part is also important when you submit your property to the FHA for appraisal purposes. In addition to determining whether the buyer is financially able to repay the loan, the FHA will appraise the property being sold to determine what the market value is at the present time. Once the market value is established, the appraiser will decide the amount of mortgage funds the FHA will insure on the property. If the FHA decides to insure the mortgage, its Appraisal Section will issue a written commitment indicating what size mortgage it will insure. This commitment is good only for a certain period of time and will expire if not used.

One of the principal activities of the FHA is to insure mortgages on one- to four-unit family houses. Subject to limitations when the mortgagor (borrower) lives in the home, the FHA insures mortgages representing up to 97 percent of the property value as appraised by its staff. This means that the borrower must pay at least 3 percent of the value as a down payment. A mortgagor sixty-two years or older may borrow the down payment and closing costs from an approved FHA source. The term of repayment of a house mortgage insured under Section 203(b) of the National Housing Act cannot be more than thirty years for an existing building. In addition to house mortgages insured under Section 203(b), insurance is also authorized under Section 203 for the following other catagories: (1) no-down-payment loans for veterans, (2) disaster loans, (3) riot-area loans, and (4) low-cost rural housing. For specific instructions and guidance, contact the Housing Assistance Administration at a Housing and Urban Development (HUD) regional office located in one of the following cities:

New York, New York
Philadelphia, Pennsylvania
Atlanta, Georgia
Chicago, Illinois
Fort Worth, Texas
San Francisco, California
Kansas City, Missouri
Seattle, Washington
Boston, Massachusetts

VA-Guaranteed and VA-Insured Loans A World War II veteran, a veteran of the Korean conflict, a widow of a World

War II or Korean conflict veteran, or a cold-war veteran is entitled to participate in the GI home loan program if he or she meets certain requirements. There are several facets of VA-backed loans that make them attractive to both the buyer and the lender. For example, the interest rate ceiling on these loans is regulated by statute so as to be adjusted to the needs prevalent in the money market. Also, qualified veterans can now pay more than the appraised value of a home, although the price must not be greater than the VA's estimate of reasonable worth.

With a guaranteed loan, the VA agrees to pay the lending institution, upon the veteran's default, a specified portion of the loan less an amount recovered when the lender sells the house to liquidate the security. However, with an insured loan, the VA agrees to indemnify the lending institution against the veteran's default up to an amount in the lender's insurance reserve or the unpaid balance on the loan, whichever is less.

The important thing to remember is that lenders usually feel safe and protected against losses with a GI-backed loan.

Private Mortgage Insurers Private insurers of conventional home mortgages do not loan money. These companies merely insure a portion of the funds loaned by a lending institution. Private insurers usually work much faster than government agencies in processing loans and getting them approved. The private mortgage insurance allows the lending institution to loan a greater portion of the value of the property, and the terms are usually more lenient. Your buyer can discuss this method of financing with a loan officer at his savings and loan association or bank.

Assuming the Seller's Mortgage If your property has an existing mortgage balance, investigate to see whether your mortgage is assumable. If your mortgage can be assumed, it might be to the buyer's advantage to do so, especially if the interest rate is less than the prevailing rate. The assumption clause does not appear in home mortgages frequently these days, but have an attorney check your mortgage document just to be certain. If your mortgage allows an assumption, it could be very beneficial to you. In the event your mortgage is assumable, find out whether there is any penalty and, if so, how much it will amount to.

Purchase-Money Mortgage No chapter on home financing would be complete without discussing the possibility of the seller's taking back a purchase-money mortgage. If the property you own is free and clear of debt, you might consider taking back a mortgage on your house. Of course, you would use this method of financing the buyer only if you did not need the cash proceeds yourself. By extending a mortgage to the buyer, you are providing the mortgage funds yourself and should expect to earn a good return on your investment. Let us assume that you sold your home, with no indebtedness, for $20,000 and that you are willing to accept $5,000 in cash and take back a $15,000 purchase-money mortgage at 7½ percent interest for twenty years. This investment would provide you with a monthly income of $120.84. Over a twenty-year period, you would receive $29,001 in principal and interest (use the tables in Chapter 9). This method of financing real estate is quite common.

Where to Go for a Loan If your buyer is uncertain as to where to go to obtain a mortgage, suggest that he first go to the commercial bank where he has his checking account or savings account. The other equally likely source of mortgage funds is the savings and loan association that has his passbook or savings account. These are two excellent sources of money. After all, these institutions know the buyer, and he has established a financial track record with them. Of course, the lender will require the buyer to complete a credit application to see whether he has a history of meeting his financial obligations. His age, length of employment, and character will also be verified. The lending institution will appraise the house to determine the fair market value for loan purposes.

Another source of mortgage funds is your own bank or savings and loan association. If you have been a customer for a period of years, you can reasonably expect them to assist you in providing a mortgage for your buyer. Make your lending institution understand that you will be depositing some or all of the proceeds from the sale of your property into their institution and that this deserves some consideration. Do not be shy when talking to lenders; they are in business to loan money.

A third approach is to investigate whether the buyer's employer is in a position to influence a lending institution that the employer favors with his business accounts. It is very common for a buyer's employer to be extremely helpful at a time like this, especially if the buyer is a cherished employee. Bring this matter up and strongly suggest that the buyer talk to his employer concerning a mortgage.

When a Mortgage Source Is Found

The lender will usually require the borrower to complete a loan application, which necessitates providing the borrower's name and address, the location of the property being mortgaged, the legal description, the amount of the loan needed, the length of time the loan is needed, and the borrower's income and place of employment. After the property has been appraised and a credit report on the borrower has been received, the loan will go to a loan committee for approval. The lending institution will then notify the applicant, who in turn should inform you as to the lender's decision.

Once the loan commitment has been made by the lender and

accepted by the applicant, a number of legal steps must take place prior to closing the loan and sale. These include, but are not limited to, the title being examined, the title insurance policy being issued indicating the lender's interest in the property, and verification that past real estate taxes have been paid and that the deed and mortgage documents have been drawn. The legal steps just mentioned should be handled by your attorney. A good real estate attorney is an integral part of a successful real estate sale.

Renting Your Home versus Selling

Possibly you have considered renting your home to generate income and provide a tax shelter. Renting is a mistake, and here is why.

If your home and lot could be sold for, say, $25,000, a general rule of thumb indicates that the monthly rental should be 1 percent of the gross value, or $250. This 1 percent ratio decreases as the value of the home goes substantially above $25,000.

If you were to allow a tenant to move into your home, the expenses would be:

Loss of at least 6% reinvestment interest on $25,000	$1,500
2% annual depreciation	500
Repairs and maintenance (1½ months' rental)	375
Estimated real estate taxes	650
Management and renting (10% of gross)	300
10% vacancy or collection loss	300
Total expense	$3,625
Gross income (12 months × $250)	3,000
Estimated loss per year	$ 625

A loss of $625 on the above property is very realistic; it could be more. Add to this loss the risk and expense of major repairs which might arise, legal problems, and other possibilities, and you have an economically unviable situation.

Granted, renting your home will offer you a tax shelter, but it will afford little else. It will usually end up costing you money out of your pocket and causing you a tremendous amount of grief.

It is always better to sell at the best possible price and then reinvest that money in some other form of real estate or other sound investment.

In concluding this chapter on financing, it should be clear that mortgages are the most widely used form of real estate financing. Since most properties are not acquired for all cash, almost every real estate buyer must find some outside source of funds, and the mortgage loan is usually the best choice.

7
Legal and Tax Aspects

Legal Aspects*

Both the buyer and the seller of real estate should be represented by attorneys. An unbelievable number of real estate transactions end up in court because either the buyer or the seller, or both, did not retain an attorney. Try to find an attorney who does a great deal of real property work with an active real estate practice. Most attorneys are happy to discuss their fee in advance so that you will know beforehand how much the legal cost will be. The fee is small, considering your exposure if a transaction is not handled properly.

It is not a good idea to draft the real estate contract yourself, even though you have a perfect right to do so. If you are

*I wish to give special credit to Mr. Donald J. Brumlik, attorney-at-law, whose review of this chapter and constructive comments on the subject of legal and tax aspects add significantly to the overall authority and experience standing behind this work.

planning to use a prepared real estate contract form, submit the form contract to your attorney for his approval before signing the document. Although your attorney should review or draft the contract you use, you should be re..sonably familiar with some of the major elements that must be included in any agreement between the buyer and the seller. The contract should always contain an adequate description of the property, using a street address or legal description with the actual or approximate size of the land. Any easements or other restrictions running with the land should be listed. The price and terms of the transaction, along with any leases, are to be included. Any personal property that is either included or excluded from the transaction is to be listed in order to eliminate any misunderstanding. A provision for a cash deposit to bind the contract is very important. Do not sign the contract without receiving an earnest-money check! The type of deed by which title is to be conveyed and the date for the transfer of title are also required. Always enter the date on which the contract was signed by both buyer and seller. Needless to say, there may be myriad other provisions, but the ones just mentioned are the essential elements of any real estate agreement.

The following contract is considered to be a standard contract not particularly weighted in either the buyer's or the seller's favor. However, the term "standard sales contract" is a misnomer, and any contract with this kind of heading should be read as carefully as you would read any legal document.

RESIDENTIAL REAL ESTATE SALE CONTRACT

1. _____(Purchaser)

agrees to purchase at a price of $_____ on the terms set

forth herein, the following described real estate in _____

County, State of _____ (if legal description is not

included herein at time of execution, _____ is

authorized to insert it thereafter), commonly known as _____

_____, and with approximate lot

dimensions of _____ X _____, together with the following personal property presently located thereon (strike items not applicable): (*a*) storm and screen doors and windows; (*b*) awnings; (*c*) outdoor television antenna; (*d*) wall-to-wall hallway and stair carpeting; (*e*) window shades and draperies and supporting fixtures; (*f*) venetian blinds; (*g*) electric, plumbing, and other attached

fixtures as installed; (*h*) water softener; (*i*) refrigerator(s); (*j*) _____

range(s); and also _____.

2. _____ (Seller)
(insert names of all owners and their respective spouses)

agrees to sell the real estate and the property, if any, described above at the price and terms set forth herein, and to convey or cause to be conveyed to

Purchaser or nominee title thereto (in joint tenancy) by a recordable _____

_____ deed, with release of dower and homestead rights, and a proper bill of sale, subject only to (*a*) covenants, conditions, and restrictions of record; (*b*) private, public, and utility easements and roads and highways, if any; (*c*) party-wall rights and agreements, if any; (*d*) existing leases and tenancies; (*e*) special taxes or assessments for improvements not yet completed; (*f*) installments not due at the date hereof of any special tax or assessment for improvements heretofore completed; (*g*) mortgage or trust deed specified

below, if any; (*h*) general taxes for the year _____ and subsequent years;

and to _____.

3. Purchaser has paid $_____ (and will pay within _____ days the

additional sum of $_____) as earnest money to be applied on the purchase price and agrees to pay or satisfy the balance of the purchase price, plus or minus prorations, at the time of closing as follows (strike subparagraph not applicable):

(*a*) The payment of $ _____.

(*b*) The acceptance of the title to the real estate by Purchaser subject to a mortgage (trust deed) of record securing a principal indebtedness (which

the Purchaser (does) (does not) agree to assume) aggregating $ _____

bearing interest at the rate of _____% a year, and the payment of a sum which represents the difference between the amount due on the indebtedness at the time of closing and the balance of the purchase price.

4. This contract is subject to the condition that Purchaser be able to procure

within _____ days a firm commitment for a loan to be secured by a mortgage

or trust deed on the real estate in the amount of $ _____, or such lesser

sum as Purchaser accepts, with interest not to exceed _____% a year to

be amortized over _____ years, the commission and service charges for

such a loan not to exceed _____%. If, after making every reasonable effort, Purchaser is unable to procure such commitment within the time specified herein and so notified Seller thereof within that time, this contract shall become null and void and all earnest money shall be returned to Purchaser; provided that if Seller, at his option, within a like period of time following Purchaser's notice, procures for Purchaser such a commitment or notified Purchaser that Seller will accept a purchase-money mortgage upon the same terms, this contract shall remain in full force and effect (strike paragraph if inapplicable).

5. The time of closing shall be on _____, or 20 days after notice that financing has been procured if above paragraph 4 is operative, or on the date, if any, to which such time is extended by reason of paragraph 2 of the Conditions and Stipulations hereafter becoming operative (whichever date is

later), unless subsequently mutually agreed otherwise, at the office of

_____ or of the mortgage lender, if any, provided title is shown to be good or is accepted by Purchaser.

6. Seller shall deliver possession to Purchaser on or before _____ days after the sale has been closed. Seller agrees to pay Purchaser the sum of $ _____ for each day Seller remains in possession between the time of closing and the time possession is delivered.

7. The earnest money shall be held by _____
for the mutual benefit of the parties.

8. Seller agrees to deliver possession of the real estate in the same condition as it is at the date of this contract, ordinary wear and tear excepted.

9. A duplicate original of this contract, duly executed by the Seller and his

spouse, if any, shall be delivered to the Purchaser within _____
days from the date below; otherwise, at the Purchaser's option, this contract shall become null and void and the earnest money shall be refunded to the Purchaser.

This contract is subject to the following Conditions and Stipulations:

CONDITIONS AND STIPULATIONS

1. Seller shall deliver or cause to be delivered to Purchaser or Purchaser's agent, not less than 5 days prior to the time of closing, a title commitment for

an owner's title insurance policy issued by _____ Title Insurance Company in the amount of the purchase price, covering title to the real estate on or after the date hereof, showing title in the intended grantor subject only to (a) the general exceptions contained in the policy, (b) the title exceptions set forth above, and (c) title exceptions pertaining to liens or encumbrances of a definite or ascertainable amount which may be removed by the payment of money at the time of closing and which the Seller may so remove at that time by using the funds to be paid upon the delivery of the deed (all of which are herein referred to as the permitted exceptions). The title commitment shall be conclusive evidence of good title as therein shown as to all matters insured by the policy, subject only to the exceptions as therein stated. Seller also shall furnish Purchaser an affidavit of title in customary form covering the date of closing and showing title in Seller subject only to the permitted exceptions in foregoing items (b) and (c) and unpermitted exceptions, if any, as to which the title insurer commits to extend insurance in the manner specified in paragraph 2 below.

2. If the title commitment discloses unpermitted exceptions, Seller shall have 30 days from the date of delivery thereof to have the exceptions removed from the commitment or to have the title insurer commit to insure against loss or damage that may be occasioned by such exceptions, and, in such event, the time of closing shall be 35 days after delivery of the commitment or the time specified in paragraph 5, whichever is later. If Seller fails to have the exceptions removed or, in the alternative, to obtain the commitment for title insurance specified above as to such exceptions within the specified time, Purchaser may terminate

this contract or may elect, upon notice to Seller within 10 days after the expiration of the 30-day period, to take title as it then is with the right to deduct from the purchase price liens or encumbrances of a definite or ascertainable amount. If Purchaser does not so elect, this contract shall become null and void without further actions of the parties.

3. Rents, premiums under assignable insurance policies, water and other utility charges, fuels, prepaid service contracts, general taxes, accrued interest on mortgage indebtedness, if any, and other similar items shall be adjusted ratably as of the time of closing. If the amount of the current general taxes is not then ascertainable, the adjustment thereof shall be on the basis of the amount of the most recent ascertainable taxes. All prorations are final unless otherwise provided herein. Existing leases and assignable insurance policies, if any, shall then be assigned to Purchaser. Seller shall pay the amount of any stamp tax imposed by law on the transfer of title and shall furnish a completed Real Estate Transfer Declaration signed by the Seller or the Seller's agent in the form required pursuant to the Real Estate Transfer Tax Act of the State

of _____.

4. The provisions of the Uniform Vendor and Purchaser Risk Act of the State

of _____ shall be applicable to this contract.

5. If this contract is terminated without Purchaser's fault, the earnest money shall be returned to the Purchaser, but if the termination is caused by the Purchaser's fault, then at the option of the Seller and upon notice to the Purchaser, the earnest money shall be forfeited to the Seller and applied first to the payment of Seller's expenses, the balance, if any, to be retained by the Seller as liquidated damages.

6. At the election of Seller or Purchaser upon notice to the other party not less than 5 days prior to the time of closing, this sale shall be closed through an

escrow with _____ Title Insurance Company in accordance with the general provisions of the usual form of Deed and Money Escrow Agreement

then in use by _____ Title Insurance Company, with such special provisions inserted in the escrow agreement as may be required to conform with this contract. Upon the creation of such an escrow, anything herein to the contrary notwithstanding, payment of purchase price and delivery of deed shall be made through the escrow and this contract and the earnest money shall be deposited in the escrow. The cost of the escrow shall be divided equally between Seller and Purchaser (strike paragraph if inapplicable).

7. Time is of the essence of this contract.

8. All notices herein required shall be in writing and shall be served on the parties at the addresses following their signatures. The mailing of a notice registered or certified mail, return receipt requested, shall be sufficient service.

Dated_____

Purchaser_____   (Address)_____

Purchaser_____   (Address)_____

Seller_____   (Address)_____

Seller_____   (Address)_____

The sample contract you have just read is the form generally used for residential sales. It can be used for the sale of small-income property, with slight modification, but it should not be used for the sale of apartment buildings over four units. Slight alteration of this contract form may be necessary in various states.

The term "closing" is used loosely in the real estate business. At times it is used improperly to refer to the signing of a contract by buyer and seller. Technically, the closing of a transaction occurs when the full purchase price is paid, there is a delivery of the deed, and certain other details are completed in connection with the transfer of the subject property. Most of the closing details should be handled by your attorney, but the following list will allow you to become familiar with some of the nomenclature associated with real estate closings in connection with houses, vacant land, and income properties. The list is certainly not meant to be definitive, and not all the terms listed below will be used in any one transaction. Some of the terms are followed by an asterisk, which indicates that the term is defined in the Glossary at the end of the book. The other terms are self-explanatory.

1. Assignments:*
   Leases*
   Lease with an option to extend the term insurance policy

Guarantees*
Real estate management contract
Utility contracts
2. Bill of sale* for personal property:
Free-standing range
Refrigerator
Movable air conditioner
Furniture
Other personalty
3. Financing:
Note*
Mortgage*
Second mortgage*
Loan payment book
Loan application
Interest rate*
Term*
Point*
4. Insurance:
Canceled policy
New policy
Prorated insurance premium
5. Statements:
Closing statement*
Prorate*
Rent schedule*
6. Taxes:
Income tax
State and local taxes
Receipted real estate tax bills
Personal property tax
7. Title to real estate:
Title guarantee policy*
Abstract of title*

Quitclaim deed*
Warranty deed*
Trust deed*
Survey*
Lien*
Judgment*

Closing Costs the Seller Usually Pays

Do not neglect to consider closing costs or underestimate their impact on the net sales price you will receive. After the sale contract is signed, but prior to putting the proceeds of the sale in your pocket, be prepared to deduct the following costs from the gross sales price:

1. The remaining balance on your mortgage must be deducted.

2. Legal fees, usually amounting to between ½ and 1 percent, depending on the sale price, must be deducted. There is usually a minimum fee, but to be safe, discuss this with your attorney prior to closing so that you will know what amount will be deducted for his fee.

3. Escrow fees are paid only if your sale is closed through an escrow account. The escrow fee is usually split between buyer and seller, and although the rate can vary, it will generally run between $20 and $50 for the seller in the sale of a residence.

4. Documentary or tax stamps that are placed on the deed generally cost 50 cents per $500 in sales price. Example: Assume the building sold is free and clear of indebtedness and is sold for $40,000. The revenue stamps will cost the seller $40.

5. Sometimes a mortgage document is written so that if the remaining mortgage balance is prepaid before a certain date, there is a penalty to the mortgagor-seller. This can take from ½ to 2 percent of the mortgage balance. A careful examination of your mortgage document will reveal any prepayment penalty clause that exists. Shortly after you decide to sell your real estate,

be sure to obtain a copy of your mortgage document from the lender if you do not already have one. A copy of the corresponding note should also be in your possession.

6. If possession of the property is not given to the buyer upon closing, the seller may have to pay the buyer an amount per day, as rent, to stay in possession if the sale contract so provides. If the seller stays on after the closing, an amount is usually placed in escrow to assure the buyer that the per diem charge will be paid. It is common to expect a charge of $10 per day, but this charge is negotiable.

7. The proration of taxes and utilities, charging the seller for expenses, which represents a credit to the buyer, for the period of time during the month or year that the seller was in possession, will also be a deduction.

8. Under certain circumstances, a buyer will not be able to negotiate a mortage unless the seller and/or buyer pays a lender's commission. This fee is a percentage of the mortgage and is usually referred to as "points." Historically, when financing real estate, a lender will charge, in addition to the interest rate, a point. A point in the real estate field is 1 percent of the total loan amount. For example, paying a point for a $50,000 loan will amount to a $500 charge to the borrower to be paid in cash. Years ago, lenders justified charging points to cover overhead costs. Presently, however, points are being charged to cover more than just the start-up costs of the loan. They are used as a method of increasing interest income in states where the usury laws prohibit charging interest rates beyond state maximums. Points are used in connection with both FHA-insured and VA-guaranteed loans.

Points are also charged as prepayment penalties by lenders who do not want loans with high interest rates paid off when the interest rate begins to drop. Often a mortgage will provide that points will be charged the borrower if he attempts to pay off the loan in the early years of the term.

Whether points are deductible on your tax return as interest depends on what the points cover. You are allowed to deduct points if the charge is for your use of the money and is not for specific services performed by the lender which are charged separately, such as title report, escrow fees, and charges for drafti ·· documents.

9. Title charges for a title insurance policy are the cost of the seller. This charge will depend on how long it has been since the title company last cleared title or on whether there are any complications that affect the title. Title complications can be in the form of judgments, claims, or liens which cloud the title. The sale usually cannot be consummated until those matters are cleared and the seller can convey clear title. The buyer has the right to accept the title with certain defects if he so chooses; however, if there is a lender involved, probably he will not.

10. The last cost can be by far the most expensive to the seller. Generally, this cost runs between 6 and 10 percent of the sales price, but you are going to eliminate it—the real estate broker's commission. The broker's commission can exceed the total of all the other expenses.

This will give you a general idea of what amounts should be deducted from the gross selling price. Too often, closing costs are neglected or are not explained to the seller until the closing takes place. Discuss closing costs with your attorney well in advance of the closing date.

Taxes

The primary purpose of this book is to instruct you in how to sell your real property, not to offer legal or tax advice. Discuss the income tax ramifications connected with the sale of your property with your lawyer or accountant. All I am attempting to do is to point out that there are legal and tax considerations involved in every sale and that you should consult an expert to handle your specific situation.

Generally speaking, the sale of your home affects your income tax as follows. If you sold your house at a profit and are under sixty-five years of age, you do not pay a tax on the profit if you buy or build another house and qualify under certain rules explained below. The deferment of tax on the sale of your house is possible if these rules apply to you. If you do not qualify, your gain (profit) is taxed at capital gains rates if you owned the property for more than six months.

The deferment of tax on the profit realized on the sale of your house, discussed above, is possible if you qualify under the following three rules:

1. *Principal-home rule.* This rule requires that you have used your old house as your principal residence and now use or intend to use your new house as your principal residence. You are entitled to have only one principal residence for the purpose of deferring tax. You are not allowed to defer the tax on the profitable sale of a second house, such as a vacation home. It is interesting to note that tax deferment is not restricted to the sale and acquisition of single-family detached dwellings. You are allowed to defer tax on the sale and acquisition of a condominium apartment, cooperative apartment, or mobile home which you are using as your principal residence.

2. *Time rule.* If you buy a house, you must use it within one year before or after you sell your old house. However, if you build a house, you must build and use it within one year before or eighteen months after you sell your old house. The eighteen-month rule has restrictions that could prevent you from taking advantage of it, and you should discuss it with your lawyer or accountant.

3. *Investment rule.* In order to defer tax on the entire profit you make, you must buy or build a house at a cost equal to,

or more than, the amount you received from the sale of your old house. To determine your gain (profit) on the sale and the exact amount of the gain that is not subject to tax, you must calculate the amount realized on the sale, the adjusted sales price, and the actual cost of your new house. If the cost of your new house is equal to, or greater than, the adjusted ₁ales price of your old house, then none of the actual gain is taxed in the year that you sell your house.

The "amount realized" is the selling price of your old house less expenses paid for advertising, legal and title services, and commissions. Any existing mortgage balance on your old house is to be included in the selling price, whether or not the buyer has assumed your mortgage. The difference between the amount realized and the cost of your old house is the amount of your actual gain.

The "adjusted sales price" is the amount realized less the cost of materials necessary to prepare your house for sale. These include such items as wallpaper, paint, and other fix-up items. Include only the cost of work that was performed ninety days prior to the contract date.

The cost of your new house includes not only the cash you paid but also any mortgage on the property. Lawyers' fees and brokers' commissions are considered part of the cost of your new house.

If you sold your house at a profit and are sixty-five years old or over on the sale date, you can, within limits discussed later in this chapter, avoid the tax on the sale of your house. This rule regarding special tax treatment applies only to those sixty-five or over and differs from the rules under which you merely defer the payment of tax until you sell your house without purchasing another. If you are over sixty-five and you sell your home at a profit, you may avoid the tax on the profit attributed to the first $20,000 of the adjusted sales price of your home. To obtain this benefit, you must (1) elect to avoid the tax, (2) be over sixty-five on or before the date of sale, and (3) have owned and used the home as your principal residence for at least five of the eight years preceding the day of sale.

Complete tax avoidance is allowed only on the gain attributed to the first $20,000 of the adjusted sales price. If the adjusted sales price is over $20,000, only a proportionate part of the gain is tax-free. For example, if the adjusted sales price is $40,000, only one-half of the gain is not taxed if the proceeds are not reinvested. However, if you are over sixty-five, and if the adjusted sales price is $40,000 and you reinvest the proceeds from the sale of your house in a new house, a combination of the deferment rule previously explained and the exclusion rule for people over sixty-five may work to your tax advantage.

If you sold at a loss, you may not deduct your loss. Losses on the sale of property devoted to personal use are nondeductible.

Again, you should discuss the matter of taxes with a competent tax counsel.

A word of advice concerning the "For Sale" sign: Allow it to remain up after the contract is signed and continue to take the names and telephone numbers of prospects until your buyer has his mortgage commitment. If your contract is contingent on the buyer's procuring a mortgage, you technically do not have the property sold until that event takes place. So play it safe and keep the sign up until the buyer has a mortgage.

8

Condominiums, Cooperatives, and Vacant Land

Condominiums and Cooperatives

Having purchased a condominium or cooperative, chances are that you have already been made aware of the differences between the two types of dwelling units. But it may be a good idea to review them.

In purchasing a condominium, you will have ownership of a unit in a building, together with an individual interest in the land and common areas. Common areas include parts of the building such as lobbies, halls, stairs, elevators, entrances, exits, roof, and other structural parts. Common areas can also include walks, streets, a clubhouse, and a swimming pool. Owners of a unit in a multistory building must have access to hallways, elevators, and stairways. Condominium-type ownership is used in commercial and industrial buildings as well as apartment houses, row houses, and recreational developments. Your own unit has a separate real estate tax bill which is issued to you, and the unit may be sold, mortgaged, or rented separately. When you purchased your condominium, you received a deed which was recorded separately.

Most states have enacted laws authorizing and regulating condominiums which require the sponsor to file a declaration of condominium with the local government. This declaration is the constitution of the condominium and usually prescribes the manner in which units can be sold or leased. Your individual unit can be offered in the marketplace in the same way that a single-family detached home is, and the market will determine the price. However, generally you are bound by the declaration to offer your unit first to the board of governors who manage the complex if such a group has been created. This "right of first refusal" allows management to purchase your unit at market value in order to protect the other owners. If management does not buy, the owner is then allowed to offer his unit on the open market. Condominium statutes that recognize management's right of first refusal on the proposed sale of a unit provide that it cannot be used to discriminate on account of race, creed, color, or national origin.

The condominium owner can finance his particular unit, and it is this ability to finance that creates a greater market for condominiums than for cooperatives and helps bring a higher price for them. The market for cooperatives is somewhat limited because the buyer is usually required to make a larger cash investment and assume the seller's obligation for the underlying mortgage.

A condominium owner is usually free to sell his unit on any terms that can be agreed upon by him and the buyer. An existing mortgage does not hamper the sale. The unit may be sold for all cash, it may be sold for cash subject to any existing mortgage on the unit, or the buyer can arrange a new mortgage.

The only joint liability that the buyer assumes is the payment of assessments for maintenance of the common areas. An underlying mortgage subject to foreclosure for which the buyer may be made liable does not exist, as it does with a cooperative.

The new buyer will be interested in the monthly maintenance assessments for your unit, so be prepared to discuss this matter.

The following advantages of condominium ownership should be pointed out to a prospective buyer:

1. The condominium owner does not pay rent to a landlord.

2. The buyer's mortgage interest and real estate taxes are deductible items for income tax purposes.

3. Increase in equity occurs as mortgage payments are made.

4. There is appreciation of real estate.

A condominium differs from a cooperative in the way title is held and in terms of the mortgage, transfer of title, taxation, and payment of the operating expenses. In the case of a cooperative, the apartment building usually is owned by a corporation which issues shares of stock that are allocated to each apartment unit in proportion to its rental value. However, the condominium owner has a "fee simple" title to the unit, together with an individual interest in the common areas. The cooperative owner's stock entitles him to a long-term lease, generally referred to as a "proprietary lease." The tenant in the cooperative agrees to pay as rental his share of the annual expenses of the corporation.

In the case of a condominium, the fee title in the unit and ownership of the individual interest in the common areas may be given by the owner as security for a mortgage. In the case of a cooperative, an underlying mortgage is obtained on the whole property, and the stockholder's equity in the property is subject to the mortgage. The condominium unit is subject to real estate taxes separately, but the maintenance expense for the common areas is prorated among the unit owners in proportion to the value of the whole property. Mortgage payments, operating expenses, and real estate taxes in the cooperative are paid by management and then prorated among the holders of the proprietary leases according to a formula spelled out in the document creating the cooperative.

When transferring title, the condominium owner executes a deed to his unit as though it were a single-family detached house. A cooperative apartment is sold by transfer of the shares of stock and the proprietary lease.

In a cooperative apartment, if the underlying mortgage on the building is paid down substantially, the buyer will be required to invest a large amount of cash representing the difference between the tenant's pro rata share of the mortgage balance and the selling price of his shares of stock. Very frequently the seller agrees to accept less cash from the buyer and loan him the balance, making his cooperative more salable.

The following advantages of owning stock in a cooperative should be pointed out to a prospective buyer:

1. Rental is reasonable since it is based on the actual cost of operating the building.

2. The owner is entitled to an income tax deduction for a proportionate share of real estate taxes and mortgage interest paid by the apartment-house corporation.

3. There is an increase in equity as the pro rata share of the mortgage is paid down.

4. There is participation in the operation of the building by election of the board of directors which controls operations.

5. There is possible gain on the resale of stock.

In advertising your condominium or cooperative, as with a single-family detached home, it is important to write a good newspaper ad and display signs whenever possible. In large condominium projects, be certain to notify all the other owners, in addition to the board of governors, since they are the most likely people to be interested in choosing the new buyer. Each of the other condominium owners probably has a friend or relative looking for a new home. It is helpful to put a Property Information Sheet in their mailboxes or pin up a sign in the laundry room to notify your neighbors.

Selling Vacant Land

Assuming that you have properly exposed your parcel of vacant land by displaying a sign, placing a newspaper ad, and preparing a Property Information Sheet to distribute, there are still other factors that will determine the price that you are able to obtain.

Land value depends to a great extent on its use and ability to produce revenue. When its capacity to produce income changes, its value changes. If the land is suitable for apartment buildings, it has a certain value; if it will accommodate a home-site or recreational facility, chances are that its value is different.

The location of the land is extremely important. Is it in the path of progress? Is it near transportation, schools, shopping, or a resort area? Location, then, will also affect the price that you receive for your land.

You had better consider these factors when placing a value on your land. Chances are that you know of contiguous land, or a parcel nearby, that was sold, and for what price. How does your parcel compare? If you know the total price and acreage, merely divide the total acres into the total selling price to arrive at the selling price per acre. Example: If a 10-acre parcel of land with similar characteristics to yours, in the same area, sold for $25,000, this would reflect a sale price of $2,500 per acre. If the size of your parcel is 8 acres, it is reasonable to expect that your land might obtain a sales price of around $20,000. If a parcel amounting to ¾ acre in size sells for $50,000 and land is selling on a square foot basis, you would compute the value as follows: Referring to the square footage table in

Chapter 9, you see that an acre consists of 43,560 square feet; therefore, ¾ acre is 32,670 square feet. If the $50,000 sales price is divided by 32,670 square feet (¾ acre), the price per square foot is $1.53. To compute the square foot area of your parcel, multiply the width times the length. Then apply a comparable per-square-foot price to determine the selling price of your parcel.

The continuing sprawl of our cities, with transfer from rural to urban use of land, requires other methods of evaluating vacant-land value. How do we determine the present value of land located within a municipality? The estimated market value is usually determined by the price per front foot of a lot or parcel. The per front foot value is usually placed on a lot of standard depth, not under the influence of a corner. Factors such as variations in depth, riparian rights, or adjacency to a corner lot can alter the value. In some cities, reference books are published with the current front foot values printed by neighborhood. Ask your lawyer, accountant, or banker whether such a book exists for your city.

Obviously, this discussion of how to determine the value of your vacant land is oversimplified, since no two pieces of property, even if contiguous and containing the same area, will be identical. Real estate is not like stock certificates or other identical assets; however, prices obtained for similar parcels will be an excellent guide in pricing your vacant land.

Installment Land Sale   If the buyer of your land is unable to obtain financing, you may be in a position to extend credit to him by receiving payment from him over two or more taxable years. You can then take advantage of the installment sale method. By deferring receipt of full payment, you report as income only a percentage of your gain, allocated to the payments you received during each year. So, when selling your land, be sure that unless you obtain all cash, you do not accept more than a 29 percent down payment. The reason is that all the gain would be taxable in the year of sale. Also considered in your 29 percent down-payment calculation would be any mortgage payments paid to you in the year of sale. It is possible that if you sell the land for less than 29 percent down payment, the sale might qualify as an installment sale. This law actually says 30 percent, but it is wise to use 29 percent in order to be certain not to exceed the 30 percent limit. It is possible to pay your capital gains tax a portion at a time, in the same proportion as the cash you receive. On the other hand, if you sell your land outright for all cash and do not use the installment sale method, and if you owned the land for six months or more, your gain (profit) is taxed at lower rates than the rate on ordinary income. Your profit is considered to be a long-term capital gain. Again, as I have mentioned in other sections of this book, the legal ramifications of a real estate transaction and tax laws should be handled by qualified attorneys or accountants, and you should seek their advice before entering into a sale agreement.

In addition to putting up signs and placing ads in the newspapers, there are other avenues to explore when trying to advertise your vacant land. One excellent source of customers is local developers or general building contractors. Usually, you can get a list of the local builders from either the classified telephone book or the builders' association in your area. By mailing your Property Information Sheet to these people, you zero in on a specific market. Remember that developers and builders must have land to stay in business. You will find that they know what they want and how much they can afford to pay, and you can often negotiate a quick sale with this type of buyer. You can also attract the builder and developer by advertising in real estate trade publications.

9

Tables

The tables on the following pages are reference tools to be used when buying or selling real estate. The information is very concise, and it can actually be used when negotiating a transaction. These tables will be extremely helpful to both the novice and the sophisticated real estate investor.

This material, in addition to other portions of this book, has been read and approved by certified public accountants and legal counsel.

Payment Table For Monthly Mortgage Loans*

The following table shows the monthly payments required to amortize a loan in a given number of years.

EXAMPLE: What is the monthly payment of principal and interest on a $25,000 loan at 8 percent interest for a term of twenty-five years?

First go to the 8 percent interest table and read down the amount column to $25,000. Then read across the term line to twenty-five years; the answer is $190.81. To find the annual payment, multiply the monthly payment of $190.81 times 12, or $2,290.

---

*These tables have been prepared as accurately as possible; the publishers do not, however, guarantee complete freedom from error.

MONTHLY PAYMENT
6% REQUIRED TO AMORTIZE A LOAN

TERM AMOUNT	15 YEARS	14 YEARS	13 YEARS	12 YEARS	11 YEARS	10 YEARS	9 YEARS	8 YEARS	7 YEARS	6 YEARS	5 YEARS	4 YEARS	3 YEARS	2 YEARS	1 YEAR
$100	.84	.88	.93	.98	1.04	1.11	1.20	1.32	1.46	1.66	1.93	2.35	3.04	4.43	8.61
200	1.68	1.76	1.85	1.95	2.07	2.22	2.40	2.63	2.92	3.31	3.86	4.70	6.08	8.86	17.21
300	2.52	2.64	2.77	2.92	3.10	3.32	3.60	3.94	4.38	4.97	5.79	7.04	9.12	13.29	25.81
400	3.36	3.51	3.69	3.89	4.14	4.43	4.79	5.25	5.83	6.62	7.72	9.39	12.16	17.72	34.42
500	4.20	4.39	4.61	4.87	5.17	5.54	5.99	6.56	7.29	8.27	9.65	11.73	15.20	22.15	43.02
600	5.04	5.27	5.53	5.84	6.20	6.64	7.19	7.87	8.75	9.93	11.58	14.08	18.24	26.58	51.62
700	5.88	6.15	6.45	6.81	7.24	7.75	8.38	9.18	10.21	11.58	13.51	16.42	21.28	31.01	60.23
800	6.72	7.02	7.37	7.78	8.27	8.86	9.58	10.49	11.66	13.24	15.44	18.77	24.32	35.43	68.83
900	7.56	7.90	8.29	8.75	9.30	9.96	10.78	11.80	13.12	14.89	17.37	21.11	27.35	39.86	77.43
1000	8.40	8.78	9.21	9.73	10.33	11.07	11.97	13.11	14.58	16.54	19.30	23.46	30.39	44.29	86.04
2000	16.80	17.55	18.42	19.45	20.66	22.14	23.94	26.22	29.15	33.08	38.60	46.91	60.78	88.58	172.07
3000	25.20	26.32	27.63	29.17	30.99	33.20	35.91	39.32	43.72	49.62	57.90	70.36	91.17	132.87	258.10
4000	33.60	35.10	36.84	38.89	41.32	44.27	47.88	52.43	58.30	66.16	77.20	93.81	121.56	177.15	344.14
5000	42.00	43.87	46.05	48.61	51.65	55.33	59.85	65.53	72.87	82.70	96.50	117.26	151.95	221.44	430.17
6000	50.40	52.64	55.26	58.33	61.98	66.40	71.82	78.64	87.44	99.23	115.80	140.71	182.34	265.73	516.20
7000	58.80	61.42	64.47	68.05	72.31	77.46	83.79	91.74	102.02	115.77	135.09	164.16	212.73	310.02	602.23
8000	67.20	70.19	73.67	77.77	82.64	88.53	95.76	104.85	116.59	132.31	154.39	187.62	243.11	354.30	688.27
9000	75.59	78.96	82.88	87.49	92.97	99.59	107.73	117.96	131.16	148.85	173.69	211.02	273.50	398.59	774.30
10000	83.99	87.74	92.09	97.21	103.30	110.66	119.70	131.06	145.74	165.39	192.99	234.52	303.89	442.88	860.33
11000	92.39	96.51	101.30	106.93	113.63	121.72	131.67	144.17	160.31	181.92	212.29	257.97	334.28	487.17	946.36
12000	100.79	105.28	110.51	116.65	123.96	132.79	143.64	157.27	174.88	198.46	231.59	281.42	364.67	531.45	1032.40
13000	109.19	114.06	119.72	126.37	134.29	143.85	155.61	170.38	189.46	215.00	250.89	304.87	395.06	575.74	1118.43
14000	117.59	122.83	128.93	136.09	144.62	154.92	167.58	183.48	204.03	231.54	270.18	328.32	425.45	620.03	1204.46
15000	125.99	131.60	138.13	145.81	154.95	165.98	179.55	196.59	218.61	248.08	289.48	351.77	455.83	664.32	1290.49
16000	134.39	140.38	147.34	155.53	165.28	177.05	191.51	209.69	233.18	264.62	308.78	375.23	486.22	708.60	1376.53
17000	142.79	149.15	156.55	165.25	175.61	188.11	203.48	222.80	247.75	281.15	328.08	398.68	516.61	752.89	1462.56
18000	151.18	157.92	165.76	174.97	185.94	199.24	215.46	235.91	262.32	297.69	347.38	422.13	547.00	797.18	1548.59
19000	159.58	166.70	174.97	184.69	196.27	210.24	227.42	249.01	276.90	314.23	366.68	445.58	577.39	841.47	1634.62
20000	167.98	175.47	184.18	194.41	206.60	221.31	239.39	262.12	291.47	330.77	385.98	469.03	607.78	885.75	1720.66
21000	176.38	184.24	193.39	204.13	216.92	232.37	251.35	275.22	306.04	347.31	405.27	492.48	638.17	930.04	1806.69
22000	184.78	193.01	202.59	213.85	227.25	243.44	263.33	288.33	320.62	363.84	424.57	515.93	668.55	974.33	1892.72
23000	193.18	201.79	211.80	223.57	237.58	254.50	275.30	301.43	335.19	380.38	443.87	539.38	698.94	1018.62	1978.75
24000	201.58	210.56	221.01	233.30	247.90	265.57	287.27	314.54	349.76	396.92	463.17	562.84	729.33	1062.90	2064.79
25000	209.98	219.33	230.22	243.02	258.24	276.63	299.24	327.64	364.34	413.46	482.47	586.29	759.72	1107.19	2150.82
26000	218.37	228.11	239.43	252.74	268.57	287.70	311.21	340.75	378.91	430.00	501.77	609.74	790.10	1151.48	2236.85
27000	226.77	236.88	248.64	262.46	278.89	298.76	323.18	353.86	393.48	446.53	521.07	633.19	820.50	1195.77	2322.88
28000	235.17	245.65	257.85	272.18	289.23	309.83	335.15	366.96	408.06	463.07	540.36	656.64	850.89	1240.05	2408.92
29000	243.57	254.43	267.05	281.90	299.56	320.89	347.12	380.07	422.63	479.61	559.66	680.09	881.28	1284.34	2494.95
30000	251.97	263.20	276.26	291.62	309.89	331.96	359.09	393.17	437.20	496.15	578.96	703.54	911.66	1328.63	2580.98
35000	293.96	307.07	322.31	340.22	361.54	387.28	418.93	458.70	510.07	578.84	675.45	820.80	1063.61	1550.06	3011.15
40000	335.96	350.93	368.35	388.82	413.19	442.61	478.78	524.24	582.94	661.53	771.95	938.06	1215.55	1771.50	3441.31
45000	377.95	394.80	414.39	437.42	464.83	497.93	538.63	589.76	655.80	744.22	868.44	1055.31	1367.49	1992.94	3871.47
50000	419.95	438.66	460.44	486.03	516.48	553.26	598.47	655.28	728.67	826.91	964.93	1172.57	1519.43	2214.38	4301.63

MONTHLY PAYMENT
REQUIRED TO AMORTIZE A LOAN

6%

TERM AMOUNT	35 YEARS	30 YEARS	28 YEARS	27 YEARS	26 YEARS	25 YEARS	24 YEARS	23 YEARS	22 YEARS	21 YEARS	20 YEARS	19 YEARS	18 YEARS	17 YEARS	16 YEARS
$100	.57	.60	.62	.62	.63	.64	.66	.67	.68	.70	.72	.74	.76	.78	.81
200	1.14	1.19	1.23	1.24	1.26	1.28	1.31	1.33	1.36	1.39	1.43	1.47	1.51	1.56	1.62
300	1.70	1.79	1.84	1.86	1.89	1.92	1.96	2.00	2.04	2.09	2.14	2.20	2.27	2.34	2.43
400	2.27	2.38	2.45	2.48	2.52	2.56	2.61	2.66	2.72	2.78	2.85	2.93	3.02	3.12	3.23
500	2.83	2.98	3.06	3.10	3.15	3.20	3.26	3.33	3.40	3.48	3.57	3.66	3.78	3.90	4.04
600	3.40	3.57	3.67	3.72	3.78	3.84	3.91	3.99	4.08	4.17	4.28	4.40	4.53	4.68	4.85
700	3.96	4.17	4.28	4.34	4.41	4.48	4.57	4.66	4.76	4.87	4.99	5.13	5.28	5.46	5.66
800	4.53	4.76	4.89	4.96	5.04	5.12	5.22	5.32	5.43	5.56	5.70	5.86	6.04	6.24	6.46
900	5.09	5.36	5.50	5.58	5.67	5.76	5.87	5.99	6.11	6.26	6.41	6.59	6.79	7.02	7.27
1000	5.66	5.95	6.11	6.20	6.30	6.40	6.52	6.65	6.79	6.95	7.13	7.32	7.55	7.80	8.08
2000	11.31	11.90	12.21	12.39	12.59	12.80	13.04	13.29	13.58	13.90	14.25	14.64	15.09	15.59	16.15
3000	16.96	17.85	18.32	18.59	18.88	19.20	19.55	19.94	20.37	20.84	21.37	21.96	22.63	23.38	24.23
4000	22.62	23.80	24.42	24.78	25.17	25.60	26.07	26.58	27.15	27.79	28.49	29.28	30.17	31.17	32.30
5000	28.27	29.75	30.53	30.97	31.46	32.00	32.58	33.23	33.94	34.74	35.61	36.60	37.71	38.96	40.38
6000	33.92	35.69	36.63	37.17	37.75	38.39	39.10	39.87	40.73	41.68	42.74	43.92	45.25	46.75	48.45
7000	39.57	41.64	42.74	43.36	44.04	44.79	45.61	46.52	47.52	48.62	49.86	51.24	52.79	54.54	56.52
8000	45.23	47.59	48.84	49.56	50.34	51.19	52.13	53.16	54.30	55.57	56.98	58.56	60.33	62.33	64.60
9000	50.88	53.54	54.95	55.75	56.63	57.59	58.64	59.81	61.09	62.52	64.10	65.88	67.87	70.12	72.67
10000	56.53	59.49	61.05	61.94	62.92	63.99	65.16	66.45	67.88	69.46	71.22	73.19	75.41	77.90	80.75
11000	62.18	65.44	67.16	68.14	69.21	70.38	71.67	73.09	74.67	76.41	78.35	80.51	82.95	85.70	88.82
12000	67.84	71.38	73.26	74.33	75.50	76.78	78.19	79.74	81.45	83.35	85.47	87.83	90.49	93.49	96.89
13000	73.49	77.33	79.37	80.53	81.79	83.18	84.70	86.38	88.24	90.30	92.59	95.15	98.03	101.28	104.97
14000	79.14	83.28	85.47	86.72	88.08	89.58	91.22	93.03	95.03	97.24	99.71	102.47	105.57	109.07	113.04
15000	84.79	89.23	91.58	92.91	94.38	95.98	97.73	99.67	101.81	104.19	106.83	109.79	113.11	116.86	121.12
16000	90.45	95.18	97.68	99.11	100.67	102.37	104.25	106.32	108.60	111.13	113.96	117.11	120.65	124.65	129.19
17000	96.10	101.12	103.79	105.30	106.96	108.77	110.77	112.96	115.39	118.08	121.08	124.43	128.19	132.44	137.26
18000	101.75	107.07	109.89	111.50	113.25	115.17	117.28	119.61	122.18	125.03	128.20	131.75	135.73	140.23	145.34
19000	107.40	113.02	116.00	117.69	119.54	121.57	123.80	126.25	128.96	131.97	135.32	139.06	143.27	148.02	153.41
20000	113.06	118.97	122.10	123.88	125.83	127.97	130.31	132.90	135.75	138.92	142.44	146.38	150.81	155.81	161.49
21000	118.71	124.92	128.21	130.08	132.12	134.36	136.83	139.54	142.54	145.86	149.56	153.70	158.35	163.60	169.56
22000	124.36	130.87	134.31	136.27	138.41	140.76	143.34	146.18	149.33	152.81	156.69	161.02	165.89	171.39	177.63
23000	130.01	136.81	140.42	142.47	144.71	147.16	149.86	152.83	156.11	159.75	163.81	168.34	173.43	179.18	185.71
24000	135.67	142.76	146.52	148.66	151.00	153.56	156.37	159.47	162.90	166.70	170.93	175.66	180.97	186.97	193.78
25000	141.32	148.71	152.63	154.85	157.29	159.96	162.89	166.12	169.69	173.65	178.05	182.98	188.51	194.76	201.86
26000	146.97	154.66	158.73	161.05	163.58	166.35	169.40	172.76	176.47	180.59	185.17	190.30	196.05	202.55	209.93
27000	152.62	160.61	164.84	167.24	169.87	172.75	175.92	179.41	183.26	187.54	192.30	197.62	203.59	210.34	218.01
28000	158.28	166.56	170.94	173.44	176.16	179.15	182.43	186.05	190.05	194.48	199.42	204.94	211.13	218.13	226.08
29000	163.93	172.50	177.05	179.63	182.45	185.55	188.95	192.70	196.84	201.43	206.54	212.25	218.67	225.92	234.15
30000	169.58	178.45	183.15	185.82	188.75	191.95	195.46	199.34	203.62	208.37	213.66	219.57	226.21	233.71	242.23
35000	197.84	208.19	213.68	216.79	220.20	223.94	228.04	232.56	237.56	243.10	249.27	256.17	263.91	272.66	282.60
40000	226.11	237.93	244.20	247.76	251.66	255.93	260.62	265.79	271.50	277.83	284.88	292.76	301.62	311.61	322.97
45000	254.37	267.68	274.72	278.73	283.12	287.92	293.19	299.01	305.43	312.56	320.49	329.36	339.32	350.56	363.34
50000	282.63	297.42	305.25	309.70	314.57	319.91	325.77	332.23	339.37	347.29	356.10	365.95	377.02	389.51	403.71

TERM AMOUNT	1 YEAR	2 YEARS	3 YEARS	4 YEARS	5 YEARS	6 YEARS	7 YEARS	8 YEARS	9 YEARS	10 YEARS	11 YEARS	12 YEARS	13 YEARS	14 YEARS	15 YEARS
$100	8.62	4.44	3.05	2.36	1.95	1.67	1.47	1.33	1.21	1.12	1.05	.99	.94	.90	.86
200	17.23	8.88	6.10	4.72	3.89	3.34	2.94	2.65	2.42	2.24	2.10	1.97	1.87	1.79	1.71
300	25.85	13.32	9.15	7.07	5.83	5.00	4.41	3.97	3.63	3.36	3.14	2.96	2.81	2.68	2.56
400	34.46	17.76	12.20	9.43	7.77	6.67	5.88	5.29	4.84	4.48	4.19	3.94	3.74	3.57	3.42
500	43.08	22.20	15.25	11.79	9.71	8.33	7.35	6.62	6.05	5.60	5.23	4.93	4.67	4.46	4.27
600	51.69	26.64	18.30	14.14	11.65	10.00	8.82	7.94	7.26	6.72	6.28	5.91	5.61	5.35	5.12
700	60.31	31.08	21.35	16.50	13.59	11.66	10.29	9.26	8.47	7.84	7.32	6.90	6.54	6.24	5.98
800	68.92	35.52	24.40	18.86	15.53	13.33	11.76	10.58	9.68	8.96	8.37	7.88	7.47	7.13	6.83
900	77.54	39.96	27.45	21.21	17.48	14.99	13.23	11.91	10.89	10.07	9.41	8.87	8.41	8.02	7.68
1000	86.15	44.40	30.50	23.57	19.42	16.66	14.70	13.23	12.10	11.19	10.46	9.85	9.34	8.91	8.54
2000	172.29	88.80	61.00	47.13	38.83	33.31	29.39	26.45	24.20	22.38	20.91	19.70	18.68	17.81	17.07
3000	258.44	133.20	91.50	70.69	58.24	49.96	44.08	39.68	36.28	33.57	31.37	29.55	28.02	26.71	25.60
4000	344.58	177.59	122.00	94.26	77.65	66.62	58.77	52.90	48.37	44.76	41.82	39.39	37.35	35.62	34.13
5000	430.73	221.99	152.50	117.82	97.07	83.27	73.46	66.13	60.46	55.94	52.27	49.24	46.69	44.52	42.66
6000	516.87	266.39	183.00	141.38	116.48	99.92	88.15	79.35	72.55	67.13	62.73	59.09	56.03	53.42	51.19
7000	603.02	310.79	213.50	164.95	135.89	116.58	102.84	92.58	84.64	78.32	73.18	68.93	65.36	62.33	59.72
8000	689.16	355.18	244.00	188.51	155.30	133.23	117.53	105.80	96.73	89.51	83.64	78.78	74.70	71.23	68.25
9000	775.31	399.58	274.50	212.07	174.71	149.88	132.22	119.02	108.87	100.69	94.09	88.63	84.04	80.13	76.78
10000	861.45	443.98	305.00	235.64	194.13	166.54	146.91	132.25	120.90	111.88	104.54	98.47	93.37	89.04	85.31
11000	947.60	488.38	335.49	259.20	213.54	183.19	161.60	145.47	133.00	123.07	115.00	108.32	102.71	97.94	93.84
12000	1033.74	532.77	365.99	282.76	232.95	199.84	176.29	158.70	145.09	134.26	125.45	118.17	112.05	106.84	102.37
13000	1119.89	577.17	396.49	306.33	252.36	216.50	190.98	171.92	157.18	145.44	135.91	128.01	121.38	115.75	110.90
14000	1206.03	621.57	426.99	329.89	271.77	233.15	205.67	185.15	169.27	156.63	146.36	137.86	130.77	124.65	119.44
15000	1292.17	665.96	457.49	353.45	291.19	249.80	220.36	198.37	181.36	167.82	156.81	147.71	140.06	133.55	127.97
16000	1378.32	710.36	487.99	377.01	310.61	266.46	235.05	211.60	193.45	179.00	167.27	157.55	149.39	142.46	136.50
17000	1464.46	754.76	518.49	400.58	330.01	283.11	249.74	224.82	205.54	190.20	177.72	167.40	158.73	151.36	145.03
18000	1550.61	799.16	548.99	424.14	349.42	299.76	264.43	238.04	217.63	201.38	188.18	177.25	168.07	160.26	153.56
19000	1636.75	843.55	579.49	447.70	368.83	316.42	279.12	251.27	229.72	212.57	198.63	187.09	177.40	169.17	162.09
20000	1722.90	887.95	609.99	471.27	388.25	333.07	293.81	264.49	241.81	223.76	209.08	196.94	186.74	178.07	170.62
21000	1809.04	932.35	640.49	494.83	407.66	349.72	308.50	277.72	253.90	234.95	219.54	206.79	196.08	186.97	179.15
22000	1895.19	976.75	670.98	518.39	427.07	366.38	323.19	290.94	265.99	246.13	229.99	216.63	205.42	195.88	187.68
23000	1981.33	1021.14	701.48	541.96	446.48	383.03	337.88	304.17	278.08	257.32	240.45	226.48	214.75	204.78	196.21
24000	2067.48	1065.54	731.98	565.52	465.89	399.68	352.57	317.39	290.17	268.51	250.90	236.33	224.09	213.68	204.74
25000	2153.62	1109.94	762.48	589.08	485.31	416.34	367.26	330.62	302.26	279.70	261.35	246.17	233.43	222.59	213.27
26000	2239.77	1154.34	792.98	612.65	504.72	432.99	381.95	343.84	314.35	290.88	271.81	256.02	242.76	231.49	221.80
27000	2325.91	1198.73	823.48	636.21	524.13	449.64	396.64	357.06	326.44	302.07	282.26	265.87	252.10	240.39	230.34
28000	2412.06	1243.13	853.98	659.77	543.54	466.30	411.33	370.29	338.53	313.26	292.72	275.71	261.44	249.30	238.87
29000	2498.20	1287.53	884.48	683.34	562.95	482.95	426.02	383.51	350.62	324.45	303.17	285.56	270.77	258.20	247.40
30000	2584.34	1331.92	914.98	706.90	582.37	499.60	440.71	396.74	362.71	335.64	313.62	295.41	280.11	267.10	255.93
35000	3015.07	1553.91	1067.47	824.71	679.43	582.87	514.16	462.86	423.16	391.57	365.89	344.68	326.79	311.62	298.58
40000	3445.79	1775.90	1219.97	942.53	776.49	666.14	587.62	528.98	483.61	447.51	418.16	393.88	373.48	356.14	341.24
45000	3876.51	1997.88	1372.46	1060.35	873.55	749.40	661.07	595.10	544.06	503.45	470.43	443.11	420.16	400.65	383.89
50000	4307.24	2219.87	1524.96	1178.16	970.61	832.67	734.52	661.23	604.51	559.39	522.70	492.34	466.85	445.17	426.54

MONTHLY PAYMENT
REQUIRED TO AMORTIZE A LOAN

6¼ %

TERM AMOUNT	16 YEARS	17 YEARS	18 YEARS	19 YEARS	20 YEARS	21 YEARS	22 YEARS	23 YEARS	24 YEARS	25 YEARS	26 YEARS	27 YEARS	28 YEARS	30 YEARS	35 YEARS
$100	.83	.80	.77	.75	.73	.71	.70	.68	.67	.66	.65	.64	.63	.62	.59
200	1.65	1.59	1.54	1.50	1.46	1.42	1.39	1.36	1.34	1.31	1.29	1.27	1.26	1.23	1.17
300	2.47	2.38	2.31	2.24	2.18	2.13	2.08	2.04	2.00	1.97	1.94	1.91	1.88	1.84	1.75
400	3.29	3.18	3.08	2.99	2.91	2.84	2.78	2.72	2.67	2.62	2.58	2.54	2.51	2.45	2.33
500	4.11	3.97	3.84	3.73	3.64	3.55	3.47	3.40	3.34	3.28	3.23	3.18	3.13	3.06	2.91
600	4.93	4.76	4.61	4.48	4.36	4.26	4.16	4.08	4.00	3.93	3.87	3.81	3.76	3.67	3.49
700	5.75	5.55	5.38	5.23	5.09	4.97	4.86	4.76	4.67	4.59	4.51	4.45	4.39	4.28	4.08
800	6.57	6.35	6.15	5.97	5.82	5.68	5.55	5.44	5.34	5.24	5.16	5.08	5.01	4.89	4.66
900	7.39	7.14	6.91	6.72	6.54	6.38	6.24	6.12	6.00	5.90	5.80	5.72	5.64	5.50	5.24
1000	8.21	7.93	7.68	7.46	7.27	7.09	6.94	6.80	6.67	6.55	6.45	6.35	6.26	6.11	5.82
2000	16.42	15.86	15.36	14.92	14.53	14.18	13.87	13.59	13.33	13.10	12.89	12.69	12.52	12.22	11.64
3000	24.63	23.78	23.04	22.38	21.79	21.27	20.80	20.38	19.99	19.65	19.33	19.04	18.78	18.32	17.45
4000	32.84	31.71	30.72	29.84	29.06	28.36	27.73	27.17	26.66	26.19	25.77	25.39	25.04	24.43	23.27
5000	41.04	39.63	38.39	37.30	36.32	35.45	34.66	33.96	33.32	32.74	32.22	31.74	31.30	30.53	29.09
6000	49.25	47.56	46.07	44.75	43.58	42.53	41.59	40.75	39.98	39.29	38.66	38.08	37.56	36.64	34.90
7000	57.46	55.49	53.75	52.21	50.84	49.62	48.53	47.54	46.65	45.84	45.10	44.44	43.82	42.74	40.72
8000	65.67	63.41	61.43	59.67	58.11	56.71	55.46	54.33	53.31	52.38	51.54	50.78	50.08	48.85	46.54
9000	73.88	71.34	69.10	67.13	65.37	63.80	62.39	61.12	59.97	58.93	57.99	57.12	56.34	54.95	52.35
10000	82.08	79.26	76.78	74.59	72.63	70.88	69.32	67.91	66.64	65.48	64.43	63.47	62.59	61.06	58.17
11000	90.29	87.19	84.46	82.04	79.90	77.98	76.25	74.70	73.30	72.03	70.87	69.82	68.85	67.16	63.99
12000	98.50	95.11	92.14	89.50	87.16	85.06	83.18	81.49	79.96	78.57	77.31	76.16	75.11	73.27	69.80
13000	106.71	103.04	99.81	96.96	94.42	92.15	90.12	88.28	86.62	85.12	83.75	82.51	81.37	79.37	75.62
14000	114.92	110.97	107.49	104.42	101.68	99.24	97.05	95.07	93.29	91.67	90.20	88.86	87.63	85.48	81.44
15000	123.12	118.89	115.17	111.88	108.95	106.33	103.98	101.86	99.95	98.22	96.64	95.20	93.89	91.58	87.25
16000	131.33	126.82	122.85	119.33	116.21	113.42	110.92	108.65	106.61	104.76	103.08	101.55	100.15	97.69	93.07
17000	139.54	134.74	130.52	126.79	123.47	120.51	117.84	115.44	113.28	111.31	109.52	107.90	106.41	103.80	98.89
18000	147.75	142.67	138.20	134.25	130.74	127.59	124.77	122.23	119.94	117.86	115.97	114.25	112.67	109.90	104.70
19000	155.95	150.59	145.88	141.71	138.00	134.68	131.71	129.03	126.60	124.41	122.41	120.59	118.93	116.01	110.52
20000	164.16	158.52	153.56	149.17	145.26	141.77	138.64	135.82	133.27	130.95	128.85	126.93	125.18	122.11	116.34
21000	172.37	166.45	161.23	156.63	152.52	148.86	145.57	142.61	139.93	137.50	135.29	133.28	131.44	128.22	122.15
22000	180.58	174.37	168.91	164.08	159.79	155.95	152.50	149.40	146.59	144.05	141.74	139.63	137.70	134.32	127.97
23000	188.79	182.30	176.59	171.54	167.05	163.04	159.43	156.19	153.25	150.60	148.18	145.97	143.96	140.43	133.79
24000	196.99	190.22	184.27	179.00	174.31	170.12	166.36	162.98	159.92	157.14	154.62	152.32	150.22	146.53	139.60
25000	205.20	198.15	191.95	186.46	181.58	177.21	173.30	169.77	166.58	163.69	161.06	158.67	156.48	152.64	145.42
26000	213.41	206.07	199.62	193.92	188.84	184.30	180.23	176.56	173.24	170.24	167.50	165.01	162.74	158.74	151.24
27000	221.62	214.00	207.30	201.37	196.10	191.39	187.16	183.35	179.91	176.79	173.95	171.36	169.00	164.85	157.05
28000	229.83	221.93	214.98	208.83	203.36	198.48	194.10	190.14	186.57	183.33	180.39	177.71	175.26	170.95	162.87
29000	238.03	229.85	222.66	216.29	210.63	205.57	201.02	196.93	193.23	189.88	186.83	184.05	181.51	177.06	168.69
30000	246.24	237.78	230.33	223.75	217.89	212.66	207.95	203.72	199.90	196.43	193.27	190.40	187.77	183.16	174.50
35000	287.28	277.41	268.72	261.00	254.20	248.09	242.61	237.67	233.21	229.16	225.49	222.13	219.07	213.69	203.59
40000	328.32	317.04	307.11	298.33	290.50	283.54	277.27	271.63	266.53	261.90	257.70	253.86	250.36	244.22	232.67
45000	369.36	356.66	345.50	335.62	326.83	318.98	311.93	305.58	299.84	294.64	289.91	285.60	281.66	274.74	261.75
50000	410.40	396.29	383.89	372.91	363.15	354.42	346.59	339.53	333.16	327.38	322.12	317.33	312.95	305.27	290.84

MONTHLY PAYMENT
6½% REQUIRED TO AMORTIZE A LOAN

TERM AMOUNT	1 YEAR	2 YEARS	3 YEARS	4 YEARS	5 YEARS	6 YEARS	7 YEARS	8 YEARS	9 YEARS	10 YEARS	11 YEARS	12 YEARS	13 YEARS	14 YEARS	15 YEARS
$100	8.63	4.46	3.07	2.37	1.96	1.68	1.49	1.34	1.23	1.14	1.06	1.00	.95	.91	.87
200	17.26	8.91	6.13	4.74	3.91	3.36	2.97	2.67	2.45	2.27	2.12	2.00	1.90	1.81	1.74
300	25.88	13.36	9.19	7.11	5.86	5.04	4.45	4.01	3.67	3.40	3.18	3.00	2.84	2.72	2.60
400	34.51	17.81	12.25	9.48	7.82	6.71	5.93	5.34	4.89	4.53	4.24	3.99	3.79	3.62	3.47
500	43.13	22.26	15.31	11.84	9.77	8.39	7.41	6.68	6.11	5.66	5.29	4.99	4.74	4.52	4.34
600	51.76	26.71	18.37	14.21	11.72	10.07	8.89	8.01	7.33	6.79	6.35	5.99	5.68	5.43	5.20
700	60.38	31.16	21.43	16.58	13.67	11.74	10.37	9.35	8.55	7.92	7.41	6.99	6.63	6.33	6.07
800	69.01	35.61	24.49	18.95	15.63	13.42	11.85	10.68	9.77	9.05	8.47	7.98	7.58	7.23	6.94
900	77.64	40.06	27.55	21.31	17.58	15.10	13.33	12.01	11.00	10.18	9.53	8.98	8.52	8.14	7.80
1000	86.26	44.51	30.61	23.68	19.53	16.77	14.81	13.35	12.22	11.32	10.58	9.98	9.47	9.04	8.67
2000	172.52	89.02	61.21	47.36	39.06	33.54	29.62	26.70	24.43	22.63	21.16	19.93	18.94	18.07	17.33
3000	258.78	133.53	91.83	71.03	58.58	50.31	44.43	40.04	36.64	33.94	31.74	29.93	28.40	27.11	26.00
4000	345.03	178.03	122.44	94.71	78.11	67.08	59.24	53.38	48.85	45.25	42.32	39.90	37.87	36.14	34.66
5000	431.29	222.54	153.05	118.38	97.63	83.85	74.04	66.72	61.06	56.56	52.90	49.87	47.33	45.18	43.32
6000	517.55	267.05	183.66	142.06	117.16	100.62	88.85	80.07	73.27	67.87	63.48	59.85	56.80	54.21	51.99
7000	603.80	311.56	214.27	165.73	136.69	117.39	103.66	93.41	85.48	79.18	74.06	69.82	66.27	63.24	60.65
8000	690.06	356.06	244.88	189.41	156.21	134.16	118.47	106.76	97.70	90.49	84.64	79.80	75.73	72.28	69.31
9000	776.32	400.57	275.49	213.08	175.74	150.92	133.27	120.10	109.91	101.80	95.22	89.77	85.20	81.31	77.98
10000	862.57	445.08	306.10	236.76	195.26	167.69	148.08	133.44	122.12	113.11	105.80	99.74	94.66	90.35	86.64
11000	948.83	489.58	336.71	260.43	214.79	184.46	162.89	146.79	134.33	124.42	116.38	109.72	104.13	99.38	95.31
12000	1035.09	534.09	367.32	284.11	234.31	201.23	177.70	160.13	146.54	135.74	126.96	119.69	113.60	108.42	103.97
13000	1121.34	578.60	397.93	307.78	253.84	218.00	192.50	173.47	158.75	147.05	137.53	129.67	123.06	117.45	112.63
14000	1207.60	623.11	428.55	331.46	273.37	234.77	207.31	186.82	170.96	158.36	148.11	139.64	132.53	126.48	121.30
15000	1293.86	667.61	459.15	355.13	292.89	251.54	222.12	200.16	183.18	169.67	158.69	149.61	141.99	135.52	129.96
16000	1380.11	712.12	489.76	378.81	312.42	268.31	236.93	213.51	195.39	180.98	169.27	159.56	151.46	144.55	138.62
17000	1466.37	756.63	520.37	402.48	331.94	285.08	251.74	226.85	207.60	192.29	179.85	169.56	160.93	153.59	147.29
18000	1552.63	801.14	550.98	426.16	351.47	301.84	266.54	240.19	219.81	203.60	190.43	179.54	170.39	162.62	155.95
19000	1638.88	845.64	581.59	449.83	370.99	318.61	281.35	253.54	232.02	214.90	201.01	189.51	179.86	171.66	164.62
20000	1725.14	890.15	612.20	473.51	390.52	335.38	296.16	266.88	244.23	226.22	211.59	199.48	189.32	180.69	173.28
21000	1811.40	934.66	642.81	497.18	410.05	352.15	310.97	280.22	256.44	237.53	222.17	209.46	198.79	189.72	181.94
22000	1897.65	979.16	673.42	520.86	429.57	368.92	325.77	293.57	268.65	248.85	232.75	219.43	208.26	198.76	190.61
23000	1983.91	1023.67	704.03	544.53	449.10	385.69	340.58	306.91	280.87	260.16	243.33	229.41	217.72	207.79	199.27
24000	2070.17	1068.18	734.64	568.21	468.62	402.46	355.39	320.26	293.08	271.47	253.91	239.38	227.19	216.83	207.93
25000	2156.42	1112.69	765.25	591.88	488.15	419.23	370.20	333.60	305.29	282.78	264.48	249.35	236.65	225.86	216.60
26000	2242.68	1157.19	795.86	615.56	507.67	436.00	385.00	346.94	317.50	294.09	275.06	259.33	246.12	234.90	225.26
27000	2328.94	1201.70	826.47	639.23	527.20	452.76	399.81	360.29	329.71	305.40	285.64	269.30	255.58	243.93	233.92
28000	2415.19	1246.21	857.08	662.91	546.73	469.53	414.62	373.63	341.92	316.71	296.22	279.27	265.05	252.96	242.59
29000	2501.45	1290.72	887.69	686.58	566.25	486.30	429.43	386.97	354.13	328.02	306.80	289.25	274.52	262.00	251.25
30000	2587.71	1335.22	918.30	710.26	585.78	503.07	444.24	400.32	366.35	339.33	317.38	299.22	283.98	271.03	259.91
35000	3018.99	1557.76	1071.35	828.64	683.41	586.92	518.27	467.04	427.40	395.89	370.28	349.09	331.31	316.20	303.23
40000	3450.27	1780.30	1224.39	947.01	781.03	670.76	592.31	533.76	488.46	452.44	423.17	398.96	378.66	361.38	346.55
45000	3881.56	2002.83	1377.44	1065.39	878.66	754.60	666.35	600.48	549.52	509.00	476.07	448.83	425.97	406.55	389.87
50000	4312.84	2225.37	1530.49	1183.76	976.29	838.45	740.39	667.19	610.57	565.55	528.96	498.70	473.30	451.72	433.19

MONTHLY PAYMENT
REQUIRED TO AMORTIZE A LOAN — 6½%

TERM AMOUNT	35 YEARS	30 YEARS	28 YEARS	27 YEARS	26 YEARS	25 YEARS	24 YEARS	23 YEARS	22 YEARS	21 YEARS	20 YEARS	19 YEARS	18 YEARS	17 YEARS	16 YEARS
$100	.60	.63	.65	.66	.66	.67	.69	.70	.71	.73	.75	.76	.79	.81	.84
200	1.20	1.26	1.29	1.31	1.32	1.34	1.37	1.39	1.42	1.45	1.49	1.52	1.57	1.62	1.67
300	1.80	1.88	1.93	1.96	1.98	2.01	2.05	2.09	2.13	2.17	2.23	2.28	2.35	2.42	2.51
400	2.40	2.51	2.57	2.61	2.64	2.68	2.73	2.78	2.84	2.90	2.97	3.04	3.13	3.23	3.34
500	3.00	3.14	3.21	3.26	3.30	3.35	3.41	3.47	3.54	3.62	3.71	3.80	3.91	4.04	4.18
600	3.59	3.76	3.85	3.91	3.96	4.02	4.09	4.17	4.25	4.34	4.45	4.56	4.69	4.84	5.01
700	4.19	4.39	4.50	4.56	4.62	4.69	4.77	4.86	4.96	5.07	5.19	5.32	5.48	5.65	5.84
800	4.79	5.02	5.14	5.21	5.28	5.36	5.45	5.56	5.67	5.79	5.93	6.08	6.26	6.45	6.68
900	5.39	5.64	5.78	5.86	5.94	6.03	6.14	6.25	6.37	6.51	6.67	6.84	7.04	7.26	7.51
1000	5.99	6.27	6.42	6.51	6.60	6.70	6.82	6.94	7.08	7.24	7.41	7.60	7.82	8.07	8.35
2000	11.97	12.53	12.83	13.01	13.19	13.40	13.63	13.88	14.16	14.47	14.82	15.20	15.64	16.13	16.69
3000	17.95	18.80	19.25	19.51	19.79	20.10	20.44	20.82	21.24	21.70	22.22	22.80	23.45	24.19	25.03
4000	23.93	25.06	25.66	26.01	26.38	26.80	27.25	27.76	28.31	28.93	29.63	30.40	31.27	32.25	33.38
5000	29.92	31.33	32.08	32.51	32.98	33.50	34.07	34.70	35.39	36.17	37.03	37.99	39.09	40.32	41.72
6000	35.90	37.59	38.49	39.01	39.57	40.19	40.88	41.63	42.47	43.40	44.44	45.60	46.90	48.38	50.06
7000	41.88	43.85	44.91	45.51	46.17	46.89	47.69	48.57	49.55	50.63	51.84	53.19	54.72	56.44	58.40
8000	47.86	50.12	51.32	52.01	52.76	53.59	54.50	55.51	56.62	57.86	59.25	60.79	62.53	64.50	66.75
9000	53.85	56.38	57.74	58.51	59.36	60.29	61.31	62.45	63.70	65.10	66.65	68.39	70.35	72.57	75.09
10000	59.83	62.65	64.15	65.01	65.95	66.99	68.13	69.39	70.78	72.33	74.06	75.99	78.17	80.63	83.43
11000	65.81	68.91	70.57	71.51	72.55	73.69	74.94	76.32	77.86	79.56	81.46	83.59	85.98	88.69	91.77
12000	71.79	75.17	76.98	78.01	79.14	80.38	81.75	83.26	84.93	86.79	88.87	91.19	93.80	96.75	100.12
13000	77.78	81.44	83.39	84.51	85.74	87.08	88.56	90.20	92.01	94.02	96.27	98.79	101.62	104.82	108.46
14000	83.76	87.70	89.81	91.01	92.33	93.78	95.38	97.14	99.09	101.26	103.68	106.39	109.43	112.88	116.80
15000	89.74	93.97	96.22	97.51	98.93	100.48	102.19	104.08	106.17	108.49	111.08	113.98	117.25	120.94	125.15
16000	95.72	100.23	102.64	104.01	105.52	107.18	109.00	111.01	113.24	115.72	118.49	121.58	125.06	129.00	133.49
17000	101.71	106.49	109.05	110.51	112.12	113.88	115.81	117.95	120.32	122.95	125.89	129.18	132.88	137.07	141.83
18000	107.69	112.76	115.47	117.01	118.71	120.57	122.62	124.89	127.40	130.19	133.30	136.78	140.70	145.13	150.17
19000	113.67	119.02	121.88	123.52	125.31	127.27	129.44	131.83	134.48	137.42	140.70	144.38	148.51	153.19	158.52
20000	119.65	125.29	128.30	130.02	131.90	133.97	136.25	138.77	141.55	144.65	148.11	151.98	156.33	161.25	166.86
21000	125.63	131.55	134.71	136.52	138.49	140.67	143.06	145.70	148.63	151.88	155.51	159.57	164.15	169.32	175.20
22000	131.62	137.81	141.13	143.02	145.09	147.37	149.87	152.64	155.71	159.11	162.92	167.17	171.96	177.38	183.54
23000	137.60	144.08	147.54	149.52	151.68	154.06	156.69	159.58	162.78	166.35	170.32	174.77	179.78	185.44	191.89
24000	143.58	150.34	153.96	156.02	158.28	160.76	163.50	166.52	169.86	173.58	177.73	182.37	187.59	193.50	200.23
25000	149.56	156.61	160.37	162.52	164.87	167.46	170.31	173.46	176.94	180.81	185.13	189.97	195.41	201.57	208.57
26000	155.55	162.87	166.78	169.02	171.47	174.16	177.12	180.39	184.02	188.04	192.54	197.57	203.23	209.63	216.91
27000	161.53	169.13	173.20	175.52	178.06	180.86	183.93	187.33	191.09	195.28	199.94	205.16	211.04	217.69	225.26
28000	167.51	175.40	179.61	182.02	184.66	187.56	190.75	194.27	198.17	202.51	207.35	212.76	218.86	225.75	233.60
29000	173.49	181.66	186.03	188.52	191.25	194.25	197.56	201.21	205.25	209.74	214.75	220.36	226.67	233.82	241.94
30000	179.48	187.93	192.44	195.02	197.85	200.95	204.37	208.15	212.33	216.97	222.16	227.96	234.49	241.88	250.29
35000	209.39	219.25	224.52	227.52	230.82	234.44	238.43	242.84	247.72	253.13	259.18	265.95	273.57	282.19	292.00
40000	239.30	250.57	256.59	260.03	263.80	267.93	272.49	277.53	283.10	289.30	296.21	303.94	312.65	322.50	333.71
45000	269.21	281.89	288.66	292.53	296.77	301.43	306.55	312.22	318.49	325.46	333.23	341.94	351.73	362.82	375.43
50000	299.12	313.21	320.73	325.03	329.74	334.92	340.61	346.91	353.87	361.62	370.26	379.93	390.81	403.13	417.14

TERM AMOUNT	1 YEAR	2 YEARS	3 YEARS	4 YEARS	5 YEARS	6 YEARS	7 YEARS	8 YEARS	9 YEARS	10 YEARS	11 YEARS	12 YEARS	13 YEARS	14 YEARS	15 YEARS
$100	8.64	4.47	3.08	2.38	1.97	1.69	1.50	1.35	1.24	1.15	1.08	1.02	.96	.92	.88
200	17.28	8.93	6.15	4.76	3.93	3.38	2.99	2.70	2.47	2.29	2.15	2.03	1.92	1.84	1.76
300	25.92	13.39	9.22	7.14	5.90	5.07	4.48	4.04	3.70	3.44	3.22	3.04	2.88	2.75	2.64
400	34.55	17.85	12.29	9.52	7.86	6.76	5.98	5.39	4.94	4.58	4.29	4.05	3.84	3.67	3.52
500	43.19	22.31	15.37	11.90	9.82	8.45	7.47	6.74	6.17	5.72	5.36	5.06	4.80	4.59	4.40
600	51.83	26.78	18.44	14.28	11.79	10.14	8.96	8.08	7.40	6.87	6.43	6.07	5.76	5.50	5.28
700	60.46	31.24	21.51	16.66	13.75	11.82	10.45	9.43	8.64	8.01	7.50	7.08	6.72	6.42	6.16
800	69.10	35.70	24.58	19.03	15.72	13.51	11.95	10.78	9.87	9.15	8.57	8.09	7.68	7.34	7.04
900	77.74	40.16	27.65	21.41	17.68	15.20	13.44	12.12	11.10	10.30	9.64	9.10	8.64	8.25	7.92
1000	86.37	44.62	30.73	23.79	19.64	16.89	14.93	13.47	12.34	11.44	10.71	10.11	9.60	9.17	8.80
2000	172.74	89.24	61.45	47.58	39.28	33.77	29.86	26.93	24.67	22.87	21.42	20.21	19.20	18.34	17.60
3000	259.11	133.86	92.17	71.37	58.92	50.66	44.78	40.40	37.00	34.31	32.13	30.31	28.79	27.50	26.40
4000	345.48	178.47	122.89	95.15	78.56	67.54	59.71	53.86	49.34	45.74	42.83	40.41	38.39	36.67	35.20
5000	431.85	223.09	153.61	118.94	98.20	84.43	74.63	67.32	61.67	57.18	53.53	50.51	47.98	45.84	43.99
6000	518.22	267.71	184.33	142.73	117.84	101.31	89.56	80.79	74.00	68.61	64.24	60.62	57.58	55.00	52.79
7000	604.59	312.33	215.05	166.52	137.48	118.20	104.48	94.25	86.34	80.05	74.94	70.72	67.18	64.17	61.59
8000	690.95	356.94	245.77	190.30	157.12	135.08	119.41	107.71	98.67	91.48	85.65	80.82	76.77	73.33	70.39
9000	777.32	401.56	276.49	214.09	176.76	151.97	134.34	121.18	111.01	102.92	96.35	90.92	86.37	82.50	79.18
10000	863.69	446.18	307.21	237.88	196.40	168.85	149.26	134.64	123.34	114.35	107.06	101.02	95.96	91.67	87.98
11000	950.06	490.79	337.93	261.67	216.04	185.74	164.19	148.11	135.67	125.79	117.76	111.13	105.56	100.83	96.78
12000	1036.43	535.41	368.65	285.45	235.68	202.62	179.11	161.57	148.00	137.22	128.47	121.23	115.15	110.00	105.58
13000	1122.80	580.03	399.37	309.24	255.32	219.51	194.04	175.03	160.34	148.66	139.17	131.33	124.75	119.17	114.37
14000	1209.17	624.65	430.09	333.03	274.96	236.39	208.96	188.50	172.67	160.09	149.88	141.43	134.35	128.33	123.17
15000	1295.54	669.26	460.81	356.82	294.60	253.28	223.89	201.96	185.00	171.53	160.58	151.53	143.94	137.50	131.97
16000	1381.90	713.88	491.53	380.60	314.24	270.16	238.81	215.42	197.34	182.96	171.29	161.63	153.54	146.66	140.77
17000	1468.27	758.50	522.25	404.39	333.88	287.05	253.74	228.89	209.67	194.40	181.99	171.73	163.13	155.83	149.56
18000	1554.64	803.12	552.97	428.18	353.52	303.93	268.67	242.35	222.00	205.83	192.70	181.84	172.73	165.00	158.36
19000	1641.01	847.73	583.69	451.97	373.16	320.82	283.59	255.81	234.34	217.27	203.40	191.94	182.33	174.16	167.16
20000	1727.38	892.35	614.42	475.75	392.80	337.70	298.52	269.28	246.67	228.70	214.11	202.04	191.92	183.33	175.96
21000	1813.75	936.97	645.14	499.54	412.44	354.59	313.44	282.74	259.00	240.14	224.81	212.14	201.52	192.50	184.75
22000	1900.12	981.58	675.86	523.33	432.08	371.47	328.37	296.21	271.34	251.57	235.52	222.25	211.11	201.66	193.55
23000	1986.49	1026.20	706.58	547.12	451.72	388.35	343.29	309.67	283.67	263.01	246.22	232.35	220.71	210.83	202.35
24000	2072.85	1070.82	737.30	570.90	471.36	405.24	358.22	323.13	296.00	274.44	256.93	242.45	230.31	219.99	211.15
25000	2159.22	1115.44	768.02	594.69	491.00	422.12	373.14	336.60	308.34	285.88	267.63	252.55	239.90	229.16	219.95
26000	2245.59	1160.05	798.74	618.48	510.64	439.01	388.07	350.06	320.67	297.31	278.34	262.65	249.50	238.33	228.74
27000	2331.96	1204.67	829.46	642.27	530.28	455.89	403.00	363.52	333.00	308.75	289.04	272.76	259.00	247.49	237.54
28000	2418.33	1249.29	860.18	666.05	549.92	472.78	417.92	376.99	345.34	320.18	299.75	282.86	268.69	256.66	246.34
29000	2504.70	1293.90	890.90	689.84	569.56	489.66	432.85	390.45	357.67	331.62	310.45	292.96	278.29	265.83	255.14
30000	2591.07	1338.52	921.62	713.63	589.20	506.55	447.77	403.91	370.00	343.05	321.16	303.06	287.88	274.99	263.93
35000	3022.91	1561.61	1075.22	832.56	687.40	590.97	522.40	471.23	431.67	400.22	374.68	353.57	335.86	320.82	307.92
40000	3454.75	1784.70	1228.83	951.50	785.60	675.40	597.03	538.55	493.33	457.40	428.21	404.08	383.84	366.65	351.91
45000	3886.60	2007.78	1382.43	1070.44	883.79	759.82	671.66	605.87	555.00	514.57	481.74	454.59	431.82	412.48	395.90
50000	4318.44	2230.87	1536.03	1189.38	981.99	844.24	746.28	673.19	616.67	571.75	535.26	505.10	479.80	458.32	439.89

MONTHLY PAYMENT
REQUIRED TO AMORTIZE A LOAN

6¾ %

TERM AMOUNT	16 YEARS	17 YEARS	18 YEARS	19 YEARS	20 YEARS	21 YEARS	22 YEARS	23 YEARS	24 YEARS	25 YEARS	26 YEARS	27 YEARS	28 YEARS	30 YEARS	35 YEARS
$100	.85	.83	.80	.78	.76	.74	.73	.71	.70	.69	.68	.67	.66	.65	.62
200	1.70	1.65	1.60	1.55	1.51	1.48	1.45	1.42	1.40	1.38	1.35	1.34	1.32	1.29	1.23
300	2.55	2.47	2.39	2.33	2.27	2.22	2.17	2.13	2.09	2.06	2.03	2.00	1.98	1.93	1.85
400	3.40	3.29	3.19	3.10	3.02	2.96	2.89	2.84	2.79	2.75	2.70	2.67	2.63	2.57	2.46
500	4.24	4.11	3.98	3.88	3.78	3.69	3.62	3.55	3.49	3.43	3.38	3.33	3.29	3.22	3.08
600	5.09	4.93	4.78	4.65	4.53	4.43	4.34	4.26	4.18	4.12	4.05	4.00	3.95	3.86	3.69
700	5.94	5.75	5.57	5.42	5.29	5.17	5.06	4.97	4.88	4.80	4.73	4.66	4.61	4.50	4.31
800	6.79	6.57	6.37	6.20	6.04	5.90	5.78	5.67	5.58	5.49	5.40	5.33	5.26	5.14	4.92
900	7.64	7.39	7.17	6.97	6.80	6.64	6.51	6.38	6.27	6.17	6.08	6.00	5.92	5.79	5.54
1000	8.48	8.21	7.96	7.75	7.55	7.38	7.23	7.09	6.97	6.86	6.75	6.66	6.58	6.43	6.15
2000	16.96	16.41	15.92	15.49	15.10	14.76	14.45	14.18	13.93	13.71	13.50	13.32	13.15	12.85	12.30
3000	25.44	24.61	23.87	23.23	22.65	22.14	21.68	21.27	20.89	20.56	20.25	19.97	19.72	19.28	18.45
4000	33.92	32.81	31.83	30.97	30.20	29.52	28.90	28.35	27.86	27.41	27.00	26.63	26.29	25.70	24.60
5000	42.40	41.01	39.78	38.71	37.75	36.89	36.13	35.44	34.82	34.26	33.75	33.29	32.86	32.13	30.75
6000	50.88	49.21	47.74	46.45	45.30	44.27	43.35	42.53	41.78	41.11	40.50	39.94	39.44	38.55	36.90
7000	59.35	57.41	55.70	54.19	52.84	51.65	50.58	49.61	48.74	47.96	47.25	46.60	46.01	44.97	43.05
8000	67.83	65.61	63.65	61.93	60.39	59.03	57.80	56.70	55.71	54.81	53.99	53.25	52.58	51.40	49.20
9000	76.31	73.81	71.61	69.67	67.94	66.40	65.03	63.79	62.67	61.66	60.74	59.91	59.15	57.82	55.35
10000	84.79	82.01	79.56	77.41	75.49	73.78	72.25	70.87	69.63	68.51	67.49	66.57	65.72	64.25	61.50
11000	93.27	90.21	87.52	85.15	83.04	81.16	79.47	77.96	76.60	75.36	74.24	73.22	72.29	70.67	67.65
12000	101.75	98.41	95.48	92.89	90.59	88.54	86.70	85.05	83.56	82.21	80.99	79.88	78.87	77.10	73.80
13000	110.23	106.61	103.43	100.63	98.13	95.91	93.92	92.13	90.52	89.06	87.74	86.53	85.44	83.52	79.95
14000	118.70	114.81	111.39	108.37	105.68	103.29	101.15	99.22	97.48	95.91	94.49	93.19	92.01	89.94	86.10
15000	127.18	123.01	119.34	116.11	113.23	110.67	108.37	106.31	104.45	102.76	101.24	99.85	98.58	96.37	92.25
16000	135.66	131.21	127.30	123.85	120.78	118.05	115.60	113.39	111.41	109.61	107.98	106.50	105.15	102.79	98.40
17000	144.14	139.41	135.26	131.59	128.33	125.42	122.82	120.48	118.37	116.46	114.73	113.16	111.72	109.22	104.55
18000	152.62	147.61	143.21	139.33	135.88	132.80	130.05	127.57	125.33	123.31	121.48	119.81	118.30	115.64	110.70
19000	161.10	155.81	151.17	147.07	143.43	140.18	137.27	134.66	132.30	130.16	128.23	126.47	124.87	122.07	116.85
20000	169.58	164.01	159.12	154.81	150.97	147.56	144.49	141.74	139.26	137.01	134.98	133.13	131.44	128.49	123.00
21000	178.05	172.21	167.08	162.55	158.52	154.93	151.72	148.83	146.22	143.87	141.73	139.78	138.01	134.92	129.15
22000	186.53	180.41	175.03	170.29	166.07	162.31	158.94	155.92	153.19	150.72	148.48	146.44	144.58	141.34	135.30
23000	195.01	188.61	182.99	178.03	173.62	169.69	166.17	163.00	160.15	157.57	155.22	153.10	151.16	147.76	141.45
24000	203.49	196.81	190.95	185.77	181.17	177.07	173.39	170.09	167.11	164.42	161.97	159.75	157.73	154.19	147.60
25000	211.97	205.01	198.90	193.51	188.72	184.44	180.62	177.18	174.07	171.27	168.72	166.41	164.30	160.61	153.75
26000	220.45	213.21	206.86	201.25	196.26	191.82	187.84	184.26	181.04	178.12	175.47	173.06	170.87	167.04	159.90
27000	228.93	221.41	214.81	208.99	203.81	199.20	195.07	191.35	188.00	184.97	182.22	179.72	177.44	173.46	166.05
28000	237.40	229.61	222.77	216.73	211.36	206.58	202.29	198.44	194.96	191.82	188.97	186.38	184.01	179.88	172.20
29000	245.88	237.81	230.73	224.47	218.90	213.95	209.51	205.52	201.92	198.67	195.72	193.03	190.59	186.31	178.35
30000	254.36	246.01	238.68	232.21	226.46	221.33	216.74	212.61	208.89	205.52	202.47	199.69	197.16	192.73	184.50
35000	296.75	287.01	278.46	270.91	264.20	258.22	252.86	248.04	243.70	239.77	236.21	232.97	230.02	224.85	215.25
40000	339.15	328.02	318.24	309.60	301.94	295.11	288.98	283.48	278.52	274.02	269.95	266.25	262.88	256.98	245.99
45000	381.54	369.02	358.02	348.31	339.68	331.99	325.11	318.91	313.33	308.28	303.70	299.53	295.73	289.10	276.74
50000	423.93	410.02	397.80	387.01	377.43	368.88	361.23	354.35	348.14	342.53	337.44	332.81	328.59	321.22	307.49

7%
MONTHLY PAYMENT
REQUIRED TO AMORTIZE A LOAN

TERM AMOUNT	1 YEAR	2 YEARS	3 YEARS	4 YEARS	5 YEARS	6 YEARS	7 YEARS	8 YEARS	9 YEARS	10 YEARS	11 YEARS	12 YEARS	13 YEARS	14 YEARS	15 YEARS
$100	8.65	4.48	3.09	2.39	1.98	1.71	1.51	1.36	1.25	1.16	1.09	1.03	.98	.93	.90
200	17.30	8.95	6.17	4.78	3.96	3.41	3.01	2.72	2.50	2.32	2.17	2.05	1.95	1.86	1.79
300	25.95	13.42	9.25	7.17	5.93	5.11	4.52	4.08	3.74	3.47	3.25	3.07	2.92	2.79	2.68
400	34.60	17.90	12.34	9.56	7.91	6.81	6.02	5.44	4.99	4.63	4.34	4.10	3.90	3.72	3.58
500	43.25	22.37	15.42	11.95	9.88	8.51	7.53	6.80	6.23	5.78	5.42	5.12	4.87	4.65	4.47
600	51.89	26.84	18.50	14.34	11.86	10.21	9.03	8.16	7.48	6.94	6.50	6.14	5.84	5.58	5.36
700	60.54	31.31	21.59	16.73	13.83	11.91	10.54	9.51	8.72	8.10	7.59	7.17	6.81	6.51	6.26
800	69.19	35.79	24.67	19.12	15.81	13.61	12.04	10.87	9.97	9.25	8.67	8.19	7.79	7.44	7.15
900	77.84	40.26	27.75	21.51	17.78	15.31	13.54	12.23	11.22	10.41	9.75	9.21	8.76	8.37	8.04
1000	86.49	44.73	30.84	23.90	19.76	17.01	15.05	13.59	12.46	11.56	10.84	10.24	9.73	9.30	8.94
2000	172.97	89.46	61.67	47.80	39.51	34.01	30.09	27.17	24.92	23.12	21.67	20.47	19.46	18.60	17.87
3000	259.45	134.19	92.50	71.70	59.27	51.01	45.14	40.76	37.37	34.68	32.50	30.70	29.19	27.90	26.80
4000	345.93	178.91	123.33	95.60	79.02	68.01	60.18	54.34	49.83	46.24	43.33	40.93	38.91	37.20	35.73
5000	432.41	223.64	154.16	119.50	98.78	85.01	75.23	67.93	62.28	57.80	54.16	51.16	48.64	46.50	44.67
6000	518.89	268.37	184.99	143.40	118.53	102.01	90.27	81.51	74.74	69.36	65.00	61.39	58.37	55.80	53.60
7000	605.37	313.10	215.82	167.30	138.28	119.01	105.31	95.09	87.19	80.92	75.83	71.62	68.09	65.10	62.53
8000	691.85	357.82	246.66	191.20	158.04	136.01	120.36	108.68	99.65	92.48	86.66	81.85	77.82	74.40	71.46
9000	778.33	402.55	277.49	215.10	177.79	153.01	135.40	122.26	112.11	104.04	97.49	92.08	87.55	83.70	80.40
10000	864.81	447.28	308.32	239.00	197.55	170.02	150.44	135.85	124.56	115.60	108.32	102.31	97.27	93.00	89.33
11000	951.29	492.01	339.15	262.90	217.30	187.02	165.49	149.43	137.02	127.16	119.15	112.54	107.00	102.29	98.26
12000	1037.77	536.73	369.98	286.80	237.05	204.02	180.53	163.01	149.47	138.72	129.99	122.77	116.73	111.59	107.19
13000	1124.25	581.46	400.81	310.70	256.81	221.02	195.58	176.60	161.93	150.28	140.82	133.00	126.45	120.89	116.13
14000	1210.73	626.19	431.64	334.60	276.56	238.02	210.62	190.18	174.38	161.84	151.65	143.23	136.18	130.19	125.06
15000	1297.22	670.91	462.47	358.50	296.32	255.02	225.66	203.77	186.84	173.40	162.48	153.46	145.91	139.49	133.99
16000	1383.70	715.64	493.31	382.40	316.07	272.02	240.71	217.35	199.30	184.96	173.31	163.69	155.63	148.79	142.92
17000	1470.18	760.37	524.14	406.30	335.82	289.02	255.75	230.93	211.75	196.51	184.15	173.93	165.36	158.09	151.86
18000	1556.66	805.10	554.97	430.20	355.58	306.02	270.79	244.52	224.21	208.07	194.98	184.16	175.09	167.39	160.79
19000	1643.14	849.82	585.80	454.10	375.33	323.03	285.84	258.10	236.66	219.63	205.81	194.39	184.81	176.69	169.72
20000	1729.62	894.55	616.63	478.00	395.09	340.03	300.88	271.69	249.12	231.19	216.64	204.62	194.54	185.99	178.65
21000	1816.10	939.28	647.46	501.90	414.84	357.03	315.93	285.27	261.57	242.75	227.47	214.85	204.27	195.29	187.59
22000	1902.58	984.01	678.30	525.80	434.59	374.03	330.97	298.85	274.03	254.31	238.30	225.08	213.99	204.58	196.52
23000	1989.06	1028.73	709.13	549.70	454.35	391.03	346.01	312.44	286.49	265.87	249.14	235.31	223.72	213.88	205.45
24000	2075.54	1073.46	739.96	573.60	474.10	408.03	361.06	326.02	298.94	277.43	259.97	245.54	233.45	223.18	214.38
25000	2162.02	1118.19	770.79	597.50	493.86	425.03	376.10	339.61	311.40	288.99	270.80	255.77	243.17	232.48	223.32
26000	2248.50	1162.91	801.62	621.40	513.61	442.03	391.15	353.19	323.85	300.55	281.63	266.00	252.90	241.78	232.25
27000	2334.98	1207.64	832.45	645.30	533.36	459.04	406.19	366.77	336.31	312.11	292.46	276.23	262.63	251.08	241.18
28000	2421.46	1252.37	863.28	669.20	553.12	476.04	421.24	380.36	348.76	323.67	303.29	286.46	272.35	260.38	250.11
29000	2507.94	1297.10	894.12	693.10	572.87	493.04	436.28	393.94	361.22	335.23	314.13	296.69	282.08	269.68	259.05
30000	2594.43	1341.82	924.95	717.00	592.63	510.04	451.32	407.53	373.68	346.79	324.96	306.92	291.81	278.98	267.98
35000	3026.83	1565.46	1079.10	836.50	691.37	595.04	526.54	475.45	435.95	404.58	379.12	358.08	340.44	325.47	312.64
40000	3459.23	1789.10	1233.26	956.00	790.17	680.05	601.76	543.37	498.23	462.38	433.28	409.23	389.07	371.97	357.30
45000	3891.64	2012.73	1387.42	1075.50	888.94	765.06	676.98	611.29	560.51	520.18	487.43	460.38	437.71	418.46	401.97
50000	4324.06	2236.37	1541.58	1195.00	987.71	850.06	752.20	679.21	622.79	577.97	541.59	511.54	486.34	464.96	446.63

MONTHLY PAYMENT
REQUIRED TO AMORTIZE A LOAN

7%

TERM AMOUNT	35 YEARS	30 YEARS	28 YEARS	27 YEARS	26 YEARS	25 YEARS	24 YEARS	23 YEARS	22 YEARS	21 YEARS	20 YEARS	19 YEARS	18 YEARS	17 YEARS	16 YEARS
$100	.64	.66	.68	.69	.70	.71	.72	.73	.74	.76	.77	.79	.81	.84	.87
200	1.27	1.32	1.35	1.37	1.39	1.41	1.43	1.45	1.48	1.51	1.54	1.58	1.62	1.67	1.73
300	1.90	1.98	2.02	2.05	2.08	2.11	2.14	2.18	2.22	2.26	2.31	2.37	2.43	2.51	2.59
400	2.53	2.64	2.70	2.73	2.77	2.81	2.85	2.90	2.95	3.01	3.08	3.16	3.24	3.34	3.45
500	3.16	3.30	3.37	3.41	3.46	3.51	3.56	3.62	3.69	3.77	3.85	3.95	4.05	4.17	4.31
600	3.80	3.96	4.04	4.09	4.15	4.21	4.27	4.35	4.43	4.52	4.62	4.73	4.86	5.01	5.17
700	4.43	4.62	4.72	4.77	4.84	4.91	4.99	5.07	5.17	5.27	5.39	5.52	5.67	5.84	6.04
800	5.06	5.27	5.39	5.46	5.53	5.61	5.70	5.79	5.90	6.02	6.16	6.31	6.48	6.68	6.90
900	5.69	5.93	6.06	6.14	6.22	6.31	6.41	6.52	6.64	6.78	6.93	7.10	7.29	7.51	7.76
1000	6.32	6.59	6.74	6.82	6.91	7.01	7.12	7.24	7.38	7.53	7.70	7.89	8.10	8.34	8.62
2000	12.64	13.18	13.47	13.63	13.81	14.01	14.23	14.48	14.75	15.05	15.39	15.77	16.20	16.68	17.24
3000	18.96	19.76	20.20	20.44	20.72	21.01	21.35	21.72	22.12	22.58	23.08	23.65	24.30	25.02	25.85
4000	25.28	26.35	26.93	27.26	27.62	28.02	28.46	28.95	29.50	30.10	30.78	31.54	32.39	33.36	34.47
5000	31.60	32.94	33.66	34.07	34.53	35.03	35.58	36.19	36.87	37.63	38.47	39.42	40.49	41.70	43.08
6000	37.92	39.52	40.39	40.88	41.43	42.03	42.69	43.43	44.24	45.15	46.16	47.30	48.59	50.04	51.70
7000	44.24	46.11	47.12	47.70	48.33	49.03	49.81	50.66	51.61	52.67	53.85	55.18	56.68	58.38	60.31
8000	50.55	52.69	53.85	54.51	55.24	56.04	56.92	57.90	58.98	60.20	61.55	63.07	64.78	66.72	68.93
9000	56.87	59.28	60.58	61.32	62.14	63.04	64.04	65.14	66.36	67.72	69.24	70.95	72.88	75.06	77.54
10000	63.19	65.87	67.31	68.14	69.05	70.05	71.15	72.38	73.73	75.25	76.94	78.83	80.97	83.40	86.16
11000	69.51	72.45	74.04	74.95	75.95	77.05	78.27	79.61	81.11	82.77	84.63	86.72	89.07	91.74	94.77
12000	75.83	79.04	80.77	81.76	82.85	84.05	85.38	86.85	88.48	90.29	92.32	94.60	97.17	100.07	103.39
13000	82.15	85.62	87.50	88.58	89.76	91.06	92.50	94.09	95.85	97.82	100.00	102.48	105.26	108.41	112.01
14000	88.47	92.21	94.23	95.39	96.66	98.06	99.61	101.32	103.22	105.34	107.71	110.36	113.36	116.75	120.62
15000	94.78	98.80	100.96	102.20	103.57	105.07	106.73	108.56	110.60	112.87	115.40	118.25	121.46	125.09	129.24
16000	101.10	105.38	107.69	109.01	110.47	112.07	113.84	115.80	117.97	120.39	123.09	126.13	129.55	133.43	137.85
17000	107.42	111.97	114.42	115.83	117.37	119.08	120.95	123.03	125.34	127.91	130.78	134.01	137.65	141.77	146.47
18000	113.74	118.55	121.15	122.64	124.28	126.08	128.07	130.27	132.72	135.44	138.48	141.90	145.75	150.11	155.08
19000	120.06	125.14	127.88	129.45	131.18	133.09	135.18	137.52	140.11	142.96	146.14	149.78	153.84	158.45	163.70
20000	126.38	131.73	134.61	136.27	138.09	140.09	142.30	144.75	147.46	150.49	153.87	157.66	161.94	166.79	172.31
21000	132.70	138.31	141.34	143.08	144.99	147.09	149.41	151.98	154.83	158.01	161.56	165.54	170.04	175.13	180.93
22000	139.01	144.90	148.07	149.89	151.89	154.10	156.53	159.22	162.21	165.53	169.30	173.43	178.13	183.47	189.54
23000	145.33	151.48	154.80	156.71	158.80	161.10	163.64	166.46	169.58	173.06	176.95	181.31	186.23	191.81	198.16
24000	151.65	158.07	161.53	163.52	165.70	168.10	170.76	173.69	176.95	180.58	184.64	189.19	194.33	200.14	206.78
25000	157.97	164.66	168.26	170.33	172.61	175.11	177.87	180.93	184.33	188.11	192.33	197.08	202.42	208.48	215.39
26000	164.29	171.24	175.00	177.15	179.51	182.11	184.99	188.17	191.70	195.63	200.00	204.96	210.52	216.82	224.01
27000	170.61	177.83	181.73	183.96	186.41	189.12	192.10	195.40	199.07	203.15	207.72	212.84	218.62	225.16	232.62
28000	176.93	184.41	188.46	190.77	193.32	196.12	199.22	202.64	206.44	210.68	215.41	220.73	226.71	233.50	241.24
29000	183.25	191.00	195.19	197.59	200.22	203.13	206.33	209.88	213.81	218.21	223.11	228.61	234.81	241.84	249.85
30000	189.56	197.59	201.92	204.40	207.13	210.13	213.45	217.12	221.19	225.73	230.80	236.49	242.91	250.18	258.47
35000	221.16	230.52	235.57	238.46	241.65	245.15	249.02	253.30	258.05	263.35	269.26	275.90	283.39	291.88	301.55
40000	252.75	263.45	269.22	272.53	276.17	280.17	284.60	289.49	294.92	300.99	307.73	315.32	323.87	333.57	344.62
45000	284.34	296.38	302.87	306.60	310.69	315.19	320.17	325.67	331.78	338.59	346.19	354.73	364.36	375.27	387.70
50000	315.94	329.31	336.52	340.66	345.21	350.21	355.74	361.86	369.65	376.21	384.66	394.15	404.84	416.96	430.78

MONTHLY PAYMENT
7¼ % REQUIRED TO AMORTIZE A LOAN

TERM AMOUNT	1 YEAR	2 YEARS	3 YEARS	4 YEARS	5 YEARS	6 YEARS	7 YEARS	8 YEARS	9 YEARS	10 YEARS	11 YEARS	12 YEARS	13 YEARS	14 YEARS	15 YEARS
$100	8.66	4.49	3.10	2.41	1.99	1.72	1.52	1.38	1.26	1.17	1.10	1.04	.99	.95	.91
200	17.32	8.97	6.19	4.81	3.98	3.43	3.04	2.75	2.52	2.34	2.20	2.08	1.98	1.89	1.82
300	25.98	13.46	9.29	7.21	5.97	5.14	4.55	4.12	3.78	3.51	3.29	3.11	2.96	2.83	2.73
400	34.64	17.94	12.38	9.61	7.95	6.85	6.07	5.49	5.04	4.68	4.39	4.15	3.95	3.78	3.63
500	43.30	22.42	15.48	12.01	9.94	8.56	7.59	6.86	6.29	5.85	5.48	5.19	4.93	4.72	4.54
600	51.96	26.91	18.57	14.41	11.93	10.28	9.10	8.23	7.55	7.02	6.58	6.22	5.92	5.66	5.45
700	60.62	31.39	21.66	16.81	13.91	11.99	10.62	9.60	8.81	8.18	7.68	7.26	6.91	6.61	6.35
800	69.28	35.87	24.76	19.22	15.90	13.70	12.14	10.97	10.07	9.35	8.77	8.29	7.89	7.55	7.26
900	77.94	40.36	27.85	21.62	17.89	15.41	13.65	12.34	11.33	10.52	9.87	9.33	8.88	8.49	8.17
1000	86.60	44.84	30.95	24.02	19.87	17.12	15.17	13.71	12.58	11.69	10.96	10.37	9.86	9.44	9.07
2000	173.19	89.68	61.89	48.03	39.74	34.24	30.33	27.41	25.16	23.37	21.92	20.73	19.72	18.87	18.14
3000	259.78	134.52	92.83	72.04	59.61	51.36	45.49	41.12	37.74	35.06	32.88	31.09	29.58	28.30	27.21
4000	346.38	179.35	123.77	96.06	79.48	68.48	60.66	54.82	50.32	46.74	43.84	41.45	39.44	37.74	36.28
5000	432.97	224.19	154.72	120.07	99.35	85.59	75.82	68.53	62.90	58.43	54.80	51.81	49.30	47.17	45.35
6000	519.56	269.03	185.66	144.08	119.22	102.71	90.98	82.23	75.48	70.11	65.76	62.17	59.16	56.60	54.42
7000	606.15	313.86	216.60	168.09	139.09	119.83	106.14	95.94	88.06	81.80	76.72	72.53	69.01	66.03	63.48
8000	692.75	358.70	247.54	192.11	158.95	136.95	121.31	109.64	100.64	93.48	87.68	82.89	78.87	75.47	72.55
9000	779.34	403.54	278.49	216.12	178.82	154.06	136.47	123.35	113.21	105.17	98.64	93.25	88.73	84.90	81.62
10000	865.93	448.38	309.43	240.13	198.69	171.18	151.63	137.05	125.79	116.85	109.60	103.61	98.59	94.33	90.69
11000	952.52	493.22	340.37	264.14	218.56	188.30	166.79	150.76	138.37	128.54	120.56	113.97	108.45	103.77	99.76
12000	1039.12	538.05	371.31	288.16	238.43	205.42	181.96	164.46	150.95	140.22	131.51	124.33	118.30	113.20	108.83
13000	1125.71	582.89	402.26	312.17	258.30	222.53	197.12	178.17	163.53	151.90	142.47	134.69	128.16	122.63	117.89
14000	1212.30	627.73	433.20	336.18	278.17	239.65	212.28	191.87	176.11	163.59	153.43	145.05	138.02	132.06	126.96
15000	1298.89	672.57	464.14	360.19	298.04	256.77	227.44	205.58	188.69	175.27	164.39	155.41	147.88	141.50	136.03
16000	1385.49	717.40	495.08	384.21	317.90	273.89	242.61	219.28	201.27	186.96	175.35	165.77	157.74	150.93	145.10
17000	1472.08	762.24	526.03	408.22	337.77	291.01	257.77	232.99	213.84	198.64	186.31	176.13	167.60	160.36	154.17
18000	1558.67	807.08	556.97	432.23	357.64	308.12	272.93	246.69	226.42	210.33	197.27	186.49	177.45	169.80	163.24
19000	1645.26	851.92	587.91	456.24	377.51	325.24	288.09	260.40	239.00	222.01	208.23	196.85	187.31	179.23	172.30
20000	1731.86	896.75	618.85	480.26	397.38	342.36	303.26	274.10	251.58	233.70	219.19	207.21	197.17	188.66	181.37
21000	1818.45	941.59	649.80	504.27	417.25	359.48	318.42	287.81	264.16	245.38	230.15	217.57	207.03	198.09	190.44
22000	1905.04	986.43	680.74	528.28	437.12	376.59	333.58	301.51	276.74	257.07	241.11	227.93	216.89	207.53	199.51
23000	1991.64	1031.26	711.68	552.29	456.98	393.71	348.74	315.22	289.32	268.75	252.07	238.29	226.75	216.96	208.58
24000	2078.23	1076.10	742.62	576.31	476.85	410.83	363.91	328.92	301.90	280.44	263.02	248.65	236.60	226.39	217.65
25000	2164.82	1120.94	773.57	600.32	496.72	427.95	379.07	342.63	314.47	292.12	273.98	259.01	246.46	235.83	226.71
26000	2251.41	1165.78	804.51	624.33	516.59	445.06	394.23	356.33	327.05	303.80	284.94	269.37	256.32	245.26	235.78
27000	2338.01	1210.61	835.45	648.34	536.46	462.18	409.39	370.04	339.63	315.49	295.90	279.73	266.18	254.69	244.85
28000	2424.60	1255.45	866.39	672.36	556.33	479.30	424.56	383.74	352.21	327.17	306.86	290.09	276.04	264.12	253.92
29000	2511.19	1300.29	897.34	696.37	576.20	496.42	439.72	397.45	364.79	338.86	317.82	300.45	285.90	273.56	262.99
30000	2597.78	1345.13	928.28	720.38	596.07	513.54	454.88	411.15	377.37	350.54	328.78	310.81	295.75	282.99	272.06
35000	3030.75	1569.31	1082.99	840.45	695.41	599.12	530.70	479.68	440.26	408.97	383.57	362.61	345.05	330.15	317.40
40000	3463.71	1793.50	1237.70	960.51	794.75	684.71	606.51	548.20	503.15	467.39	438.37	414.41	394.34	377.32	362.74
45000	3896.67	2017.69	1392.42	1080.57	894.10	770.30	682.32	616.73	566.05	525.81	493.11	466.21	443.63	424.48	408.08
50000	4329.64	2241.87	1547.13	1200.63	993.44	855.89	758.14	685.25	628.94	584.24	547.96	518.01	492.92	471.65	453.42

MONTHLY PAYMENT
REQUIRED TO AMORTIZE A LOAN   7¼ %

TERM AMOUNT	35 YEARS	30 YEARS	28 YEARS	27 YEARS	26 YEARS	25 YEARS	24 YEARS	23 YEARS	22 YEARS	21 YEARS	20 YEARS	19 YEARS	18 YEARS	17 YEARS	16 YEARS
$100	.65	.68	.69	.70	.71	.72	.73	.74	.76	.77	.79	.81	.83	.85	.88
200	1.30	1.35	1.38	1.40	1.42	1.44	1.46	1.48	1.51	1.54	1.57	1.61	1.65	1.70	1.76
300	1.95	2.03	2.07	2.10	2.12	2.15	2.19	2.22	2.26	2.31	2.36	2.41	2.48	2.55	2.63
400	2.60	2.70	2.76	2.79	2.83	2.87	2.91	2.96	3.01	3.07	3.14	3.22	3.30	3.40	3.51
500	3.25	3.38	3.45	3.49	3.54	3.58	3.64	3.70	3.77	3.84	3.92	4.02	4.12	4.24	4.38
600	3.90	4.05	4.14	4.19	4.24	4.30	4.37	4.44	4.52	4.61	4.71	4.82	4.95	5.09	5.26
700	4.55	4.73	4.83	4.88	4.95	5.02	5.09	5.18	5.27	5.38	5.49	5.62	5.77	5.94	6.13
800	5.20	5.40	5.52	5.58	5.65	5.73	5.82	5.92	6.02	6.14	6.28	6.43	6.60	6.79	7.01
900	5.85	6.08	6.21	6.28	6.36	6.45	6.55	6.65	6.78	6.91	7.06	7.23	7.42	7.64	7.88
1000	6.49	6.75	6.90	6.97	7.07	7.16	7.27	7.39	7.53	7.68	7.84	8.03	8.24	8.48	8.76
2000	12.98	13.50	13.79	13.95	14.13	14.32	14.54	14.78	15.05	15.35	15.68	16.06	16.48	16.96	17.51
3000	19.47	20.25	20.68	20.92	21.19	21.48	21.81	22.17	22.57	23.02	23.52	24.09	24.72	25.44	26.27
4000	25.96	27.00	27.57	27.89	28.25	28.64	29.08	29.56	30.09	30.69	31.36	32.11	32.96	33.92	35.02
5000	32.45	33.75	34.46	34.86	35.31	35.80	36.34	36.95	37.62	38.36	39.20	40.14	41.20	42.40	43.77
6000	38.94	40.50	41.35	41.83	42.37	42.96	43.61	44.34	45.14	46.04	47.04	48.17	49.44	50.88	52.53
7000	45.43	47.25	48.24	48.81	49.43	50.12	50.88	51.72	52.66	53.71	54.88	56.20	57.68	59.36	61.28
8000	51.92	54.00	55.13	55.78	56.49	57.28	58.15	59.11	60.18	61.38	62.72	64.22	65.91	67.84	70.03
9000	58.41	60.75	62.02	62.75	63.55	64.44	65.42	66.50	67.71	69.05	70.56	72.25	74.15	76.32	78.79
10000	64.89	67.50	68.91	69.72	70.61	71.60	72.68	73.89	75.23	76.72	78.39	80.27	82.39	84.80	87.54
11000	71.38	74.25	75.80	76.69	77.67	78.76	79.95	81.28	82.75	84.40	86.23	88.30	90.63	93.27	96.29
12000	77.87	81.00	82.69	83.66	84.73	85.92	87.22	88.67	90.27	92.07	94.07	96.33	98.87	101.75	105.05
13000	84.36	87.75	89.58	90.64	91.80	93.07	94.49	96.06	97.80	99.74	101.91	104.36	107.11	110.23	113.80
14000	90.85	94.49	96.47	97.61	98.86	100.23	101.76	103.44	105.32	107.41	109.75	112.38	115.35	118.71	122.55
15000	97.34	101.24	103.36	104.58	105.92	107.39	109.02	110.83	112.84	115.08	117.59	120.41	123.59	127.19	131.31
16000	103.83	107.99	110.25	111.55	112.98	114.55	116.29	118.22	120.36	122.75	125.43	128.44	131.82	135.67	140.06
17000	110.32	114.74	117.14	118.52	120.04	121.71	123.56	125.61	127.89	130.43	133.27	136.46	140.06	144.15	148.81
18000	116.81	121.49	124.03	125.49	127.10	128.87	130.83	133.00	135.41	138.10	141.11	144.49	148.30	152.63	157.57
19000	123.30	128.24	130.92	132.46	134.16	136.03	138.10	140.39	142.93	145.77	148.95	152.51	156.54	161.11	166.32
20000	129.78	134.99	137.81	139.44	141.22	143.19	145.36	147.77	150.45	153.44	156.78	160.54	164.78	169.59	175.07
21000	136.27	141.74	144.70	146.41	148.28	150.35	152.63	155.16	157.98	161.12	164.62	168.57	173.02	178.07	183.83
22000	142.76	148.49	151.59	153.38	155.34	157.51	159.90	162.55	165.50	168.79	172.46	176.59	181.26	186.54	192.58
23000	149.25	155.24	158.49	160.35	162.40	164.67	167.17	169.94	173.02	176.46	180.30	184.62	189.49	195.02	201.33
24000	155.74	161.99	165.38	167.32	169.46	171.83	174.44	177.33	180.54	184.13	188.14	192.65	197.73	203.50	210.09
25000	162.23	168.74	172.27	174.29	176.52	178.98	181.70	184.72	188.07	191.80	195.98	200.67	205.97	211.98	218.84
26000	168.72	175.49	179.16	181.27	183.59	186.14	188.97	192.11	195.59	199.47	203.82	208.70	214.21	220.46	227.59
27000	175.21	182.24	186.05	188.24	190.65	193.30	196.24	199.49	203.11	207.14	211.66	216.73	222.45	228.94	236.35
28000	181.70	188.98	192.94	195.21	197.71	200.46	203.51	206.88	210.63	214.82	219.50	224.75	230.69	237.42	245.10
29000	188.19	195.73	199.83	202.18	204.77	207.62	210.78	214.27	218.16	222.49	227.34	232.78	238.93	245.90	253.85
30000	194.67	202.48	206.72	209.15	211.83	214.78	218.04	221.66	225.68	230.16	235.18	240.80	247.17	254.38	262.61
35000	227.12	236.23	241.17	244.01	247.13	250.58	254.38	258.60	263.29	268.52	274.37	280.94	288.36	296.77	306.37
40000	259.56	269.97	275.62	278.87	282.44	286.37	290.72	295.54	300.90	306.88	313.56	321.08	329.55	339.17	350.14
45000	292.01	303.72	310.08	313.72	317.74	322.16	327.06	332.49	338.52	345.24	352.76	361.21	370.75	381.56	393.91
50000	324.45	337.47	344.53	348.58	353.04	357.96	363.40	369.43	376.13	383.60	391.95	401.34	411.94	423.96	437.67

MONTHLY PAYMENT
7½ % REQUIRED TO AMORTIZE A LOAN

TERM AMOUNT	1 YEAR	2 YEARS	3 YEARS	4 YEARS	5 YEARS	6 YEARS	7 YEARS	8 YEARS	9 YEARS	10 YEARS	11 YEARS	12 YEARS	13 YEARS	14 YEARS	15 YEARS
$100	8.68	4.50	3.11	2.42	2.00	1.73	1.53	1.39	1.28	1.19	1.11	1.05	1.00	.96	.93
200	17.35	8.99	6.22	4.83	4.00	3.45	3.06	2.77	2.55	2.37	2.22	2.10	2.00	1.92	1.85
300	26.02	13.49	9.32	7.24	6.00	5.18	4.59	4.15	3.82	3.55	3.33	3.15	3.00	2.88	2.77
400	34.69	17.98	12.43	9.66	8.00	6.90	6.12	5.54	5.09	4.73	4.44	4.20	4.00	3.83	3.69
500	43.36	22.48	15.53	12.07	10.00	8.62	7.65	6.92	6.36	5.91	5.55	5.25	5.00	4.79	4.61
600	52.03	26.97	18.64	14.48	12.00	10.35	9.17	8.30	7.63	7.09	6.66	6.30	6.00	5.75	5.53
700	60.70	31.47	21.74	16.89	13.99	12.07	10.70	9.68	8.90	8.27	7.77	7.35	7.00	6.70	6.45
800	69.37	35.96	24.85	19.31	15.99	13.79	12.23	11.07	10.17	9.45	8.87	8.40	8.00	7.66	7.37
900	78.04	40.46	27.95	21.72	17.99	15.52	13.76	12.45	11.44	10.63	9.98	9.45	9.00	8.62	8.29
1000	86.71	44.95	31.06	24.13	19.99	17.24	15.29	13.83	12.71	11.82	11.09	10.50	10.00	9.57	9.21
2000	173.41	89.90	62.11	48.26	39.97	34.47	30.57	27.66	25.41	23.63	22.18	20.99	19.99	19.14	18.42
3000	260.12	134.85	93.17	72.38	59.96	51.71	45.85	41.48	38.11	35.44	33.27	31.48	29.98	28.71	27.62
4000	346.82	179.80	124.22	96.51	79.94	68.94	61.13	55.31	50.82	47.25	44.36	41.97	39.97	38.27	36.83
5000	433.53	224.74	155.27	120.63	99.92	86.18	76.41	69.14	63.52	59.06	55.44	52.47	49.95	47.84	46.03
6000	520.23	269.69	186.33	144.76	119.90	103.41	91.70	82.96	76.22	70.87	66.53	62.95	59.95	57.41	55.24
7000	606.94	314.64	217.38	168.88	139.89	120.65	106.98	96.79	88.92	82.68	77.62	73.44	69.93	66.98	64.44
8000	693.64	359.59	248.43	193.01	159.87	137.88	122.26	110.62	101.67	94.50	88.70	83.93	79.93	76.54	73.65
9000	780.35	404.53	279.49	217.13	179.86	155.12	137.54	124.44	114.33	106.30	99.79	94.91	89.91	86.11	82.85
10000	867.05	449.48	310.54	241.26	199.82	172.35	152.82	138.27	127.03	118.11	110.88	104.91	99.90	95.68	92.06
11000	953.75	494.43	341.59	265.39	219.81	189.59	168.10	152.09	139.73	129.92	121.96	115.40	109.90	105.25	101.26
12000	1040.46	539.38	372.65	289.51	239.81	206.82	183.39	165.92	152.43	141.73	133.05	125.89	119.89	114.81	110.47
13000	1127.16	584.32	403.70	313.64	259.79	224.06	198.67	179.75	165.14	153.54	144.14	136.38	129.88	124.38	119.67
14000	1213.87	629.27	434.76	337.76	279.77	241.29	213.95	193.57	177.84	165.35	155.23	146.87	139.88	133.95	128.88
15000	1300.57	674.22	465.81	361.89	299.71	258.53	229.23	207.40	190.54	177.16	166.31	157.36	149.86	143.52	138.08
16000	1387.28	719.17	496.86	386.01	319.74	275.76	244.51	221.23	203.24	188.97	177.40	167.85	159.86	153.08	147.29
17000	1473.98	764.11	527.92	410.14	339.73	292.99	259.80	235.05	215.95	200.78	188.49	178.34	169.85	162.65	156.49
18000	1560.69	809.06	558.97	434.26	359.71	310.23	275.08	248.88	228.65	212.59	199.57	188.83	179.84	172.22	165.70
19000	1647.39	854.01	590.02	458.39	379.69	327.46	290.36	262.70	241.35	224.40	210.66	199.32	189.83	181.79	174.90
20000	1734.10	898.96	621.08	482.51	399.68	344.70	305.64	276.53	254.05	236.21	221.75	209.81	199.82	191.35	184.11
21000	1820.80	943.90	652.13	506.64	419.66	361.93	320.92	290.36	266.76	248.02	232.84	220.30	209.81	200.92	193.31
22000	1907.50	988.85	683.18	530.77	439.59	379.17	336.20	304.18	279.46	259.84	243.92	230.79	219.80	210.49	202.52
23000	1994.21	1033.80	714.24	554.89	459.63	396.40	351.49	318.01	292.16	271.65	255.01	241.28	229.79	220.06	211.72
24000	2080.91	1078.75	745.29	579.02	479.61	413.64	366.77	331.84	304.86	283.46	266.10	251.77	239.78	229.62	220.93
25000	2167.62	1123.69	776.35	603.14	499.59	430.87	382.05	345.66	317.56	295.27	277.19	262.27	249.77	239.19	230.13
26000	2254.32	1168.64	807.40	627.27	519.58	448.11	397.33	359.49	330.27	307.08	288.27	272.76	259.76	248.76	239.34
27000	2341.03	1213.59	838.45	651.39	539.56	465.34	412.61	373.32	342.97	318.90	299.36	283.25	269.76	258.33	248.54
28000	2427.73	1258.54	869.51	675.52	559.54	482.58	427.90	387.14	355.67	330.70	310.45	293.74	279.75	267.89	257.75
29000	2514.44	1303.48	900.56	699.64	579.53	499.81	443.18	400.97	368.37	342.51	321.53	304.23	289.74	277.46	266.95
30000	2601.14	1348.43	931.61	723.77	599.51	517.05	458.46	414.80	381.08	354.32	332.62	314.72	299.73	287.03	276.16
35000	3034.66	1573.17	1086.88	844.40	699.43	603.22	534.54	483.93	444.59	413.37	388.06	367.17	349.68	334.87	322.18
40000	3468.19	1797.91	1242.15	965.02	799.35	689.39	611.28	553.06	508.10	472.42	443.49	419.62	399.64	382.70	368.21
45000	3901.71	2022.64	1397.42	1085.65	899.26	775.57	687.69	622.19	571.61	531.48	498.93	472.07	449.59	430.54	414.24
50000	4335.23	2247.38	1552.69	1206.28	999.18	861.74	764.09	691.32	635.12	590.53	554.37	524.53	499.55	478.38	460.26

MONTHLY PAYMENT
REQUIRED TO AMORTIZE A LOAN

7½ %

TERM AMOUNT	35 YEARS	30 YEARS	28 YEARS	27 YEARS	26 YEARS	25 YEARS	24 YEARS	23 YEARS	22 YEARS	21 YEARS	20 YEARS	19 YEARS	18 YEARS	17 YEARS	16 YEARS
$100	.67	.70	.71	.72	.73	.74	.75	.76	.77	.79	.81	.82	.85	.87	.90
200	1.35	1.40	1.43	1.44	1.46	1.48	1.50	1.52	1.55	1.58	1.61	1.65	1.69	1.74	1.79
300	2.02	2.10	2.14	2.16	2.19	2.22	2.25	2.28	2.32	2.37	2.42	2.47	2.54	2.61	2.69
400	2.70	2.80	2.85	2.88	2.92	2.96	3.00	3.05	3.10	3.16	3.22	3.30	3.38	3.47	3.58
500	3.37	3.50	3.56	3.60	3.65	3.70	3.75	3.81	3.87	3.95	4.03	4.12	4.23	4.34	4.48
600	4.05	4.20	4.28	4.32	4.38	4.43	4.50	4.57	4.65	4.73	4.83	4.94	5.07	5.21	5.38
700	4.72	4.89	4.99	5.04	5.11	5.17	5.25	5.33	5.42	5.52	5.64	5.77	5.92	6.08	6.27
800	5.39	5.59	5.70	5.77	5.84	5.91	6.00	6.09	6.20	6.31	6.44	6.59	6.76	6.95	7.17
900	6.07	6.29	6.42	6.49	6.56	6.65	6.75	6.85	6.97	7.10	7.25	7.42	7.61	7.82	8.06
1000	6.74	6.99	7.13	7.21	7.29	7.39	7.50	7.61	7.74	7.89	8.06	8.24	8.45	8.69	8.96
2000	13.48	13.98	14.26	14.41	14.59	14.78	14.99	15.23	15.49	15.78	16.11	16.48	16.90	17.37	17.92
3000	20.23	20.98	21.39	21.62	21.88	22.17	22.49	22.84	23.23	23.67	24.17	24.72	25.35	26.06	26.88
4000	26.97	27.97	28.51	28.83	29.18	29.56	29.99	30.46	30.98	31.57	32.22	32.96	33.80	34.75	35.83
5000	33.71	34.96	35.64	36.04	36.47	36.95	37.48	38.07	38.72	39.46	40.28	41.20	42.25	43.44	44.79
6000	40.45	41.95	42.77	43.24	43.77	44.34	44.98	45.69	46.47	47.35	48.33	49.45	50.70	52.12	53.75
7000	47.20	48.95	49.90	50.45	51.06	51.74	52.48	53.30	54.21	55.24	56.39	57.69	59.15	60.81	62.71
8000	53.94	55.94	57.03	57.66	58.35	59.13	59.97	60.92	61.95	63.13	64.45	65.93	67.60	69.50	71.67
9000	60.68	62.93	64.16	64.86	65.65	66.52	67.47	68.53	69.70	71.02	72.50	74.17	76.06	78.19	80.63
10000	67.42	69.92	71.29	72.07	72.94	73.91	74.97	76.15	77.44	78.91	80.56	82.41	84.51	86.87	89.58
11000	74.17	76.91	78.42	79.28	80.24	81.30	82.46	83.76	85.19	86.81	88.61	90.65	92.96	95.56	98.54
12000	80.91	83.91	85.54	86.49	87.53	88.69	89.96	91.38	92.93	94.70	96.67	98.89	101.41	104.25	107.50
13000	87.65	90.90	92.67	93.69	94.83	96.08	97.46	98.99	100.68	102.59	104.73	107.13	109.86	112.93	116.46
14000	94.39	97.89	99.80	100.90	102.12	103.47	104.95	106.60	108.42	110.48	112.78	115.37	118.31	121.62	125.42
15000	101.14	104.88	106.93	108.11	109.41	110.86	112.45	114.22	116.16	118.37	120.84	123.61	126.76	130.31	134.38
16000	107.88	111.87	114.06	115.31	116.71	118.25	119.95	121.83	123.91	126.26	128.89	131.85	135.21	139.00	143.33
17000	114.62	118.87	121.19	122.52	124.00	125.64	127.44	129.45	131.65	134.15	136.95	140.09	143.66	147.68	152.29
18000	121.36	125.86	128.32	129.73	131.30	133.03	134.94	137.06	139.40	142.04	145.00	148.34	152.11	156.37	161.25
19000	128.11	132.85	135.44	136.94	138.59	140.43	142.44	144.68	147.14	149.94	153.06	156.58	160.56	165.06	170.21
20000	134.85	139.84	142.57	144.14	145.89	147.82	149.93	152.29	154.89	157.83	161.12	164.82	169.01	173.75	179.17
21000	141.59	146.84	149.70	151.35	153.18	155.21	157.43	159.91	162.63	165.72	169.17	173.06	177.46	182.43	188.13
22000	148.33	153.83	156.83	158.56	160.47	162.60	164.93	167.52	170.37	173.61	177.23	181.30	185.91	191.12	197.08
23000	155.08	160.82	163.96	165.76	167.77	169.99	172.42	175.14	178.12	181.50	185.28	189.54	194.36	199.81	206.04
24000	161.82	167.81	171.09	172.97	175.06	177.38	179.92	182.75	185.86	189.39	193.34	197.78	202.81	208.49	215.00
25000	168.56	174.80	178.22	180.18	182.36	184.77	187.42	190.37	193.61	197.28	201.40	206.02	211.27	217.18	223.96
26000	175.30	181.80	185.35	187.38	189.65	192.16	194.91	197.98	201.35	205.18	209.45	214.26	219.72	225.87	232.92
27000	182.05	188.79	192.47	194.59	196.95	199.55	202.41	205.60	209.10	213.07	217.51	222.50	228.17	234.56	241.88
28000	188.79	195.78	199.60	201.80	204.24	206.94	209.91	213.21	216.84	220.96	225.56	230.74	236.62	243.24	250.83
29000	195.53	202.77	206.73	209.01	211.53	214.33	217.40	220.82	224.58	228.85	233.62	238.99	245.07	251.93	259.79
30000	202.27	209.76	213.86	216.21	218.83	221.72	224.90	228.44	232.33	236.74	241.67	247.23	253.52	260.62	268.75
35000	235.98	244.73	249.50	252.25	255.30	258.68	262.38	266.51	271.05	276.30	281.95	288.43	295.77	304.05	313.54
40000	269.70	279.69	285.15	288.28	291.77	295.63	299.87	304.59	309.77	315.66	322.23	329.63	338.02	347.49	358.33
45000	303.41	314.65	320.79	324.32	328.24	332.59	337.35	342.66	348.49	355.01	362.51	370.84	380.28	390.93	403.13
50000	337.12	349.61	356.43	360.36	364.72	369.54	374.84	380.73	387.21	394.57	402.79	412.04	422.53	434.36	447.92

MONTHLY PAYMENT
REQUIRED TO AMORTIZE A LOAN

7¾ %

TERM AMOUNT	1 YEAR	2 YEARS	3 YEARS	4 YEARS	5 YEARS	6 YEARS	7 YEARS	8 YEARS	9 YEARS	10 YEARS	11 YEARS	12 YEARS	13 YEARS	14 YEARS	15 YEARS
$100	8.69	4.51	3.12	2.43	2.01	1.74	1.55	1.40	1.29	1.20	1.13	1.07	1.02	.98	.94
200	17.37	9.02	6.24	4.85	4.02	3.48	3.09	2.79	2.57	2.39	2.25	2.13	2.03	1.95	1.87
300	26.05	13.52	9.35	7.28	6.03	5.21	4.63	4.19	3.85	3.59	3.37	3.19	3.04	2.92	2.81
400	34.73	18.03	12.47	9.70	8.04	6.95	6.17	5.58	5.14	4.78	4.49	4.25	4.05	3.89	3.74
500	43.41	22.53	15.59	12.12	10.05	8.68	7.71	6.98	6.47	5.97	5.61	5.32	5.07	4.86	4.68
600	52.09	27.04	18.70	14.55	12.06	10.42	9.25	8.37	7.70	7.17	6.73	6.38	6.08	5.83	5.61
700	60.78	31.55	21.82	16.97	14.07	12.15	10.79	9.77	8.98	8.36	7.86	7.44	7.09	6.80	6.55
800	69.46	36.05	24.94	19.40	16.08	13.89	12.33	11.16	10.27	9.55	8.98	8.50	8.10	7.77	7.48
900	78.14	40.56	28.05	21.82	18.09	15.62	13.87	12.56	11.55	10.75	10.10	9.56	9.12	8.74	8.41
1000	86.82	45.06	31.17	24.24	20.10	17.36	15.41	13.95	12.83	11.94	11.22	10.63	10.13	9.71	9.35
2000	173.64	90.12	62.33	48.48	40.20	34.71	30.81	27.90	25.66	23.88	22.44	21.25	20.25	19.41	18.69
3000	260.45	135.18	93.50	72.96	60.30	52.06	46.21	41.85	38.48	35.82	33.65	31.87	30.38	29.11	28.03
4000	347.27	180.24	124.66	96.96	80.40	69.41	61.61	55.80	51.31	47.76	44.87	42.49	40.50	38.82	37.38
5000	434.09	225.29	155.83	121.20	100.50	86.77	77.01	69.75	64.14	59.69	56.09	53.11	50.63	48.52	46.72
6000	520.90	270.35	186.99	145.44	120.60	104.12	92.41	83.69	76.96	71.63	67.32	63.73	60.75	58.22	56.06
7000	607.72	315.41	218.16	169.67	140.70	121.47	107.81	97.64	89.79	83.56	78.52	74.36	70.87	67.93	65.41
8000	694.54	360.47	249.32	193.91	160.79	138.82	123.22	111.59	102.62	95.50	89.73	84.98	81.00	77.63	74.75
9000	781.35	405.52	280.49	218.15	180.89	156.17	138.62	125.54	115.44	107.44	100.95	95.60	91.12	87.33	84.09
10000	868.17	450.58	311.65	242.39	200.99	173.53	154.02	139.49	128.27	119.37	112.17	106.22	101.25	97.04	93.43
11000	954.99	495.64	342.82	266.63	221.09	190.88	169.42	153.44	141.10	131.31	123.38	116.84	111.37	106.74	102.78
12000	1041.80	540.70	373.98	290.87	241.19	208.23	184.82	167.38	153.92	143.25	134.63	127.46	121.49	116.44	112.12
13000	1128.62	585.76	405.15	315.11	261.29	225.58	200.22	181.33	166.75	155.19	145.81	138.08	131.62	126.14	121.46
14000	1215.43	630.81	436.31	339.34	281.39	242.93	215.62	195.28	179.58	167.12	157.03	148.71	141.74	135.85	130.81
15000	1302.25	675.87	467.48	363.58	301.49	260.29	231.02	209.23	192.40	179.06	168.46	159.33	151.87	145.55	140.15
16000	1389.07	720.93	498.64	387.82	321.58	277.64	246.43	223.18	205.23	191.00	179.46	169.95	161.99	155.25	149.49
17000	1475.88	765.99	529.81	412.06	341.68	294.99	261.83	237.12	218.06	202.93	190.68	180.57	172.11	164.96	158.83
18000	1562.70	811.05	560.97	436.30	361.78	312.34	277.23	251.07	230.88	214.87	201.89	191.19	182.24	174.66	168.18
19000	1649.52	856.10	592.14	460.54	381.88	329.69	292.63	265.02	243.71	226.81	213.11	201.81	192.36	184.36	177.52
20000	1736.33	901.16	623.30	484.78	401.98	347.05	308.03	278.97	256.56	238.74	224.33	212.43	202.49	194.07	186.86
21000	1823.15	946.22	654.47	509.01	422.08	364.40	323.43	292.92	269.39	250.68	235.54	223.06	212.61	203.77	196.21
22000	1909.97	991.27	685.63	533.25	442.18	381.75	338.84	306.87	282.19	262.62	246.76	233.68	222.74	213.47	205.55
23000	1996.78	1036.33	716.80	557.49	462.28	399.10	354.24	320.81	295.07	274.56	257.97	244.30	232.86	223.17	214.89
24000	2083.60	1081.39	747.96	581.73	482.37	416.45	369.64	334.76	307.84	286.49	269.19	254.92	242.98	232.88	224.23
25000	2170.42	1126.45	779.13	605.97	502.47	433.81	385.04	348.71	320.67	298.43	280.41	265.54	253.11	242.58	233.58
26000	2257.23	1171.51	810.29	630.21	522.57	451.16	400.44	362.66	333.50	310.37	291.62	276.16	263.23	252.28	242.92
27000	2344.05	1216.56	841.46	654.45	542.67	468.51	415.84	376.61	346.33	322.31	302.84	286.78	273.36	261.99	252.26
28000	2430.86	1261.62	872.62	678.68	562.77	485.86	431.24	390.55	359.15	334.24	314.05	297.41	283.48	271.69	261.61
29000	2517.68	1306.68	903.79	702.92	582.87	503.21	446.65	404.50	371.98	346.18	325.27	308.03	293.60	281.39	270.95
30000	2604.50	1351.74	934.95	727.16	602.97	520.57	462.05	418.45	384.81	358.11	336.49	318.65	303.73	291.10	280.29
35000	3038.58	1577.02	1090.77	848.35	703.46	607.33	539.05	488.19	448.94	417.80	392.57	371.76	354.35	339.61	327.01
40000	3472.66	1802.31	1246.60	969.55	803.95	694.09	616.06	557.93	513.07	477.48	448.65	424.86	404.97	388.13	373.72
45000	3906.74	2027.60	1402.43	1090.74	904.45	780.85	693.07	627.67	577.20	537.15	504.73	477.95	455.59	436.64	420.43
50000	4340.83	2252.89	1558.25	1211.93	1004.94	867.61	770.08	697.42	641.33	596.85	560.81	531.08	506.21	485.16	467.15

MONTHLY PAYMENT
REQUIRED TO AMORTIZE A LOAN

7¾ %

TERM AMOUNT	16 YEARS	17 YEARS	18 YEARS	19 YEARS	20 YEARS	21 YEARS	22 YEARS	23 YEARS	24 YEARS	25 YEARS	26 YEARS	27 YEARS	28 YEARS	30 YEARS	35 YEARS
$100	.91	.88	.86	.84	.82	.80	.79	.77	.76	.75	.74	.73	.73	.71	.69
200	1.81	1.76	1.71	1.67	1.63	1.60	1.57	1.54	1.52	1.50	1.48	1.46	1.45	1.42	1.37
300	2.71	2.63	2.56	2.50	2.45	2.40	2.35	2.31	2.28	2.25	2.22	2.19	2.17	2.13	2.06
400	3.62	3.51	3.42	3.33	3.26	3.19	3.14	3.08	3.04	2.99	2.96	2.92	2.89	2.84	2.74
500	4.52	4.39	4.27	4.16	4.07	3.99	3.92	3.85	3.79	3.74	3.70	3.65	3.61	3.54	3.42
600	5.42	5.26	5.12	5.00	4.89	4.79	4.70	4.62	4.55	4.49	4.43	4.38	4.33	4.25	4.11
700	6.33	6.14	5.97	5.83	5.70	5.58	5.48	5.39	5.31	5.24	5.17	5.11	5.06	4.96	4.79
800	7.23	7.01	6.83	6.66	6.51	6.38	6.27	6.16	6.07	5.98	5.91	5.84	5.78	5.67	5.47
900	8.13	7.89	7.68	7.49	7.33	7.18	7.05	6.93	6.83	6.73	6.65	6.57	6.50	6.38	6.16
1000	9.04	8.77	8.53	8.32	8.14	7.98	7.83	7.70	7.58	7.48	7.38	7.30	7.22	7.08	6.84
2000	18.07	17.53	17.06	16.64	16.27	15.95	15.66	15.40	15.16	14.95	14.76	14.59	14.43	14.16	13.67
3000	27.10	26.29	25.58	24.96	24.41	23.92	23.48	23.09	22.74	22.42	22.14	21.88	21.65	21.24	20.51
4000	36.13	35.05	34.11	33.28	32.54	31.89	31.31	30.79	30.32	29.90	29.52	29.17	28.86	28.32	27.34
5000	45.17	43.82	42.63	41.60	40.68	39.86	39.13	38.48	37.90	37.37	36.90	36.46	36.08	35.40	34.17
6000	54.20	52.58	51.16	49.91	48.81	47.83	46.96	46.18	45.48	44.84	44.27	43.76	43.29	42.48	41.01
7000	63.23	61.34	59.69	58.23	56.94	55.80	54.78	53.87	53.05	52.32	51.65	51.05	50.51	49.56	47.84
8000	72.26	70.10	68.21	66.55	65.08	63.77	62.61	61.57	60.63	59.79	59.03	58.34	57.72	56.64	54.68
9000	81.29	78.86	76.74	74.87	73.21	71.74	70.43	69.26	68.21	67.26	66.41	65.64	64.94	63.72	61.51
10000	90.33	87.63	85.26	83.19	81.35	79.69	78.26	76.96	75.79	74.74	73.79	72.93	72.15	70.80	68.34
11000	99.36	96.39	93.79	91.50	89.48	87.69	86.09	84.65	83.37	82.21	81.17	80.22	79.37	77.88	75.18
12000	108.39	105.15	102.32	99.82	97.62	95.66	93.91	92.35	90.95	89.68	88.54	87.51	86.58	84.96	82.01
13000	117.42	113.91	110.84	108.14	105.75	103.60	101.74	100.04	98.52	97.16	95.92	94.81	93.80	92.04	88.85
14000	126.46	122.67	119.37	116.46	113.88	111.60	109.56	107.74	106.10	104.63	103.30	102.10	101.01	99.12	95.68
15000	135.49	131.44	127.89	124.78	122.02	119.57	117.39	115.43	113.68	112.10	110.68	109.39	108.23	106.20	102.51
16000	144.52	140.20	136.42	133.09	130.29	127.54	125.21	123.13	121.26	119.58	118.06	116.68	115.44	113.28	109.35
17000	153.55	148.96	144.94	141.41	138.29	135.51	133.04	130.82	128.84	127.05	125.44	123.98	122.65	120.36	116.18
18000	162.58	157.72	153.47	149.73	146.42	143.48	140.86	138.52	136.42	134.52	132.81	131.27	129.87	127.44	123.01
19000	171.62	166.49	161.99	158.05	154.56	151.43	148.69	146.21	143.99	142.00	140.19	138.56	137.08	134.52	129.85
20000	180.65	175.25	170.52	166.37	162.69	159.43	156.51	153.91	151.57	149.47	147.57	145.85	144.30	141.60	136.68
21000	189.68	184.01	179.05	174.68	170.82	167.40	164.34	161.61	159.15	156.94	154.95	153.15	151.51	148.68	143.52
22000	198.71	192.77	187.57	183.00	178.96	175.37	172.16	169.30	166.73	164.42	162.33	160.44	158.73	155.76	150.35
23000	207.74	201.53	196.10	191.32	187.09	183.34	179.99	177.00	174.31	171.89	169.71	167.73	165.94	162.84	157.18
24000	216.78	210.30	204.63	199.64	195.23	191.31	187.82	184.69	181.89	179.36	177.08	175.02	173.16	169.92	164.02
25000	225.81	219.06	213.15	207.96	203.36	199.28	195.64	192.39	189.46	186.84	184.46	182.32	180.37	177.00	170.85
26000	234.84	227.82	221.68	216.27	211.49	207.25	203.47	200.08	197.04	194.31	191.84	189.61	187.59	184.08	177.69
27000	243.87	236.58	230.20	224.59	219.63	215.22	211.29	207.78	204.62	201.78	199.22	196.90	194.80	191.16	184.52
28000	252.91	245.34	238.73	232.91	227.76	223.19	219.12	215.47	212.20	209.25	206.60	204.19	202.02	198.24	191.35
29000	261.94	254.11	247.26	241.23	235.90	231.16	226.94	223.17	219.78	216.73	213.98	211.49	209.23	205.37	198.19
30000	270.97	262.87	255.78	249.55	244.03	239.13	234.77	230.86	227.36	224.20	221.35	218.78	216.45	212.40	205.02
35000	316.13	306.68	298.41	291.14	284.70	278.99	273.90	269.34	265.25	261.57	258.24	255.24	252.57	247.80	239.19
40000	361.29	350.49	341.04	332.73	325.37	318.85	313.02	307.82	303.14	298.93	295.14	291.70	288.59	283.20	273.36
45000	406.45	394.30	383.67	374.32	366.05	358.70	352.15	346.29	341.03	336.30	332.03	328.17	324.67	318.60	307.53
50000	451.61	438.11	426.30	415.91	406.72	398.56	391.28	384.77	378.92	373.67	368.92	364.63	360.74	354.00	341.70

MONTHLY PAYMENT
8% — REQUIRED TO AMORTIZE A LOAN

TERM AMOUNT	1 YEAR	2 YEARS	3 YEARS	4 YEARS	5 YEARS	6 YEARS	7 YEARS	8 YEARS	9 YEARS	10 YEARS	11 YEARS	12 YEARS	13 YEARS	14 YEARS	15 YEARS
$100	8.70	4.52	3.13	2.44	2.03	1.75	1.56	1.41	1.30	1.21	1.14	1.08	1.03	.99	.95
200	17.39	9.04	6.26	4.88	4.05	3.50	3.11	2.82	2.60	2.42	2.27	2.16	2.06	1.97	1.90
300	26.08	13.56	9.39	7.31	6.07	5.25	4.66	4.23	3.89	3.62	3.41	3.23	3.08	2.96	2.85
400	34.78	18.07	12.52	9.75	8.09	6.99	6.21	5.63	5.19	4.83	4.54	4.31	4.11	3.94	3.80
500	43.47	22.59	15.64	12.18	10.11	8.74	7.77	7.04	6.48	6.04	5.68	5.38	5.13	4.92	4.75
600	52.16	27.11	18.77	14.62	12.13	10.49	9.32	8.45	7.78	7.24	6.81	6.46	6.16	5.91	5.69
700	60.85	31.62	21.90	17.05	14.15	12.23	10.87	9.85	9.07	8.45	7.95	7.53	7.19	6.89	6.64
800	69.55	36.14	25.03	19.49	16.17	13.98	12.42	11.26	10.37	9.66	9.08	8.61	8.21	7.88	7.59
900	78.24	40.66	28.15	21.92	18.20	15.73	13.97	12.67	11.66	10.86	10.22	9.68	9.24	8.86	8.54
1000	86.93	45.17	31.28	24.36	20.22	17.47	15.53	14.08	12.96	12.07	11.35	10.76	10.26	9.84	9.49
2000	173.86	90.34	62.56	48.71	40.43	34.94	31.05	28.15	25.91	24.13	22.70	21.51	20.52	19.68	18.97
3000	260.79	135.51	93.83	73.06	60.64	52.41	46.57	42.22	38.86	36.20	34.04	32.26	30.78	29.52	28.45
4000	347.72	180.68	125.11	97.41	80.86	69.88	62.09	56.29	51.81	48.26	45.39	43.02	41.00	39.36	37.93
5000	434.65	225.84	156.39	121.76	101.08	87.35	77.61	70.36	64.76	60.33	56.73	53.77	51.30	49.20	47.41
6000	521.57	271.01	187.66	146.12	121.29	104.82	93.13	84.43	77.71	72.39	68.08	64.52	61.55	59.04	56.89
7000	608.50	316.18	218.94	170.47	141.50	122.29	108.66	98.50	90.66	84.45	79.42	75.28	71.81	68.88	66.38
8000	695.43	361.35	250.22	194.82	161.72	139.76	124.18	112.57	103.62	96.52	90.77	86.03	82.07	78.72	75.86
9000	782.36	406.52	281.49	219.17	181.93	157.23	139.70	126.64	116.57	108.58	102.11	96.78	92.33	88.56	85.34
10000	869.29	451.68	312.77	243.52	202.15	174.70	155.22	140.71	129.52	120.65	113.46	107.54	102.59	98.40	94.82
11000	956.22	496.85	344.04	267.88	222.36	192.17	170.74	154.78	142.47	132.71	124.81	118.29	112.85	108.24	104.30
12000	1043.14	542.02	375.32	292.23	242.57	209.64	186.26	168.85	155.42	144.77	136.15	129.04	123.11	118.08	113.78
13000	1130.07	587.19	406.60	316.58	262.79	227.11	201.78	182.92	168.37	156.84	147.50	139.80	133.36	127.92	123.26
14000	1217.00	632.36	437.87	340.93	283.00	244.58	217.31	196.99	181.32	168.90	158.84	150.55	143.62	137.76	132.75
15000	1303.93	677.52	469.15	365.28	303.22	262.05	232.83	211.06	194.28	180.97	170.19	161.30	153.88	147.60	142.23
16000	1390.86	722.69	500.43	389.63	323.43	279.52	248.35	225.13	207.23	193.03	181.53	172.06	164.14	157.44	151.71
17000	1477.79	767.86	531.70	413.99	343.65	296.99	263.87	239.21	220.18	205.09	192.88	182.81	174.39	167.28	161.19
18000	1564.71	813.03	562.98	438.34	363.86	314.46	279.39	253.28	233.13	217.16	204.22	193.56	184.65	177.11	170.67
19000	1651.64	858.20	594.26	462.69	384.07	331.93	294.91	267.35	246.08	229.22	215.57	204.32	194.91	186.95	180.15
20000	1738.57	903.36	625.53	487.04	404.29	349.40	310.43	281.42	259.03	241.29	226.91	215.07	205.17	196.79	189.64
21000	1825.50	948.53	656.81	511.39	424.50	366.87	325.96	295.49	271.98	253.35	238.26	225.82	215.43	206.63	199.12
22000	1912.43	993.70	688.08	535.74	444.72	384.34	341.48	309.56	284.93	265.41	249.61	236.58	225.69	216.47	208.60
23000	1999.35	1038.87	719.36	560.10	464.93	401.81	357.00	323.63	297.89	277.48	260.95	247.33	235.94	226.31	218.08
24000	2086.28	1084.04	750.64	584.45	485.14	419.28	372.52	337.70	310.84	289.54	272.30	258.08	246.20	236.15	227.56
25000	2173.21	1129.20	781.91	608.80	505.36	436.75	388.04	351.77	323.79	301.61	283.64	268.84	256.46	245.99	237.04
26000	2260.14	1174.37	813.19	633.15	525.57	454.22	403.56	365.84	336.74	313.67	294.99	279.59	266.72	255.83	246.52
27000	2347.07	1219.54	844.47	657.51	545.79	471.69	419.08	379.91	349.69	325.74	306.33	290.30	276.98	265.67	256.01
28000	2434.00	1264.71	875.74	681.86	566.00	489.16	434.61	393.98	362.64	337.80	317.68	301.10	287.24	275.51	265.49
29000	2520.92	1309.88	907.02	706.21	586.22	506.63	450.13	408.05	375.59	349.86	329.02	311.85	297.49	285.35	274.97
30000	2607.85	1355.04	938.30	730.56	606.43	524.10	465.65	422.12	388.55	361.93	340.37	322.60	307.75	295.19	284.45
35000	3042.49	1580.88	1094.68	852.32	707.50	611.45	543.26	492.48	453.30	422.25	397.10	376.37	359.04	344.38	331.86
40000	3477.14	1806.72	1251.06	974.06	808.57	698.80	620.86	562.83	518.06	482.57	453.82	430.14	410.33	393.58	379.27
45000	3911.78	2032.56	1407.44	1095.84	909.64	786.14	698.47	633.18	582.82	542.89	510.55	483.90	461.63	442.78	426.67
50000	4346.42	2258.40	1563.82	1217.60	1010.71	873.49	776.08	703.54	647.57	603.21	567.28	537.67	512.92	491.98	474.08

MONTHLY PAYMENT
REQUIRED TO AMORTIZE A LOAN — 8%

TERM AMOUNT	35 YEARS	30 YEARS	28 YEARS	27 YEARS	26 YEARS	25 YEARS	24 YEARS	23 YEARS	22 YEARS	21 YEARS	20 YEARS	19 YEARS	18 YEARS	17 YEARS	16 YEARS
$100	.71	.73	.74	.75	.76	.77	.78	.79	.80	.82	.83	.85	.87	.90	.92
200	1.41	1.45	1.48	1.50	1.51	1.53	1.55	1.58	1.60	1.63	1.66	1.70	1.74	1.79	1.84
300	2.11	2.18	2.22	2.24	2.27	2.29	2.33	2.36	2.40	2.44	2.49	2.54	2.61	2.68	2.76
400	2.81	2.90	2.96	2.99	3.02	3.06	3.10	3.15	3.20	3.25	3.32	3.39	3.47	3.57	3.67
500	3.51	3.63	3.69	3.73	3.77	3.82	3.87	3.93	3.99	4.07	4.15	4.24	4.34	4.46	4.59
600	4.21	4.35	4.43	4.48	4.53	4.58	4.65	4.72	4.79	4.88	4.98	5.08	5.21	5.35	5.51
700	4.91	5.08	5.17	5.22	5.28	5.35	5.42	5.50	5.59	5.69	5.80	5.93	6.07	6.24	6.43
800	5.61	5.80	5.91	5.97	6.04	6.11	6.19	6.29	6.39	6.50	6.63	6.78	6.94	7.13	7.34
900	6.31	6.53	6.65	6.71	6.79	6.87	6.97	7.07	7.19	7.32	7.46	7.62	7.81	8.02	8.26
1000	7.01	7.25	7.38	7.46	7.54	7.64	7.74	7.86	7.98	8.13	8.29	8.47	8.68	8.91	9.18
2000	14.02	14.50	14.76	14.91	15.08	15.27	15.48	15.71	15.96	16.25	16.57	16.94	17.35	17.82	18.35
3000	21.03	21.75	22.14	22.37	22.62	22.90	23.21	23.56	23.94	24.37	24.86	25.40	26.02	26.72	27.52
4000	28.04	28.99	29.52	29.82	30.16	30.53	30.95	31.41	31.92	32.49	33.14	33.87	34.69	35.63	36.70
5000	35.05	36.24	36.90	37.28	37.70	38.17	38.68	39.26	39.90	40.62	41.42	42.33	43.36	44.53	45.87
6000	42.05	43.49	44.28	44.73	45.24	45.80	46.42	47.11	47.88	48.74	49.71	50.80	52.03	53.44	55.04
7000	49.06	50.73	51.66	52.19	52.78	53.43	54.15	54.96	55.86	56.86	57.99	59.26	60.70	62.34	64.22
8000	56.07	57.98	59.04	59.64	60.32	61.06	61.89	62.81	63.84	64.98	66.27	67.73	69.37	71.25	73.39
9000	63.08	65.23	66.41	67.10	67.86	68.69	69.62	70.66	71.81	73.11	74.56	76.19	78.04	80.15	82.56
10000	70.10	72.48	73.79	74.55	75.39	76.33	77.36	78.51	79.77	81.23	82.84	84.66	86.72	89.06	91.74
11000	77.10	79.72	81.17	82.01	82.93	83.96	85.10	86.37	87.77	89.35	91.12	93.12	95.39	97.96	100.91
12000	84.10	86.97	88.55	89.46	90.47	91.59	92.83	94.21	95.75	97.47	99.41	101.59	104.06	106.87	110.08
13000	91.11	94.22	95.93	96.92	98.01	99.22	100.57	102.06	103.73	105.60	107.69	110.05	112.73	115.77	119.25
14000	98.12	101.46	103.31	104.37	105.55	106.85	108.30	109.91	111.71	113.72	115.98	118.52	121.40	124.68	128.43
15000	105.13	108.71	110.69	111.83	113.09	114.49	116.04	117.76	119.69	121.84	124.26	126.98	130.07	133.58	137.60
16000	112.13	115.96	118.07	119.28	120.63	122.12	123.77	125.61	127.67	129.96	132.55	135.45	138.74	142.49	146.77
17000	119.15	123.21	125.44	126.74	128.17	129.75	131.51	133.46	135.66	138.09	140.83	143.92	147.41	151.39	155.95
18000	126.15	130.45	132.82	134.19	135.71	137.38	139.24	141.31	143.62	146.21	149.11	152.38	156.08	160.30	165.12
19000	133.16	137.70	140.20	141.64	143.25	145.02	146.98	149.16	151.60	154.33	157.39	160.85	164.76	169.31	174.29
20000	140.17	144.95	147.58	149.10	150.78	152.65	154.71	157.00	159.58	162.45	165.68	169.31	173.43	178.11	183.47
21000	147.18	152.19	154.96	156.56	158.32	160.28	162.45	164.87	167.56	170.57	173.96	177.78	182.10	187.01	192.64
22000	154.19	159.44	162.34	164.01	165.86	167.91	170.19	172.72	175.54	178.92	182.24	186.24	190.77	195.92	201.81
23000	161.20	166.69	169.72	171.47	173.40	175.54	177.92	180.57	183.52	186.82	190.53	194.71	199.44	204.82	210.99
24000	168.20	173.94	177.10	178.92	180.94	183.18	185.66	188.42	191.50	194.94	198.81	203.17	208.11	213.73	220.16
25000	175.22	181.18	184.47	186.38	188.48	190.81	193.39	196.27	199.47	203.06	207.09	211.64	216.78	222.63	229.33
26000	182.22	188.43	191.85	193.83	196.02	198.44	201.12	204.12	207.35	211.19	215.38	220.10	225.45	231.54	238.50
27000	189.23	195.68	199.23	201.29	203.56	206.07	208.86	211.97	215.43	219.31	223.66	228.57	234.12	240.44	247.68
28000	196.24	202.92	206.61	208.74	211.10	213.70	216.60	219.82	223.41	227.43	231.95	237.03	242.79	249.35	256.85
29000	203.24	210.17	213.99	216.20	218.64	221.34	224.33	227.67	231.39	235.55	240.23	245.50	251.47	258.26	266.02
30000	210.25	217.42	221.37	223.65	226.17	228.97	232.07	235.52	239.37	243.68	248.51	253.96	260.14	267.16	275.20
35000	245.29	253.65	258.26	260.93	263.87	267.13	270.75	274.77	279.26	284.29	289.93	296.29	303.49	311.69	321.06
40000	280.34	289.89	295.16	298.20	301.56	305.29	309.42	314.02	319.16	324.90	331.35	338.62	346.85	356.21	366.93
45000	315.38	326.12	332.05	335.47	339.26	343.45	348.10	353.28	359.05	365.51	372.77	380.94	390.20	400.74	412.79
50000	350.42	362.36	368.94	372.75	376.95	381.61	386.78	392.53	398.94	406.12	414.18	423.27	433.56	445.26	458.66

TERM AMOUNT	1 YEAR	2 YEARS	3 YEARS	4 YEARS	5 YEARS	6 YEARS	7 YEARS	8 YEARS	9 YEARS	10 YEARS	11 YEARS	12 YEARS	13 YEARS	14 YEARS	15 YEARS
$100	8.71	4.53	3.14	2.45	2.04	1.76	1.57	1.42	1.31	1.22	1.15	1.09	1.04	1.00	.97
200	17.41	9.06	6.28	4.90	4.07	3.52	3.13	2.84	2.62	2.44	2.30	2.18	2.08	2.00	1.93
300	26.12	13.59	9.42	7.34	6.10	5.28	4.70	4.26	3.93	3.66	3.45	3.27	3.12	3.00	2.89
400	34.82	18.12	12.56	9.79	8.14	7.04	6.26	5.68	5.24	4.88	4.60	4.36	4.16	4.00	3.85
500	43.53	22.64	15.70	12.24	10.17	8.80	7.83	7.10	6.54	6.10	5.74	5.45	5.20	4.99	4.82
600	52.23	27.17	18.84	14.68	12.20	10.56	9.39	8.52	7.85	7.32	6.89	6.54	6.24	5.99	5.78
700	60.93	31.70	21.98	17.13	14.24	12.32	10.95	9.94	9.16	8.54	8.04	7.63	7.28	6.99	6.74
800	69.64	36.23	25.12	19.58	16.27	14.08	12.52	11.36	10.47	9.76	9.19	8.71	8.32	7.99	7.70
900	78.34	40.76	28.25	22.02	18.30	15.83	14.08	12.78	11.77	10.98	10.33	9.80	9.36	8.98	8.66
1000	87.05	45.28	31.39	24.47	20.33	17.59	15.65	14.20	13.08	12.20	11.48	10.88	10.40	9.98	9.63
2000	174.09	90.56	62.78	48.94	40.66	35.18	31.29	28.39	26.16	24.39	22.96	21.78	20.79	19.96	19.25
3000	261.13	135.84	94.17	73.40	60.99	52.77	46.93	42.59	39.24	36.58	34.43	32.66	31.18	29.94	28.87
4000	348.17	181.12	125.56	97.87	81.32	70.36	62.57	56.78	52.31	48.77	45.91	43.55	41.58	39.91	38.49
5000	435.21	226.40	156.94	122.33	101.65	87.94	78.21	70.97	65.39	60.96	57.38	54.43	51.97	49.89	48.11
6000	522.25	271.67	188.33	146.80	121.98	105.53	93.86	85.17	78.47	73.16	68.86	65.32	62.36	59.87	57.73
7000	609.29	316.95	219.72	171.26	142.31	123.12	109.50	99.36	91.54	85.35	80.33	76.21	72.76	69.84	67.35
8000	696.33	362.23	251.11	195.73	162.64	140.70	125.14	113.55	104.62	97.54	91.81	87.09	83.15	79.82	76.96
9000	783.37	407.51	282.50	220.19	182.97	158.30	140.78	127.75	117.70	109.73	103.29	97.98	93.54	89.80	86.59
10000	870.41	452.79	313.88	244.66	203.30	175.88	156.42	141.94	130.77	121.92	114.76	108.86	103.94	99.77	96.22
11000	957.45	498.07	345.27	269.12	223.63	193.47	172.07	156.13	143.85	134.12	126.24	119.75	114.33	109.75	105.84
12000	1044.49	543.34	376.66	293.59	243.96	211.06	187.71	170.33	156.93	146.31	137.71	130.64	124.72	119.73	115.46
13000	1131.53	588.62	408.05	318.05	264.29	228.65	203.35	184.52	170.00	158.50	149.19	141.52	135.12	129.68	125.08
14000	1218.57	633.90	439.44	342.52	284.62	246.23	218.99	198.71	183.08	170.69	160.66	152.41	145.51	139.68	134.70
15000	1305.61	679.18	470.82	366.99	304.95	263.82	234.63	212.91	196.16	182.88	172.14	163.29	155.90	149.66	144.32
16000	1392.65	724.46	502.21	391.45	325.28	281.41	250.28	227.10	209.23	195.07	183.62	174.18	166.30	159.63	153.94
17000	1479.69	769.74	533.60	415.92	345.61	299.00	265.92	241.29	222.31	207.27	195.09	185.06	176.69	169.61	163.56
18000	1566.73	815.01	564.99	440.38	365.94	316.59	281.56	255.49	235.39	219.46	206.57	195.95	187.08	179.59	173.18
19000	1653.77	860.29	596.38	464.85	386.27	334.17	297.20	269.68	248.46	231.65	218.04	206.84	197.48	189.56	182.81
20000	1740.81	905.57	627.76	489.31	406.60	351.76	312.84	283.88	261.54	243.84	229.52	217.72	207.87	199.54	192.43
21000	1827.85	950.85	659.15	513.78	426.93	369.35	328.49	298.07	274.62	256.03	240.99	228.61	218.26	209.52	202.05
22000	1914.89	996.13	690.54	538.24	447.26	386.94	344.13	312.26	287.69	268.23	252.47	239.49	228.65	219.49	211.67
23000	2001.93	1041.40	721.93	562.71	467.59	404.52	359.77	326.46	300.77	280.42	263.95	250.38	239.05	229.47	221.29
24000	2088.97	1086.68	753.31	587.17	487.92	422.11	375.41	340.65	313.85	292.61	275.42	261.27	249.44	239.45	230.91
25000	2176.01	1131.96	784.70	611.64	508.25	439.70	391.05	354.84	326.92	304.80	286.90	272.15	259.83	249.42	240.53
26000	2263.05	1177.24	816.09	636.10	528.58	457.29	406.69	369.04	340.00	316.99	298.37	283.04	270.23	259.40	250.15
27000	2350.09	1222.52	847.48	660.57	548.91	474.88	422.34	383.23	353.08	329.18	309.85	293.92	280.62	269.38	259.77
28000	2437.13	1267.80	878.87	685.04	569.24	492.46	437.98	397.42	366.15	341.38	321.32	304.81	291.01	279.35	269.40
29000	2524.17	1313.07	910.25	709.50	589.57	510.05	453.62	411.62	379.23	353.57	332.80	315.69	301.41	289.33	279.02
30000	2611.21	1358.35	941.64	733.97	609.90	527.64	469.26	425.81	392.31	365.76	344.27	326.58	311.80	299.31	288.64
35000	3046.41	1584.74	1098.58	856.29	711.55	615.58	547.47	496.78	457.69	426.72	401.65	381.01	363.77	349.19	336.74
40000	3481.61	1811.13	1255.52	978.62	813.20	703.52	625.68	567.75	523.07	487.68	459.03	435.44	415.73	399.07	384.85
45000	3916.81	2037.53	1412.46	1100.30	914.85	791.46	703.89	638.71	588.46	548.64	516.41	489.87	467.67	448.96	432.95
50000	4352.01	2263.92	1569.40	1223.27	1016.50	879.40	782.10	709.68	653.84	609.60	573.79	544.30	519.66	498.84	481.06

MONTHLY PAYMENT
REQUIRED TO AMORTIZE A LOAN

8¼%

TERM AMOUNT	35 YEARS	30 YEARS	28 YEARS	27 YEARS	26 YEARS	25 YEARS	24 YEARS	23 YEARS	22 YEARS	21 YEARS	20 YEARS	19 YEARS	18 YEARS	17 YEARS	16 YEARS
$100	.72	.75	.76	.77	.78	.78	.79	.81	.82	.83	.85	.87	.89	.91	.94
200	1.44	1.49	1.51	1.53	1.55	1.56	1.58	1.61	1.63	1.66	1.69	1.73	1.77	1.81	1.87
300	2.16	2.23	2.27	2.29	2.32	2.34	2.37	2.41	2.44	2.49	2.54	2.59	2.65	2.72	2.80
400	2.88	2.97	3.02	3.05	3.09	3.12	3.16	3.21	3.26	3.31	3.38	3.45	3.53	3.62	3.73
500	3.60	3.71	3.78	3.81	3.86	3.90	3.95	4.01	4.07	4.14	4.22	4.31	4.41	4.53	4.66
600	4.32	4.45	4.53	4.58	4.63	4.68	4.74	4.81	4.88	4.97	5.07	5.17	5.30	5.43	5.59
700	5.03	5.20	5.29	5.34	5.40	5.46	5.53	5.61	5.70	5.80	5.91	6.03	6.18	6.34	6.53
800	5.75	5.94	6.04	6.10	6.17	6.24	6.32	6.41	6.51	6.62	6.75	6.90	7.06	7.24	7.46
900	6.47	6.68	6.79	6.86	6.94	7.02	7.11	7.21	7.32	7.45	7.60	7.76	7.94	8.15	8.39
1000	7.19	7.42	7.55	7.62	7.71	7.80	7.90	8.01	8.14	8.28	8.44	8.62	8.82	9.05	9.32
2000	14.37	14.84	15.09	15.24	15.41	15.59	15.79	16.02	16.27	16.55	16.87	17.23	17.64	18.10	18.63
3000	21.56	22.25	22.64	22.86	23.11	23.38	23.69	24.03	24.40	24.83	25.31	25.85	26.46	27.15	27.95
4000	28.74	29.67	30.18	30.48	30.81	31.17	31.58	32.03	32.54	33.10	33.74	34.46	35.27	36.20	37.26
5000	35.92	37.08	37.73	38.10	38.51	38.97	39.47	40.04	40.67	41.38	42.18	43.07	44.09	45.25	46.58
6000	43.11	44.50	45.27	45.72	46.21	46.76	47.37	48.05	48.80	49.65	50.61	51.69	52.91	54.30	55.89
7000	50.29	51.91	52.81	53.33	53.91	54.55	55.26	56.06	56.94	57.93	59.04	60.30	61.73	63.35	65.20
8000	57.48	59.33	60.36	60.95	61.61	62.34	63.16	64.06	65.07	66.20	67.48	68.91	70.54	72.40	74.52
9000	64.66	66.75	67.90	68.57	69.31	70.14	71.05	72.07	73.20	74.48	75.91	77.53	79.36	81.45	83.84
10000	71.84	74.16	75.45	76.19	77.01	77.93	78.94	80.07	81.34	82.75	84.35	86.14	88.18	90.49	93.15
11000	79.03	81.58	82.99	83.81	84.72	85.72	86.84	88.08	89.47	91.03	92.78	94.76	97.00	99.54	102.47
12000	86.21	88.99	90.53	91.43	92.42	93.51	94.73	96.09	97.60	99.30	101.21	103.37	105.81	108.59	111.78
13000	93.40	96.41	98.08	99.05	100.12	101.30	102.62	104.10	105.74	107.58	109.65	111.98	114.63	117.64	121.10
14000	100.58	103.82	105.62	106.66	107.82	109.10	110.52	112.10	113.87	115.85	118.08	120.60	123.45	126.69	130.41
15000	107.76	111.24	113.17	114.28	115.52	116.89	118.41	120.11	122.00	124.13	126.52	129.21	132.26	135.74	139.73
16000	114.95	118.66	120.71	121.90	123.22	124.68	126.31	128.12	130.14	132.40	134.95	137.82	141.08	144.79	149.04
17000	122.13	126.07	128.25	129.52	130.92	132.47	134.20	136.12	138.27	140.68	143.38	146.44	149.90	153.84	158.36
18000	129.31	133.49	135.80	137.14	138.62	140.27	142.09	144.13	146.40	148.95	151.82	155.05	158.72	162.89	167.67
19000	136.50	140.90	143.34	144.76	146.32	148.06	149.99	152.14	154.54	157.23	160.25	163.66	167.53	171.94	176.99
20000	143.68	148.32	150.89	152.38	154.02	155.85	157.88	160.14	162.67	165.50	168.69	172.28	176.35	180.99	186.30
21000	150.87	155.73	158.43	159.99	161.72	163.64	165.78	168.15	170.80	173.78	177.12	180.89	185.17	190.04	195.62
22000	158.05	163.15	165.98	167.61	169.42	171.44	173.67	176.16	178.94	182.05	185.55	189.51	193.99	199.09	204.93
23000	165.23	170.56	173.52	175.23	177.13	179.23	181.56	184.16	187.07	190.33	193.99	198.12	202.80	208.14	214.25
24000	172.42	177.98	181.06	182.85	184.83	187.02	189.46	192.17	195.20	198.60	202.42	206.73	211.62	217.19	223.56
25000	179.60	185.40	188.61	190.47	192.53	194.81	197.35	200.18	203.34	206.88	210.86	215.35	220.44	226.24	232.88
26000	186.79	192.81	196.15	198.09	200.23	202.60	205.24	208.19	211.47	215.15	219.29	223.96	229.25	235.28	242.19
27000	193.97	200.23	203.70	205.71	207.93	210.40	213.14	216.19	219.60	223.43	227.72	232.57	238.07	244.33	251.51
28000	201.15	207.64	211.24	213.32	215.63	218.19	221.03	224.20	227.74	231.70	236.16	241.19	246.89	253.38	260.82
29000	208.34	215.06	218.78	220.94	223.33	225.98	228.93	232.21	235.87	239.98	244.59	249.80	255.71	262.43	270.14
30000	215.52	222.47	226.33	228.56	231.03	233.77	236.82	240.21	244.00	248.25	253.03	258.42	264.52	271.48	279.45
35000	251.44	259.55	264.05	266.66	269.54	272.74	276.29	280.25	284.67	289.63	295.20	301.49	308.61	316.73	326.03
40000	287.36	296.63	301.77	304.75	308.04	311.70	315.76	320.28	325.34	331.00	337.37	344.55	352.70	361.97	372.60
45000	323.28	333.71	339.49	342.84	346.55	350.66	355.23	360.32	366.00	372.37	379.54	387.62	396.78	407.22	419.17
50000	359.20	370.79	377.21	380.93	385.05	389.62	394.70	400.35	406.67	413.75	421.71	430.69	440.87	452.47	465.75

MONTHLY PAYMENT
8½ % REQUIRED TO AMORTIZE A LOAN

TERM AMOUNT	15 YEARS	14 YEARS	13 YEARS	12 YEARS	11 YEARS	10 YEARS	9 YEARS	8 YEARS	7 YEARS	6 YEARS	5 YEARS	4 YEARS	3 YEARS	2 YEARS	1 YEAR
$100	.98	1.02	1.06	1.11	1.17	1.24	1.33	1.44	1.58	1.78	2.05	2.46	3.15	4.54	8.72
200	1.96	2.03	2.11	2.21	2.33	2.47	2.65	2.87	3.16	3.55	4.09	4.92	6.30	9.08	17.44
300	2.93	3.04	3.16	3.31	3.49	3.70	3.97	4.30	4.73	5.32	6.14	7.38	9.45	13.62	26.15
400	3.91	4.05	4.22	4.41	4.65	4.93	5.29	5.73	6.31	7.09	8.18	9.84	12.60	18.16	34.87
500	4.88	5.06	5.27	5.51	5.81	6.17	6.61	7.16	7.89	8.86	10.23	12.29	15.75	22.70	43.58
600	5.86	6.07	6.32	6.62	6.97	7.40	7.93	8.60	9.46	10.63	12.27	14.75	18.90	27.24	52.30
700	6.84	7.09	7.38	7.72	8.13	8.63	9.25	10.03	11.04	12.40	14.32	17.21	22.05	31.78	61.01
800	7.81	8.10	8.43	8.82	9.29	9.86	10.57	11.46	12.62	14.17	16.36	19.67	25.20	36.32	69.73
900	8.79	9.11	9.48	9.92	10.45	11.09	11.89	12.89	14.19	15.94	18.41	22.13	28.35	40.85	78.44
1000	9.77	10.12	10.53	11.02	11.61	12.33	13.21	14.32	15.77	17.72	20.45	24.58	31.50	45.39	87.16
2000	19.53	20.23	21.06	22.04	23.22	24.65	26.41	28.64	31.53	35.42	40.90	49.16	63.00	90.78	174.31
3000	29.29	30.35	31.59	33.06	34.82	36.97	39.61	42.96	47.29	53.12	61.34	73.74	94.50	136.17	261.46
4000	39.05	40.46	42.12	44.08	46.43	49.29	52.87	57.27	63.06	70.83	81.79	98.32	126.00	181.56	348.61
5000	48.81	50.58	52.65	55.10	58.04	61.61	66.00	71.59	78.82	88.54	102.23	122.90	157.50	226.95	435.76
6000	58.57	60.69	63.18	66.12	69.64	73.93	79.22	85.91	94.58	106.24	122.68	147.48	189.00	272.34	522.92
7000	68.34	70.81	73.71	77.14	81.25	86.25	92.42	100.22	110.34	123.95	143.12	172.06	220.50	317.73	610.07
8000	78.10	80.92	84.24	88.16	92.86	98.57	105.63	114.54	126.11	141.65	163.57	196.64	252.00	363.11	697.22
9000	87.86	91.04	94.77	99.18	104.46	110.89	118.83	128.86	141.87	159.36	184.02	221.22	283.50	408.50	784.37
10000	97.62	101.15	105.29	110.20	116.07	123.21	132.03	143.17	157.63	177.07	204.46	245.80	315.00	453.89	871.52
11000	107.38	111.27	115.82	121.22	127.68	135.53	145.23	157.49	173.40	194.77	224.91	270.37	346.50	499.28	958.68
12000	117.14	121.38	126.35	132.23	139.28	147.85	158.44	171.81	189.16	212.48	245.36	294.95	378.00	544.67	1045.83
13000	126.91	131.50	136.88	143.25	150.89	160.17	171.64	186.12	204.92	230.18	265.80	319.53	409.50	590.06	1132.98
14000	136.67	141.61	147.41	154.27	162.50	172.49	184.84	200.44	220.68	247.89	286.25	344.11	441.00	635.45	1220.13
15000	146.43	151.73	157.94	165.29	174.10	184.81	198.04	214.76	236.45	265.60	306.69	368.69	472.50	680.83	1307.28
16000	156.19	161.84	168.47	176.31	185.71	197.13	211.25	229.07	252.21	283.30	327.14	393.27	504.00	726.22	1394.43
17000	165.95	171.96	179.00	187.33	197.32	209.45	224.45	243.39	267.97	301.01	347.59	417.85	535.50	771.61	1481.59
18000	175.71	182.07	189.53	198.35	208.92	221.77	237.65	257.71	283.74	318.72	368.03	442.43	567.00	817.00	1568.74
19000	185.47	192.19	200.05	209.37	220.53	234.09	250.86	272.03	299.50	336.42	388.48	467.01	598.50	862.39	1655.89
20000	195.24	202.30	210.58	220.39	232.14	246.41	264.06	286.34	315.26	354.13	408.92	491.59	630.00	907.78	1743.04
21000	205.00	212.42	221.11	231.41	243.74	258.73	277.26	300.66	331.02	371.84	429.37	516.17	661.50	953.17	1830.19
22000	214.76	222.53	231.64	242.43	255.35	271.05	290.46	314.98	346.79	389.54	449.81	540.74	693.00	998.55	1917.35
23000	224.52	232.65	242.17	253.45	266.95	283.37	303.66	329.29	362.55	407.25	470.26	565.32	724.50	1043.94	2004.50
24000	234.28	242.76	252.70	264.47	278.56	295.69	316.87	343.61	378.31	424.95	490.71	589.90	756.00	1089.33	2091.65
25000	244.04	252.88	263.23	275.48	290.17	308.00	330.07	357.93	394.08	442.66	511.15	614.48	787.49	1134.72	2178.80
26000	253.81	262.99	273.76	286.50	301.77	320.33	343.27	372.24	409.84	460.37	531.60	639.06	818.99	1180.11	2265.95
27000	263.57	273.11	284.29	297.52	313.38	332.65	356.47	386.56	425.60	478.07	552.04	663.64	850.49	1225.50	2353.11
28000	273.33	283.22	294.81	308.54	324.99	344.97	369.68	400.88	441.36	495.78	572.49	688.22	881.99	1270.89	2440.26
29000	283.09	293.33	305.34	319.56	336.59	357.29	382.88	415.19	457.13	513.49	592.94	712.80	913.49	1316.27	2527.41
30000	292.85	303.45	315.87	330.58	348.20	369.61	396.08	429.51	472.89	531.19	613.38	737.38	944.99	1361.66	2614.56
35000	341.66	354.02	368.52	385.68	406.23	431.21	462.09	501.10	551.70	619.72	715.61	860.27	1102.49	1588.61	3050.32
40000	390.47	404.60	421.16	440.77	464.27	492.81	528.11	572.68	630.52	708.25	817.84	983.17	1259.99	1815.55	3486.08
45000	439.28	455.17	473.81	495.87	522.30	554.42	594.12	644.27	709.33	796.79	920.07	1106.06	1417.49	2042.49	3921.84
50000	488.08	505.75	526.45	550.96	580.33	616.02	660.13	715.85	788.15	885.32	1022.30	1228.96	1574.98	2269.43	4357.60

MONTHLY PAYMENT
REQUIRED TO AMORTIZE A LOAN

8½ %

TERM AMOUNT	35 YEARS	30 YEARS	28 YEARS	27 YEARS	26 YEARS	25 YEARS	24 YEARS	23 YEARS	22 YEARS	21 YEARS	20 YEARS	19 YEARS	18 YEARS	17 YEARS	16 YEARS
$100	.75	.77	.78	.79	.80	.81	.82	.83	.84	.85	.87	.89	.91	.93	.95
200	1.49	1.54	1.56	1.58	1.59	1.61	1.63	1.65	1.68	1.70	1.74	1.77	1.81	1.86	1.91
300	2.24	2.31	2.34	2.37	2.39	2.42	2.45	2.48	2.52	2.56	2.60	2.66	2.72	2.78	2.86
400	2.99	3.08	3.13	3.15	3.19	3.22	3.26	3.30	3.35	3.41	3.47	3.54	3.62	3.71	3.82
500	3.73	3.84	3.91	3.94	3.98	4.03	4.08	4.13	4.19	4.26	4.34	4.43	4.53	4.64	4.77
600	4.48	4.61	4.69	4.73	4.78	4.83	4.89	4.96	5.03	5.11	5.21	5.31	5.43	5.57	5.73
700	5.23	5.38	5.47	5.52	5.57	5.64	5.71	5.78	5.87	5.97	6.07	6.20	6.34	6.50	6.68
800	5.97	6.15	6.25	6.31	6.37	6.44	6.52	6.61	6.71	6.82	6.94	7.08	7.24	7.43	7.64
900	6.72	6.92	7.03	7.10	7.17	7.25	7.34	7.43	7.55	7.67	7.81	7.97	8.15	8.35	8.59
1000	7.47	7.69	7.81	7.88	7.96	8.05	8.15	8.26	8.38	8.52	8.68	8.85	9.05	9.28	9.54
2000	14.94	15.38	15.63	15.77	15.93	16.10	16.30	16.52	16.77	17.04	17.36	17.71	18.11	18.57	19.09
3000	22.41	23.07	23.44	23.65	23.89	24.16	24.45	24.78	25.15	25.57	26.03	26.56	27.16	27.85	28.63
4000	29.87	30.76	31.25	31.54	31.86	32.21	32.60	33.04	33.54	34.09	34.71	35.42	36.22	37.13	38.18
5000	37.34	38.45	39.06	39.42	39.82	40.26	40.75	41.30	41.92	42.61	43.39	44.27	45.27	46.41	47.72
6000	44.81	46.14	46.88	47.31	47.78	48.31	48.91	49.56	50.30	51.13	52.07	53.13	54.33	55.70	57.27
7000	52.28	53.82	54.69	55.19	55.75	56.37	57.06	57.83	58.69	59.66	60.75	61.98	63.38	64.98	66.81
8000	59.75	61.51	62.50	63.07	63.71	64.42	65.21	66.09	67.07	68.18	69.43	70.84	72.44	74.26	76.36
9000	67.22	69.20	70.31	70.96	71.67	72.47	73.36	74.35	75.46	76.70	78.10	79.69	81.49	83.55	85.90
10000	74.69	76.89	78.13	78.84	79.64	80.52	81.51	82.61	83.84	85.22	86.78	88.54	90.55	92.83	95.45
11000	82.15	84.58	85.94	86.73	87.60	88.58	89.66	90.87	92.22	93.75	95.46	97.40	99.60	102.11	104.99
12000	89.62	92.27	93.75	94.61	95.57	96.63	97.81	99.13	100.61	102.27	104.14	106.25	108.65	111.39	114.54
13000	97.09	99.96	101.56	102.50	103.53	104.68	105.96	107.39	108.99	110.79	112.82	115.11	117.71	120.68	124.08
14000	104.56	107.65	109.38	110.38	111.49	112.73	114.11	115.65	117.38	119.31	121.49	123.96	126.76	129.96	133.63
15000	112.03	115.34	117.19	118.26	119.46	120.78	122.26	123.91	125.76	127.84	130.17	132.82	135.82	139.24	143.17
16000	119.50	123.03	125.00	126.15	127.42	128.84	130.41	132.17	134.14	136.36	138.85	141.67	144.87	148.53	152.72
17000	126.97	130.72	132.81	134.03	135.38	136.89	138.57	140.43	142.53	144.88	147.53	150.52	153.93	157.81	162.26
18000	134.43	138.41	140.63	141.92	143.35	144.94	146.72	148.69	150.91	153.40	156.21	159.38	162.98	167.09	171.81
19000	141.90	146.09	148.44	149.80	151.31	152.99	154.87	156.96	159.30	161.93	164.89	168.23	172.04	176.38	181.35
20000	149.37	153.78	156.25	157.69	159.28	161.05	163.02	165.22	167.68	170.45	173.56	177.09	181.09	185.66	190.90
21000	156.84	161.47	164.06	165.57	167.24	169.10	171.17	173.48	176.06	178.97	182.24	185.94	190.14	194.94	200.44
22000	164.31	169.16	171.88	173.45	175.20	177.15	179.32	181.74	184.45	187.49	190.92	194.80	199.20	204.22	209.99
23000	171.78	176.85	179.69	181.34	183.17	185.20	187.47	190.00	192.83	196.02	199.60	203.65	208.25	213.51	219.53
24000	179.25	184.54	187.50	189.22	191.13	193.26	195.62	198.26	201.22	204.54	208.28	212.51	217.31	222.79	229.08
25000	186.72	192.23	195.32	197.11	199.10	201.31	203.77	206.52	209.60	213.06	216.96	221.36	226.36	232.07	238.62
26000	194.18	199.92	203.13	204.99	207.06	209.36	211.92	214.78	217.98	221.58	225.63	230.21	235.42	241.36	248.17
27000	201.65	207.61	210.94	212.88	215.02	217.41	220.07	223.04	226.37	230.10	234.31	239.07	244.47	250.64	257.71
28000	209.12	215.30	218.75	220.76	222.99	225.46	228.23	231.30	234.75	238.63	242.99	247.92	253.53	259.92	267.26
29000	216.59	222.99	226.57	228.64	230.95	233.52	236.38	239.56	243.14	247.15	251.67	256.78	262.58	269.20	276.80
30000	224.06	230.68	234.38	236.53	238.91	241.57	244.53	247.82	251.52	255.67	260.35	265.63	271.64	278.49	286.35
35000	261.40	269.12	273.44	275.95	278.73	281.83	285.28	289.13	293.44	298.28	303.74	309.90	316.91	324.90	334.07
40000	298.74	307.57	312.50	315.37	318.55	322.09	326.04	330.43	335.36	340.90	347.13	354.18	362.18	371.32	381.80
45000	336.09	346.01	351.57	354.79	358.37	362.35	366.79	371.74	377.28	383.51	390.52	398.45	407.45	417.73	429.52
50000	373.43	384.46	390.63	394.22	398.19	402.62	407.55	413.04	419.20	426.12	433.91	442.72	452.73	464.15	477.25

MONTHLY PAYMENT
REQUIRED TO AMORTIZE A LOAN

TERM AMOUNT	1 YEAR	2 YEARS	3 YEARS	4 YEARS	5 YEARS	6 YEARS	7 YEARS	8 YEARS	9 YEARS	10 YEARS	11 YEARS	12 YEARS	13 YEARS	14 YEARS	15 YEARS
$100	8.73	4.55	3.17	2.47	2.06	1.79	1.59	1.45	1.34	1.25	1.18	1.12	1.07	1.03	1.00
200	17.46	9.10	6.33	4.94	4.12	3.57	3.18	2.89	2.67	2.49	2.35	2.24	2.14	2.06	1.99
300	26.18	13.65	9.49	7.41	6.17	5.35	4.77	4.34	4.00	3.74	3.53	3.35	3.20	3.08	2.98
400	34.91	18.20	12.65	9.88	8.23	7.14	6.36	5.78	5.34	4.98	4.70	4.47	4.27	4.11	3.97
500	43.64	22.75	15.81	12.35	10.29	8.92	7.95	7.23	6.67	6.23	5.87	5.58	5.34	5.13	4.96
600	52.36	27.30	18.97	14.82	12.34	10.70	9.54	8.67	8.00	7.47	7.05	6.70	6.40	6.16	5.95
700	61.09	31.85	22.13	17.29	14.40	12.48	11.12	10.11	9.34	8.72	8.22	7.81	7.47	7.18	6.94
800	69.82	36.40	25.29	19.76	16.45	14.27	12.71	11.56	10.67	9.96	9.40	8.93	8.54	8.21	7.93
900	78.54	40.95	28.46	22.23	18.51	16.05	14.30	13.00	12.00	11.21	10.57	10.04	9.60	9.23	8.92
1000	87.27	45.50	31.62	24.70	20.57	17.83	15.89	14.45	13.33	12.45	11.74	11.16	10.67	10.26	9.91
2000	174.53	91.00	63.23	49.39	41.13	35.66	31.77	28.89	26.66	24.90	23.48	22.31	21.34	20.51	19.81
3000	261.80	136.50	94.84	74.08	61.69	53.48	47.66	43.33	39.99	37.35	35.22	33.46	32.00	30.77	29.71
4000	349.06	182.00	126.45	98.78	82.25	71.31	63.54	57.77	53.32	49.80	46.96	44.62	42.67	41.02	39.62
5000	436.32	227.50	158.06	123.47	102.82	89.13	79.43	72.21	66.65	62.25	58.70	55.77	53.33	51.27	49.52
6000	523.59	273.00	189.67	148.16	123.38	106.96	95.31	86.65	79.98	74.70	70.43	66.92	64.00	61.53	59.42
7000	610.85	318.50	221.28	172.86	143.94	124.78	111.19	101.09	93.31	87.15	82.17	78.08	74.66	71.78	69.33
8000	698.11	364.00	252.90	197.55	164.50	142.61	127.08	115.53	106.64	99.60	93.91	89.23	85.33	82.04	79.23
9000	785.38	409.50	284.51	222.24	185.06	160.43	142.96	129.97	119.97	112.05	105.65	100.38	95.99	92.29	89.13
10000	872.64	454.99	316.12	246.94	205.63	178.26	158.85	144.41	133.30	124.50	117.39	111.54	106.66	102.54	99.03
11000	959.90	500.49	347.73	271.63	226.19	196.08	174.73	158.85	146.62	136.95	129.12	122.69	117.32	112.80	108.94
12000	1047.17	545.99	379.34	296.32	246.75	213.91	190.61	173.29	159.95	149.40	140.86	133.84	127.99	123.05	118.84
13000	1134.43	591.49	410.95	321.01	267.31	231.73	206.50	187.74	173.28	161.85	152.60	145.00	138.66	133.30	128.74
14000	1221.70	636.99	442.56	345.71	287.88	249.56	222.38	202.18	186.61	174.29	164.34	156.15	149.32	143.56	138.65
15000	1308.96	682.49	474.18	370.40	308.44	267.38	238.27	216.62	199.94	186.74	176.08	167.30	159.99	153.81	148.55
16000	1396.22	727.99	505.79	395.09	329.00	285.21	254.15	231.06	213.27	199.19	187.81	178.46	170.65	164.07	158.45
17000	1483.49	773.49	537.40	419.79	349.56	303.03	270.03	245.50	226.60	211.64	199.55	189.61	181.32	174.32	168.36
18000	1570.75	818.99	569.01	444.48	370.12	320.86	285.92	259.94	239.93	224.09	211.29	200.76	191.98	184.57	178.26
19000	1658.01	864.49	600.62	469.17	390.69	338.68	301.80	274.38	253.26	236.54	223.03	211.92	202.65	194.83	188.16
20000	1745.28	909.98	632.23	493.87	411.25	356.51	317.69	288.82	266.59	248.99	234.77	223.07	213.31	205.08	198.06
21000	1832.54	955.48	663.84	518.56	431.81	374.33	333.57	303.26	279.91	261.44	246.50	234.22	223.98	215.33	207.97
22000	1919.80	1000.98	695.46	543.25	452.37	392.16	349.46	317.70	293.24	273.89	258.24	245.38	234.64	225.59	217.87
23000	2007.07	1046.48	727.07	567.94	472.93	409.98	365.34	332.14	306.57	286.34	269.98	256.53	245.31	235.84	227.77
24000	2094.33	1091.98	758.68	592.64	493.50	427.81	381.22	346.58	319.90	298.79	281.72	267.68	255.98	246.10	237.68
25000	2181.60	1137.48	790.29	617.33	514.06	445.63	397.11	361.02	333.23	311.24	293.46	278.84	266.64	256.35	247.58
26000	2268.86	1182.98	821.90	642.02	534.62	463.46	412.99	375.47	346.56	323.69	305.19	289.99	277.31	266.60	257.48
27000	2356.12	1228.48	853.51	666.72	555.18	481.28	428.88	389.91	359.89	336.13	316.93	301.14	287.97	276.86	267.38
28000	2443.39	1273.98	885.12	691.41	575.75	499.11	444.76	404.35	373.22	348.58	328.67	312.30	298.64	287.11	277.29
29000	2530.65	1319.48	916.74	716.10	596.31	516.93	460.65	418.79	386.55	361.03	340.41	323.45	309.30	297.36	287.19
30000	2617.91	1364.97	948.35	740.80	616.87	534.76	476.53	433.23	399.88	373.48	352.15	334.60	319.97	307.62	297.09
35000	3054.23	1592.47	1106.40	864.26	719.68	623.88	555.95	505.43	466.52	435.73	410.84	390.37	373.30	358.89	346.61
40000	3490.55	1819.96	1264.46	987.73	822.49	713.01	635.37	577.64	533.17	497.97	469.53	446.13	426.62	410.16	396.12
45000	3926.87	2047.46	1422.52	1111.19	925.30	802.13	714.79	649.84	599.81	560.22	528.22	501.90	479.95	461.43	445.64
50000	4363.19	2274.95	1580.58	1234.66	1028.11	891.26	794.20	722.04	666.46	622.47	586.91	557.67	533.28	512.69	495.15

MONTHLY PAYMENT
REQUIRED TO AMORTIZE A LOAN 8¾%

TERM AMOUNT	16 YEARS	17 YEARS	18 YEARS	19 YEARS	20 YEARS	21 YEARS	22 YEARS	23 YEARS	24 YEARS	25 YEARS	26 YEARS	27 YEARS	28 YEARS	30 YEARS	35 YEARS
$100	.97	.94	.92	.90	.88	.86	.85	.84	.83	.82	.81	.80	.79	.78	.76
200	1.93	1.87	1.83	1.79	1.75	1.72	1.69	1.67	1.65	1.63	1.61	1.59	1.58	1.56	1.51
300	2.89	2.81	2.74	2.68	2.63	2.58	2.54	2.50	2.47	2.44	2.41	2.39	2.37	2.33	2.27
400	3.85	3.74	3.65	3.57	3.50	3.44	3.38	3.33	3.29	3.25	3.22	3.18	3.16	3.11	3.02
500	4.81	4.68	4.56	4.46	4.37	4.30	4.23	4.17	4.11	4.06	4.02	3.98	3.94	3.88	3.77
600	5.77	5.61	5.47	5.35	5.25	5.15	5.07	5.00	4.93	4.87	4.82	4.77	4.73	4.66	4.53
700	6.73	6.54	6.38	6.24	6.12	6.01	5.92	5.83	5.75	5.69	5.62	5.57	5.52	5.43	5.28
800	7.69	7.48	7.30	7.14	7.00	6.87	6.76	6.66	6.58	6.50	6.43	6.36	6.31	6.21	6.04
900	8.65	8.41	8.21	8.03	7.87	7.73	7.61	7.50	7.40	7.31	7.23	7.16	7.10	6.99	6.79
1000	9.61	9.35	9.12	8.92	8.74	8.59	8.45	8.33	8.22	8.12	8.03	7.95	7.88	7.76	7.54
2000	19.21	18.69	18.23	17.83	17.48	17.17	16.90	16.65	16.43	16.24	16.06	15.90	15.76	15.52	15.08
3000	28.81	28.03	27.34	26.75	26.22	25.75	25.34	24.97	24.65	24.35	24.09	23.85	23.64	23.27	22.62
4000	38.41	37.37	36.45	35.66	34.96	34.34	33.79	33.30	32.86	32.47	32.12	31.80	31.52	31.03	30.16
5000	48.01	46.71	45.57	44.57	43.70	42.92	42.23	41.62	41.07	40.59	40.15	39.75	39.40	38.79	37.70
6000	57.61	56.05	54.68	53.49	52.43	51.50	50.68	49.94	49.29	48.70	48.18	47.70	47.28	46.54	45.24
7000	67.21	65.39	63.79	62.40	61.17	60.09	59.12	58.27	57.50	56.82	56.20	55.65	55.15	54.30	52.77
8000	76.82	74.73	72.91	71.31	69.91	68.67	67.57	66.59	65.72	64.93	64.23	63.60	63.03	62.06	60.31
9000	86.42	84.07	82.02	80.23	78.65	77.25	76.02	74.91	73.93	73.05	72.26	71.55	70.91	69.81	67.85
10000	96.02	93.41	91.13	89.14	87.39	85.84	84.46	83.24	82.14	81.17	80.29	79.50	78.79	77.57	75.39
11000	105.62	102.75	100.25	98.05	96.13	94.42	92.91	91.56	90.36	89.28	88.32	87.45	86.67	85.32	82.93
12000	115.22	112.09	109.36	106.97	104.86	103.00	101.35	99.88	98.57	97.40	96.35	95.40	94.55	93.08	90.47
13000	124.82	121.43	118.47	115.88	113.60	111.59	109.80	108.21	106.79	105.51	104.37	103.35	102.42	100.84	98.01
14000	134.43	130.77	127.58	124.80	122.34	120.17	118.24	116.53	115.00	113.63	112.40	111.30	110.30	108.59	105.54
15000	144.03	140.11	136.70	133.71	131.08	128.75	126.69	124.85	123.21	121.74	120.46	119.25	118.18	116.35	113.08
16000	153.63	149.45	145.81	142.62	139.82	137.34	135.14	133.18	131.43	129.86	128.46	127.20	126.06	124.11	120.62
17000	163.23	158.79	154.92	151.53	148.55	145.92	143.58	141.50	139.64	137.98	136.49	135.15	133.94	131.86	128.16
18000	172.83	168.13	164.04	160.45	157.29	154.50	152.03	149.82	147.86	146.09	144.54	143.10	141.82	139.62	135.70
19000	182.43	177.47	173.15	169.36	166.03	163.09	160.47	158.15	156.07	154.21	152.56	151.04	149.69	147.37	143.24
20000	192.03	186.81	182.26	178.27	174.77	171.67	168.92	166.47	164.28	162.33	160.57	158.99	157.57	155.13	150.77
21000	201.63	196.15	191.37	187.19	183.51	180.25	177.36	174.79	172.50	170.44	168.60	166.89	165.45	162.89	158.31
22000	211.24	205.49	200.49	196.10	192.25	188.84	185.81	183.12	180.71	178.56	176.63	174.89	173.34	170.64	165.85
23000	220.84	214.83	209.60	205.02	200.98	197.42	194.26	191.44	188.93	186.68	184.66	182.84	181.21	178.40	173.39
24000	230.44	224.17	218.71	213.93	209.72	206.00	202.70	199.76	197.14	194.79	192.69	190.74	189.06	186.16	180.93
25000	240.04	233.51	227.83	222.84	218.46	214.59	211.15	208.09	205.35	202.91	200.71	198.74	196.96	193.91	188.47
26000	249.64	242.85	236.94	231.76	227.20	223.17	219.59	216.41	213.57	211.02	208.74	206.69	204.84	201.67	196.01
27000	259.24	252.19	246.05	240.67	235.94	231.75	228.04	224.73	221.78	219.14	216.77	214.64	212.72	209.43	203.54
28000	268.84	261.53	255.16	249.59	244.68	240.33	236.48	233.06	230.00	227.26	224.80	222.59	220.60	217.18	211.08
29000	278.45	270.87	264.28	258.50	253.41	248.92	244.93	241.38	238.21	235.37	232.83	230.49	228.48	224.94	218.62
30000	288.05	280.21	273.39	267.42	262.15	257.50	253.38	249.70	246.42	243.37	240.86	238.49	236.36	232.69	226.16
35000	336.05	326.92	318.95	311.98	305.84	300.42	295.60	291.32	287.49	284.07	281.00	278.24	275.75	271.48	263.85
40000	384.06	373.62	364.52	356.55	349.53	343.33	337.83	332.94	328.56	324.66	321.14	317.99	315.14	310.26	301.54
45000	432.07	420.32	410.08	401.12	393.22	386.25	380.06	374.55	369.63	365.23	361.28	357.73	354.53	349.04	339.24
50000	480.07	467.02	455.65	445.68	436.92	429.17	422.29	416.17	410.70	405.81	401.42	397.48	393.92	387.82	376.93

MONTHLY PAYMENT
9% REQUIRED TO AMORTIZE A LOAN

TERM AMOUNT	1 YEAR	2 YEARS	3 YEARS	4 YEARS	5 YEARS	6 YEARS	7 YEARS	8 YEARS	9 YEARS	10 YEARS	11 YEARS	12 YEARS	13 YEARS	14 YEARS	15 YEARS
$100	8.74	4.57	3.18	2.49	2.07	1.80	1.61	1.46	1.35	1.26	1.19	1.13	1.09	1.04	1.01
200	17.48	9.13	6.35	4.97	4.14	3.59	3.21	2.92	2.70	2.52	2.38	2.26	2.17	2.08	2.01
300	26.22	13.69	9.52	7.45	6.21	5.39	4.81	4.37	4.04	3.78	3.57	3.39	3.25	3.12	3.02
400	34.96	18.25	12.69	9.93	8.28	7.18	6.41	5.83	5.39	5.04	4.75	4.52	4.33	4.16	4.02
500	43.69	22.81	15.87	12.41	10.34	8.98	8.01	7.29	6.73	6.29	5.94	5.65	5.41	5.20	5.03
600	52.43	27.37	19.04	14.89	12.41	10.77	9.61	8.74	8.08	7.55	7.13	6.78	6.49	6.24	6.03
700	61.17	31.93	22.21	17.37	14.48	12.57	11.21	10.20	9.42	8.81	8.31	7.91	7.57	7.28	7.04
800	69.91	36.49	25.38	19.85	16.55	14.36	12.81	11.66	10.77	10.07	9.50	9.04	8.65	8.32	8.04
900	78.64	41.05	28.56	22.33	18.62	16.15	14.41	13.11	12.12	11.33	10.69	10.16	9.73	9.36	9.05
1000	87.38	45.61	31.73	24.81	20.68	17.95	16.01	14.57	13.46	12.58	11.88	11.29	10.81	10.40	10.05
2000	174.76	91.22	63.45	49.62	41.36	35.89	32.02	29.14	26.92	25.16	23.75	22.58	21.61	20.79	20.10
3000	262.13	136.83	95.18	74.43	62.04	53.84	48.02	43.70	40.37	37.74	35.62	33.87	32.41	31.19	30.14
4000	349.51	182.44	126.90	99.23	82.72	71.78	64.03	58.27	53.83	50.32	47.49	45.16	43.22	41.58	40.19
5000	436.88	228.05	158.62	124.04	103.40	89.73	80.03	72.83	67.29	62.90	59.36	56.44	54.02	51.97	50.23
6000	524.26	273.66	190.35	148.85	124.08	107.67	96.04	87.40	80.74	75.48	71.23	67.73	64.82	62.37	60.28
7000	611.63	319.27	222.07	173.66	144.76	125.61	112.05	101.96	94.20	88.06	83.10	79.02	75.62	72.76	70.32
8000	699.01	364.88	253.79	198.46	165.43	143.56	128.05	116.53	107.65	100.64	94.97	90.31	86.43	83.15	80.37
9000	786.38	410.49	285.52	223.27	186.11	161.50	144.06	131.09	121.11	113.21	106.84	101.60	97.23	93.55	90.41
10000	873.76	456.10	317.24	248.08	206.79	179.45	160.06	145.66	134.57	125.79	118.71	112.88	108.03	103.94	100.46
11000	961.13	501.71	348.96	272.88	227.47	197.39	176.07	160.22	148.02	138.37	130.58	124.17	118.84	114.33	110.50
12000	1048.51	547.32	380.69	297.69	248.15	215.33	192.08	174.79	161.48	150.95	142.45	135.46	129.64	124.73	120.55
13000	1135.88	592.93	412.41	322.50	268.83	233.28	208.08	189.35	174.93	163.53	154.32	146.75	140.44	135.12	130.59
14000	1223.26	638.54	444.13	347.30	289.51	251.22	224.09	203.92	188.39	176.11	166.19	158.04	151.24	145.52	140.64
15000	1310.63	684.15	475.86	372.11	310.19	269.17	240.09	218.48	201.85	188.69	178.06	169.32	162.05	155.91	150.68
16000	1398.01	729.76	507.58	396.92	330.86	287.11	256.10	233.05	215.30	201.27	189.93	180.61	172.85	166.30	160.73
17000	1485.39	775.37	539.30	421.73	351.54	305.06	272.10	247.61	228.76	213.85	201.80	191.90	183.65	176.70	170.77
18000	1572.76	820.97	571.03	446.53	372.22	323.00	288.11	262.18	242.21	226.42	213.67	203.19	194.46	187.09	180.82
19000	1660.14	866.58	602.75	471.34	392.90	340.94	304.12	276.74	255.67	239.00	225.54	214.48	205.26	197.48	190.86
20000	1747.51	912.19	634.47	496.15	413.58	358.89	320.12	291.31	269.13	251.58	237.41	225.76	216.06	207.88	200.91
21000	1834.89	957.80	666.20	520.95	434.26	376.83	336.13	305.87	282.58	264.16	249.28	237.05	226.86	218.27	210.95
22000	1922.26	1003.41	697.92	545.76	454.94	394.78	352.13	320.44	296.04	276.74	261.15	248.34	237.67	228.66	221.00
23000	2009.64	1049.02	729.64	570.57	475.62	412.72	368.14	335.00	309.49	289.32	273.02	259.63	248.47	239.06	231.04
24000	2097.01	1094.63	761.37	595.38	496.30	430.67	384.15	349.57	322.95	301.90	284.89	270.92	259.27	249.45	241.09
25000	2184.39	1140.24	793.09	620.18	516.97	448.61	400.15	364.13	336.41	314.48	296.76	282.20	270.07	259.84	251.13
26000	2271.76	1185.85	824.81	644.99	537.65	466.55	416.16	378.70	349.86	327.06	308.63	293.49	280.88	270.24	261.18
27000	2359.14	1231.46	856.54	669.80	558.33	484.50	432.16	393.26	363.32	339.63	320.50	304.78	291.68	280.63	271.23
28000	2446.51	1277.07	888.26	694.60	579.01	502.44	448.17	407.83	376.77	352.21	332.37	316.07	302.48	291.03	281.27
29000	2533.89	1322.68	919.98	719.41	599.69	520.38	464.17	422.39	390.23	364.79	344.24	327.36	313.28	301.42	291.32
30000	2621.26	1368.29	951.71	744.22	620.37	538.33	480.18	436.96	403.69	377.37	356.11	338.64	324.09	311.81	301.36
35000	3058.14	1596.33	1110.32	868.25	723.76	628.05	560.21	509.78	470.97	440.26	415.46	395.08	378.10	363.78	351.59
40000	3495.02	1824.37	1268.94	992.29	827.15	717.77	640.24	582.61	538.25	503.16	474.82	451.52	432.11	415.75	401.81
45000	3931.89	2052.43	1427.56	1116.33	930.55	807.49	720.27	655.44	605.53	566.05	534.17	507.96	486.13	467.72	452.04
50000	4368.77	2280.48	1586.17	1240.36	1033.94	897.21	800.30	728.26	672.81	628.95	593.52	564.40	540.14	519.68	502.26

MONTHLY PAYMENT
REQUIRED TO AMORTIZE A LOAN 9%

TERM AMOUNT	16 YEARS	17 YEARS	18 YEARS	19 YEARS	20 YEARS	21 YEARS	22 YEARS	23 YEARS	24 YEARS	25 YEARS	26 YEARS	27 YEARS	28 YEARS	30 YEARS	35 YEARS
$100	.98	.95	.93	.91	.89	.88	.87	.85	.84	.83	.83	.82	.81	.80	.78
200	1.96	1.91	1.87	1.83	1.79	1.76	1.74	1.71	1.69	1.67	1.66	1.64	1.63	1.60	1.56
300	2.95	2.87	2.80	2.75	2.69	2.65	2.61	2.57	2.54	2.51	2.49	2.46	2.44	2.41	2.35
400	3.93	3.83	3.74	3.66	3.59	3.53	3.48	3.43	3.39	3.35	3.32	3.29	3.26	3.21	3.13
500	4.92	4.79	4.68	4.58	4.49	4.42	4.35	4.29	4.24	4.19	4.15	4.11	4.08	4.02	3.91
600	5.90	5.75	5.61	5.50	5.39	5.30	5.22	5.15	5.09	5.03	4.98	4.93	4.89	4.82	4.70
700	6.89	6.71	6.55	6.41	6.29	6.19	6.09	6.01	5.94	5.87	5.81	5.76	5.71	5.63	5.48
800	7.87	7.67	7.49	7.33	7.19	7.07	6.96	6.87	6.78	6.71	6.64	6.58	6.53	6.43	6.27
900	8.86	8.62	8.42	8.25	8.09	7.96	7.84	7.73	7.63	7.55	7.47	7.40	7.34	7.24	7.05
1000	9.84	9.58	9.36	9.16	8.99	8.84	8.71	8.59	8.48	8.39	8.30	8.23	8.16	8.04	7.83
2000	19.69	19.17	18.72	18.33	17.99	17.69	17.42	17.18	16.97	16.78	16.61	16.46	16.32	16.09	15.67
3000	29.53	28.76	28.09	27.50	26.99	26.53	26.13	25.77	25.46	25.17	24.92	24.69	24.48	24.13	23.51
4000	39.38	38.35	37.45	36.67	35.98	35.38	34.84	34.37	33.94	33.56	33.22	32.92	32.65	32.18	31.35
5000	49.22	47.94	46.82	45.84	44.98	44.22	43.55	42.95	42.43	41.95	41.53	41.15	40.81	40.23	39.19
6000	59.07	57.52	56.18	55.01	53.98	53.07	52.27	51.55	50.92	50.35	49.84	49.38	48.97	48.27	47.03
7000	68.91	67.11	65.55	64.18	62.98	61.92	60.98	60.15	59.40	58.74	58.15	57.61	57.14	56.32	54.87
8000	78.76	76.70	74.91	73.35	71.97	70.76	69.69	68.74	67.89	67.13	66.45	65.84	65.30	64.36	62.71
9000	88.60	86.29	84.28	82.52	80.97	79.61	78.40	77.32	76.38	75.52	74.76	74.08	73.46	72.41	70.55
10000	98.45	95.88	93.64	91.68	89.97	88.45	87.11	85.92	84.86	83.91	83.07	82.31	81.62	80.46	78.39
11000	108.29	105.46	103.00	100.85	98.96	97.30	95.82	94.51	93.35	92.31	91.37	90.54	89.79	88.50	86.23
12000	118.14	115.05	112.37	110.02	107.96	106.14	104.54	103.11	101.84	100.70	99.68	98.77	97.95	96.55	94.07
13000	127.98	124.64	121.73	119.19	116.96	114.99	113.25	111.70	110.32	109.09	107.96	107.00	106.11	104.60	101.91
14000	137.83	134.23	131.10	128.36	125.96	123.84	121.96	120.29	118.81	117.48	116.25	115.23	114.28	112.69	109.75
15000	147.67	143.82	140.46	137.53	134.95	132.68	130.67	128.89	127.30	125.87	124.60	123.46	122.44	120.69	117.59
16000	157.52	153.40	149.83	146.70	143.95	141.53	139.38	137.48	135.78	134.27	132.91	131.69	130.60	128.73	125.43
17000	167.36	162.99	159.19	155.87	152.95	150.37	148.10	146.07	144.27	142.66	141.22	139.93	138.77	136.78	133.27
18000	177.21	172.58	168.56	165.04	161.95	159.22	156.81	154.66	152.76	151.05	149.52	148.16	146.93	144.83	141.11
19000	187.05	182.17	177.92	174.21	170.94	168.07	165.52	163.26	161.24	159.44	157.83	156.39	155.09	152.87	148.95
20000	196.90	191.76	187.29	183.37	179.94	176.91	174.23	171.85	169.73	167.83	166.14	164.62	163.25	160.92	156.79
21000	206.74	201.35	196.65	192.54	188.94	185.76	182.94	180.44	178.22	176.23	174.45	172.85	171.42	168.97	164.67
22000	216.59	210.93	206.01	201.71	197.93	194.60	191.65	189.03	186.70	184.62	182.75	181.08	179.58	177.01	172.55
23000	226.43	220.52	215.38	210.88	206.93	203.45	200.37	197.63	195.19	193.01	191.06	189.31	187.74	185.06	180.43
24000	236.28	230.11	224.74	220.05	215.93	212.29	209.08	206.22	203.68	201.40	199.37	197.54	195.91	193.10	188.15
25000	246.12	239.70	234.11	229.22	224.93	221.14	217.79	214.81	212.16	209.79	207.68	205.78	204.07	201.15	195.99
26000	255.97	249.29	243.47	238.39	233.92	229.99	226.50	223.41	220.65	218.19	215.98	214.01	212.23	209.20	203.83
27000	265.81	258.87	252.84	247.56	242.92	238.83	235.22	232.00	229.14	226.58	224.29	222.24	220.40	217.24	211.67
28000	275.66	268.46	262.20	256.73	251.92	247.68	243.94	240.59	237.62	235.02	232.60	230.47	228.56	225.29	219.51
29000	285.50	278.05	271.57	265.90	260.92	256.52	252.66	249.18	246.11	243.46	240.90	238.70	236.72	233.34	227.35
30000	295.35	287.64	280.93	275.06	269.91	265.37	261.35	257.78	254.60	251.75	249.21	246.93	244.88	241.38	235.19
35000	344.57	335.58	327.75	320.91	314.90	309.60	304.91	300.74	297.03	293.71	290.75	288.09	285.70	281.61	274.39
40000	393.80	383.52	374.58	366.75	359.89	353.83	348.47	343.70	339.46	335.67	332.28	329.24	326.51	321.84	313.59
45000	443.03	431.46	421.40	412.60	404.87	398.06	392.03	386.67	381.90	377.63	373.82	370.40	367.33	362.07	352.79
50000	492.25	479.40	468.22	458.44	449.86	442.29	435.58	429.53	424.33	419.59	415.36	411.56	408.14	402.31	391.99

MONTHLY PAYMENT
REQUIRED TO AMORTIZE A LOAN

TERM AMOUNT	1 YEAR	2 YEARS	3 YEARS	4 YEARS	5 YEARS	6 YEARS	7 YEARS	8 YEARS	9 YEARS	10 YEARS	11 YEARS	12 YEARS	13 YEARS	14 YEARS	15 YEARS
$100	8.75	4.58	3.19	2.50	2.08	1.81	1.62	1.47	1.36	1.28	1.21	1.15	1.10	1.06	1.02
200	17.50	9.15	6.37	5.00	4.16	3.62	3.23	2.94	2.72	2.55	2.41	2.29	2.19	2.11	2.04
300	26.25	13.72	9.56	7.48	6.24	5.42	4.84	4.41	4.08	3.82	3.61	3.43	3.29	3.17	3.06
400	35.00	18.29	12.74	9.97	8.32	7.23	6.46	5.88	5.44	5.09	4.81	4.57	4.38	4.22	4.08
500	43.75	22.86	15.92	12.47	10.40	9.04	8.07	7.35	6.80	6.36	6.01	5.72	5.48	5.27	5.10
600	52.50	27.44	19.11	14.96	12.48	10.84	9.68	8.82	8.16	7.63	7.21	6.86	6.57	6.33	6.12
700	61.25	32.01	22.29	17.45	14.56	12.65	11.29	10.29	9.51	8.90	8.41	8.00	7.66	7.38	7.14
800	70.00	36.58	25.47	19.94	16.64	14.46	12.91	11.76	10.87	10.17	9.61	9.14	8.76	8.43	8.16
900	78.74	41.15	28.66	22.43	18.72	16.26	14.52	13.23	12.23	11.44	10.81	10.29	9.85	9.49	9.17
1000	87.49	45.72	31.84	24.93	20.80	18.07	16.13	14.69	13.59	12.71	12.01	11.43	10.95	10.54	10.19
2000	174.98	91.44	63.68	49.85	41.60	36.13	32.26	29.38	27.17	25.42	24.01	22.85	21.89	21.07	20.38
3000	262.47	137.16	95.51	74.77	62.39	54.20	48.39	44.07	40.76	38.13	36.01	34.28	32.83	31.61	30.57
4000	349.95	182.88	127.35	99.69	83.19	72.26	64.52	58.76	54.34	50.84	48.02	45.70	43.77	42.14	40.76
5000	437.44	228.60	159.18	124.61	103.98	90.32	80.64	73.45	67.92	63.55	60.02	57.12	54.71	52.68	50.95
6000	524.93	274.32	191.02	149.53	124.78	108.39	96.77	88.14	81.51	76.26	72.02	68.55	65.65	63.21	61.13
7000	612.40	320.04	222.85	174.46	145.57	126.45	112.90	102.83	95.09	88.97	84.03	79.97	76.59	73.74	71.32
8000	699.90	365.76	254.69	199.38	166.37	144.51	129.03	117.52	108.67	101.68	96.03	91.39	87.53	84.28	81.51
9000	787.39	411.48	286.52	224.30	187.17	162.58	145.16	132.21	122.26	114.39	108.03	102.82	98.47	94.81	91.70
10000	874.88	457.20	318.36	249.22	207.96	180.64	161.28	146.90	135.84	127.10	120.04	114.24	109.41	105.35	101.89
11000	962.36	502.92	350.19	274.14	228.76	198.70	177.41	161.59	149.42	139.80	132.04	125.66	120.35	115.88	112.08
12000	1049.85	548.64	382.03	299.06	249.55	216.77	193.54	176.28	163.01	152.51	144.04	137.09	131.29	126.42	122.26
13000	1137.34	594.36	413.86	323.99	270.35	234.83	209.67	190.97	176.59	165.22	156.05	148.51	142.24	136.95	132.45
14000	1224.82	640.08	445.70	348.91	291.14	252.90	225.80	205.66	190.17	177.93	168.05	159.93	153.18	147.48	142.64
15000	1312.31	685.80	477.54	373.83	311.94	270.96	241.92	220.35	203.76	190.64	180.05	171.36	164.12	158.02	152.83
16000	1399.80	731.52	509.37	398.75	332.73	289.02	258.05	235.04	217.34	203.35	192.06	182.78	175.06	168.55	163.00
17000	1487.28	777.24	541.21	423.67	353.53	307.09	274.18	249.73	230.93	216.06	204.06	194.20	186.00	179.09	173.21
18000	1574.77	822.96	573.04	448.59	374.33	325.15	290.31	264.42	244.51	228.77	216.06	205.63	196.94	189.62	183.39
19000	1662.26	868.68	604.88	473.51	395.12	343.22	306.44	279.11	258.09	241.48	228.07	217.05	207.88	200.16	193.58
20000	1749.75	914.40	636.71	498.43	415.92	361.28	322.56	293.80	271.68	254.19	240.07	228.48	218.82	210.69	203.77
21000	1837.23	960.12	668.55	523.36	436.71	379.34	338.69	308.49	285.26	266.90	252.07	239.90	229.76	221.22	213.96
22000	1924.72	1005.84	700.38	548.28	457.51	397.40	354.82	323.18	298.84	279.60	264.08	251.32	240.70	231.76	224.15
23000	2012.21	1051.56	732.22	573.20	478.30	415.47	370.95	337.87	312.43	292.31	276.08	262.75	251.64	242.29	234.34
24000	2099.69	1097.28	764.05	598.12	499.10	433.53	387.08	352.56	326.01	305.01	288.08	274.17	262.58	252.83	244.52
25000	2187.18	1143.00	795.89	623.04	519.89	451.59	403.20	367.25	339.59	317.73	300.08	285.59	273.53	263.36	254.71
26000	2274.67	1188.72	827.73	647.96	540.69	469.66	419.33	381.94	353.18	330.44	312.09	297.02	284.47	273.89	264.90
27000	2362.15	1234.44	859.56	672.88	561.49	487.72	435.46	396.63	366.76	343.15	324.09	308.44	295.41	284.43	275.09
28000	2449.64	1280.16	891.40	697.81	582.28	505.79	451.59	411.32	380.34	355.86	336.09	319.86	306.35	294.96	285.28
29000	2537.13	1325.88	923.23	722.73	603.08	523.85	467.72	426.01	393.93	368.57	348.10	331.29	317.29	305.50	295.47
30000	2624.62	1371.60	955.07	747.65	623.87	541.91	483.84	440.70	407.51	381.28	360.10	342.71	328.23	316.03	305.65
35000	3062.05	1600.20	1114.24	872.26	727.85	632.23	564.48	514.15	475.43	444.82	420.12	399.83	382.93	368.70	356.60
40000	3499.49	1828.80	1273.42	996.86	831.83	722.55	645.12	587.60	543.35	508.37	480.13	456.95	437.64	421.37	407.54
45000	3936.92	2057.40	1432.60	1121.47	935.81	812.87	725.76	661.05	611.26	571.91	540.15	514.06	492.34	474.04	458.48
50000	4374.36	2286.00	1591.78	1246.08	1039.78	903.18	806.40	734.50	679.18	635.46	600.16	571.18	547.05	526.72	509.42

MONTHLY PAYMENT
REQUIRED TO AMORTIZE A LOAN 9¼ %

TERM AMOUNT	16 YEARS	17 YEARS	18 YEARS	19 YEARS	20 YEARS	21 YEARS	22 YEARS	23 YEARS	24 YEARS	25 YEARS	26 YEARS	27 YEARS	28 YEARS	30 YEARS	35 YEARS
$100	.99	.97	.95	.93	.91	.89	.88	.87	.86	.85	.84	.83	.83	.82	.79
200	1.98	1.93	1.89	1.85	1.81	1.78	1.76	1.73	1.71	1.69	1.68	1.66	1.65	1.63	1.58
300	2.97	2.90	2.83	2.77	2.72	2.67	2.63	2.60	2.57	2.54	2.51	2.49	2.47	2.44	2.37
400	3.96	3.86	3.77	3.69	3.62	3.56	3.51	3.46	3.42	3.38	3.35	3.32	3.29	3.25	3.16
500	4.94	4.82	4.71	4.61	4.53	4.45	4.39	4.33	4.27	4.23	4.19	4.15	4.11	4.06	3.95
600	5.94	5.79	5.65	5.54	5.43	5.34	5.26	5.19	5.13	5.07	5.02	4.98	4.94	4.87	4.74
700	6.93	6.75	6.59	6.46	6.34	6.23	6.14	6.06	5.98	5.92	5.86	5.80	5.76	5.68	5.53
800	7.92	7.71	7.53	7.38	7.24	7.11	7.01	6.92	6.84	6.76	6.69	6.63	6.58	6.49	6.32
900	8.91	8.68	8.48	8.30	8.15	8.01	7.89	7.78	7.69	7.61	7.53	7.46	7.40	7.30	7.11
1000	9.90	9.64	9.42	9.22	9.05	8.90	8.77	8.65	8.54	8.45	8.37	8.29	8.22	8.11	7.90
2000	19.79	19.28	18.83	18.44	18.10	17.80	17.53	17.29	17.08	16.89	16.73	16.57	16.44	16.21	15.80
3000	29.68	28.91	28.24	27.66	27.14	26.69	26.29	25.94	25.62	25.34	25.09	24.86	24.66	24.31	23.70
4000	39.57	38.55	37.65	36.88	36.19	35.59	35.05	34.58	34.16	33.78	33.45	33.14	32.87	32.41	31.59
5000	49.46	48.18	47.07	46.09	45.24	44.48	43.82	43.23	42.70	42.23	41.81	41.43	41.09	40.51	39.49
6000	59.35	57.82	56.48	55.31	54.28	53.38	52.58	51.87	51.24	50.67	50.17	49.71	49.31	48.61	47.39
7000	69.25	67.45	65.89	64.53	63.33	62.28	61.34	60.51	59.78	59.12	58.53	58.00	57.53	56.71	55.29
8000	79.14	77.09	75.30	73.75	72.38	71.17	70.10	69.16	68.31	67.56	66.89	66.28	65.74	64.82	63.18
9000	89.03	86.72	84.72	82.96	81.42	80.07	78.87	77.80	76.85	76.01	75.25	74.57	73.96	72.92	71.08
10000	98.92	96.36	94.13	92.18	90.47	88.96	87.63	86.45	85.39	84.45	83.61	82.85	82.18	81.02	78.98
11000	108.81	105.99	103.54	101.40	99.52	97.86	96.39	95.09	93.93	92.89	91.97	91.14	90.39	89.12	86.88
12000	118.70	115.63	112.95	110.62	108.56	106.75	105.15	103.73	102.47	101.34	100.33	99.42	98.61	97.22	94.77
13000	128.60	125.26	122.37	119.83	117.61	115.65	113.92	112.38	111.01	109.78	108.69	107.71	106.83	105.32	102.67
14000	138.49	134.90	131.78	129.05	126.66	124.55	122.68	121.02	119.55	118.23	117.05	115.99	115.05	113.42	110.57
15000	148.38	144.53	141.19	138.27	135.70	133.44	131.44	129.67	128.08	126.67	125.41	124.28	123.26	121.53	118.46
16000	158.27	154.17	150.60	147.49	144.75	142.34	140.20	138.31	136.62	135.12	133.77	132.56	131.48	129.63	126.36
17000	168.16	163.80	160.02	156.70	153.80	151.23	148.97	146.95	145.16	143.56	142.13	140.85	139.70	137.73	134.26
18000	178.05	173.44	169.43	165.92	162.84	160.13	157.73	155.60	153.70	152.01	150.49	149.13	147.91	145.83	142.16
19000	187.94	183.07	178.84	175.14	171.89	169.03	166.49	164.24	162.24	160.45	158.85	157.42	156.13	153.93	150.05
20000	197.84	192.71	188.25	184.36	180.94	177.92	175.25	172.89	170.78	168.89	167.21	165.70	164.35	162.03	157.95
21000	207.73	202.34	197.66	193.57	189.98	186.82	184.02	181.53	179.32	177.34	175.57	173.99	172.57	170.13	165.85
22000	217.62	211.98	207.08	202.79	199.03	195.71	192.78	190.17	187.85	185.78	183.93	182.27	180.78	178.23	173.75
23000	227.51	221.61	216.49	212.01	208.08	204.61	201.54	198.82	196.39	194.23	192.29	190.56	189.00	186.34	181.64
24000	237.40	231.25	225.90	221.23	217.12	213.50	210.30	207.46	204.93	202.67	200.65	198.84	197.22	194.44	189.54
25000	247.29	240.89	235.31	230.45	226.17	222.40	219.07	216.11	213.47	211.12	209.01	207.13	205.43	202.54	197.44
26000	257.19	250.52	244.73	239.66	235.21	231.30	227.83	224.75	222.01	219.56	217.37	215.41	213.65	210.64	205.33
27000	267.08	260.16	254.14	248.88	244.26	240.19	236.59	233.39	230.55	228.01	225.73	223.70	221.87	218.74	213.23
28000	276.97	269.79	263.55	258.10	253.31	249.09	245.35	242.04	239.09	236.45	234.09	231.98	230.09	226.84	221.13
29000	286.86	279.43	272.96	267.32	262.36	257.98	254.12	250.68	247.62	244.90	242.45	240.27	238.30	234.95	229.03
30000	296.75	289.06	282.38	276.53	271.40	266.88	262.88	259.33	256.16	253.34	250.82	248.55	246.52	243.05	236.92
35000	346.21	337.24	329.44	322.62	316.64	311.36	306.69	302.55	298.86	295.56	292.62	289.98	287.61	283.55	276.41
40000	395.67	385.41	376.50	368.71	361.87	355.84	350.50	345.77	341.55	337.78	334.42	331.40	328.69	324.06	315.90
45000	445.13	433.59	423.56	414.80	407.10	400.33	394.32	388.99	384.24	380.01	376.22	372.83	369.78	364.56	355.38
50000	494.58	481.77	470.62	460.89	452.33	444.80	438.13	432.21	426.93	422.23	418.02	414.25	410.86	405.08	394.87

MONTHLY PAYMENT
9½% REQUIRED TO AMORTIZE A LOAN

TERM AMOUNT	1 YEAR	2 YEARS	3 YEARS	4 YEARS	5 YEARS	6 YEARS	7 YEARS	8 YEARS	9 YEARS	10 YEARS	11 YEARS	12 YEARS	13 YEARS	14 YEARS	15 YEARS
$100	8.76	4.59	3.20	2.51	2.10	1.82	1.63	1.49	1.38	1.29	1.22	1.16	1.11	1.07	1.04
200	17.52	9.17	6.39	5.01	4.19	3.64	3.26	2.97	2.75	2.57	2.43	2.32	2.22	2.14	2.07
300	26.28	13.75	9.59	7.52	6.28	5.46	4.88	4.45	4.12	3.86	3.65	3.47	3.33	3.21	3.10
400	35.04	18.34	12.78	10.02	8.37	7.28	6.51	5.93	5.49	5.14	4.86	4.63	4.44	4.28	4.14
500	43.80	22.92	15.98	12.52	10.46	9.10	8.13	7.41	6.86	6.42	6.07	5.78	5.54	5.34	5.17
600	52.56	27.50	19.17	15.03	12.55	10.92	9.76	8.89	8.23	7.71	7.29	6.94	6.65	6.41	6.20
700	61.32	32.09	22.37	17.53	14.64	12.73	11.38	10.38	9.60	8.99	8.50	8.10	7.76	7.48	7.24
800	70.08	36.67	25.56	20.03	16.74	14.55	13.01	11.86	10.97	10.28	9.71	9.25	8.87	8.55	8.27
900	78.84	41.25	28.76	22.54	18.83	16.37	14.63	13.34	12.35	11.56	10.93	10.41	9.98	9.61	9.30
1000	87.60	45.84	31.95	25.04	20.92	18.19	16.26	14.82	13.72	12.84	12.14	11.56	11.08	10.68	10.34
2000	175.20	91.67	63.90	50.08	41.83	36.37	32.51	29.64	27.43	25.68	24.28	23.12	22.16	21.36	20.67
3000	262.80	137.50	95.85	75.11	62.74	54.56	48.76	44.45	41.14	38.52	36.42	34.68	33.24	32.03	31.00
4000	350.40	183.33	127.80	100.15	83.66	72.74	65.01	59.27	54.85	51.36	48.55	46.24	44.32	42.71	41.33
5000	438.00	229.16	159.74	125.18	104.57	90.92	81.26	74.08	68.56	64.20	60.69	57.80	55.40	53.38	51.67
6000	525.60	274.99	191.69	150.22	125.48	109.11	97.51	88.90	82.27	77.04	72.83	69.36	66.48	64.06	62.00
7000	613.20	320.82	223.64	175.26	146.39	127.29	113.76	103.71	95.99	89.88	84.96	80.92	77.56	74.73	72.33
8000	700.79	366.65	255.59	200.29	167.31	145.47	130.01	118.53	109.70	102.72	97.10	92.48	88.64	85.41	82.66
9000	788.39	412.48	287.53	225.33	188.23	163.66	146.26	133.34	123.41	115.56	109.24	104.04	99.72	96.09	93.00
10000	875.99	458.31	319.48	250.35	209.13	181.84	162.51	148.16	137.12	128.40	121.37	115.60	110.80	106.76	103.33
11000	963.59	504.14	351.43	275.38	230.04	200.02	178.76	162.97	150.83	141.24	133.51	127.16	121.88	117.44	113.66
12000	1051.19	549.97	383.38	300.44	250.96	218.21	195.01	177.79	164.54	154.08	145.65	138.72	132.96	128.11	123.99
13000	1138.79	595.80	415.32	325.47	271.87	236.39	211.26	192.60	178.26	166.92	157.78	150.28	144.04	138.79	134.32
14000	1226.39	641.63	447.27	350.51	292.78	254.57	227.51	207.42	191.97	179.76	169.92	161.84	155.12	149.46	144.66
15000	1313.98	687.46	479.22	375.54	313.70	272.76	243.76	222.23	205.69	192.60	182.06	173.40	166.20	160.14	154.99
16000	1401.58	733.29	511.17	400.58	334.61	290.94	260.01	237.05	219.39	205.44	194.19	184.92	177.28	170.82	165.32
17000	1489.18	779.12	543.11	425.62	355.52	309.12	276.26	251.87	233.10	218.28	206.33	196.52	188.36	181.49	175.65
18000	1576.78	824.95	575.06	450.65	376.43	327.31	292.51	266.68	246.81	231.11	218.47	208.08	199.44	192.17	185.99
19000	1664.38	870.78	607.01	475.69	397.35	345.49	308.76	281.50	260.53	243.95	230.60	219.60	210.52	202.84	196.32
20000	1751.98	916.61	638.96	500.72	418.26	363.67	325.02	296.31	274.26	256.80	242.74	231.20	221.60	213.52	206.65
21000	1839.58	962.44	670.90	525.76	439.17	381.86	341.27	311.13	287.95	269.64	254.88	242.76	232.68	224.19	216.98
22000	1927.17	1008.27	702.85	550.80	460.08	400.04	357.52	325.94	301.66	282.48	267.01	254.32	243.76	234.87	227.31
23000	2014.77	1054.11	734.80	575.83	481.00	418.22	373.77	340.76	315.37	295.32	279.15	265.88	254.84	245.54	237.65
24000	2102.37	1099.94	766.75	600.87	501.91	436.41	390.02	355.57	329.08	308.16	291.29	277.44	265.92	256.22	247.98
25000	2189.97	1145.77	798.69	625.90	522.82	454.59	406.27	370.39	342.80	321.00	303.42	289.00	277.00	266.90	258.31
26000	2277.57	1191.60	830.64	650.94	543.73	472.77	422.52	385.20	356.51	333.84	315.56	300.56	288.08	277.57	268.64
27000	2365.17	1237.43	862.59	675.98	564.64	490.96	438.77	400.02	370.22	346.68	327.70	312.12	299.16	288.25	278.98
28000	2452.77	1283.26	894.54	701.01	585.56	509.14	455.02	414.83	383.93	359.52	339.83	323.68	310.24	298.92	289.31
29000	2540.37	1329.09	926.49	726.05	606.47	527.32	471.27	429.65	397.64	372.36	351.97	335.24	321.32	309.60	299.64
30000	2627.96	1374.92	958.44	751.08	627.39	545.51	487.52	444.46	411.35	385.20	364.11	346.80	332.40	320.27	309.97
35000	3065.96	1604.07	1118.17	876.26	731.95	636.42	568.77	518.54	479.91	449.40	424.79	404.60	387.79	373.65	361.63
40000	3503.95	1833.23	1277.91	1001.44	836.51	727.34	650.03	592.62	548.47	513.60	485.47	462.39	443.19	427.03	413.30
45000	3941.94	2062.39	1437.65	1126.62	941.08	818.26	731.28	666.69	617.03	577.80	546.16	520.19	498.59	480.41	464.96
50000	4379.94	2291.53	1597.38	1251.80	1045.64	909.17	812.53	740.77	685.59	647.00	606.84	577.99	553.99	533.79	516.62

MONTHLY PAYMENT
REQUIRED TO AMORTIZE A LOAN 9½ %

TERM AMOUNT	35 YEARS	30 YEARS	28 YEARS	27 YEARS	26 YEARS	25 YEARS	24 YEARS	23 YEARS	22 YEARS	21 YEARS	20 YEARS	19 YEARS	18 YEARS	17 YEARS	16 YEARS
$100	.81	.83	.84	.85	.86	.87	.88	.89	.90	.91	.93	.94	.96	.98	1.01
200	1.62	1.66	1.68	1.70	1.71	1.73	1.75	1.77	1.79	1.82	1.85	1.88	1.92	1.96	2.01
300	2.43	2.49	2.52	2.54	2.56	2.59	2.62	2.65	2.68	2.72	2.77	2.82	2.87	2.94	3.02
400	3.24	3.32	3.36	3.39	3.42	3.45	3.49	3.53	3.57	3.63	3.69	3.75	3.83	3.92	4.02
500	4.04	4.14	4.20	4.23	4.27	4.31	4.36	4.41	4.46	4.53	4.61	4.69	4.79	4.90	5.02
600	4.85	4.97	5.04	5.08	5.12	5.17	5.23	5.29	5.36	5.44	5.53	5.63	5.74	5.88	6.03
700	5.66	5.80	5.88	5.92	5.97	6.03	6.10	6.17	6.25	6.34	6.45	6.56	6.70	6.85	7.03
800	6.47	6.63	6.72	6.77	6.83	6.89	6.97	7.05	7.14	7.25	7.37	7.50	7.66	7.83	8.04
900	7.28	7.45	7.55	7.61	7.68	7.75	7.84	7.93	8.04	8.15	8.29	8.44	8.61	8.81	9.04
1000	8.08	8.28	8.39	8.46	8.53	8.62	8.71	8.81	8.93	9.06	9.21	9.38	9.57	9.79	10.04
2000	16.16	16.56	16.78	16.91	17.06	17.23	17.41	17.62	17.85	18.11	18.41	18.75	19.13	19.57	20.08
3000	24.24	24.83	25.17	25.37	25.59	25.84	26.11	26.42	26.77	27.17	27.61	28.12	28.70	29.36	30.12
4000	32.32	33.11	33.56	33.82	34.12	34.45	34.81	35.23	35.69	36.22	36.81	37.49	38.26	39.14	40.16
5000	40.40	41.38	41.95	42.28	42.64	43.06	43.52	44.03	44.61	45.27	46.01	46.86	47.82	48.93	50.20
6000	48.47	49.66	50.33	50.73	51.17	51.67	52.22	52.84	53.54	54.33	55.22	56.23	57.39	58.71	60.23
7000	56.55	57.93	58.72	59.18	59.70	60.28	60.92	61.64	62.46	63.38	64.42	65.60	66.95	68.49	70.27
8000	64.63	66.21	67.11	67.64	68.23	68.89	69.62	70.45	71.38	72.43	73.62	74.97	76.51	78.28	80.31
9000	72.71	74.48	75.50	76.09	76.76	77.50	78.33	79.26	80.31	81.49	82.83	84.34	86.08	88.06	90.35
10000	80.79	82.76	83.89	84.55	85.28	86.11	87.03	88.06	89.23	90.54	92.03	93.72	95.64	97.85	100.39
11000	88.86	91.04	92.27	93.00	93.81	94.72	95.73	96.87	98.15	99.59	101.23	103.09	105.20	107.63	110.42
12000	96.94	99.31	100.66	101.46	102.34	103.33	104.43	105.68	107.07	108.65	110.43	112.46	114.77	117.41	120.46
13000	105.02	107.59	109.05	109.91	110.87	111.94	113.13	114.48	115.99	117.70	119.63	121.83	124.33	127.20	130.50
14000	113.10	115.86	117.44	118.36	119.40	120.55	121.84	123.29	124.92	126.76	128.84	131.20	133.89	136.98	140.54
15000	121.18	124.14	125.83	126.82	127.92	129.16	130.54	132.09	133.84	135.81	138.04	140.57	143.46	146.77	150.58
16000	129.25	132.41	134.22	135.27	136.45	137.77	139.24	140.90	142.76	144.86	147.24	149.94	153.02	156.55	160.61
17000	137.33	140.69	142.60	143.73	144.98	146.38	147.95	149.71	151.69	153.91	156.44	159.31	162.59	166.33	170.65
18000	145.41	148.96	150.99	152.18	153.51	154.99	156.65	158.51	160.61	162.97	165.65	168.68	172.15	176.12	180.69
19000	153.49	157.24	159.38	160.63	162.04	163.60	165.35	167.32	169.53	172.02	174.85	178.05	181.71	185.90	190.73
20000	161.57	165.52	167.77	169.09	170.56	172.21	174.05	176.12	178.45	181.08	184.05	187.43	191.28	195.69	200.77
21000	169.64	173.79	176.16	177.54	179.09	180.82	182.76	184.93	187.37	190.13	193.25	196.80	200.84	205.47	210.80
22000	177.72	182.07	184.54	186.00	187.62	189.43	191.46	193.74	196.30	199.19	202.46	206.17	210.40	215.25	220.84
23000	185.80	190.34	192.93	194.45	196.14	198.04	200.16	202.54	205.22	208.24	211.66	215.54	219.97	225.04	230.88
24000	193.88	198.62	201.32	202.91	204.67	206.65	208.86	211.35	214.14	217.29	220.86	224.91	229.53	234.82	240.92
25000	201.96	206.89	209.71	211.36	213.20	215.26	217.57	220.15	223.06	226.35	230.06	234.28	239.09	244.61	250.96
26000	210.04	215.17	218.10	219.82	221.73	223.87	226.27	228.96	231.99	235.40	239.26	243.65	248.66	254.39	260.99
27000	218.11	223.44	226.49	228.27	230.26	232.48	234.97	237.77	240.90	244.45	248.46	253.02	258.22	264.17	271.03
28000	226.19	231.72	234.87	236.72	238.79	241.09	243.67	246.57	249.83	253.51	257.67	262.39	267.78	273.96	281.07
29000	234.27	240.00	243.26	245.18	247.31	249.70	252.38	255.38	258.75	262.56	266.87	271.77	277.35	283.74	291.11
30000	242.35	248.27	251.65	253.63	255.84	258.31	261.08	264.18	267.68	271.62	276.07	281.14	286.91	293.53	301.15
35000	282.74	289.65	293.59	295.90	298.48	301.36	304.59	308.21	312.28	316.88	322.08	327.99	334.73	342.45	351.34
40000	323.13	331.03	335.53	338.17	341.12	344.42	348.10	352.24	356.90	362.15	368.10	374.85	382.55	391.37	401.53
45000	363.52	372.40	377.47	380.45	383.76	387.47	391.62	396.27	401.51	407.42	414.11	421.70	430.37	440.29	451.72
50000	403.91	413.78	419.41	422.72	426.40	430.52	435.13	440.30	446.12	452.69	460.12	468.56	478.18	489.21	501.91

MONTHLY PAYMENT
9¾ % REQUIRED TO AMORTIZE A LOAN

TERM AMOUNT	1 YEAR	2 YEARS	3 YEARS	4 YEARS	5 YEARS	6 YEARS	7 YEARS	8 YEARS	9 YEARS	10 YEARS	11 YEARS	12 YEARS	13 YEARS	14 YEARS	15 YEARS
$100	8.78	4.60	3.21	2.52	2.11	1.84	1.64	1.50	1.39	1.30	1.23	1.17	1.13	1.09	1.05
200	17.55	9.19	6.42	5.04	4.21	3.67	3.28	2.99	2.77	2.60	2.46	2.34	2.26	2.17	2.10
300	26.32	13.79	9.62	7.55	6.31	5.50	4.92	4.49	4.16	3.90	3.69	3.51	3.37	3.25	3.15
400	35.09	18.38	12.83	10.07	8.42	7.33	6.55	5.98	5.54	5.19	4.91	4.68	4.49	4.33	4.20
500	43.86	22.98	16.04	12.58	10.52	9.16	8.19	7.48	6.93	6.49	6.14	5.85	5.61	5.41	5.24
600	52.63	27.57	19.24	15.10	12.62	10.99	9.83	8.97	8.31	7.79	7.37	7.02	6.74	6.50	6.29
700	61.40	32.16	22.45	17.61	14.73	12.82	11.47	10.46	9.69	9.08	8.59	8.19	7.86	7.58	7.34
800	70.17	36.76	25.66	20.13	16.83	14.65	13.10	11.96	11.08	10.38	9.82	9.36	8.98	8.66	8.39
900	78.94	41.35	28.86	22.64	18.93	16.48	14.74	13.45	12.46	11.68	11.05	10.53	10.10	9.74	9.43
1000	87.72	45.95	32.06	25.16	21.04	18.31	16.38	14.95	13.85	12.98	12.28	11.70	11.22	10.82	10.48
2000	175.43	91.89	64.12	50.31	42.07	36.61	32.75	29.89	27.69	25.95	24.55	23.40	22.44	21.64	20.96
3000	263.14	137.83	96.18	75.46	63.10	54.92	49.13	44.83	41.53	38.92	36.82	35.09	33.66	32.46	31.44
4000	350.85	183.77	128.24	100.61	84.13	73.22	65.50	59.77	55.37	51.89	49.09	46.79	44.88	43.28	41.91
5000	438.56	229.71	160.30	125.76	105.16	91.52	81.87	74.71	69.21	64.86	61.36	58.49	56.10	54.09	52.39
6000	526.27	275.65	192.36	150.91	126.19	109.83	98.25	89.65	83.05	77.83	73.63	70.18	67.32	64.91	62.87
7000	613.98	321.59	224.42	176.06	147.22	128.13	114.62	104.59	96.89	90.80	85.90	81.88	78.54	75.73	73.34
8000	701.69	367.53	256.48	201.21	168.25	146.43	130.99	119.53	110.73	103.78	98.17	93.58	89.76	86.55	83.82
9000	789.40	413.47	288.54	226.36	189.28	164.74	147.37	134.48	124.57	116.75	110.44	105.27	100.98	97.37	94.30
10000	877.12	459.42	320.60	251.51	210.34	183.04	163.74	149.42	138.41	129.72	122.71	116.97	112.20	108.18	104.78
11000	964.82	505.36	352.66	276.66	231.34	201.34	180.11	164.36	152.25	142.69	134.98	128.67	123.42	119.00	115.25
12000	1052.53	551.30	384.71	301.81	252.37	219.65	196.49	179.30	166.09	155.66	147.26	140.36	134.64	129.82	125.73
13000	1140.24	597.24	416.78	326.96	273.40	237.95	212.86	194.24	179.93	168.63	159.53	152.06	145.86	140.64	136.21
14000	1227.95	643.18	448.84	352.11	294.43	256.25	229.23	209.18	193.77	181.60	171.80	163.76	157.08	151.46	146.68
15000	1315.66	689.12	480.90	377.27	315.46	274.56	245.61	224.12	207.61	194.58	184.07	175.45	168.30	162.27	157.16
16000	1403.37	735.06	512.96	402.42	336.49	292.86	261.98	239.06	221.45	207.55	196.34	187.15	179.51	173.09	167.64
17000	1491.08	781.00	545.02	427.57	357.52	311.17	278.35	254.00	235.29	220.52	208.61	198.85	190.73	183.91	178.12
18000	1578.79	826.94	577.08	452.72	378.55	329.47	294.73	268.95	249.13	233.46	220.88	210.54	201.95	194.73	188.59
19000	1666.50	872.88	609.14	477.87	399.58	347.77	311.10	283.89	262.97	246.46	233.15	222.24	213.17	205.54	199.07
20000	1754.21	918.83	641.20	503.02	420.61	366.08	327.48	298.83	276.81	259.43	245.42	233.94	224.39	216.36	209.55
21000	1841.92	964.77	673.26	528.17	441.64	384.38	343.85	313.77	290.65	272.40	257.69	245.63	235.61	227.18	220.02
22000	1929.63	1010.71	705.31	553.32	462.67	402.68	360.22	328.71	304.49	285.37	269.96	257.33	246.83	238.00	230.50
23000	2017.34	1056.65	737.38	578.47	483.70	420.99	376.60	343.65	318.33	298.35	282.24	269.03	258.05	248.82	240.98
24000	2105.05	1102.59	769.44	603.62	504.73	439.29	392.97	358.59	332.17	311.32	294.51	280.72	269.27	259.63	251.45
25000	2192.76	1148.53	801.50	628.77	525.76	457.59	409.34	373.53	346.01	324.29	306.78	292.42	280.49	270.45	261.93
26000	2280.47	1194.47	833.56	653.92	546.79	475.90	425.72	388.47	359.85	337.26	319.05	304.12	291.71	281.27	272.41
27000	2368.18	1240.41	865.62	679.07	567.82	494.20	442.09	403.42	373.69	350.23	331.32	315.81	302.93	292.09	282.89
28000	2455.89	1286.35	897.68	704.22	588.85	512.50	458.46	418.36	387.53	363.20	343.59	327.51	314.15	302.91	293.36
29000	2543.60	1332.29	929.74	729.37	609.88	530.81	474.84	433.30	401.37	376.17	355.86	339.21	325.36	313.72	303.84
30000	2631.31	1378.24	961.80	754.52	630.91	549.11	491.21	448.24	415.21	389.15	368.13	350.90	336.58	324.54	314.32
35000	3069.87	1607.94	1122.10	880.28	736.06	640.63	573.08	522.94	484.41	454.00	429.49	409.39	392.68	378.63	366.70
40000	3508.42	1837.65	1282.40	1006.03	841.21	732.15	654.95	597.65	553.62	518.86	490.84	467.87	448.78	432.72	419.09
45000	3946.97	2067.35	1442.70	1131.79	946.36	823.66	736.81	672.36	622.82	583.57	552.20	526.35	504.87	486.81	471.47
50000	4385.52	2297.06	1603.00	1257.54	1051.51	915.18	818.68	747.06	692.02	648.57	613.55	584.84	560.97	540.90	523.86

MONTHLY PAYMENT
REQUIRED TO AMORTIZE A LOAN 9¾%

TERM AMOUNT	16 YEARS	17 YEARS	18 YEARS	19 YEARS	20 YEARS	21 YEARS	22 YEARS	23 YEARS	24 YEARS	25 YEARS	26 YEARS	27 YEARS	28 YEARS	30 YEARS	35 YEARS
$100	1.02	1.00	.98	.96	.94	.93	.91	.90	.89	.88	.87	.87	.86	.85	.83
200	2.04	1.99	1.95	1.91	1.88	1.85	1.82	1.80	1.78	1.76	1.74	1.73	1.72	1.70	1.66
300	3.06	2.99	2.92	2.86	2.81	2.77	2.73	2.70	2.67	2.64	2.61	2.59	2.57	2.54	2.48
400	4.08	3.98	3.89	3.82	3.75	3.69	3.64	3.59	3.55	3.52	3.48	3.45	3.43	3.39	3.31
500	5.10	4.97	4.86	4.77	4.68	4.61	4.55	4.49	4.44	4.39	4.35	4.32	4.29	4.23	4.13
600	6.12	5.97	5.83	5.72	5.62	5.53	5.45	5.39	5.33	5.27	5.22	5.18	5.14	5.08	4.96
700	7.14	6.96	6.81	6.67	6.56	6.45	6.36	6.28	6.21	6.15	6.09	6.04	6.00	5.92	5.79
800	8.15	7.95	7.78	7.63	7.49	7.38	7.27	7.18	7.10	7.03	6.96	6.90	6.85	6.77	6.61
900	9.17	8.95	8.75	8.58	8.43	8.30	8.18	8.08	7.99	7.90	7.83	7.77	7.71	7.61	7.44
1000	10.19	9.94	9.72	9.53	9.36	9.22	9.09	8.97	8.87	8.78	8.70	8.63	8.57	8.46	8.26
2000	20.38	19.87	19.44	19.06	18.72	18.43	18.17	17.94	17.74	17.56	17.40	17.25	17.13	16.91	16.52
3000	30.56	29.81	29.15	28.58	28.08	27.64	27.25	26.91	26.61	26.34	26.09	25.88	25.69	25.36	24.78
4000	40.75	39.74	38.87	38.11	37.44	36.86	36.34	35.88	35.47	35.11	34.79	34.50	34.25	33.81	33.04
5000	50.93	49.67	48.58	47.63	46.80	46.07	45.42	44.85	44.34	43.89	43.48	43.13	42.81	42.26	41.30
6000	61.12	59.61	58.30	57.16	56.16	55.28	54.50	53.82	53.21	52.67	52.18	51.75	51.37	50.71	49.56
7000	71.30	69.54	68.01	66.68	65.52	64.49	63.59	62.79	62.08	61.44	60.88	60.38	59.93	59.16	57.82
8000	81.49	79.48	77.73	76.21	74.88	73.71	72.67	71.76	70.94	70.22	69.57	69.00	68.49	67.61	66.08
9000	91.67	89.41	87.45	85.73	84.24	82.92	81.75	80.73	79.81	79.00	78.27	77.63	77.05	76.06	74.34
10000	101.86	99.34	97.16	95.26	93.59	92.13	90.84	89.69	88.68	87.78	86.97	86.25	85.61	84.51	82.60
11000	112.04	109.28	106.88	104.79	102.95	101.34	99.92	98.66	97.55	96.55	95.67	94.88	94.17	92.96	90.86
12000	122.23	119.21	116.59	114.31	112.31	110.56	109.00	107.63	106.41	105.33	104.36	103.50	102.73	101.41	99.12
13000	132.41	129.14	126.31	123.84	121.67	119.77	118.09	116.60	115.28	114.11	113.06	112.12	111.29	109.86	107.38
14000	142.60	139.08	136.02	133.36	131.03	128.98	127.17	125.57	124.15	122.88	121.76	120.75	119.85	118.31	115.64
15000	152.78	149.01	145.74	142.89	140.39	138.19	136.25	134.54	133.02	131.66	130.45	129.37	128.41	126.76	123.90
16000	162.97	158.95	155.46	152.41	149.75	147.41	145.34	143.51	141.88	140.44	139.15	138.00	136.97	135.22	132.16
17000	173.16	168.88	165.17	161.94	159.11	156.62	154.42	152.48	150.75	149.22	147.85	146.62	145.53	143.67	140.42
18000	183.34	178.81	174.89	171.46	168.47	165.83	163.50	161.45	159.62	157.99	156.54	155.25	154.09	152.12	148.68
19000	193.53	188.75	184.60	180.99	177.83	175.04	172.59	170.41	168.49	166.77	165.24	163.87	162.65	160.57	156.94
20000	203.71	198.68	194.32	190.52	187.18	184.26	181.67	179.38	177.35	175.55	173.94	172.50	171.21	169.02	165.20
21000	213.90	208.62	204.03	200.04	196.54	193.47	190.75	188.35	186.22	184.32	182.63	181.12	179.77	177.47	173.46
22000	224.08	218.55	213.75	209.57	205.90	202.68	199.84	197.32	195.09	193.10	191.33	189.75	188.33	185.92	181.72
23000	234.27	228.48	223.47	219.09	215.26	211.89	208.92	206.29	203.96	201.88	200.03	198.37	196.89	194.37	189.98
24000	244.45	238.42	233.18	228.62	224.62	221.11	218.00	215.26	212.82	210.65	208.72	206.99	205.45	202.82	198.24
25000	254.64	248.35	242.90	238.14	233.98	230.32	227.09	224.23	221.69	219.43	217.42	215.62	214.01	211.27	206.50
26000	264.82	258.28	252.61	247.67	243.34	239.53	236.17	233.20	230.56	228.21	226.11	224.24	222.57	219.72	214.76
27000	275.01	268.22	262.33	257.19	252.70	248.74	245.25	242.17	239.43	236.99	234.81	232.87	231.13	228.17	223.02
28000	285.19	278.15	272.04	266.72	262.06	257.96	254.34	251.14	248.29	245.76	243.51	241.49	239.69	236.62	231.28
29000	295.38	288.09	281.76	276.25	271.42	267.17	263.42	260.10	257.16	254.54	252.20	250.12	248.25	245.07	239.54
30000	305.56	298.02	291.48	285.77	280.77	276.38	272.50	269.07	266.03	263.32	260.90	258.74	256.81	253.52	247.80
35000	356.49	347.69	340.05	333.40	327.57	322.44	317.92	313.92	310.36	307.20	304.38	301.87	299.61	295.78	289.10
40000	407.42	397.36	388.63	381.03	374.36	368.51	363.34	358.76	354.70	351.09	347.87	344.99	342.44	338.03	330.40
45000	458.34	447.03	437.21	428.65	421.16	414.57	408.75	403.61	399.04	394.97	391.35	388.11	385.21	380.28	371.70
50000	509.27	496.70	485.79	476.28	467.95	460.63	454.17	448.45	443.38	438.86	434.83	431.23	428.01	422.54	412.99

MONTHLY PAYMENT
10% REQUIRED TO AMORTIZE A LOAN

TERM AMOUNT	1 YEAR	2 YEARS	3 YEARS	4 YEARS	5 YEARS	6 YEARS	7 YEARS	8 YEARS	9 YEARS	10 YEARS	11 YEARS	12 YEARS	13 YEARS	14 YEARS	15 YEARS
$100	8.79	4.61	3.22	2.53	2.12	1.85	1.65	1.51	1.40	1.32	1.25	1.19	1.14	1.10	1.07
200	17.57	9.22	6.44	5.06	4.23	3.69	3.30	3.02	2.80	2.63	2.49	2.37	2.28	2.20	2.13
300	26.35	13.82	9.66	7.58	6.35	5.53	4.95	4.53	4.20	3.94	3.73	3.56	3.41	3.29	3.19
400	35.13	18.43	12.87	10.11	8.46	7.37	6.60	6.03	5.59	5.25	4.97	4.74	4.55	4.39	4.25
500	43.92	23.03	16.09	12.64	10.58	9.22	8.25	7.54	6.99	6.56	6.21	5.92	5.68	5.49	5.32
600	52.70	27.64	19.31	15.16	12.69	11.06	9.90	9.05	8.39	7.87	7.45	7.11	6.82	6.58	6.38
700	61.48	32.24	22.53	17.69	14.81	12.90	11.55	10.55	9.78	9.18	8.69	8.29	7.96	7.68	7.44
800	70.26	36.85	25.74	20.22	16.92	14.74	13.20	12.06	11.18	10.49	9.93	9.47	9.09	8.77	8.50
900	79.04	41.45	28.96	22.74	19.04	16.59	14.85	13.57	12.58	11.80	11.17	10.66	10.23	9.87	9.57
1000	87.83	46.06	32.18	25.27	21.15	18.43	16.50	15.07	13.97	13.11	12.41	11.84	11.36	10.97	10.63
2000	175.65	92.11	64.35	50.54	42.30	36.85	33.00	30.14	27.94	26.21	24.82	23.67	22.72	21.93	21.25
3000	263.47	138.16	96.52	75.80	63.45	55.28	49.50	45.21	41.91	39.32	37.22	35.51	34.08	32.89	31.87
4000	351.29	184.21	128.69	101.07	84.60	73.70	65.99	60.27	55.88	52.42	49.63	47.34	45.43	43.85	42.50
5000	439.11	230.26	160.87	126.34	105.74	92.13	82.49	75.34	69.85	65.52	62.03	59.18	56.80	54.81	53.12
6000	526.94	276.31	193.04	151.60	126.89	110.55	98.99	90.41	83.82	78.63	74.44	71.01	68.16	65.77	63.74
7000	614.76	322.37	225.21	176.86	148.04	128.97	115.48	105.48	97.79	91.73	86.85	82.84	79.51	76.73	74.36
8000	702.58	368.42	257.38	202.13	169.19	147.40	131.98	120.54	111.76	104.83	99.25	94.68	90.88	87.69	84.99
9000	790.40	414.47	289.56	227.40	190.33	165.82	148.48	135.61	125.73	117.94	111.66	106.51	102.24	98.65	95.61
10000	878.22	460.52	321.73	252.67	211.48	184.25	164.97	150.68	139.70	131.04	124.06	118.35	113.60	109.61	106.23
11000	966.05	506.57	353.90	277.93	232.63	202.67	181.47	165.75	153.67	144.14	136.47	130.18	124.96	120.57	116.85
12000	1053.87	552.62	386.07	303.19	253.78	221.09	197.97	180.81	167.64	157.25	148.87	142.02	136.32	131.54	127.48
13000	1141.69	598.68	418.25	328.46	274.93	239.52	214.46	195.88	181.61	170.35	161.28	153.85	147.68	142.50	138.10
14000	1229.51	644.73	450.42	353.72	296.07	257.94	230.96	210.95	195.58	183.45	173.69	165.68	159.04	153.46	148.72
15000	1317.33	690.78	482.59	378.99	317.22	276.37	247.46	226.02	209.55	196.56	186.09	177.52	170.39	164.42	159.35
16000	1405.16	736.83	514.76	404.25	338.37	294.79	263.96	241.08	223.52	209.66	198.50	189.35	181.75	175.38	169.97
17000	1492.98	782.88	546.93	429.52	359.52	313.21	280.45	256.15	237.49	222.76	210.90	201.19	193.11	186.34	180.59
18000	1580.80	828.93	579.11	454.79	380.66	331.64	296.95	271.22	251.45	235.87	223.31	213.02	204.47	197.30	191.21
19000	1668.62	874.99	611.28	480.05	401.81	350.06	313.45	286.29	265.42	248.97	235.71	224.86	215.83	208.26	201.84
20000	1756.44	921.04	643.45	505.32	422.96	368.49	329.94	301.35	279.39	262.07	248.12	236.69	227.19	219.22	212.46
21000	1844.26	967.09	675.62	530.58	444.11	386.91	346.44	316.42	293.36	275.18	260.53	248.52	238.55	230.18	223.08
22000	1932.09	1013.14	707.80	555.85	465.26	405.33	362.94	331.49	307.33	288.28	272.93	260.36	249.91	241.14	233.70
23000	2019.91	1059.19	739.97	581.11	486.40	423.76	379.43	346.56	321.30	301.38	285.34	272.19	261.28	252.11	244.33
24000	2107.73	1105.24	772.14	606.38	507.55	442.18	395.93	361.62	335.27	314.49	297.74	284.03	272.64	263.07	254.95
25000	2195.55	1151.30	804.31	631.64	528.70	460.61	412.43	376.69	349.24	327.59	310.15	295.86	284.00	274.03	265.57
26000	2283.37	1197.35	836.49	656.91	549.85	479.03	428.92	391.76	363.21	340.69	322.55	307.70	295.36	284.99	276.20
27000	2371.20	1243.40	868.66	682.18	570.99	497.45	445.42	406.82	377.18	353.80	334.96	319.53	306.72	295.95	286.82
28000	2459.02	1289.45	900.83	707.44	592.14	515.88	461.92	421.89	391.15	366.90	347.37	331.36	318.07	306.91	297.44
29000	2546.84	1335.50	933.00	732.71	613.29	534.30	478.42	436.96	405.12	380.00	359.77	343.20	329.43	317.87	308.06
30000	2634.66	1381.55	965.18	757.97	634.44	552.73	494.91	452.02	419.09	393.11	372.18	355.03	340.79	328.83	318.69
35000	3073.77	1611.81	1126.04	884.30	740.17	644.85	577.40	527.36	488.94	458.62	434.21	414.20	397.59	383.64	371.80
40000	3512.88	1842.07	1286.90	1010.63	845.91	736.97	659.88	602.70	558.78	524.14	496.23	473.38	454.39	438.44	424.91
45000	3951.99	2072.33	1447.76	1136.96	951.65	829.09	742.37	678.04	628.63	589.66	558.26	532.55	511.19	493.25	478.03
50000	4391.10	2302.59	1608.62	1263.28	1057.39	921.21	824.85	753.37	698.48	655.17	620.29	591.72	567.99	548.05	531.14

MONTHLY PAYMENT
REQUIRED TO AMORTIZE A LOAN

10 %

TERM AMOUNT	16 YEARS	17 YEARS	18 YEARS	19 YEARS	20 YEARS	21 YEARS	22 YEARS	23 YEARS	24 YEARS	25 YEARS	26 YEARS	27 YEARS	28 YEARS	30 YEARS	35 YEARS
$100	1.04	1.01	.99	.97	.96	.94	.93	.92	.91	.90	.89	.88	.88	.87	.85
200	2.07	2.03	1.98	1.94	1.91	1.88	1.85	1.83	1.81	1.79	1.78	1.76	1.75	1.73	1.69
300	3.11	3.04	2.97	2.91	2.86	2.82	2.78	2.74	2.71	2.69	2.66	2.64	2.62	2.59	2.54
400	4.14	4.04	3.95	3.88	3.81	3.75	3.70	3.66	3.62	3.58	3.55	3.52	3.50	3.46	3.38
500	5.17	5.05	4.94	4.85	4.76	4.69	4.63	4.57	4.52	4.48	4.44	4.40	4.37	4.32	4.23
600	6.21	6.06	5.93	5.81	5.71	5.63	5.55	5.48	5.42	5.37	5.32	5.28	5.24	5.18	5.07
700	7.24	7.06	6.91	6.78	6.67	6.57	6.48	6.40	6.33	6.27	6.21	6.16	6.12	6.04	5.91
800	8.27	8.07	7.90	7.75	7.62	7.50	7.40	7.31	7.23	7.16	7.10	7.04	6.99	6.91	6.76
900	9.31	9.08	8.89	8.72	8.57	8.44	8.33	8.22	8.13	8.06	7.98	7.92	7.86	7.77	7.60
1000	10.34	10.09	9.87	9.69	9.52	9.38	9.25	9.14	9.04	8.95	8.87	8.80	8.74	8.63	8.45
2000	20.67	20.17	19.74	19.37	19.04	18.75	18.50	18.27	18.07	17.90	17.74	17.60	17.47	17.26	16.89
3000	31.01	30.26	29.61	29.05	28.55	28.12	27.74	27.40	27.10	26.84	26.60	26.39	26.20	25.89	25.33
4000	41.34	40.34	39.48	38.73	38.07	37.49	36.99	36.54	36.14	35.78	35.47	35.19	34.94	34.51	33.77
5000	51.67	50.43	49.35	48.41	47.58	46.87	46.23	45.67	45.17	44.73	44.34	43.98	43.67	43.14	42.22
6000	62.01	60.51	59.22	58.09	57.10	56.24	55.48	54.80	54.20	53.67	53.20	52.78	52.40	51.77	50.66
7000	72.34	70.60	69.09	67.77	66.62	65.61	64.72	63.94	63.24	62.62	62.07	61.58	61.14	60.39	59.10
8000	82.67	80.68	78.96	77.45	76.14	74.98	73.97	73.07	72.27	71.56	70.93	70.37	69.87	69.02	67.54
9000	93.01	90.77	88.82	87.13	85.65	84.36	83.21	82.20	81.30	80.51	79.80	79.17	78.60	77.65	75.99
10000	103.34	100.85	98.69	96.81	95.17	93.73	92.46	91.33	90.34	89.45	88.67	87.96	87.34	86.27	84.43
11000	113.67	110.93	108.56	106.50	104.69	103.10	101.70	100.47	99.37	98.40	97.53	96.76	96.07	94.90	92.87
12000	124.01	121.02	118.43	116.18	114.20	112.47	110.95	109.60	108.40	107.34	106.40	105.56	104.80	103.53	101.31
13000	134.34	131.10	128.30	125.86	123.72	121.85	120.19	118.73	117.44	116.29	115.26	114.35	113.54	112.15	109.76
14000	144.67	141.19	138.17	135.54	133.24	131.22	129.44	127.87	126.47	125.23	124.13	123.15	122.27	120.78	118.20
15000	155.01	151.27	148.04	145.22	142.75	140.59	138.68	137.00	135.50	134.18	133.00	131.94	131.00	129.41	126.64
16000	165.34	161.36	157.91	154.90	152.27	149.96	147.93	146.13	144.54	143.12	141.86	140.74	139.74	138.03	135.08
17000	175.67	171.44	167.77	164.58	161.79	159.33	157.17	155.26	153.57	152.07	150.73	149.53	148.47	146.66	143.52
18000	186.01	181.53	177.64	174.26	171.30	168.71	166.42	164.40	162.60	161.01	159.60	158.33	157.20	155.29	151.97
19000	196.34	191.61	187.51	183.94	180.82	178.08	175.66	173.53	171.64	169.96	168.46	167.12	165.93	163.91	160.41
20000	206.67	201.69	197.38	193.62	190.34	187.45	184.91	182.66	180.67	178.90	177.33	175.92	174.67	172.54	168.85
21000	217.01	211.78	207.25	203.30	199.85	196.82	194.16	191.80	189.70	187.85	186.19	184.72	183.40	181.17	177.29
22000	227.34	221.86	217.12	212.98	209.37	206.20	203.40	200.93	198.74	196.79	195.06	193.51	192.13	189.80	185.74
23000	237.68	231.95	226.99	222.67	218.89	215.57	212.65	210.06	207.77	205.74	203.93	202.31	200.87	198.42	194.18
24000	248.01	242.03	236.86	232.35	228.40	224.94	221.89	219.19	216.80	214.68	212.79	211.11	209.60	207.05	202.62
25000	258.34	252.12	246.72	242.03	237.94	234.32	231.14	228.33	225.84	223.63	221.66	219.90	218.33	215.67	211.06
26000	268.68	262.20	256.59	251.71	247.44	243.69	240.38	237.41	234.90	232.57	230.52	228.70	227.07	224.30	219.50
27000	279.01	272.29	266.46	261.39	256.95	253.06	249.63	246.59	243.90	241.52	239.39	237.49	235.80	232.93	227.95
28000	289.34	282.37	276.33	271.07	266.47	262.44	258.87	255.73	252.94	250.46	248.26	246.29	244.53	241.56	236.39
29000	299.68	292.45	286.20	280.75	275.99	271.80	268.12	264.86	261.97	259.41	257.12	255.09	253.27	250.18	244.83
30000	310.01	302.54	296.07	290.43	285.50	281.18	277.36	273.99	271.00	268.35	265.99	263.88	262.00	258.81	253.27
35000	361.68	352.96	345.41	338.84	333.09	328.04	323.59	319.66	316.17	313.08	310.32	307.86	305.66	301.94	295.49
40000	413.34	403.38	394.76	387.24	380.67	374.90	369.82	365.32	361.34	357.80	354.65	351.86	349.33	345.07	337.70
45000	465.01	453.81	444.10	435.65	428.25	421.76	416.04	410.99	406.50	402.52	398.98	395.82	393.00	388.21	379.91
50000	516.68	504.23	493.44	484.05	475.84	468.62	462.27	456.65	451.67	447.25	443.31	439.80	436.66	431.34	422.12

MONTHLY PAYMENT
10¼% REQUIRED TO AMORTIZE A LOAN

TERM AMOUNT	1 YEAR	2 YEARS	3 YEARS	4 YEARS	5 YEARS	6 YEARS	7 YEARS	8 YEARS	9 YEARS	10 YEARS	11 YEARS	12 YEARS	13 YEARS	14 YEARS	15 YEARS
$100	8.80	4.62	3.23	2.54	2.13	1.86	1.67	1.52	1.41	1.33	1.26	1.20	1.16	1.12	1.08
200	17.59	9.24	6.46	5.08	4.26	3.71	3.33	3.04	2.82	2.65	2.51	2.40	2.31	2.23	2.16
300	26.39	13.85	9.69	7.62	6.38	5.57	4.99	4.56	4.23	3.98	3.77	3.60	3.46	3.34	3.24
400	35.18	18.47	12.92	10.16	8.51	7.42	6.65	6.08	5.64	5.30	5.02	4.79	4.61	4.45	4.31
500	43.97	23.09	16.15	12.70	10.64	9.28	8.32	7.60	7.05	6.62	6.28	5.99	5.76	5.56	5.39
600	52.77	27.70	19.38	15.23	12.76	11.13	9.98	9.12	8.46	7.95	7.53	7.19	6.91	6.67	6.47
700	61.56	32.32	22.60	17.77	14.89	12.99	11.64	10.64	9.87	9.27	8.78	8.39	8.06	7.78	7.54
800	70.35	36.93	25.83	20.31	17.02	14.84	13.30	12.16	11.28	10.59	10.04	9.58	9.21	8.89	8.62
900	79.15	41.55	29.06	22.85	19.14	16.70	14.96	13.68	12.69	11.92	11.29	10.78	10.36	10.00	9.70
1000	87.94	46.17	32.29	25.39	21.27	18.55	16.63	15.20	14.10	13.24	12.55	11.98	11.51	11.11	10.77
2000	175.87	92.33	64.57	50.77	42.54	37.09	33.25	30.39	28.20	26.48	25.09	23.95	23.01	22.21	21.54
3000	263.81	138.49	96.86	76.15	63.80	55.64	49.87	45.59	42.30	39.71	37.63	35.92	34.51	33.32	32.31
4000	351.74	184.65	129.14	101.53	85.07	74.18	66.49	60.78	56.40	52.95	50.17	47.90	46.01	44.42	43.08
5000	439.67	230.82	161.43	126.91	106.33	92.73	83.11	75.98	70.50	66.18	62.71	59.87	57.51	55.53	53.85
6000	527.61	276.98	193.71	152.29	127.60	111.27	99.73	91.17	84.60	79.42	75.25	71.84	69.01	66.63	64.62
7000	615.54	323.14	226.00	177.67	148.86	129.82	116.35	106.36	98.70	92.66	87.79	83.81	80.51	77.74	75.39
8000	703.47	369.30	258.28	203.05	170.13	148.36	132.97	121.56	112.80	105.89	100.33	95.79	92.01	88.84	86.16
9000	791.41	415.47	290.57	228.43	191.40	166.90	149.59	136.75	126.90	119.13	112.88	107.76	103.51	99.95	96.93
10000	879.34	461.63	322.85	253.81	212.66	185.45	166.21	151.95	141.00	132.36	125.42	119.73	115.01	111.05	107.70
11000	967.27	507.79	355.14	279.19	233.93	203.99	182.83	167.14	155.09	145.60	137.96	131.70	126.51	122.16	118.47
12000	1055.21	553.95	387.42	304.57	255.19	222.54	199.45	182.33	169.19	158.84	150.50	143.68	138.01	133.26	129.23
13000	1143.14	600.12	419.71	329.95	276.46	241.09	216.07	197.53	183.29	172.07	163.04	155.65	149.51	144.37	140.00
14000	1231.07	646.28	451.99	355.33	297.72	259.63	232.69	212.72	197.39	185.31	175.58	167.62	161.02	155.47	150.77
15000	1319.01	692.44	484.28	380.72	318.99	278.18	249.32	227.92	211.49	198.54	188.12	179.59	172.52	166.58	161.54
16000	1406.94	738.60	516.56	406.10	340.25	296.72	265.94	243.11	225.59	211.78	200.66	191.57	184.02	177.68	172.31
17000	1494.87	784.76	548.85	431.48	361.52	315.27	282.56	258.31	239.69	225.02	213.21	203.54	195.52	188.79	183.08
18000	1582.81	830.93	581.13	456.86	382.79	333.81	299.18	273.50	253.79	238.25	225.75	215.51	207.02	199.89	193.85
19000	1670.74	877.09	613.42	482.24	404.05	352.36	315.80	288.69	267.89	251.49	238.29	227.48	218.52	210.99	204.62
20000	1758.67	923.25	645.70	507.62	425.32	370.90	332.42	303.89	281.99	264.72	250.83	239.46	230.02	222.10	215.39
21000	1846.61	969.41	677.99	533.00	446.58	389.45	349.04	319.08	296.09	277.96	263.37	251.43	241.52	233.20	226.16
22000	1934.54	1015.58	710.27	558.38	467.85	407.99	365.66	334.28	310.19	291.20	275.91	263.40	253.02	244.31	236.93
23000	2022.47	1061.74	742.56	583.76	489.11	426.54	382.28	349.47	324.28	304.43	288.45	275.37	264.52	255.41	247.70
24000	2110.41	1107.90	774.84	609.14	510.38	445.08	398.90	364.66	338.38	317.67	300.99	287.35	276.02	266.52	258.46
25000	2198.34	1154.06	807.13	634.52	531.65	463.63	415.52	379.86	352.48	330.90	313.54	299.32	287.52	277.62	269.23
26000	2286.27	1200.23	839.41	659.90	552.91	482.17	432.14	395.05	366.58	344.14	326.08	311.29	299.02	288.73	280.00
27000	2374.21	1246.39	871.70	685.28	574.18	500.72	448.76	410.25	380.68	357.38	338.62	323.26	310.52	299.83	290.77
28000	2462.14	1292.55	903.98	710.66	595.44	519.26	465.38	425.44	394.78	370.61	351.16	335.24	322.03	310.94	301.54
29000	2550.07	1338.71	936.27	736.05	616.71	537.81	482.00	440.64	408.88	383.85	363.70	347.21	333.53	322.04	312.31
30000	2638.01	1384.88	968.55	761.43	637.97	556.35	498.63	455.83	422.98	397.08	376.24	359.18	345.03	333.15	323.08
35000	3077.68	1615.69	1129.98	888.33	744.30	649.08	581.73	531.80	493.47	463.26	438.95	419.05	402.53	388.67	376.93
40000	3517.34	1846.50	1291.40	1015.23	850.63	741.80	664.83	607.77	563.97	529.44	501.65	478.92	460.03	444.19	430.77
45000	3957.01	2077.31	1452.83	1142.14	956.96	834.52	747.94	683.74	634.47	595.62	564.36	538.77	517.54	499.72	484.62
50000	4396.68	2308.12	1614.25	1269.04	1063.29	927.25	831.04	759.71	704.96	661.80	627.07	598.63	575.04	555.24	538.46

MONTHLY PAYMENT
REQUIRED TO AMORTIZE A LOAN   10¼%

TERM AMOUNT	35 YEARS	30 YEARS	28 YEARS	27 YEARS	26 YEARS	25 YEARS	24 YEARS	23 YEARS	22 YEARS	21 YEARS	20 YEARS	19 YEARS	18 YEARS	17 YEARS	16 YEARS
$100	.87	.89	.90	.90	.91	.92	.93	.93	.95	.96	.97	.99	1.01	1.03	1.05
200	1.73	1.77	1.79	1.80	1.81	1.83	1.85	1.86	1.89	1.91	1.94	1.97	2.01	2.05	2.10
300	2.59	2.65	2.68	2.70	2.72	2.74	2.77	2.79	2.83	2.86	2.91	2.96	3.01	3.08	3.15
400	3.46	3.53	3.57	3.59	3.62	3.65	3.69	3.72	3.77	3.82	3.88	3.94	4.01	4.10	4.20
500	4.32	4.41	4.46	4.49	4.52	4.56	4.61	4.65	4.71	4.77	4.84	4.92	5.02	5.12	5.25
600	5.18	5.29	5.35	5.39	5.43	5.47	5.53	5.58	5.65	5.72	5.81	5.91	6.02	6.15	6.29
700	6.04	6.17	6.24	6.28	6.33	6.38	6.45	6.51	6.59	6.68	6.78	6.89	7.02	7.18	7.34
800	6.91	7.05	7.13	7.18	7.23	7.30	7.37	7.44	7.53	7.63	7.75	7.87	8.03	8.19	8.39
900	7.77	7.93	8.02	8.07	8.14	8.21	8.29	8.37	8.47	8.58	8.71	8.86	9.03	9.22	9.44
1000	8.63	8.81	8.91	8.97	9.04	9.12	9.21	9.30	9.41	9.54	9.68	9.84	10.03	10.24	10.49
2000	17.26	17.61	17.82	17.94	18.08	18.23	18.41	18.60	18.82	19.07	19.36	19.68	20.05	20.48	20.97
3000	25.88	26.42	26.73	26.91	27.11	27.35	27.61	27.90	28.23	28.60	29.03	29.52	30.07	30.72	31.45
4000	34.51	35.22	35.63	35.88	36.15	36.46	36.81	37.20	37.64	38.14	38.71	39.35	40.10	40.95	41.94
5000	43.13	44.02	44.54	44.85	45.19	45.57	46.01	46.49	47.05	47.67	48.38	49.19	50.12	51.19	52.42
6000	51.76	52.83	53.45	53.81	54.22	54.69	55.21	55.79	56.46	57.20	58.06	59.03	60.14	61.42	62.90
7000	60.38	61.63	62.35	62.78	63.26	63.80	64.41	65.09	65.86	66.74	67.73	68.87	70.16	71.66	73.38
8000	69.01	70.43	71.26	71.75	72.30	72.91	73.61	74.39	75.27	76.27	77.41	78.70	80.19	81.89	83.87
9000	77.64	79.24	80.17	80.72	81.33	82.03	82.81	83.69	84.68	85.81	87.09	88.54	90.21	92.13	94.35
10000	86.26	88.04	89.08	89.69	90.37	91.14	92.01	92.98	94.09	95.34	96.76	98.38	100.23	102.37	104.83
11000	94.89	96.84	97.98	98.65	99.40	100.25	101.21	102.28	103.49	104.87	106.43	108.21	110.28	112.60	115.31
12000	103.51	105.65	106.89	107.62	108.44	109.37	110.41	111.58	112.90	114.41	116.11	118.05	120.28	122.84	125.80
13000	112.14	114.45	115.80	116.59	117.48	118.48	119.61	120.88	122.31	123.94	125.78	127.89	130.30	133.07	136.28
14000	120.76	123.26	124.70	125.56	126.52	127.59	128.81	130.17	131.72	133.47	135.46	137.73	140.33	143.31	146.76
15000	129.39	132.06	133.61	134.53	135.55	136.71	138.01	139.47	141.13	143.01	145.14	157.56	150.35	153.55	157.24
16000	138.01	140.86	142.52	143.50	144.59	145.82	147.21	148.77	150.54	152.54	154.81	157.40	160.37	163.78	167.73
17000	146.64	149.67	151.43	152.46	153.63	154.94	156.41	158.07	159.94	162.07	164.49	167.24	170.39	174.02	178.20
18000	155.27	158.47	160.33	161.43	162.66	164.05	165.61	167.37	169.35	171.61	174.16	177.08	180.42	184.25	188.69
19000	163.89	167.27	169.24	170.40	171.70	173.16	174.81	176.66	178.76	181.14	183.83	186.91	190.44	194.49	199.17
20000	172.52	176.08	178.15	179.37	180.74	182.28	184.01	185.96	188.17	190.67	193.51	196.75	200.46	204.72	209.65
21000	181.14	184.88	187.05	188.34	189.77	191.39	193.21	195.26	197.58	200.20	203.19	206.59	210.48	214.96	220.13
22000	189.77	193.68	195.96	197.30	198.81	200.50	202.41	204.56	206.98	209.73	212.86	216.42	220.51	225.19	230.62
23000	198.39	202.49	204.87	206.27	207.85	209.62	211.61	213.86	216.39	219.27	222.54	226.26	230.53	235.43	241.10
24000	207.02	211.29	213.77	215.24	216.88	218.73	220.81	223.15	225.80	228.80	232.21	236.10	240.55	245.67	251.58
25000	215.65	220.10	222.68	224.21	225.92	227.85	230.01	232.45	235.21	238.33	241.89	245.94	250.57	255.91	262.07
26000	224.27	228.90	231.59	233.18	234.96	236.96	239.21	241.75	244.62	247.87	251.56	255.77	260.60	266.14	272.55
27000	232.90	237.70	240.49	242.14	243.99	246.07	248.41	251.05	254.03	257.40	261.24	265.61	270.62	276.38	283.03
28000	241.52	246.51	249.40	251.11	253.03	255.19	257.61	260.34	263.43	266.93	270.91	275.45	280.64	286.61	293.51
29000	250.15	255.31	258.31	260.08	262.07	264.30	266.81	269.64	272.84	276.46	280.59	285.29	290.66	296.85	303.99
30000	258.77	264.11	267.22	269.05	271.10	273.41	276.01	278.94	282.25	286.00	290.26	295.12	300.69	307.09	314.48
35000	301.90	308.13	311.75	313.89	316.29	318.98	322.01	325.43	329.29	333.67	338.64	344.31	350.80	358.27	366.89
40000	345.03	352.15	356.62	358.57	361.47	364.55	368.01	371.92	376.33	381.33	387.02	393.53	400.91	409.31	419.31
45000	388.16	396.17	400.82	403.57	406.65	410.12	414.01	418.41	423.37	429.00	435.39	442.68	451.03	460.63	471.72
50000	431.29	440.19	445.36	448.41	451.84	455.69	460.02	464.90	470.41	476.66	483.77	491.87	501.14	511.81	524.13

MONTHLY PAYMENT
10½ % REQUIRED TO AMORTIZE A LOAN

TERM AMOUNT	15 YEARS	14 YEARS	13 YEARS	12 YEARS	11 YEARS	10 YEARS	9 YEARS	8 YEARS	7 YEARS	6 YEARS	5 YEARS	4 YEARS	3 YEARS	2 YEARS	1 YEAR
$100	1.10	1.13	1.17	1.22	1.27	1.34	1.43	1.54	1.68	1.87	2.14	2.55	3.24	4.63	8.81
200	2.19	2.25	2.33	2.43	2.54	2.68	2.85	3.07	3.35	3.74	4.28	5.10	6.48	9.26	17.61
300	3.28	3.38	3.50	3.64	3.81	4.02	4.27	4.60	5.03	5.60	6.42	7.65	9.72	13.89	26.42
400	4.37	4.50	4.66	4.85	5.08	5.35	5.70	6.13	6.70	7.47	8.56	10.20	12.96	18.51	35.22
500	5.46	5.63	5.83	6.06	6.34	6.69	7.12	7.67	8.38	9.34	10.70	12.75	16.20	23.14	44.03
600	6.55	6.75	6.99	7.27	7.61	8.03	8.54	9.20	10.05	11.20	12.84	15.30	19.44	27.77	52.83
700	7.65	7.88	8.15	8.48	8.88	9.36	9.97	10.73	11.73	13.07	14.97	17.85	22.68	32.40	61.64
800	8.74	9.00	9.32	9.69	10.15	10.70	11.39	12.26	13.40	14.94	17.11	20.40	25.92	37.02	70.44
900	9.83	10.13	10.48	10.91	11.41	12.04	12.81	13.79	15.08	16.80	19.25	22.95	29.16	41.65	79.25
1000	10.92	11.25	11.65	12.12	12.68	13.37	14.23	15.33	16.75	18.67	21.39	25.50	32.40	46.28	88.05
2000	21.84	22.50	23.29	24.23	25.36	26.74	28.46	30.65	33.49	37.34	42.77	51.00	64.80	92.55	176.09
3000	32.75	33.75	34.93	36.34	38.04	40.11	42.69	45.97	50.24	56.00	64.16	76.49	97.20	138.82	264.14
4000	43.67	45.00	46.58	48.45	50.71	53.48	56.92	61.29	66.98	74.67	85.54	101.99	129.60	185.10	352.18
5000	54.59	56.25	58.22	60.56	63.39	66.85	71.15	76.61	83.73	93.34	106.92	127.49	161.99	231.37	440.23
6000	65.50	67.50	69.86	72.67	76.07	80.22	85.38	91.93	100.47	112.00	128.31	152.98	194.39	277.64	528.27
7000	76.42	78.75	81.50	84.79	88.75	93.59	99.61	107.25	117.22	130.67	149.69	178.48	226.79	323.92	616.32
8000	87.34	90.00	93.15	96.90	101.42	106.96	113.84	122.58	133.96	149.33	171.08	203.97	259.19	370.19	704.36
9000	98.25	101.25	104.79	109.01	114.10	120.33	128.07	137.90	150.71	168.00	192.46	229.47	291.59	416.46	792.41
10000	109.17	112.50	116.43	121.12	126.78	133.70	142.30	153.22	167.45	186.67	213.84	254.97	323.98	462.74	880.45
11000	120.09	123.75	128.07	133.23	139.46	147.07	156.53	168.54	184.20	205.33	235.23	280.46	356.38	509.01	968.50
12000	131.00	135.00	139.72	145.34	152.14	160.44	170.76	183.86	200.94	224.00	256.61	305.96	388.78	555.28	1056.54
13000	141.92	146.25	151.36	157.46	164.81	173.80	184.99	199.18	217.69	242.66	277.99	331.45	421.17	601.55	1144.59
14000	152.83	157.49	163.00	169.57	177.49	187.17	199.22	214.50	234.43	261.33	299.38	356.95	453.57	647.83	1232.63
15000	163.75	168.74	174.64	181.68	190.17	200.54	213.45	229.83	251.18	280.00	320.76	382.45	485.97	694.10	1320.68
16000	174.67	179.99	186.29	193.79	202.84	213.91	227.67	245.15	267.92	298.66	342.15	407.94	518.37	740.37	1408.72
17000	185.58	191.24	197.93	205.90	215.52	227.28	241.90	260.47	284.67	317.33	363.53	433.44	550.76	786.65	1496.77
18000	196.50	202.49	209.57	218.01	228.20	240.65	256.13	275.79	301.41	335.99	384.91	458.93	583.16	832.92	1584.81
19000	207.42	213.74	221.21	230.13	240.87	254.02	270.36	291.11	318.16	354.66	406.30	484.43	615.56	879.19	1672.86
20000	218.33	224.99	232.86	242.24	253.55	267.39	284.59	306.43	334.90	373.33	427.68	509.93	647.96	925.47	1760.90
21000	229.25	236.24	244.50	254.35	266.23	280.76	298.82	321.75	351.65	391.99	449.06	535.42	680.35	971.74	1848.95
22000	240.17	247.49	256.14	266.46	278.91	294.13	313.05	337.07	368.39	410.66	470.45	560.92	712.75	1018.01	1936.99
23000	251.08	258.74	267.78	278.57	291.58	307.50	327.28	352.40	385.14	429.32	491.83	586.41	745.15	1064.29	2025.04
24000	262.00	269.99	279.43	290.68	304.26	320.87	341.51	367.72	401.88	447.99	513.21	611.91	777.55	1110.56	2113.08
25000	272.92	281.24	291.07	302.79	316.94	334.23	355.74	383.04	418.63	466.66	534.60	637.41	809.94	1156.83	2201.13
26000	283.83	292.49	302.71	314.91	329.62	347.60	369.97	398.36	435.37	485.32	555.98	662.90	842.34	1203.10	2289.17
27000	294.75	303.74	314.35	327.02	342.29	360.97	384.20	413.68	452.12	503.99	577.37	688.40	874.74	1249.38	2377.22
28000	305.66	314.98	326.00	339.13	354.97	374.34	398.43	429.00	468.86	522.65	598.75	713.89	907.14	1295.65	2465.26
29000	316.58	326.23	337.64	351.24	367.65	387.71	412.66	444.32	485.61	541.32	620.14	739.39	939.54	1341.92	2553.31
30000	327.50	337.48	349.28	363.35	380.33	401.08	426.89	459.65	502.35	559.99	641.52	764.89	971.93	1388.20	2641.35
35000	382.08	393.73	407.49	423.91	443.71	467.93	498.03	536.25	586.08	653.32	748.44	892.37	1133.92	1619.56	3081.58
40000	436.66	449.98	465.71	484.47	507.10	534.77	569.18	612.86	669.80	746.65	855.36	1019.85	1295.91	1850.93	3521.80
45000	491.24	506.22	523.92	545.03	570.49	601.62	640.33	689.47	753.52	839.98	962.28	1147.33	1457.90	2082.29	3962.03
50000	545.83	562.47	582.13	605.58	633.87	668.46	711.47	766.07	837.25	933.31	1069.20	1274.81	1619.88	2313.66	4402.25

MONTHLY PAYMENT
REQUIRED TO AMORTIZE A LOAN 10½%

TERM AMOUNT	35 YEARS	30 YEARS	28 YEARS	27 YEARS	26 YEARS	25 YEARS	24 YEARS	23 YEARS	22 YEARS	21 YEARS	20 YEARS	19 YEARS	18 YEARS	17 YEARS	16 YEARS
$100	.89	.90	.91	.92	.93	.93	.94	.95	.96	.97	.99	1.00	1.02	1.04	1.07
200	1.77	1.80	1.82	1.83	1.85	1.86	1.88	1.90	1.92	1.94	1.97	2.00	2.04	2.08	2.13
300	2.65	2.70	2.73	2.75	2.77	2.79	2.82	2.84	2.88	2.91	2.96	3.00	3.06	3.12	3.19
400	3.53	3.60	3.64	3.66	3.69	3.72	3.75	3.79	3.83	3.88	3.94	4.00	4.08	4.16	4.26
500	4.41	4.50	4.55	4.58	4.61	4.65	4.69	4.74	4.79	4.85	4.92	5.00	5.09	5.20	5.32
600	5.29	5.39	5.45	5.49	5.53	5.57	5.63	5.68	5.75	5.82	5.91	6.00	6.11	6.24	6.38
700	6.17	6.29	6.36	6.40	6.45	6.50	6.56	6.63	6.71	6.79	6.89	7.00	7.13	7.28	7.44
800	7.05	7.19	7.27	7.32	7.37	7.43	7.50	7.58	7.66	7.76	7.87	8.00	8.15	8.32	8.51
900	7.93	8.09	8.18	8.23	8.29	8.36	8.44	8.52	8.62	8.70	8.84	9.00	9.16	9.35	9.57
1000	8.81	8.99	9.09	9.15	9.21	9.29	9.37	9.47	9.58	9.70	9.84	10.00	10.18	10.39	10.64
2000	17.62	17.97	18.17	18.29	18.42	18.57	18.74	18.93	19.15	19.39	19.67	19.99	20.36	20.78	21.27
3000	26.43	26.95	27.25	27.43	27.63	27.85	28.11	28.40	28.72	29.09	29.51	29.99	30.54	31.17	31.90
4000	35.24	35.93	36.33	36.57	36.84	37.14	37.48	37.86	38.29	38.78	39.34	39.98	40.72	41.56	42.53
5000	44.05	44.91	45.41	45.71	46.05	46.42	46.85	47.32	47.86	48.48	49.18	49.98	50.89	51.95	53.17
6000	52.86	53.89	54.50	54.85	55.25	55.70	56.21	56.79	57.44	58.17	59.01	59.97	61.07	62.34	63.80
7000	61.67	62.87	63.58	63.99	64.46	64.99	65.58	66.25	67.01	67.87	68.85	69.97	71.25	72.72	74.43
8000	70.48	71.86	72.66	73.14	73.67	74.27	74.95	75.71	76.58	77.56	78.68	79.96	81.43	83.11	85.06
9000	79.29	80.84	81.74	82.28	82.88	83.55	84.32	85.18	86.15	87.26	88.52	89.96	91.60	93.50	95.70
10000	88.10	89.82	90.82	91.42	92.09	92.84	93.69	94.64	95.72	96.95	98.35	99.95	101.78	103.89	106.33
11000	96.91	98.80	99.90	100.56	101.29	102.12	103.05	104.11	105.30	106.65	108.19	109.94	111.96	114.28	116.96
12000	105.72	107.78	108.99	109.70	110.50	111.40	112.42	113.57	114.87	116.34	118.02	119.93	122.17	124.67	127.59
13000	114.53	116.76	118.07	118.84	119.71	120.69	121.79	123.03	124.44	126.04	127.86	129.93	132.31	135.05	138.23
14000	123.34	125.74	127.15	127.98	128.92	129.97	131.16	132.50	134.01	135.73	137.53	139.92	142.47	145.44	148.86
15000	132.15	134.73	136.23	137.12	138.13	139.25	140.53	141.96	143.58	145.43	147.36	149.92	152.67	155.83	159.49
16000	140.96	143.71	145.31	146.27	147.33	148.54	149.89	151.42	153.16	155.12	157.36	159.92	162.85	166.22	170.12
17000	149.77	152.69	154.40	155.41	156.54	157.82	159.26	160.89	162.73	164.82	167.03	169.91	173.02	176.60	180.76
18000	158.58	161.67	163.48	164.55	165.75	167.10	168.63	170.35	172.30	174.51	177.03	179.91	183.20	187.00	191.39
19000	167.39	170.65	172.56	173.69	174.96	176.39	178.00	179.82	181.87	184.21	186.86	189.90	193.38	197.38	202.02
20000	176.20	179.63	181.64	182.83	184.17	185.67	187.37	189.28	191.44	193.90	196.70	199.89	203.56	207.77	212.65
21000	185.01	188.61	190.72	191.97	193.38	194.95	196.73	198.74	201.02	203.60	206.53	209.89	213.74	218.16	223.28
22000	193.82	197.60	199.80	201.11	202.58	204.24	206.10	208.21	210.59	213.29	216.37	219.88	223.91	228.55	233.92
23000	202.63	206.58	208.89	210.25	211.79	213.52	215.47	217.67	220.16	222.99	226.20	229.87	234.09	238.94	244.55
24000	211.44	215.56	217.97	219.40	221.00	222.80	224.84	227.13	229.73	232.68	236.04	239.87	244.27	249.33	255.18
25000	220.25	224.54	227.05	228.54	230.21	232.09	234.21	236.60	239.30	242.38	245.87	249.87	254.44	259.71	265.81
26000	229.06	233.52	236.13	237.68	239.42	241.37	243.57	246.06	248.88	252.07	255.71	259.86	264.62	270.10	276.45
27000	237.87	242.50	245.21	246.82	248.62	250.65	252.94	255.52	258.45	261.77	265.55	269.86	274.80	280.49	287.08
28000	246.68	251.48	254.30	255.96	257.83	259.94	262.31	264.99	268.02	271.46	275.38	279.85	284.98	290.88	297.71
29000	255.48	260.47	263.38	265.10	267.04	269.22	271.68	274.45	277.59	281.16	285.22	289.84	295.15	301.27	308.34
30000	264.29	269.45	272.46	274.24	276.25	278.50	281.05	283.92	287.16	290.85	295.05	299.84	305.23	311.66	318.98
35000	308.34	314.35	317.87	319.95	322.29	324.92	327.89	331.23	335.02	339.33	344.22	349.81	356.22	363.60	372.14
40000	352.39	359.26	363.28	365.65	368.33	371.34	374.73	378.55	382.88	387.80	393.39	399.78	407.11	415.54	425.30
45000	396.44	404.17	408.69	411.36	414.37	417.75	421.57	425.87	430.74	436.27	442.57	449.76	458.00	467.48	478.46
50000	440.49	449.08	454.10	457.07	460.41	464.17	468.41	473.19	478.60	484.75	491.74	499.73	508.88	519.42	531.62

MONTHLY PAYMENT
10¾% REQUIRED TO AMORTIZE A LOAN

TERM AMOUNT	1 YEAR	2 YEARS	3 YEARS	4 YEARS	5 YEARS	6 YEARS	7 YEARS	8 YEARS	9 YEARS	10 YEARS	11 YEARS	12 YEARS	13 YEARS	14 YEARS	15 YEARS
$100	8.82	4.64	3.26	2.57	2.16	1.88	1.69	1.55	1.44	1.36	1.29	1.23	1.18	1.14	1.11
200	17.64	9.28	6.51	5.13	4.31	3.76	3.38	3.09	2.88	2.71	2.57	2.46	2.36	2.28	2.22
300	26.45	13.92	9.76	7.69	6.46	5.64	5.07	4.64	4.31	4.06	3.85	3.68	3.54	3.42	3.32
400	35.27	18.56	13.01	10.25	8.61	7.52	6.75	6.18	5.75	5.41	5.13	4.91	4.72	4.56	4.43
500	44.08	23.20	16.26	12.81	10.76	9.40	8.44	7.73	7.19	6.76	6.41	6.13	5.90	5.70	5.54
600	52.90	27.84	19.51	15.37	12.91	11.28	10.13	9.27	8.62	8.11	7.69	7.36	7.08	6.84	6.64
700	61.71	32.47	22.76	17.93	15.06	13.16	11.81	10.82	10.06	9.46	8.97	8.58	8.25	7.98	7.75
800	70.53	37.11	26.01	20.49	17.21	15.04	13.50	12.36	11.49	10.81	10.26	9.81	9.43	9.12	8.86
900	79.35	41.75	29.26	23.06	19.36	16.91	15.19	13.91	12.93	12.16	11.54	11.03	10.61	10.26	9.96
1000	88.16	46.39	32.52	25.62	21.51	18.79	16.87	15.45	14.37	13.51	12.82	12.26	11.79	11.40	11.07
2000	176.32	92.77	65.03	51.23	43.01	37.58	33.74	30.90	28.73	27.01	25.63	24.51	23.58	22.79	22.13
3000	264.47	139.16	97.54	76.84	64.51	56.37	50.61	46.35	43.09	40.51	38.45	36.76	35.36	34.19	33.20
4000	352.63	185.54	130.05	102.45	86.01	75.16	67.48	61.80	57.45	54.02	51.26	49.02	47.15	45.58	44.26
5000	440.79	231.92	162.56	128.06	107.52	93.94	84.35	77.25	71.81	67.52	64.08	61.26	58.93	56.98	55.33
6000	528.94	278.31	195.07	153.67	129.02	112.73	101.22	92.70	86.17	81.02	76.89	73.51	70.72	68.37	66.39
7000	617.10	324.69	227.58	179.29	150.52	131.52	118.09	108.15	100.53	94.53	89.70	85.77	82.50	79.77	77.46
8000	705.25	371.08	260.09	204.90	172.02	150.31	134.96	123.60	114.89	108.03	102.52	98.02	94.29	91.16	88.52
9000	793.41	417.46	292.60	230.51	193.53	169.09	151.83	139.05	129.25	121.53	115.33	110.27	106.07	102.56	99.59
10000	881.57	463.84	325.11	256.12	215.03	187.88	168.70	154.50	143.61	135.03	128.15	122.52	117.86	113.95	110.65
11000	969.73	510.23	357.62	281.73	236.53	206.67	185.57	169.94	157.97	148.54	140.96	134.77	129.64	125.35	121.71
12000	1057.88	556.61	390.13	307.34	258.03	225.46	202.44	185.39	172.33	162.04	153.77	147.02	141.43	136.74	132.78
13000	1146.04	603.00	422.64	332.95	279.53	244.24	219.31	200.84	186.69	175.54	166.59	159.27	153.21	148.13	143.84
14000	1234.20	649.38	455.15	358.57	301.04	263.03	236.18	216.29	201.05	189.05	179.40	171.52	165.00	159.53	154.91
15000	1322.35	695.76	487.66	384.18	322.54	281.82	253.05	231.74	215.41	202.55	192.22	183.77	176.78	170.92	165.97
16000	1410.51	742.15	520.17	409.79	344.04	300.61	269.92	247.19	229.77	216.05	205.03	196.03	188.57	182.32	177.04
17000	1498.66	788.53	552.68	435.40	365.54	319.39	286.79	262.64	244.13	229.56	217.84	208.28	200.35	193.71	188.10
18000	1586.82	834.91	585.19	461.01	387.05	338.18	303.66	278.09	258.49	243.06	230.66	220.53	212.14	205.11	199.17
19000	1674.98	881.30	617.70	486.62	408.55	356.97	320.52	293.54	272.85	256.56	243.47	232.78	223.92	216.50	210.23
20000	1763.13	927.68	650.21	512.24	430.05	375.76	337.39	308.99	287.21	270.06	256.29	245.03	235.71	227.90	221.29
21000	1851.29	974.07	682.72	537.85	451.55	394.54	354.26	324.43	301.57	283.57	269.10	257.29	247.49	239.29	232.36
22000	1939.45	1020.45	715.23	563.46	473.05	413.33	371.13	339.88	315.93	297.07	281.92	269.53	259.28	250.69	243.42
23000	2027.60	1066.83	747.74	589.07	494.56	432.12	388.00	355.33	330.29	310.57	294.73	281.78	271.06	262.08	254.49
24000	2115.76	1113.22	780.25	614.68	516.06	450.91	404.87	370.78	344.65	324.08	307.54	294.04	282.85	273.48	265.55
25000	2203.92	1159.60	812.76	640.29	537.56	469.69	421.74	386.23	359.01	337.58	320.36	306.29	294.63	284.87	276.62
26000	2292.07	1205.99	845.28	665.90	559.06	488.48	438.61	401.68	373.37	351.08	333.17	318.54	306.42	296.26	287.68
27000	2380.23	1252.37	877.79	691.52	580.57	507.27	455.48	417.13	387.73	364.59	345.99	330.80	318.20	307.66	298.75
28000	2468.39	1298.75	910.30	717.13	602.07	526.06	472.35	432.58	402.09	378.09	358.80	343.04	329.99	319.05	309.81
29000	2556.54	1345.14	942.81	742.74	623.57	544.84	489.22	448.03	416.45	391.59	371.61	355.29	341.77	330.45	320.87
30000	2644.70	1391.52	975.32	768.35	645.07	563.63	506.09	463.48	430.81	405.10	384.43	367.54	353.56	341.84	331.94
35000	3085.48	1623.44	1137.87	896.41	752.58	657.57	590.44	540.72	502.61	472.61	448.50	428.80	412.48	398.82	387.26
40000	3526.26	1855.36	1300.36	1024.47	860.10	751.51	674.78	617.97	574.41	540.12	512.57	490.06	471.41	455.79	442.58
45000	3967.04	2087.29	1462.90	1152.52	967.61	845.44	759.13	695.21	646.21	607.64	576.64	551.31	530.33	512.76	497.91
50000	4407.83	2319.20	1625.52	1280.58	1075.12	939.38	843.48	772.46	718.01	675.15	640.71	612.57	589.26	569.74	553.23

MONTHLY PAYMENT
REQUIRED TO AMORTIZE A LOAN — 10¾ %

TERM AMOUNT	35 YEARS	30 YEARS	28 YEARS	27 YEARS	26 YEARS	25 YEARS	24 YEARS	23 YEARS	22 YEARS	21 YEARS	20 YEARS	19 YEARS	18 YEARS	17 YEARS	16 YEARS
$100	.90	.92	.93	.94	.94	.95	.96	.97	.98	.99	1.00	1.02	1.04	1.06	1.08
200	1.80	1.84	1.86	1.87	1.88	1.90	1.91	1.93	1.95	1.98	2.00	2.04	2.07	2.11	2.16
300	2.70	2.75	2.78	2.80	2.82	2.84	2.87	2.89	2.93	2.96	3.00	3.05	3.10	3.17	3.24
400	3.60	3.67	3.71	3.73	3.76	3.79	3.82	3.86	3.90	3.95	4.00	4.07	4.14	4.22	4.32
500	4.50	4.59	4.63	4.66	4.70	4.73	4.77	4.82	4.87	4.93	5.00	5.08	5.17	5.28	5.40
600	5.40	5.50	5.56	5.59	5.63	5.68	5.73	5.78	5.85	5.92	6.00	6.10	6.20	6.33	6.47
700	6.30	6.42	6.49	6.53	6.57	6.62	6.68	6.75	6.82	6.91	7.00	7.11	7.24	7.38	7.55
800	7.20	7.33	7.41	7.46	7.51	7.57	7.63	7.71	7.80	7.89	8.00	8.13	8.27	8.44	8.63
900	8.10	8.25	8.34	8.39	8.45	8.51	8.59	8.67	8.77	8.88	9.00	9.14	9.30	9.49	9.71
1000	9.00	9.17	9.26	9.32	9.39	9.46	9.54	9.64	9.74	9.86	10.00	10.16	10.34	10.55	10.79
2000	17.99	18.33	18.52	18.64	18.77	18.91	19.08	19.27	19.48	19.72	19.99	20.31	20.67	21.09	21.57
3000	26.99	27.49	27.78	27.95	28.15	28.37	28.62	28.90	29.22	29.57	29.99	30.46	31.00	31.63	32.35
4000	35.98	36.65	37.03	37.27	37.53	37.82	38.15	38.53	38.96	39.43	39.98	40.62	41.34	42.17	43.14
5000	44.98	45.81	46.29	46.58	46.91	47.27	47.69	48.16	48.69	49.29	49.98	50.77	51.67	52.71	53.92
6000	53.97	54.97	55.55	55.90	56.29	56.73	57.23	57.79	58.43	59.15	59.98	60.92	62.00	63.25	64.70
7000	62.96	64.13	64.81	65.21	65.67	66.18	66.76	67.42	68.16	69.00	69.97	71.07	72.34	73.80	75.49
8000	71.96	73.29	74.06	74.53	75.05	75.64	76.30	77.05	77.90	78.86	79.97	81.23	82.67	84.34	86.27
9000	80.95	82.45	83.32	83.84	84.43	85.09	85.84	86.68	87.64	88.72	89.96	91.38	93.01	94.88	97.05
10000	89.94	91.61	92.58	93.16	93.81	94.54	95.37	96.31	97.37	98.58	99.95	101.53	103.34	105.42	107.84
11000	98.94	100.77	101.84	102.47	103.19	104.00	104.91	105.94	107.11	108.43	109.95	111.68	113.67	115.96	118.62
12000	107.94	109.93	111.09	111.79	112.57	113.45	114.45	115.57	116.85	118.29	119.94	121.84	124.01	126.50	129.40
13000	116.93	119.09	120.35	121.10	121.95	122.91	123.98	125.20	126.58	128.15	129.94	131.99	134.34	137.05	140.18
14000	125.93	128.25	129.61	130.42	131.33	132.36	133.52	134.83	136.32	138.01	139.94	142.14	144.67	147.59	150.97
15000	134.92	137.41	138.87	139.73	140.71	141.81	143.06	144.46	146.06	147.86	149.93	152.29	155.01	158.13	161.75
16000	143.92	146.57	148.13	149.05	150.09	151.27	152.59	154.09	155.79	157.72	159.92	162.44	165.34	168.67	172.53
17000	152.91	155.73	157.38	158.37	159.47	160.72	162.13	163.72	165.53	167.58	169.92	172.60	175.67	179.21	183.32
18000	161.90	164.89	166.64	167.68	168.85	170.17	171.67	173.35	175.27	177.44	179.91	182.75	186.01	189.75	194.10
19000	170.90	174.05	175.90	177.00	178.23	179.63	181.20	182.98	185.00	187.29	189.91	192.90	196.34	200.30	204.88
20000	179.89	183.21	185.15	186.31	187.61	189.08	190.74	192.61	194.74	197.15	199.91	203.06	206.67	210.84	215.67
21000	188.89	192.37	194.41	195.63	196.99	198.54	200.28	202.24	204.48	207.01	209.90	213.21	217.01	221.38	226.45
22000	197.88	201.53	203.67	204.94	206.38	207.99	209.82	211.87	214.21	216.87	219.89	223.36	227.34	231.92	237.23
23000	206.88	210.69	212.93	214.26	215.76	217.44	219.35	221.51	223.95	226.72	229.89	233.51	237.67	242.46	248.02
24000	215.87	219.85	222.18	223.57	225.14	226.90	228.89	231.14	233.69	236.58	239.88	243.67	248.01	253.00	258.80
25000	224.86	229.01	231.44	232.89	234.52	236.35	238.42	240.77	243.42	246.44	249.88	253.82	258.34	263.55	269.58
26000	233.86	238.17	240.70	242.20	243.90	245.81	247.96	250.40	253.16	256.30	259.87	263.97	268.67	274.09	280.36
27000	242.85	247.33	249.96	251.52	253.28	255.26	257.50	260.03	262.89	266.16	269.87	274.13	279.01	284.63	291.15
28000	251.85	256.49	259.21	260.83	262.66	264.71	267.03	269.66	272.63	276.01	279.86	284.28	289.34	295.17	301.93
29000	260.84	265.65	268.47	270.15	272.04	274.17	276.57	279.29	282.37	285.87	289.86	294.43	299.67	305.71	312.71
30000	269.84	274.81	277.73	279.46	281.42	283.62	286.11	288.92	292.11	295.73	299.86	304.58	310.00	316.25	323.50
35000	314.81	320.61	324.02	326.04	328.32	330.89	333.79	337.07	340.79	345.02	349.81	355.34	361.67	368.96	377.41
40000	359.78	366.41	370.30	372.62	375.22	378.16	381.47	385.22	389.47	394.30	399.81	406.11	413.34	421.67	431.33
45000	404.75	412.21	416.59	419.19	422.13	425.43	429.16	433.38	438.16	443.59	449.79	456.87	465.00	474.38	485.24
50000	449.72	458.01	462.88	465.77	469.03	472.70	476.84	481.53	486.84	492.88	499.76	507.63	516.67	527.09	539.16

TERM AMOUNT	1 YEAR	2 YEARS	3 YEARS	4 YEARS	5 YEARS	6 YEARS	7 YEARS	8 YEARS	9 YEARS	10 YEARS	11 YEARS	12 YEARS	13 YEARS	14 YEARS	15 YEARS
$100	8.83	4.65	3.27	2.58	2.17	1.90	1.70	1.56	1.45	1.37	1.30	1.24	1.20	1.16	1.13
200	17.66	9.30	6.53	5.15	4.33	3.79	3.40	3.12	2.90	2.73	2.60	2.48	2.39	2.31	2.25
300	26.49	13.95	9.79	7.72	6.49	5.68	5.10	4.68	4.35	4.10	3.89	3.72	3.58	3.47	3.37
400	35.31	18.60	13.05	10.30	8.65	7.57	6.80	6.24	5.80	5.46	5.19	4.96	4.78	4.62	4.49
500	44.14	23.25	16.32	12.87	10.82	9.46	8.50	7.79	7.25	6.82	6.48	6.20	5.97	5.78	5.61
600	52.97	27.90	19.58	15.44	12.98	11.35	10.20	9.35	8.70	8.19	7.78	7.44	7.16	6.93	6.73
700	61.79	32.55	22.84	18.01	15.14	13.24	11.90	10.91	10.15	9.55	9.07	8.68	8.35	8.08	7.85
800	70.62	37.20	26.10	20.59	17.30	15.13	13.60	12.47	11.60	10.91	10.37	9.92	9.55	9.24	8.98
900	79.45	41.85	29.37	23.16	19.46	17.02	15.30	14.02	13.05	12.28	11.66	11.16	10.74	10.39	10.10
1000	88.27	46.50	32.63	25.73	21.63	18.91	17.00	15.58	14.50	13.64	12.96	12.40	11.93	11.55	11.22
2000	176.54	92.99	65.25	51.46	43.25	37.82	33.99	31.16	28.99	27.28	25.91	24.79	23.86	23.09	22.43
3000	264.81	139.49	97.87	77.19	64.87	56.73	50.99	46.74	43.48	40.92	38.86	37.18	35.79	34.63	33.64
4000	353.08	185.98	130.50	102.91	86.49	75.64	67.98	62.31	57.97	54.55	51.81	49.57	47.72	46.17	44.86
5000	441.34	232.48	163.12	128.64	108.11	94.55	84.98	77.89	72.46	68.19	64.76	61.96	59.65	57.71	56.07
6000	529.61	278.97	195.74	154.37	129.73	113.46	101.97	93.47	86.95	81.83	77.71	74.35	71.57	69.25	67.28
7000	617.88	325.47	228.37	180.10	151.35	132.37	118.97	109.05	101.44	95.47	90.67	86.75	83.50	80.79	78.50
8000	706.15	371.96	260.99	205.82	172.97	151.28	135.96	124.62	115.94	109.10	103.62	99.14	95.43	92.33	89.71
9000	794.42	418.46	293.61	231.55	194.59	170.19	152.96	140.20	130.43	122.74	116.57	111.53	107.36	103.87	100.92
10000	882.68	464.95	326.24	257.28	216.21	189.10	169.95	155.78	144.92	136.38	129.52	123.92	119.29	115.41	112.14
11000	970.95	511.45	358.86	283.01	237.84	208.01	186.94	171.35	159.41	150.02	142.47	136.31	131.22	126.95	123.35
12000	1059.22	557.94	391.48	308.73	259.46	226.92	203.94	186.93	173.90	163.65	155.42	148.70	143.14	138.49	134.56
13000	1147.49	604.44	424.11	334.46	281.08	245.83	220.93	202.51	188.39	177.29	168.37	161.10	155.07	150.03	145.78
14000	1235.76	650.93	456.73	360.19	302.70	264.74	237.93	218.09	202.88	190.93	181.33	173.49	167.00	161.57	156.99
15000	1324.02	697.43	489.35	385.91	324.32	283.65	254.92	233.66	217.38	204.56	194.28	185.88	178.93	173.12	168.20
16000	1412.29	743.92	521.98	411.64	345.94	302.56	271.92	249.24	231.87	218.20	207.23	198.27	190.86	184.66	179.42
17000	1500.56	790.41	554.60	437.37	367.56	321.46	288.91	264.82	246.36	231.84	220.18	210.66	202.79	196.20	190.63
18000	1588.83	836.91	587.22	463.10	389.18	340.37	305.91	280.39	260.85	245.48	233.13	223.05	214.71	207.74	201.84
19000	1677.10	883.40	619.85	488.82	410.80	359.28	322.90	295.97	275.34	259.11	246.08	235.45	226.64	219.28	213.06
20000	1765.36	929.90	652.47	514.55	432.42	378.19	339.89	311.55	289.83	272.75	259.03	247.84	238.57	230.82	224.27
21000	1853.63	976.39	685.09	540.28	454.05	397.10	356.89	327.13	304.32	286.39	271.99	260.23	250.50	242.36	235.48
22000	1941.90	1022.89	717.72	566.00	475.67	416.01	373.88	342.70	318.81	300.03	284.94	272.62	262.43	253.90	246.70
23000	2030.17	1069.38	750.34	591.73	497.29	434.92	390.88	358.28	333.31	313.66	297.89	285.01	274.36	265.44	257.91
24000	2118.44	1115.88	782.96	617.46	518.91	453.83	407.87	373.86	347.80	327.30	310.84	297.40	286.28	276.98	269.12
25000	2206.70	1162.37	815.59	643.19	540.53	472.74	424.87	389.44	362.29	340.94	323.79	309.80	298.21	288.52	280.34
26000	2294.97	1208.87	848.21	668.91	562.15	491.65	441.86	405.01	376.78	354.57	336.74	322.19	310.14	300.06	291.55
27000	2383.24	1255.36	880.83	694.64	583.77	510.56	458.86	420.59	391.27	368.21	349.70	334.58	322.07	311.60	302.76
28000	2471.51	1301.86	913.46	720.37	605.39	529.47	475.85	436.17	405.76	381.85	362.65	346.97	334.00	323.14	313.98
29000	2559.77	1348.35	946.08	746.09	627.01	548.38	492.84	451.74	420.25	395.49	375.60	359.36	345.93	334.68	325.19
30000	2648.04	1394.85	978.70	771.82	648.63	567.29	509.84	467.32	434.75	409.12	388.55	371.75	357.85	346.23	336.40
35000	3089.38	1627.32	1141.82	900.46	756.74	661.83	594.81	545.21	507.20	477.31	453.31	433.71	417.50	403.93	392.47
40000	3530.72	1859.79	1304.94	1029.09	864.84	756.38	679.78	623.09	579.66	545.50	518.06	495.67	477.14	461.63	448.54
45000	3972.06	2092.27	1468.05	1157.73	972.95	850.93	764.76	700.98	652.12	613.68	582.82	557.63	536.78	519.34	504.60
50000	4413.40	2324.74	1631.17	1286.37	1081.05	945.47	849.73	778.86	724.57	681.87	647.58	619.59	596.42	577.04	560.67

MONTHLY PAYMENT
REQUIRED TO AMORTIZE A LOAN — 11%

TERM AMOUNT	16 YEARS	17 YEARS	18 YEARS	19 YEARS	20 YEARS	21 YEARS	22 YEARS	23 YEARS	24 YEARS	25 YEARS	26 YEARS	27 YEARS	28 YEARS	30 YEARS	35 YEARS
$100	1.11	1.09	1.07	1.05	1.03	1.02	1.01	1.00	0.99	0.98	0.97	0.97	0.96	0.95	0.94
200	2.22	2.17	2.13	2.09	2.06	2.04	2.01	1.99	1.98	1.96	1.95	1.93	1.92	1.90	1.87
300	3.33	3.26	3.20	3.14	3.10	3.06	3.02	2.99	2.96	2.94	2.92	2.90	2.88	2.86	2.81
400	4.44	4.34	4.26	4.19	4.13	4.08	4.03	3.99	3.95	3.92	3.89	3.87	3.85	3.81	3.75
500	5.54	5.43	5.33	5.24	5.16	5.09	5.04	4.99	4.94	4.90	4.87	4.83	4.81	4.76	4.68
600	6.65	6.51	6.39	6.28	6.19	6.11	6.04	5.98	5.93	5.88	5.84	5.80	5.77	5.71	5.62
700	7.76	7.60	7.46	7.33	7.23	7.13	7.05	6.98	6.92	6.86	6.81	6.77	6.73	6.67	6.56
800	8.87	8.68	8.52	8.38	8.26	8.15	8.06	7.98	7.90	7.84	7.79	7.73	7.69	7.62	7.50
900	9.98	9.77	9.59	9.43	9.29	9.17	9.07	8.97	8.89	8.82	8.76	8.70	8.65	8.57	8.43
1000	11.09	10.85	10.65	10.47	10.32	10.19	10.07	9.97	9.88	9.80	9.73	9.67	9.62	9.52	9.37
2000	22.18	21.71	21.30	20.95	20.64	20.38	20.14	19.94	19.76	19.60	19.46	19.33	19.23	19.05	18.74
3000	33.27	32.56	31.95	31.42	30.97	30.57	30.22	29.91	29.64	29.40	29.20	29.00	28.85	28.57	28.11
4000	44.36	43.42	42.60	41.90	41.29	40.75	40.29	39.88	39.52	39.20	38.93	38.67	38.46	38.09	37.48
5000	55.45	54.27	53.25	52.37	51.61	50.94	50.36	49.85	49.40	49.01	48.66	48.34	48.08	47.62	46.85
6000	66.54	65.12	63.91	62.85	61.93	61.13	60.43	59.82	59.28	58.81	58.39	58.00	57.69	57.14	56.22
7000	77.63	75.98	74.56	73.32	72.25	71.32	70.51	69.79	69.16	68.61	68.13	67.67	67.31	66.66	65.59
8000	88.72	86.83	85.21	83.80	82.57	81.51	80.58	79.76	79.04	78.41	77.86	77.34	76.92	76.19	74.96
9000	99.81	97.68	95.86	94.27	92.90	91.70	90.65	89.73	88.92	88.21	87.59	87.01	86.54	85.71	84.33
10000	110.90	108.54	106.51	104.75	103.22	101.89	100.72	99.70	98.80	98.01	97.32	96.67	96.16	95.23	93.69
11000	121.99	119.39	117.16	115.22	113.54	112.08	110.79	109.67	108.68	107.81	107.06	106.34	105.77	104.76	103.06
12000	133.08	130.25	127.81	125.70	123.86	122.26	120.87	119.64	118.56	117.61	116.79	116.01	115.39	114.28	112.43
13000	144.17	141.10	138.46	136.17	134.18	132.45	130.94	129.61	128.44	127.42	126.52	125.68	125.00	123.80	121.80
14000	155.26	151.95	149.11	146.65	144.51	142.64	141.01	139.58	138.32	137.22	136.25	135.34	134.62	133.33	131.17
15000	166.35	162.81	159.76	157.12	154.83	152.83	151.08	149.55	148.20	147.02	145.99	145.01	144.23	142.85	140.54
16000	177.43	173.66	170.42	167.60	165.15	163.02	161.16	159.52	158.08	156.82	155.72	154.68	153.85	152.37	149.91
17000	188.52	184.51	181.07	178.07	175.47	173.21	171.23	169.49	167.96	166.62	165.45	164.35	163.46	161.90	159.28
18000	199.61	195.37	191.72	188.55	185.79	183.40	181.30	179.46	177.85	176.42	175.18	174.01	173.08	171.42	168.65
19000	210.70	206.22	202.37	199.02	196.12	193.58	191.37	189.43	187.73	186.22	184.91	183.68	182.69	180.94	178.02
20000	221.79	217.08	213.02	209.50	206.44	203.77	201.44	199.40	197.61	196.02	194.65	193.35	192.31	190.46	187.39
21000	232.88	227.93	223.67	219.97	216.76	213.96	211.52	209.37	207.49	205.82	204.38	203.02	201.93	199.99	196.76
22000	243.97	238.78	234.32	230.45	227.08	224.15	221.59	219.34	217.37	215.63	214.11	212.68	211.54	209.51	206.13
23000	255.06	249.64	244.97	240.92	237.40	234.34	231.66	229.31	227.25	225.43	223.84	222.35	221.16	219.03	215.50
24000	266.15	260.49	255.62	251.40	247.72	244.53	241.73	239.28	237.13	235.23	233.58	232.02	230.77	228.56	224.87
25000	277.24	271.34	266.27	261.87	258.05	254.72	251.81	249.25	247.01	245.03	243.31	241.68	240.39	238.08	234.24
26000	288.33	282.20	276.92	272.35	268.37	264.91	261.88	259.22	256.89	254.83	253.04	251.35	250.00	247.60	243.61
27000	299.42	293.05	287.58	282.82	278.69	275.09	271.95	269.19	266.77	264.63	262.77	261.02	259.62	257.13	252.98
28000	310.51	303.91	298.23	293.30	289.01	285.28	282.02	279.16	276.65	274.43	272.51	270.69	269.23	266.65	262.35
29000	321.60	314.76	308.88	303.77	299.33	295.47	292.09	289.13	286.53	284.23	282.24	280.35	278.85	276.17	271.71
30000	332.69	325.61	319.53	314.25	309.66	305.66	302.17	299.10	296.41	294.04	291.97	290.02	288.47	285.70	281.08
35000	388.14	379.88	372.78	366.62	361.27	356.60	352.53	348.95	345.81	343.04	340.63	338.36	336.54	333.31	327.93
40000	443.59	434.15	426.04	419.00	412.87	407.55	402.89	398.80	395.21	392.05	389.29	386.70	384.62	380.93	374.78
45000	499.04	488.42	479.29	471.37	464.48	458.49	453.25	448.65	444.61	441.05	437.96	435.03	432.70	428.55	421.63
50000	554.48	542.69	532.55	523.74	516.09	509.43	503.61	498.50	494.01	490.06	486.62	483.37	480.78	476.16	468.47

MONTHLY PAYMENT
11¼% REQUIRED TO AMORTIZE A LOAN

TERM AMOUNT	1 YEAR	2 YEARS	3 YEARS	4 YEARS	5 YEARS	6 YEARS	7 YEARS	8 YEARS	9 YEARS	10 YEARS	11 YEARS	12 YEARS	13 YEARS	14 YEARS	15 YEARS
$100	8.84	4.67	3.28	2.59	2.18	1.91	1.72	1.58	1.47	1.38	1.31	1.26	1.21	1.17	1.14
200	17.68	9.33	6.55	5.17	4.35	3.81	3.43	3.15	2.93	2.76	2.62	2.51	2.42	2.34	2.28
300	26.52	13.99	9.83	7.76	6.53	5.71	5.14	4.72	4.39	4.14	3.93	3.76	3.63	3.51	3.41
400	35.36	18.65	13.10	10.34	8.70	7.62	6.85	6.29	5.85	5.51	5.24	5.02	4.83	4.68	4.54
500	44.19	23.31	16.37	12.93	10.87	9.52	8.56	7.86	7.32	6.89	6.55	6.27	6.04	5.85	5.69
600	53.03	27.97	19.65	15.51	13.05	11.42	10.28	9.43	8.78	8.27	7.86	7.52	7.25	7.02	6.82
700	61.87	32.63	22.92	18.10	15.22	13.33	11.99	11.00	10.24	9.65	9.17	8.78	8.46	8.19	7.96
800	70.71	37.29	26.19	20.68	17.40	15.23	13.70	12.57	11.70	11.02	10.48	10.03	9.66	9.35	9.10
900	79.55	41.95	29.47	23.26	19.57	17.13	15.41	14.14	13.16	12.40	11.79	11.28	10.87	10.52	10.23
1000	88.38	46.61	32.74	25.85	21.74	19.04	17.12	15.71	14.63	13.78	13.09	12.54	12.08	11.69	11.37
2000	176.76	93.22	65.48	51.69	43.48	38.07	34.24	31.42	29.25	27.55	26.18	25.07	24.15	23.38	22.73
3000	265.14	139.82	98.21	77.53	65.22	57.10	51.36	47.13	43.87	41.32	39.27	37.60	36.22	35.07	34.09
4000	353.52	186.43	130.95	103.38	86.96	76.13	68.48	62.83	58.50	55.09	52.36	50.14	48.29	46.75	45.46
5000	441.90	233.03	163.69	129.22	108.70	95.16	85.60	78.53	73.12	68.87	65.45	62.67	60.37	58.44	56.82
6000	530.28	279.64	196.42	155.06	130.44	114.19	102.72	94.24	87.74	82.64	78.54	75.20	72.44	70.13	68.18
7000	618.66	326.24	229.16	180.91	152.18	133.23	119.84	109.95	102.37	96.41	91.63	87.73	84.51	81.82	79.55
8000	707.04	372.85	261.90	206.75	173.92	152.26	136.96	125.65	116.99	110.18	104.72	100.27	96.58	93.50	90.91
9000	795.42	419.46	294.63	232.59	195.66	171.29	154.08	141.36	131.61	123.95	117.81	112.80	108.66	105.19	102.27
10000	883.80	466.06	327.37	258.44	217.40	190.32	171.20	157.06	146.24	137.73	130.90	125.33	120.73	116.88	113.63
11000	972.18	512.67	360.11	284.28	239.14	209.35	188.32	172.77	160.86	151.50	143.99	137.86	132.80	128.57	125.00
12000	1060.56	559.27	392.84	310.12	260.88	228.38	205.44	188.47	175.48	165.27	157.08	150.40	144.87	140.25	136.36
13000	1148.94	605.88	425.58	335.97	282.62	247.42	222.56	204.18	190.11	179.04	170.17	162.93	156.94	151.94	147.72
14000	1237.32	652.48	458.31	361.81	304.36	266.45	239.68	219.89	204.73	192.82	183.26	175.46	169.01	163.63	159.09
15000	1325.70	699.09	491.05	387.65	326.10	285.48	256.80	235.60	219.35	206.59	196.35	187.99	181.08	175.31	170.45
16000	1414.07	745.69	523.79	413.49	347.84	304.51	273.92	251.30	233.97	220.36	209.44	200.53	193.16	187.00	181.81
17000	1502.45	792.30	556.52	439.34	369.58	323.54	291.04	267.00	248.59	234.13	222.53	213.06	205.23	198.69	193.17
18000	1590.83	838.90	589.26	465.18	391.31	342.57	308.16	282.71	263.22	247.90	235.62	225.59	217.31	210.38	204.54
19000	1679.21	885.51	622.00	491.02	413.06	361.60	325.28	298.41	277.84	261.68	248.71	238.12	229.38	222.06	215.90
20000	1767.59	932.12	654.73	516.87	434.80	380.64	342.40	314.12	292.47	275.45	261.79	250.66	241.45	233.75	227.26
21000	1855.97	978.72	687.47	542.71	456.54	399.67	359.52	329.83	307.09	289.22	274.88	263.19	253.53	245.44	238.63
22000	1944.35	1025.33	720.21	568.55	478.28	418.70	376.64	345.53	321.71	302.99	287.97	275.72	265.60	257.13	249.99
23000	2032.73	1071.93	752.94	594.40	500.02	437.73	393.76	361.24	336.34	316.77	301.06	288.26	277.67	268.82	261.35
24000	2121.11	1118.54	785.68	620.24	521.76	456.76	410.88	376.94	350.96	330.54	314.15	300.79	289.74	280.50	272.71
25000	2209.49	1165.14	818.41	646.08	543.50	475.79	428.00	392.65	365.58	344.31	327.24	313.32	301.81	292.19	284.08
26000	2297.87	1211.75	851.15	671.93	565.24	494.83	445.12	408.35	380.21	358.08	340.33	325.85	313.88	303.88	295.44
27000	2386.25	1258.35	883.89	697.77	586.98	513.86	462.24	424.06	394.83	371.85	353.42	338.39	325.96	315.56	306.80
28000	2474.63	1304.96	916.62	723.61	608.72	532.89	479.36	439.77	409.45	385.63	366.51	350.92	338.03	327.25	318.17
29000	2563.01	1351.57	949.36	749.46	630.46	551.92	496.48	455.47	424.08	399.40	379.60	363.45	350.10	338.94	329.53
30000	2651.39	1398.17	982.10	775.30	652.20	570.95	513.60	471.18	438.70	413.17	392.69	375.98	362.17	350.63	340.89
35000	3093.28	1631.20	1145.78	904.51	760.90	666.11	599.20	549.71	511.81	482.03	458.14	438.65	422.53	409.07	397.71
40000	3535.18	1864.23	1309.46	1033.73	869.60	761.27	684.80	628.24	584.93	550.89	523.58	501.31	482.90	467.50	454.52
45000	3977.08	2097.25	1473.14	1162.95	978.30	856.42	770.40	706.76	658.05	619.75	589.03	563.97	543.26	525.94	511.33
50000	4418.97	2330.28	1636.82	1292.16	1087.00	951.58	856.00	785.29	731.16	688.61	654.48	626.64	603.62	584.38	568.15

MONTHLY PAYMENT
REQUIRED TO AMORTIZE A LOAN   11¼ %

TERM AMOUNT	35 YEARS	30 YEARS	28 YEARS	27 YEARS	26 YEARS	25 YEARS	24 YEARS	23 YEARS	22 YEARS	21 YEARS	20 YEARS	19 YEARS	18 YEARS	17 YEARS	16 YEARS
$100	.94	.96	.97	.97	.98	.98	.99	1.00	1.01	1.02	1.04	1.05	1.07	1.09	1.11
200	1.88	1.91	1.93	1.94	1.95	1.96	1.98	2.00	2.02	2.04	2.07	2.10	2.13	2.18	2.22
300	2.81	2.86	2.89	2.90	2.92	2.94	2.97	2.99	3.03	3.06	3.10	3.15	3.20	3.26	3.33
400	3.75	3.81	3.85	3.87	3.90	3.92	3.96	3.99	4.03	4.08	4.13	4.19	4.26	4.35	4.44
500	4.69	4.76	4.81	4.84	4.87	4.90	4.94	4.98	5.04	5.10	5.16	5.24	5.33	5.43	5.55
600	5.62	5.72	5.77	5.80	5.84	5.88	5.93	5.98	6.05	6.12	6.20	6.29	6.39	6.52	6.66
700	6.56	6.67	6.73	6.77	6.81	6.86	6.92	6.98	7.05	7.13	7.23	7.33	7.46	7.60	7.77
800	7.50	7.62	7.69	7.74	7.79	7.84	7.91	7.97	8.06	8.15	8.26	8.38	8.52	8.69	8.87
900	8.43	8.57	8.66	8.70	8.76	8.82	8.89	8.97	9.07	9.17	9.29	9.43	9.59	9.77	9.98
1000	9.37	9.52	9.62	9.67	9.73	9.80	9.88	9.97	10.07	10.19	10.32	10.48	10.65	10.86	11.09
2000	18.74	19.04	19.23	19.34	19.46	19.60	19.76	19.94	20.14	20.38	20.64	20.95	21.30	21.71	22.18
3000	28.10	28.56	28.84	29.00	29.19	29.40	29.64	29.90	30.21	30.56	30.96	31.42	31.95	32.56	33.27
4000	37.47	38.08	38.45	38.67	38.92	39.20	39.51	39.87	40.28	40.75	41.28	41.89	42.59	43.41	44.35
5000	46.83	47.60	48.06	48.33	48.64	48.99	49.39	49.84	50.35	50.93	51.60	52.36	53.24	54.26	55.44
6000	56.20	57.12	57.67	58.00	58.37	58.79	59.27	59.80	60.42	61.12	61.92	62.83	63.89	65.11	66.53
7000	65.56	66.64	67.28	67.67	68.10	68.59	69.14	69.77	70.49	71.30	72.23	73.30	74.54	75.96	77.61
8000	74.93	76.16	76.89	77.33	77.83	78.39	79.02	79.74	80.56	81.49	82.55	83.78	85.18	86.81	88.70
9000	84.30	85.68	86.51	87.00	87.55	88.18	88.90	89.70	90.62	91.67	92.87	94.25	95.83	97.66	99.79
10000	93.66	95.20	96.12	96.66	97.28	97.98	98.77	99.67	100.69	101.86	103.19	104.72	106.48	108.51	110.87
11000	103.03	104.72	105.73	106.33	107.01	107.78	108.65	109.64	110.76	112.04	113.51	115.19	117.12	119.36	121.96
12000	112.39	114.24	115.34	116.00	116.74	117.58	118.53	119.60	120.83	122.23	123.83	125.66	127.77	130.22	133.05
13000	121.76	123.76	124.95	125.66	126.46	127.37	128.40	129.57	130.89	132.41	134.15	136.13	138.42	141.06	144.13
14000	131.12	133.28	134.56	135.33	136.19	137.17	138.28	139.54	140.96	142.60	144.46	146.60	149.07	151.91	155.22
15000	140.49	142.80	144.17	144.99	145.92	146.97	148.16	149.50	151.03	152.78	154.78	157.07	159.71	162.76	166.31
16000	149.86	152.32	153.78	154.66	155.65	156.77	158.03	159.47	161.10	162.97	165.10	167.55	170.36	173.61	177.39
17000	159.22	161.84	163.39	164.32	165.38	166.56	167.91	169.44	171.17	173.15	175.42	178.02	181.01	184.46	188.48
18000	168.59	171.36	173.01	173.99	175.10	176.36	177.79	179.40	181.24	183.34	185.74	188.49	191.66	195.32	199.57
19000	177.95	180.88	182.62	183.66	184.83	186.16	187.66	189.37	191.31	193.52	196.06	198.96	202.30	206.17	210.65
20000	187.32	190.39	192.23	193.32	194.56	195.96	197.54	199.33	201.38	203.71	206.38	209.43	212.95	217.02	221.74
21000	196.68	199.91	201.84	202.99	204.29	205.75	207.42	209.30	211.45	213.90	216.69	219.90	223.60	227.87	232.83
22000	206.05	209.43	211.45	212.65	214.01	215.55	217.29	219.27	221.51	224.08	227.01	230.37	234.24	238.72	243.92
23000	215.42	218.95	221.06	222.32	223.74	225.35	227.17	229.23	231.58	234.27	237.33	240.85	244.89	249.57	255.00
24000	224.78	228.47	230.67	231.99	233.47	235.15	237.05	239.20	241.65	244.45	247.65	251.32	255.54	260.42	266.09
25000	234.15	237.99	240.28	241.65	243.20	244.94	246.92	249.17	251.72	254.64	257.97	261.79	266.19	271.28	277.18
26000	243.51	247.51	249.89	251.32	252.92	254.74	256.80	259.13	261.79	264.82	268.29	272.26	276.83	282.12	288.26
27000	252.88	257.03	259.50	260.98	262.65	264.54	266.68	269.10	271.86	275.01	278.61	282.73	287.48	292.97	299.35
28000	262.24	266.55	269.12	270.65	272.38	274.34	276.55	279.07	281.93	285.19	288.92	293.20	298.13	303.83	310.44
29000	271.61	276.07	278.73	280.31	282.11	284.13	286.43	289.03	291.99	295.38	299.24	303.67	308.77	314.67	321.52
30000	280.98	285.59	288.34	289.98	291.83	293.93	296.31	299.00	302.06	305.56	309.56	314.14	319.42	325.52	332.61
35000	327.80	333.19	336.39	338.31	340.47	342.92	345.68	348.83	352.41	356.49	361.15	366.50	372.66	379.78	388.04
40000	374.63	380.78	384.45	386.64	389.11	391.91	395.07	398.66	402.76	407.42	412.75	418.86	425.89	434.03	443.48
45000	421.46	428.38	432.51	434.97	437.75	440.89	444.46	448.50	453.10	458.34	464.34	471.21	479.13	488.28	498.91
50000	468.29	475.98	480.56	483.30	486.39	489.88	493.84	498.33	503.44	509.27	515.93	523.57	532.37	542.53	554.35

MONTHLY PAYMENT
11½% REQUIRED TO AMORTIZE A LOAN

TERM AMOUNT	1 YEAR	2 YEARS	3 YEARS	4 YEARS	5 YEARS	6 YEARS	7 YEARS	8 YEARS	9 YEARS	10 YEARS	11 YEARS	12 YEARS	13 YEARS	14 YEARS	15 YEARS
$100	8.85	4.68	3.29	2.60	2.19	1.92	1.73	1.59	1.48	1.40	1.33	1.27	1.23	1.19	1.16
200	17.70	9.35	6.57	5.20	4.38	3.84	3.45	3.17	2.96	2.79	2.65	2.54	2.45	2.37	2.31
300	26.55	14.02	9.86	7.79	6.56	5.75	5.18	4.76	4.43	4.18	3.97	3.81	3.67	3.56	3.46
400	35.40	18.69	13.14	10.39	8.75	7.67	6.90	6.34	5.91	5.57	5.30	5.07	4.89	4.74	4.61
500	44.25	23.36	16.43	12.98	10.93	9.58	8.63	7.92	7.38	6.96	6.62	6.34	6.11	5.92	5.76
600	53.10	28.03	19.71	15.58	13.12	11.50	10.35	9.51	8.86	8.35	7.94	7.61	7.34	7.11	6.91
700	61.95	32.71	23.00	18.17	15.31	13.41	12.08	11.09	10.33	9.74	9.26	8.88	8.56	8.29	8.06
800	70.80	37.38	26.28	20.77	17.49	15.33	13.80	12.67	11.81	11.13	10.59	10.14	9.78	9.47	9.22
900	79.65	42.05	29.57	23.37	19.68	17.24	15.53	14.26	13.28	12.52	11.91	11.41	11.00	10.66	10.37
1000	88.50	46.72	32.85	25.96	21.86	19.16	17.25	15.84	14.76	13.91	13.23	12.68	12.22	11.84	11.52
2000	176.99	93.44	65.70	51.92	43.72	38.31	34.50	31.67	29.52	27.82	26.46	25.35	24.44	23.68	23.03
3000	265.48	140.15	98.55	77.88	65.58	57.47	51.74	47.51	44.27	41.73	39.69	38.03	36.66	35.51	34.54
4000	353.97	186.87	131.40	103.84	87.44	76.62	68.99	63.34	59.03	55.64	52.92	50.70	48.87	47.35	46.06
5000	442.46	233.59	164.25	129.80	109.30	95.78	86.23	79.18	73.78	69.54	66.15	63.38	61.09	59.18	57.57
6000	530.95	280.30	197.10	155.76	131.16	114.93	103.48	95.01	88.54	83.45	79.37	76.05	73.31	71.02	69.08
7000	619.44	327.02	229.95	181.72	153.02	134.08	120.72	110.85	103.29	97.36	92.60	88.72	85.52	82.85	80.60
8000	707.93	373.74	262.80	207.68	174.88	153.24	137.97	126.68	118.05	111.27	105.83	101.40	97.74	94.69	92.11
9000	796.42	420.45	295.65	233.64	196.74	172.39	155.22	142.52	132.80	125.17	119.06	114.07	109.96	106.52	103.62
10000	884.91	467.17	328.50	259.60	218.60	191.55	172.46	158.35	147.56	139.08	132.29	126.75	122.17	118.36	115.14
11000	973.40	513.89	361.35	285.56	240.46	210.70	189.71	174.19	162.31	152.99	145.51	139.42	134.39	130.19	126.65
12000	1061.89	560.60	394.20	311.52	262.32	229.85	206.95	190.02	177.07	166.90	158.74	152.10	146.61	142.03	138.16
13000	1150.38	607.32	427.05	337.47	284.17	249.01	224.20	205.86	191.83	180.80	171.97	164.77	158.82	153.86	149.68
14000	1238.88	654.04	459.90	363.43	306.03	268.16	241.44	221.69	206.58	194.71	185.20	177.44	171.04	165.70	161.19
15000	1327.37	700.75	492.75	389.39	327.89	287.32	258.69	237.53	221.34	208.62	198.43	190.12	183.26	177.53	172.70
16000	1415.86	747.47	525.60	415.35	349.75	306.47	275.93	253.36	236.09	222.53	211.65	202.79	195.48	189.37	184.22
17000	1504.35	794.18	558.45	441.31	371.61	325.62	293.18	269.20	250.85	236.44	224.88	215.47	207.69	201.20	195.73
18000	1592.84	840.90	591.30	467.27	393.47	344.78	310.43	285.03	265.60	250.34	238.11	228.14	219.91	213.04	207.24
19000	1681.33	887.62	624.15	493.23	415.33	363.93	327.67	300.87	280.36	264.25	251.34	240.82	232.13	224.87	218.76
20000	1769.82	934.33	657.00	519.19	437.19	383.09	344.92	316.70	295.11	278.16	264.57	253.49	244.34	236.71	230.27
21000	1858.31	981.05	689.85	545.15	459.05	402.24	362.16	332.54	309.87	292.07	277.79	266.16	256.56	248.54	241.78
22000	1946.80	1027.77	722.69	571.07	480.91	421.39	379.41	348.37	324.62	305.97	291.02	278.84	268.78	260.38	253.30
23000	2035.29	1074.48	755.54	597.07	502.77	440.55	396.65	364.21	339.38	319.88	304.25	291.51	280.99	272.21	264.81
24000	2123.78	1121.20	788.39	623.03	524.63	459.70	413.90	380.04	354.13	333.79	317.48	304.19	293.21	284.05	276.32
25000	2212.27	1167.92	821.24	648.99	546.48	478.86	431.15	395.87	368.89	347.70	330.71	316.86	305.43	295.88	287.84
26000	2300.76	1214.63	854.09	674.94	568.34	498.01	448.39	411.71	383.65	361.60	343.94	329.54	317.64	307.72	299.35
27000	2388.26	1261.35	886.94	700.90	590.20	517.16	465.64	427.54	398.40	375.51	357.16	342.21	329.86	319.55	310.86
28000	2477.75	1308.07	919.79	726.86	612.06	536.32	482.88	443.38	413.16	389.42	370.39	354.88	342.08	331.39	322.37
29000	2566.24	1354.78	952.64	752.82	633.92	555.47	500.13	459.21	427.91	403.33	383.62	367.56	354.30	343.22	333.89
30000	2654.73	1401.50	985.49	778.78	655.78	574.63	517.37	475.05	442.67	417.24	396.85	380.23	366.51	355.06	345.40
35000	3097.18	1635.08	1150.08	908.57	765.08	670.40	603.60	554.22	516.44	486.78	463.00	443.60	427.60	414.23	402.97
40000	3539.63	1868.66	1313.99	1038.37	874.37	766.17	689.83	633.40	590.22	556.31	529.13	506.98	488.68	473.41	460.53
45000	3982.09	2102.25	1478.23	1168.25	983.67	861.94	776.06	712.57	664.00	625.85	595.27	570.35	549.77	532.58	518.10
50000	4424.54	2335.83	1642.48	1297.97	1092.96	957.71	862.29	791.74	737.77	695.39	661.41	633.72	610.85	591.76	575.67

MONTHLY PAYMENT
REQUIRED TO AMORTIZE A LOAN

11½%

TERM AMOUNT	35 YEARS	30 YEARS	28 YEARS	27 YEARS	26 YEARS	25 YEARS	24 YEARS	23 YEARS	22 YEARS	21 YEARS	20 YEARS	19 YEARS	18 YEARS	17 YEARS	16 YEARS
$100	.96	.98	.98	.99	1.00	1.00	1.01	1.02	1.03	1.04	1.05	1.07	1.09	1.11	1.13
200	1.92	1.95	1.96	1.97	1.99	2.00	2.01	2.03	2.05	2.08	2.10	2.13	2.17	2.21	2.25
300	2.87	2.92	2.94	2.96	2.98	3.00	3.02	3.05	3.08	3.11	3.15	3.19	3.25	3.31	3.38
400	3.83	3.89	3.92	3.94	3.97	3.99	4.02	4.06	4.10	4.15	4.20	4.26	4.33	4.41	4.50
500	4.78	4.86	4.90	4.93	4.96	4.99	5.03	5.07	5.12	5.18	5.25	5.32	5.41	5.51	5.62
600	5.74	5.83	5.88	5.91	5.95	5.99	6.03	6.09	6.15	6.22	6.29	6.38	6.49	6.61	6.75
700	6.69	6.80	6.86	6.89	6.94	6.98	7.04	7.10	7.17	7.25	7.34	7.45	7.57	7.71	7.87
800	7.65	7.77	7.84	7.88	7.93	7.98	8.04	8.11	8.19	8.29	8.39	8.51	8.65	8.81	9.00
900	8.60	8.74	8.82	8.86	8.92	8.98	9.05	9.13	9.22	9.32	9.44	9.57	9.73	9.91	10.12
1000	9.56	9.71	9.79	9.85	9.91	9.98	10.05	10.14	10.24	10.36	10.49	10.64	10.81	11.01	11.24
2000	19.11	19.41	19.58	19.69	19.81	19.95	20.10	20.28	20.48	20.71	20.97	21.27	21.62	22.02	22.48
3000	28.66	29.11	29.37	29.53	29.71	29.92	30.15	30.41	30.71	31.06	31.45	31.90	32.42	33.02	33.72
4000	38.21	38.81	39.16	39.37	39.61	39.89	40.20	40.55	40.95	41.41	41.93	42.53	43.23	44.03	44.96
5000	47.77	48.51	48.95	49.22	49.52	49.86	50.24	50.68	51.19	51.76	52.41	53.16	54.04	55.04	56.20
6000	57.32	58.21	58.74	59.06	59.42	59.83	60.29	60.82	61.42	62.11	62.89	63.80	64.84	66.04	67.44
7000	66.87	67.91	68.53	68.90	69.32	69.80	70.34	70.96	71.66	72.46	73.38	74.43	75.64	77.05	78.68
8000	76.42	77.61	78.32	78.74	79.22	79.77	80.39	81.09	81.89	82.81	83.86	85.06	86.45	88.06	89.92
9000	85.98	87.31	88.11	88.59	89.13	89.74	90.44	91.23	92.13	93.16	94.34	95.69	97.25	99.06	101.16
10000	95.53	97.01	97.90	98.43	99.03	99.71	100.48	101.36	102.37	103.51	104.82	106.32	108.06	110.07	112.40
11000	105.08	106.71	107.68	108.27	108.93	109.68	110.53	111.50	112.60	113.86	115.30	116.96	118.86	121.07	123.64
12000	114.63	116.41	117.47	118.11	118.83	119.65	120.58	121.63	122.84	124.21	125.78	127.59	129.67	132.08	134.88
13000	124.18	126.11	127.26	127.95	128.74	129.62	130.63	131.77	133.07	134.56	136.26	138.22	140.48	143.09	146.12
14000	133.73	135.81	137.05	137.80	138.64	139.59	140.68	141.91	143.31	144.91	146.75	148.85	151.28	154.09	157.36
15000	143.29	145.51	146.83	147.64	148.54	149.56	150.72	152.04	153.55	155.26	157.23	159.48	162.09	165.10	168.60
16000	152.84	155.21	156.63	157.48	158.44	159.53	160.77	162.18	163.78	165.61	167.71	170.12	172.89	176.11	179.84
17000	162.39	164.91	166.42	167.32	168.35	169.51	170.82	172.31	174.02	175.96	178.19	180.75	183.70	187.11	191.08
18000	171.95	174.61	176.21	177.17	178.25	179.48	180.87	182.45	184.25	186.31	188.67	191.38	194.50	198.12	202.32
19000	181.50	184.31	186.00	187.01	188.15	189.45	190.92	192.58	194.49	196.66	199.15	202.01	205.31	209.12	213.56
20000	191.05	194.01	195.79	196.85	198.05	199.42	200.96	202.72	204.73	207.01	209.63	212.64	216.11	220.13	224.80
21000	200.60	203.71	205.58	206.69	207.96	209.39	211.01	212.86	214.96	217.36	220.12	223.28	226.92	231.14	236.04
22000	210.15	213.41	215.36	216.54	217.86	219.36	221.06	222.99	225.20	227.71	230.60	233.91	237.72	242.14	247.28
23000	219.71	223.11	225.15	226.38	227.76	229.33	231.11	233.13	235.43	238.07	241.08	244.54	248.53	253.15	258.52
24000	229.26	232.81	234.94	236.22	237.66	239.30	241.16	243.26	245.67	248.42	251.56	255.17	259.34	264.16	269.76
25000	238.81	242.51	244.73	246.06	247.57	249.27	251.20	253.40	255.91	258.77	262.04	265.80	270.14	275.16	281.00
26000	248.36	252.22	254.52	255.90	257.47	259.24	261.25	263.54	266.14	269.12	272.52	276.44	280.95	286.17	292.24
27000	257.92	261.92	264.31	265.75	267.37	269.21	271.30	273.67	276.38	279.47	283.00	287.07	291.75	297.17	303.48
28000	267.47	271.62	274.10	275.59	277.27	279.18	281.35	283.81	286.61	289.82	293.49	297.70	302.56	308.18	314.72
29000	277.02	281.32	283.89	285.43	287.18	289.15	291.40	293.94	296.85	300.17	303.97	308.33	313.36	319.19	325.96
30000	286.57	291.02	293.68	295.27	297.08	299.12	301.44	304.08	307.09	310.52	314.45	318.96	324.17	330.19	337.20
35000	334.33	339.52	342.65	344.48	346.59	348.98	351.68	354.76	358.27	362.27	366.86	372.12	378.19	385.22	393.40
40000	382.09	388.02	391.58	393.70	396.10	398.83	401.92	405.44	409.45	414.02	419.27	425.28	432.22	440.26	449.60
45000	429.86	436.52	440.51	442.91	445.61	448.68	452.16	456.12	460.63	465.78	471.67	478.44	486.25	495.29	505.80
50000	477.62	485.02	489.46	492.12	495.13	498.54	502.40	506.80	511.81	517.53	524.08	531.60	540.28	550.32	562.00

MONTHLY PAYMENT
REQUIRED TO AMORTIZE A LOAN
11¾%

TERM AMOUNT	1 YEAR	2 YEARS	3 YEARS	4 YEARS	5 YEARS	6 YEARS	7 YEARS	8 YEARS	9 YEARS	10 YEARS	11 YEARS	12 YEARS	13 YEARS	14 YEARS	15 YEARS
$100	8.87	4.69	3.30	2.61	2.20	1.93	1.74	1.60	1.49	1.41	1.34	1.29	1.24	1.20	1.17
200	17.73	9.37	6.60	5.22	4.40	3.86	3.48	3.20	2.98	2.81	2.68	2.57	2.48	2.40	2.34
300	26.59	14.05	9.89	7.83	6.60	5.79	5.22	4.79	4.47	4.22	4.02	3.85	3.71	3.60	3.50
400	35.45	18.74	13.19	10.44	8.80	7.72	6.95	6.39	5.96	5.62	5.35	5.13	4.95	4.80	4.67
500	44.31	23.42	16.49	13.04	10.99	9.64	8.69	7.99	7.45	7.03	6.69	6.41	6.19	6.00	5.84
600	53.17	28.10	19.78	15.65	13.19	11.57	10.43	9.58	8.94	8.43	8.03	7.69	7.42	7.19	7.00
700	62.03	32.78	23.08	18.26	15.39	13.50	12.17	11.18	10.43	9.84	9.36	8.98	8.66	8.39	8.17
800	70.89	37.47	26.38	20.87	17.59	15.43	13.90	12.78	11.92	11.24	10.70	10.26	9.89	9.59	9.34
900	79.75	42.15	29.67	23.47	19.79	17.35	15.64	14.37	13.40	12.64	12.04	11.54	11.13	10.79	10.50
1000	88.61	46.83	32.97	26.08	21.98	19.28	17.38	15.97	14.89	14.05	13.37	12.82	12.37	11.99	11.67
2000	177.21	93.66	65.93	52.16	43.96	38.56	34.75	31.93	29.78	28.09	26.74	25.64	24.73	23.97	23.33
3000	265.81	140.49	98.89	78.23	65.94	57.84	52.12	47.90	44.67	42.14	40.11	38.45	37.09	35.95	35.00
4000	354.41	187.31	131.86	104.31	87.92	77.11	69.49	63.86	59.56	56.18	53.47	51.27	49.45	47.94	46.66
5000	443.02	234.14	164.82	130.38	109.90	96.39	86.86	79.83	74.45	70.22	66.84	64.09	61.82	59.92	58.33
6000	531.62	280.97	197.78	156.46	131.88	115.67	104.24	95.79	89.33	84.27	80.21	76.90	74.18	71.90	69.99
7000	620.22	327.80	230.74	182.53	153.86	134.94	121.61	111.76	104.22	98.31	93.58	89.72	86.54	83.89	81.65
8000	708.82	374.62	263.71	208.61	175.83	154.22	138.98	127.72	119.11	112.35	106.94	102.54	98.90	95.87	93.32
9000	797.42	421.45	296.67	234.68	197.81	173.50	156.35	143.68	134.00	126.40	120.31	115.35	111.27	107.85	104.98
10000	886.03	468.28	329.63	260.76	219.79	192.78	173.72	159.65	148.89	140.44	133.68	128.17	123.63	119.84	116.65
11000	974.63	515.11	362.60	286.84	241.77	212.05	191.09	175.61	163.78	154.48	147.05	140.99	135.99	131.82	128.31
12000	1063.23	561.93	395.56	312.91	263.75	231.33	208.47	191.58	178.66	168.53	160.41	153.80	148.35	143.80	139.98
13000	1151.83	608.76	428.52	338.99	285.73	250.60	225.84	207.54	193.55	182.57	173.78	166.62	160.71	155.79	151.64
14000	1240.43	655.59	461.48	365.06	307.71	269.88	243.21	223.51	208.44	196.62	187.15	179.44	173.08	167.77	163.30
15000	1329.04	702.42	494.45	391.14	329.69	289.16	260.58	239.47	223.33	210.66	200.51	192.25	185.44	179.75	174.97
16000	1417.64	749.24	527.41	417.21	351.66	308.43	277.95	255.43	238.22	224.70	213.88	205.07	197.80	191.74	186.63
17000	1506.24	796.07	560.37	443.29	373.64	327.71	295.33	271.40	253.11	238.75	227.25	217.89	210.16	203.72	198.30
18000	1594.84	842.90	593.34	469.36	395.62	346.99	312.70	287.36	267.99	252.79	240.62	230.70	222.53	215.70	209.96
19000	1683.45	889.73	626.30	495.44	417.60	366.27	330.07	303.33	282.88	266.84	253.98	243.52	234.89	227.69	221.63
20000	1772.05	936.55	659.26	521.51	439.58	385.54	347.44	319.29	297.77	280.88	267.35	256.34	247.25	239.67	233.29
21000	1860.65	983.38	692.22	547.59	461.56	404.82	364.81	335.26	312.66	294.92	280.72	269.15	259.61	251.65	244.95
22000	1949.25	1030.21	725.19	573.67	483.54	424.10	382.18	351.22	327.55	308.97	294.09	281.97	271.97	263.64	256.62
23000	2037.85	1077.04	758.15	599.74	505.52	443.37	399.56	367.18	342.43	323.01	307.45	294.79	284.34	275.62	268.28
24000	2126.46	1123.86	791.11	625.82	527.49	462.65	416.93	383.15	357.32	337.05	320.82	307.60	296.70	287.60	279.95
25000	2215.06	1170.69	824.08	651.89	549.47	481.93	434.30	399.11	372.21	351.10	334.19	320.42	309.06	299.59	291.61
26000	2303.66	1217.52	857.04	677.97	571.45	501.20	451.67	415.08	387.10	365.14	347.55	333.24	321.42	311.57	303.28
27000	2392.26	1264.35	890.00	704.04	593.43	520.48	469.04	431.04	401.99	379.18	360.92	346.05	333.79	323.55	314.94
28000	2480.86	1311.17	922.96	730.12	615.41	539.76	486.41	447.01	416.87	393.23	374.29	358.87	346.15	335.54	326.60
29000	2569.47	1358.00	955.93	756.19	637.39	559.03	503.79	462.97	431.76	407.27	387.66	371.69	358.51	347.52	338.27
30000	2658.07	1404.83	988.89	782.27	659.37	578.31	521.16	478.93	446.65	421.32	401.02	384.50	370.87	359.50	349.93
35000	3101.08	1638.96	1153.70	912.65	769.26	674.69	608.02	558.76	521.09	491.53	467.86	448.59	432.68	419.42	408.25
40000	3544.09	1873.10	1318.52	1043.02	879.15	771.08	694.88	638.58	595.53	561.75	534.70	512.67	494.49	479.34	466.58
45000	3987.10	2107.24	1483.33	1173.40	989.05	867.46	781.73	718.40	669.97	631.97	601.53	576.75	556.31	539.25	524.90
50000	4430.11	2341.38	1648.15	1303.78	1098.94	963.85	868.59	798.22	744.41	702.19	668.37	640.83	618.12	599.17	583.22

MONTHLY PAYMENT
REQUIRED TO AMORTIZE A LOAN   11¾%

TERM AMOUNT	16 YEARS	17 YEARS	18 YEARS	19 YEARS	20 YEARS	21 YEARS	22 YEARS	23 YEARS	24 YEARS	25 YEARS	26 YEARS	27 YEARS	28 YEARS	30 YEARS	35 YEARS
$100	1.14	1.12	1.10	1.08	1.07	1.06	1.05	1.04	1.03	1.02	1.01	1.01	1.00	.99	.98
200	2.28	2.24	2.20	2.16	2.13	2.11	2.09	2.07	2.05	2.03	2.01	2.01	2.00	1.98	1.95
300	3.42	3.35	3.29	3.24	3.20	3.16	3.13	3.10	3.07	3.05	3.03	3.01	3.00	2.97	2.93
400	4.56	4.47	4.39	4.32	4.26	4.21	4.17	4.13	4.09	4.06	4.04	4.01	3.99	3.96	3.90
500	5.70	5.59	5.48	5.40	5.33	5.26	5.21	5.16	5.11	5.08	5.05	5.01	4.99	4.95	4.87
600	6.84	6.70	6.58	6.48	6.39	6.31	6.25	6.19	6.14	6.09	6.05	6.02	5.99	5.93	5.85
700	7.98	7.82	7.68	7.56	7.46	7.37	7.29	7.22	7.16	7.11	7.06	7.02	6.98	6.92	6.82
800	9.12	8.94	8.77	8.64	8.52	8.42	8.33	8.25	8.18	8.12	8.07	8.02	7.98	7.91	7.80
900	10.26	10.05	9.87	9.72	9.59	9.47	9.37	9.28	9.20	9.13	9.08	9.02	8.98	8.90	8.77
1000	11.40	11.17	10.97	10.80	10.65	10.52	10.41	10.31	10.22	10.15	10.08	10.02	9.97	9.89	9.74
2000	22.79	22.33	21.93	21.59	21.30	21.04	20.81	20.62	20.44	20.29	20.16	20.04	19.94	19.77	19.48
3000	34.19	33.49	32.90	32.39	31.94	31.55	31.22	30.92	30.66	30.44	30.24	30.06	29.91	29.65	29.22
4000	45.58	44.66	43.86	43.18	42.59	42.07	41.62	41.23	40.88	40.58	40.32	40.08	39.88	39.53	38.96
5000	56.97	55.82	54.83	53.97	53.23	52.59	52.03	51.53	51.10	50.73	50.39	50.10	49.84	49.41	48.70
6000	68.37	66.98	65.79	64.77	63.88	63.10	62.43	61.84	61.32	60.87	60.47	60.12	59.81	59.30	58.44
7000	79.76	78.14	76.76	75.56	74.52	73.62	72.84	72.15	71.54	71.02	70.55	70.14	69.78	69.18	68.18
8000	91.15	89.31	87.72	86.35	85.17	84.14	83.24	82.45	81.76	81.16	80.63	80.16	79.75	79.06	77.92
9000	102.55	100.47	98.68	97.15	95.81	94.65	93.64	92.76	91.98	91.30	90.71	90.18	89.71	88.94	87.66
10000	113.94	111.63	109.65	107.94	106.46	105.17	104.05	103.06	102.20	101.45	100.78	100.22	99.68	98.82	97.40
11000	125.34	122.79	120.61	118.73	117.10	115.69	114.45	113.37	112.42	111.59	110.86	110.24	109.65	108.70	107.14
12000	136.73	133.96	131.58	129.53	127.75	126.20	124.85	123.68	122.64	121.74	120.94	120.26	119.61	118.59	116.88
13000	148.12	145.12	142.54	140.32	138.39	136.72	135.26	133.98	132.86	131.88	131.02	130.28	129.58	128.47	126.62
14000	159.52	156.28	153.51	151.11	149.04	147.23	145.66	144.29	143.08	142.03	141.10	140.28	139.55	138.35	136.36
15000	170.91	167.45	164.47	161.91	159.68	157.75	156.07	154.59	153.30	152.17	151.17	150.30	149.52	148.23	146.09
16000	182.30	178.61	175.44	172.70	170.33	168.27	166.47	164.90	163.52	162.32	161.25	160.32	159.48	158.11	155.83
17000	193.70	189.77	186.40	183.49	180.97	178.78	176.88	175.21	173.74	172.46	171.33	170.34	169.45	168.00	165.57
18000	205.09	200.93	197.36	194.28	191.62	189.30	187.28	185.51	183.96	182.60	181.41	180.35	179.42	177.88	175.31
19000	216.49	212.10	208.33	205.08	202.26	199.82	197.68	195.82	194.18	192.75	191.49	190.37	189.39	187.76	185.05
20000	227.88	223.26	219.29	215.87	212.91	210.33	208.09	206.12	204.40	202.89	201.56	200.39	199.36	197.64	194.79
21000	239.27	234.42	230.26	226.67	223.55	220.85	218.49	216.43	214.62	213.04	211.64	210.41	209.32	207.52	204.53
22000	250.67	245.58	241.22	237.46	234.20	231.37	228.90	226.74	224.84	223.18	221.72	220.43	219.29	217.41	214.27
23000	262.06	256.75	252.19	248.25	244.84	241.88	239.30	237.04	235.06	233.33	231.80	230.45	229.26	227.29	224.01
24000	273.45	267.91	263.15	259.05	255.49	252.40	249.70	247.35	245.28	243.47	241.88	240.47	239.23	237.17	233.75
25000	284.85	279.07	274.12	269.84	266.13	262.92	260.11	257.65	255.50	253.62	251.95	250.49	249.20	247.05	243.49
26000	296.24	290.24	285.08	280.63	276.78	273.43	270.51	267.96	265.72	263.76	262.03	260.51	259.16	256.93	253.23
27000	307.64	301.40	296.05	291.43	287.42	283.95	280.92	278.27	275.94	273.90	272.11	270.53	269.13	266.81	262.97
28000	319.03	312.56	307.01	302.22	298.07	294.46	291.32	288.57	286.16	284.05	282.19	280.55	279.10	276.70	272.71
29000	330.42	323.72	317.97	313.01	308.72	304.98	301.73	298.88	296.38	294.19	292.27	290.57	289.07	286.58	282.44
30000	341.82	334.89	328.94	323.81	319.36	315.50	312.13	309.18	306.60	304.34	302.34	300.59	299.04	296.46	292.18
35000	398.79	390.70	383.76	377.77	372.59	368.08	364.15	360.71	357.70	355.06	352.73	350.69	348.88	345.87	340.87
40000	455.75	446.51	438.58	431.74	425.81	420.66	416.17	412.24	408.80	405.78	403.12	400.78	398.72	395.28	389.58
45000	512.72	502.33	493.41	485.71	479.04	473.24	468.19	463.77	459.90	456.50	453.51	450.88	448.55	444.68	438.27
50000	569.69	558.14	548.23	539.67	532.27	525.83	520.21	515.30	511.00	507.23	503.90	500.98	498.39	494.09	486.97

MONTHLY PAYMENT
12% REQUIRED TO AMORTIZE A LOAN

TERM AMOUNT	1 YEAR	2 YEARS	3 YEARS	4 YEARS	5 YEARS	6 YEARS	7 YEARS	8 YEARS	9 YEARS	10 YEARS	11 YEARS	12 YEARS	13 YEARS	14 YEARS	15 YEARS
$100	8.88	4.70	3.31	2.62	2.21	1.94	1.75	1.61	1.51	1.42	1.36	1.30	1.26	1.22	1.19
200	17.75	9.39	6.62	5.24	4.42	3.88	3.50	3.22	3.01	2.84	2.71	2.60	2.51	2.43	2.37
300	26.62	14.09	9.93	7.86	6.63	5.82	5.25	4.83	4.51	4.26	4.06	3.89	3.76	3.64	3.55
400	35.49	18.78	13.24	10.48	8.84	7.76	7.00	6.44	6.01	5.68	5.41	5.19	5.01	4.86	4.73
500	44.36	23.47	16.54	13.10	11.05	9.70	8.75	8.05	7.52	7.10	6.76	6.48	6.26	6.07	5.91
600	53.23	28.17	19.85	15.72	13.26	11.64	10.50	9.66	9.02	8.51	8.11	7.78	7.51	7.28	7.09
700	62.10	32.86	23.16	18.34	15.47	13.58	12.25	11.27	10.52	9.93	9.46	9.08	8.76	8.50	8.28
800	70.98	37.56	26.47	20.96	17.68	15.52	14.00	12.88	12.02	11.35	10.81	10.37	10.01	9.71	9.46
900	79.85	42.25	29.77	23.58	19.89	17.46	15.75	14.49	13.52	12.77	12.16	11.67	11.26	10.92	10.64
1000	88.72	46.94	33.08	26.20	22.10	19.40	17.50	16.10	15.03	14.19	13.51	12.96	12.51	12.14	11.82
2000	177.43	93.88	66.16	52.39	44.20	38.80	35.00	32.19	30.05	28.37	27.02	25.92	25.02	24.27	23.64
3000	266.15	140.82	99.23	78.58	66.30	58.20	52.50	48.29	45.07	42.55	40.53	38.88	37.53	36.40	35.45
4000	354.86	187.76	132.31	104.77	88.40	77.60	70.00	64.38	60.09	56.73	54.03	51.84	50.04	48.53	47.27
5000	443.57	234.70	165.39	130.96	110.50	97.00	87.50	80.48	75.11	70.91	67.54	64.80	62.55	60.67	59.09
6000	532.29	281.64	198.46	157.16	132.60	116.40	104.99	96.57	90.13	85.09	81.05	77.76	75.05	72.80	70.90
7000	621.00	328.57	231.54	183.35	154.69	135.80	122.49	112.66	105.16	99.27	94.55	90.72	87.56	84.93	82.72
8000	709.71	375.51	264.61	209.54	176.79	155.20	139.99	128.76	120.18	113.45	108.06	103.68	100.07	97.06	94.53
9000	798.43	422.45	297.69	235.73	198.89	174.60	157.49	144.85	135.20	127.63	121.57	116.64	112.58	109.20	106.35
10000	887.14	469.39	330.77	261.92	220.99	194.00	174.99	160.95	150.22	141.81	135.08	129.60	125.09	121.33	118.17
11000	975.85	516.33	363.84	288.12	243.09	213.40	192.49	177.04	165.24	155.99	148.58	142.56	137.60	133.46	129.98
12000	1064.55	563.27	396.92	314.31	265.19	232.80	209.98	193.14	180.26	170.17	162.09	155.52	150.10	145.59	141.80
13000	1153.28	610.20	430.00	340.50	287.28	252.20	227.48	209.23	195.28	184.35	175.60	168.48	162.61	157.72	153.61
14000	1241.99	657.14	463.07	366.69	309.38	271.60	244.98	225.32	210.31	198.53	189.10	181.44	175.12	169.86	165.43
15000	1330.71	704.08	496.15	392.88	331.48	291.00	262.48	241.42	225.33	212.71	202.61	194.40	187.63	181.99	177.25
16000	1419.42	751.02	529.22	419.08	353.58	310.40	279.98	257.51	240.35	226.89	216.12	207.36	200.14	194.12	189.06
17000	1508.13	797.96	562.30	445.27	375.68	329.80	297.48	273.61	255.37	241.07	229.63	220.32	212.64	206.25	200.88
18000	1596.85	844.90	595.38	471.46	397.78	349.20	314.97	289.70	270.39	255.25	243.13	233.28	225.15	218.39	212.69
19000	1685.56	891.83	628.45	497.65	419.88	368.60	332.47	305.80	285.41	269.43	256.64	246.24	237.66	230.52	224.51
20000	1774.27	938.77	661.53	523.84	441.97	388.00	349.97	321.89	300.43	283.61	270.15	259.20	250.17	242.65	236.33
21000	1862.99	985.71	694.61	550.04	464.07	407.40	367.47	337.98	315.46	297.79	283.66	272.16	262.68	254.78	248.14
22000	1951.70	1032.65	727.68	576.23	486.17	426.80	384.97	354.08	330.48	311.97	297.16	285.11	275.19	266.91	259.96
23000	2040.41	1079.59	760.76	602.42	508.27	446.20	402.47	370.17	345.50	326.15	310.67	298.07	287.69	279.05	271.78
24000	2129.13	1126.53	793.83	628.61	530.37	465.60	419.96	386.27	360.52	340.33	324.17	311.03	300.20	291.18	283.59
25000	2217.84	1173.47	826.91	654.80	552.47	485.00	437.46	402.36	375.54	354.51	337.68	323.99	312.71	303.31	295.41
26000	2306.55	1220.40	859.99	681.00	574.56	504.40	454.96	418.45	390.56	368.69	351.19	336.95	325.22	315.44	307.22
27000	2395.27	1267.34	893.06	707.19	596.66	523.80	472.46	434.55	405.58	382.87	364.70	349.91	337.73	327.58	319.04
28000	2483.98	1314.28	926.14	733.38	618.76	543.20	489.96	450.64	420.61	397.05	378.20	362.87	350.24	339.71	330.86
29000	2572.69	1361.22	959.22	759.57	640.86	562.60	507.46	466.74	435.63	411.23	391.71	375.83	362.74	351.84	342.67
30000	2661.41	1408.16	992.29	785.76	662.96	582.00	524.95	482.83	450.65	425.41	405.22	388.79	375.25	363.97	354.49
35000	3104.98	1642.85	1157.67	916.72	773.45	679.00	612.45	563.30	525.76	496.31	472.75	453.59	437.79	424.63	413.57
40000	3546.54	1877.54	1323.05	1047.68	883.94	776.00	699.94	643.77	600.86	567.20	540.29	518.39	500.33	485.29	472.65
45000	3992.11	2112.23	1488.44	1178.64	994.44	873.00	787.43	724.25	675.97	638.12	607.82	583.18	562.88	545.96	531.73
50000	4435.68	2346.93	1653.82	1309.60	1104.93	970.00	874.92	804.72	751.08	709.02	675.36	647.98	625.42	606.62	590.81

MONTHLY PAYMENT
REQUIRED TO AMORTIZE A LOAN 12%

TERM AMOUNT	35 YEARS	30 YEARS	28 YEARS	27 YEARS	26 YEARS	25 YEARS	24 YEARS	23 YEARS	22 YEARS	21 YEARS	20 YEARS	19 YEARS	18 YEARS	17 YEARS	16 YEARS
$100	1.00	1.01	1.02	1.02	1.03	1.04	1.04	1.05	1.06	1.07	1.09	1.10	1.12	1.14	1.16
200	1.99	2.02	2.03	2.04	2.06	2.07	2.08	2.10	2.12	2.14	2.17	2.20	2.23	2.27	2.31
300	2.98	3.02	3.05	3.06	3.08	3.10	3.12	3.15	3.18	3.21	3.25	3.29	3.34	3.40	3.47
400	3.98	4.03	4.06	4.08	4.11	4.13	4.16	4.20	4.23	4.28	4.33	4.39	4.45	4.53	4.62
500	4.97	5.04	5.08	5.10	5.13	5.16	5.20	5.24	5.29	5.35	5.42	5.48	5.57	5.66	5.78
600	5.96	6.04	6.09	6.12	6.16	6.20	6.24	6.29	6.35	6.41	6.49	6.58	6.68	6.80	6.93
700	6.95	7.05	7.11	7.14	7.18	7.23	7.28	7.34	7.41	7.48	7.57	7.67	7.79	7.93	8.09
800	7.95	8.06	8.12	8.16	8.21	8.26	8.32	8.39	8.46	8.55	8.65	8.77	8.90	9.06	9.24
900	8.94	9.06	9.14	9.18	9.23	9.29	9.36	9.43	9.52	9.62	9.73	9.87	10.02	10.19	10.40
1000	9.93	10.07	10.15	10.20	10.26	10.32	10.40	10.48	10.58	10.69	10.81	10.96	11.13	11.32	11.55
2000	19.86	20.13	20.30	20.40	20.51	20.64	20.79	20.96	21.15	21.37	21.62	21.92	22.25	22.64	23.10
3000	29.79	30.20	30.45	30.60	30.77	30.96	31.18	31.44	31.73	32.05	32.43	32.87	33.38	33.96	34.65
4000	39.71	40.26	40.59	40.79	41.02	41.28	41.58	41.91	42.30	42.74	43.24	43.83	44.50	45.28	46.20
5000	49.64	50.32	50.74	50.99	51.28	51.60	51.97	52.39	52.87	53.42	54.05	54.78	55.63	56.60	57.75
6000	59.57	60.39	60.89	61.19	61.53	61.92	62.36	62.87	63.44	64.10	64.86	65.74	66.75	67.92	69.29
7000	69.49	70.45	71.03	71.39	71.78	72.24	72.75	73.34	74.02	74.79	75.67	76.69	77.87	79.24	80.84
8000	79.42	80.52	81.18	81.58	82.04	82.56	83.15	83.82	84.59	85.47	86.48	87.65	89.00	90.56	92.39
9000	89.35	90.58	91.33	91.78	92.30	92.88	93.54	94.30	95.16	96.15	97.29	98.61	100.12	101.88	103.94
10000	99.27	100.64	101.48	101.98	102.55	103.19	103.93	104.77	105.74	106.84	108.10	109.56	111.25	113.20	115.49
11000	109.20	110.71	111.62	112.18	112.80	113.51	114.33	115.25	116.31	117.52	118.91	120.52	122.37	124.52	127.04
12000	119.13	120.77	121.77	122.37	123.06	123.83	124.72	125.73	126.88	128.20	129.72	131.47	133.50	135.84	138.58
13000	129.05	130.84	131.92	132.57	133.31	134.15	135.11	136.20	137.45	138.89	140.53	142.43	144.62	147.16	150.13
14000	138.98	140.90	142.06	142.77	143.56	144.47	145.50	146.68	148.03	149.57	151.34	153.38	155.74	158.48	161.68
15000	148.91	150.96	152.21	152.96	153.82	154.79	155.90	157.16	158.60	160.25	162.15	164.34	166.87	169.80	173.23
16000	158.83	161.03	162.36	163.16	164.07	165.11	166.29	167.63	169.17	170.94	172.96	175.29	177.99	181.12	184.78
17000	168.76	171.09	172.51	173.36	174.33	175.43	176.68	178.11	179.75	181.62	183.77	186.25	189.12	192.44	196.33
18000	178.69	181.15	182.65	183.56	184.58	185.75	187.07	188.59	190.32	192.30	194.58	197.20	200.24	203.76	207.87
19000	188.61	191.22	192.80	193.75	194.84	196.07	197.47	199.07	200.89	202.99	205.39	208.16	211.36	215.08	219.42
20000	198.54	201.28	202.95	203.95	205.09	206.38	207.86	209.54	211.47	213.67	216.20	219.12	222.49	226.40	230.97
21000	208.47	211.35	213.09	214.15	215.34	216.70	218.25	220.02	222.04	224.35	227.01	230.07	233.61	237.72	242.52
22000	218.40	221.41	223.24	224.35	225.60	227.02	228.65	230.50	232.61	235.04	237.82	241.03	244.74	249.04	254.07
23000	228.32	231.47	233.39	234.54	235.85	237.34	239.04	240.97	243.18	245.72	248.63	251.98	255.86	260.36	265.62
24000	238.25	241.54	243.54	244.74	246.11	247.66	249.43	251.45	253.76	256.40	259.44	262.94	266.99	271.68	277.16
25000	248.18	251.60	253.68	254.94	256.36	257.98	259.82	261.93	264.33	267.08	270.25	273.89	278.11	283.00	288.71
26000	258.10	261.67	263.83	265.13	266.62	268.30	270.22	272.40	274.90	277.77	281.06	284.85	289.23	294.32	300.26
27000	268.03	271.73	273.98	275.33	276.87	278.62	280.61	282.88	285.48	288.45	291.87	295.81	300.36	305.64	311.81
28000	277.96	281.79	284.12	285.53	287.12	288.94	291.00	293.36	296.05	299.13	302.68	306.76	311.48	316.96	323.36
29000	287.88	291.86	294.27	295.73	297.38	299.26	301.39	303.83	306.62	309.82	313.49	317.72	322.61	328.28	334.91
30000	297.81	301.92	304.42	305.92	307.63	309.57	311.79	314.31	317.20	320.50	324.30	328.67	333.73	339.60	346.45
35000	347.44	352.24	355.15	356.91	358.90	361.17	363.75	366.69	370.06	373.92	378.35	383.45	389.35	396.20	404.20
40000	397.08	402.56	405.89	407.90	410.17	412.76	415.71	419.07	422.93	427.33	432.40	438.23	444.97	452.80	461.94
45000	446.71	452.88	456.63	458.88	461.45	464.36	467.67	471.46	475.79	480.75	486.45	493.01	500.59	509.40	519.68
50000	496.35	503.20	507.36	509.87	512.72	515.95	519.64	523.85	528.66	534.16	540.49	547.78	556.21	566.00	577.42

MONTHLY PAYMENT
12¼% REQUIRED TO AMORTIZE A LOAN

TERM AMOUNT	1 YEAR	2 YEARS	3 YEARS	4 YEARS	5 YEARS	6 YEARS	7 YEARS	8 YEARS	9 YEARS	10 YEARS	11 YEARS	12 YEARS	13 YEARS	14 YEARS	15 YEARS
$100	8.89	4.71	3.32	2.64	2.23	1.96	1.77	1.63	1.52	1.44	1.37	1.32	1.27	1.23	1.20
200	17.77	9.41	6.64	5.27	4.45	3.91	3.53	3.25	3.04	2.87	2.73	2.63	2.54	2.46	2.40
300	26.65	14.12	9.96	7.90	6.67	5.86	5.29	4.87	4.55	4.30	4.10	3.94	3.80	3.69	3.60
400	35.53	18.82	13.28	10.53	8.89	7.81	7.06	6.49	6.07	5.73	5.46	5.25	5.07	4.92	4.79
500	44.42	23.53	16.60	13.16	11.11	9.77	8.82	8.12	7.58	7.16	6.83	6.56	6.33	6.15	5.99
600	53.30	28.23	19.92	15.79	13.34	11.72	10.58	9.74	9.10	8.60	8.19	7.87	7.60	7.37	7.19
700	62.18	32.94	23.24	18.42	15.56	13.67	12.34	11.36	10.61	10.03	9.56	9.18	8.86	8.60	8.38
800	71.06	37.64	26.56	21.05	17.78	15.62	14.11	12.98	12.13	11.46	10.92	10.49	10.13	9.83	9.58
900	79.95	42.35	29.88	23.68	20.00	17.58	15.87	14.61	13.64	12.89	12.29	11.80	11.39	11.06	10.78
1000	88.83	47.05	33.19	26.31	22.22	19.53	17.63	16.23	15.16	14.32	13.65	13.11	12.66	12.29	11.97
2000	177.65	94.10	66.38	52.62	44.44	39.05	35.26	32.45	30.32	28.64	27.30	26.21	25.31	24.57	23.94
3000	266.48	141.15	99.57	78.93	66.66	58.58	52.88	48.68	45.47	42.96	40.95	39.31	37.97	36.85	35.91
4000	355.30	188.20	132.76	105.24	88.88	78.10	70.51	64.90	60.63	57.27	54.59	52.42	50.62	49.13	47.88
5000	444.13	235.25	165.95	131.55	111.10	97.62	88.13	81.13	75.78	71.59	68.24	65.52	63.28	61.41	59.85
6000	532.95	282.30	199.14	157.86	133.32	117.15	105.76	97.35	90.94	85.91	81.89	78.62	75.93	73.70	71.82
7000	621.78	329.35	232.33	184.17	155.53	136.67	123.38	113.58	106.09	100.23	95.54	91.73	88.59	85.98	83.79
8000	710.60	376.40	265.52	210.47	177.75	156.19	141.01	129.80	121.25	114.54	109.18	104.83	101.24	98.26	95.75
9000	799.43	423.45	298.71	236.78	199.97	175.72	158.63	146.03	136.40	128.86	122.83	117.93	113.90	110.54	107.72
10000	888.25	470.50	331.90	263.09	222.19	195.24	176.26	162.25	151.56	143.18	136.48	131.04	126.55	122.82	119.69
11000	977.08	517.55	365.09	289.40	244.41	214.76	193.88	178.48	166.71	157.50	150.13	144.14	139.21	135.11	131.66
12000	1065.90	564.60	398.28	315.71	266.63	234.29	211.51	194.70	181.87	171.81	163.77	157.24	151.86	147.39	143.63
13000	1154.73	611.65	431.47	342.02	288.85	253.81	229.13	210.92	197.02	186.13	177.42	170.35	164.52	159.67	155.60
14000	1243.55	658.70	464.66	368.33	311.06	273.33	246.76	227.15	212.18	200.45	191.07	183.45	177.17	171.95	167.57
15000	1332.38	705.75	497.85	394.64	333.28	292.86	264.38	243.37	227.33	214.77	204.72	196.55	189.83	184.24	179.53
16000	1421.20	752.80	531.04	420.94	355.50	312.38	282.01	259.60	242.49	229.08	218.36	209.65	202.48	196.51	191.50
17000	1510.03	799.85	564.23	447.25	377.72	331.90	299.63	275.82	257.64	243.40	232.01	222.76	215.14	208.80	203.47
18000	1598.85	846.90	597.42	473.56	399.94	351.43	317.26	292.05	272.80	257.72	245.66	235.86	227.79	221.08	215.44
19000	1687.68	893.94	630.61	499.87	422.16	370.95	334.88	308.27	287.95	272.04	259.31	248.96	240.45	233.36	227.41
20000	1776.50	940.99	663.80	526.18	444.37	390.47	352.51	324.50	303.11	286.35	272.95	262.07	253.10	245.64	239.38
21000	1865.32	988.04	696.99	552.49	466.59	410.00	370.13	340.72	318.27	300.67	286.60	275.17	265.76	257.92	251.35
22000	1954.15	1035.09	730.18	578.79	488.81	429.52	387.76	356.95	333.42	314.99	300.25	288.27	278.41	270.20	263.31
23000	2042.97	1082.14	763.37	605.10	511.03	449.04	405.39	373.17	348.58	329.30	313.90	301.38	291.07	282.49	275.28
24000	2131.80	1129.19	796.56	631.41	533.25	468.57	423.01	389.40	363.73	343.62	327.54	314.48	303.72	294.77	287.25
25000	2220.63	1176.24	829.75	657.72	555.47	488.09	440.64	405.62	378.89	357.94	341.19	327.58	316.38	307.05	299.22
26000	2309.45	1223.29	862.94	684.03	577.69	507.62	458.26	421.84	394.04	372.26	354.84	340.69	329.03	319.33	311.19
27000	2398.27	1270.34	896.13	710.34	599.90	527.14	475.89	438.07	409.20	386.57	368.49	353.78	341.69	331.62	323.16
28000	2487.10	1317.39	929.32	736.65	622.12	546.66	493.51	454.29	424.35	400.89	382.13	366.89	354.34	343.90	335.13
29000	2575.92	1364.44	962.51	762.95	644.34	566.19	511.14	470.52	439.51	415.21	395.78	379.99	367.00	356.18	347.10
30000	2664.75	1411.49	995.70	789.26	666.56	585.71	528.76	486.74	454.66	429.53	409.43	393.10	379.65	368.46	359.06
35000	3108.87	1646.74	1161.65	920.81	777.65	683.33	616.89	567.87	530.44	501.11	477.67	458.61	442.93	429.87	418.91
40000	3552.99	1881.98	1327.60	1052.35	888.74	780.94	705.01	648.99	606.22	572.70	545.91	524.13	506.20	491.28	478.75
45000	3997.12	2117.23	1493.54	1183.89	999.84	878.56	793.14	730.11	681.99	644.29	614.14	589.65	569.47	552.69	538.55
50000	4441.24	2352.48	1659.49	1315.43	1110.93	976.18	881.27	811.24	757.77	715.87	682.38	655.16	632.75	614.10	598.44

MONTHLY PAYMENT
REQUIRED TO AMORTIZE A LOAN — 12¼%

TERM AMOUNT	35 YEARS	30 YEARS	28 YEARS	27 YEARS	26 YEARS	25 YEARS	24 YEARS	23 YEARS	22 YEARS	21 YEARS	20 YEARS	19 YEARS	18 YEARS	17 YEARS	16 YEARS
$100	1.02	1.03	1.04	1.04	1.05	1.05	1.06	1.07	1.08	1.09	1.10	1.12	1.13	1.15	1.18
200	2.03	2.05	2.07	2.08	2.09	2.10	2.12	2.13	2.15	2.18	2.20	2.23	2.26	2.30	2.35
300	3.04	3.08	3.10	3.12	3.13	3.15	3.17	3.20	3.23	3.26	3.30	3.34	3.39	3.45	3.52
400	4.05	4.10	4.14	4.16	4.18	4.20	4.23	4.26	4.30	4.35	4.40	4.45	4.52	4.60	4.69
500	5.06	5.13	5.17	5.20	5.22	5.25	5.29	5.33	5.38	5.43	5.50	5.56	5.65	5.74	5.86
600	6.07	6.15	6.20	6.23	6.26	6.30	6.34	6.39	6.45	6.52	6.59	6.68	6.78	6.89	7.03
700	7.09	7.18	7.23	7.27	7.31	7.35	7.40	7.46	7.52	7.60	7.69	7.79	7.90	8.04	8.20
800	8.10	8.20	8.27	8.31	8.35	8.40	8.46	8.52	8.60	8.69	8.79	8.90	9.03	9.19	9.37
900	9.11	9.23	9.30	9.34	9.39	9.45	9.51	9.59	9.67	9.77	9.88	10.01	10.16	10.34	10.54
1000	10.12	10.25	10.33	10.38	10.44	10.50	10.57	10.65	10.75	10.86	10.98	11.12	11.29	11.48	11.71
2000	20.23	20.50	20.66	20.76	20.87	20.99	21.14	21.30	21.49	21.71	21.96	22.24	22.57	22.96	23.41
3000	30.35	30.74	30.99	31.13	31.30	31.49	31.70	31.95	32.23	32.56	32.93	33.36	33.86	34.44	35.12
4000	40.46	40.99	41.31	41.51	41.73	41.98	42.27	42.60	42.98	43.41	43.91	44.48	45.14	45.92	46.82
5000	50.58	51.24	51.64	51.88	52.16	52.48	52.84	53.25	53.72	54.26	54.88	55.60	56.43	57.39	58.52
6000	60.69	61.48	61.97	62.26	62.59	62.97	63.40	63.90	64.46	65.11	65.86	66.72	67.71	68.87	70.23
7000	70.81	71.73	72.30	72.64	73.02	73.46	73.97	74.54	75.20	75.96	76.83	77.83	79.00	80.35	81.93
8000	80.92	81.98	82.62	83.01	83.45	83.96	84.53	85.19	85.95	86.81	87.81	88.95	90.28	91.83	93.63
9000	91.04	92.22	92.95	93.39	93.89	94.45	95.10	95.84	96.69	97.66	98.78	100.07	101.57	103.31	105.34
10000	101.15	102.47	103.28	103.76	104.32	104.95	105.67	106.49	107.43	108.51	109.76	111.19	112.85	114.78	117.04
11000	111.27	112.72	113.60	114.14	114.75	115.44	116.23	117.14	118.17	119.36	120.73	122.31	124.14	126.26	128.74
12000	121.38	122.96	123.93	124.52	125.18	125.94	126.80	127.79	128.92	130.21	131.71	133.43	135.42	137.74	140.45
13000	131.50	133.21	134.26	134.89	135.61	136.43	137.37	138.44	139.66	141.06	142.68	144.55	146.71	149.22	152.15
14000	141.61	143.46	144.59	145.27	146.04	146.92	147.93	149.08	150.40	151.91	153.66	155.66	157.99	160.70	163.86
15000	151.73	153.70	154.91	155.64	156.47	157.42	158.50	159.73	161.14	162.76	164.63	166.78	169.28	172.17	175.56
16000	161.84	163.95	165.24	166.02	166.90	167.91	169.06	170.38	171.89	173.62	175.61	177.90	180.56	183.65	187.26
17000	171.96	174.20	175.57	176.39	177.34	178.41	179.63	181.03	182.63	184.47	186.58	189.02	191.85	195.13	198.97
18000	182.07	184.44	185.89	186.77	187.77	188.90	190.20	191.68	193.37	195.32	197.56	200.14	203.13	206.61	210.67
19000	192.19	194.69	196.22	197.15	198.20	199.40	200.76	202.33	204.11	206.17	208.53	211.26	214.41	218.09	222.37
20000	202.30	204.94	206.55	207.52	208.63	209.89	211.33	212.97	214.86	217.02	219.51	222.38	225.70	229.56	234.08
21000	212.42	215.18	216.88	217.90	219.06	220.38	221.90	223.62	225.60	227.87	230.48	233.49	236.98	241.04	245.78
22000	222.53	225.43	227.20	228.27	229.49	230.88	232.46	234.27	236.34	238.72	241.46	244.61	248.27	252.52	257.48
23000	232.65	235.68	237.53	238.65	239.92	241.37	243.03	244.92	247.09	249.57	252.43	255.73	259.55	264.00	269.19
24000	242.76	245.92	247.86	249.02	250.35	251.87	253.59	255.57	257.83	260.42	263.41	266.85	270.84	275.48	280.89
25000	252.88	256.17	258.18	259.40	260.78	262.36	264.16	266.22	268.57	271.27	274.38	277.97	282.12	286.95	292.59
26000	262.99	266.42	268.51	269.78	271.22	272.86	274.73	276.87	279.31	282.12	285.36	289.09	293.41	298.43	304.30
27000	273.10	276.66	278.84	280.15	281.65	283.35	285.29	287.51	290.06	292.97	296.33	300.21	304.69	309.91	316.00
28000	283.22	286.91	289.17	290.53	292.08	293.84	295.86	298.16	300.80	303.82	307.31	311.32	315.98	321.39	327.71
29000	293.33	297.16	299.49	300.90	302.51	304.34	306.42	308.81	311.54	314.68	318.28	322.44	327.26	332.86	339.41
30000	303.45	307.40	309.82	311.28	312.94	314.83	316.99	319.46	322.28	325.53	329.26	333.56	338.55	344.34	351.11
35000	354.02	358.63	361.46	363.16	365.10	367.30	369.82	372.70	376.00	379.78	384.13	389.15	394.97	401.73	409.63
40000	404.60	409.87	413.09	415.04	417.25	419.78	422.65	425.94	429.71	434.03	439.01	444.75	451.39	459.12	468.15
45000	455.17	461.10	464.71	466.92	469.41	472.25	475.49	479.19	483.42	488.28	493.88	500.44	507.82	516.51	526.67
50000	505.75	512.33	516.36	518.80	521.56	524.72	528.32	532.43	537.14	542.54	548.76	555.93	564.24	573.90	585.18

MONTHLY PAYMENT
12½ % REQUIRED TO AMORTIZE A LOAN

TERM AMOUNT	1 YEAR	2 YEARS	3 YEARS	4 YEARS	5 YEARS	6 YEARS	7 YEARS	8 YEARS	9 YEARS	10 YEARS	11 YEARS	12 YEARS	13 YEARS	14 YEARS	15 YEARS
$100	8.90	4.72	3.34	2.65	2.24	1.97	1.78	1.64	1.53	1.45	1.38	1.33	1.29	1.25	1.22
200	17.79	9.44	6.67	5.29	4.47	3.93	3.56	3.28	3.06	2.90	2.76	2.65	2.57	2.49	2.44
300	26.69	14.15	10.00	7.93	6.71	5.90	5.33	4.91	4.59	4.34	4.14	3.98	3.85	3.73	3.64
400	35.58	18.87	13.33	10.58	8.94	7.86	7.11	6.55	6.12	5.79	5.52	5.30	5.13	4.98	4.85
500	44.47	23.58	16.66	13.22	11.17	9.83	8.88	8.18	7.65	7.23	6.90	6.63	6.41	6.22	6.07
600	53.37	28.30	19.99	15.86	13.41	11.79	10.66	9.82	9.18	8.68	8.28	7.95	7.69	7.46	7.28
700	62.26	33.02	23.32	18.50	15.64	13.76	12.43	11.45	10.71	10.12	9.66	9.28	8.97	8.71	8.49
800	71.15	37.73	26.65	21.15	17.88	15.72	14.21	13.09	12.24	11.57	11.04	10.60	10.25	9.95	9.70
900	80.05	42.45	29.98	23.79	20.11	17.69	15.98	14.72	13.77	13.01	12.41	11.93	11.53	11.19	10.91
1000	88.94	47.17	33.31	26.43	22.34	19.65	17.76	16.36	15.29	14.46	13.79	13.25	12.81	12.44	12.13
2000	177.88	94.33	66.61	52.86	44.68	39.30	35.51	32.72	30.58	28.92	27.58	26.50	25.61	24.87	24.25
3000	266.81	141.49	99.92	79.28	67.02	58.95	53.26	49.07	45.87	43.37	41.37	39.75	38.41	37.30	36.37
4000	355.75	188.65	133.22	105.71	89.36	78.59	71.02	65.43	61.16	57.83	55.16	52.99	51.21	49.73	48.49
5000	444.69	235.81	166.52	132.13	111.70	98.24	88.77	81.78	76.45	72.28	68.95	66.24	64.02	62.17	60.61
6000	533.62	282.97	199.83	158.56	134.04	117.89	106.52	98.14	91.74	86.74	82.74	79.49	76.82	74.60	72.74
7000	622.56	330.13	233.13	184.98	156.38	137.54	124.03	114.49	107.03	101.19	96.52	92.74	89.62	87.03	84.86
8000	711.49	377.29	266.43	211.41	178.71	157.18	142.03	130.85	122.32	115.65	110.31	105.98	102.42	99.46	96.98
9000	800.43	424.45	299.74	237.83	201.05	176.83	159.78	147.20	137.61	130.10	124.10	119.23	115.22	111.89	109.10
10000	889.37	471.61	333.04	264.26	223.39	196.48	177.53	163.56	152.90	144.56	137.89	132.48	128.03	124.33	121.22
11000	978.30	518.77	366.34	290.68	245.73	216.12	195.28	179.91	168.19	159.01	151.68	145.72	140.83	136.76	133.35
12000	1067.24	565.93	399.65	317.11	268.07	235.77	213.04	196.27	183.48	173.47	165.47	158.97	153.63	149.19	145.47
13000	1156.17	613.09	432.95	343.53	290.40	255.42	230.79	212.62	198.77	187.92	179.25	172.22	166.43	161.62	157.59
14000	1245.11	660.25	466.25	369.96	312.75	275.07	248.54	228.98	214.06	202.38	193.04	185.47	179.24	174.06	169.71
15000	1334.05	707.41	499.56	396.39	335.09	294.71	266.29	245.34	229.35	216.83	206.83	198.71	192.04	186.49	181.83
16000	1422.98	754.57	532.86	422.81	357.42	314.36	284.05	261.69	244.64	231.29	220.62	211.96	204.84	198.92	193.95
17000	1511.92	801.73	566.16	449.24	379.76	334.01	301.80	278.05	259.93	245.74	234.41	225.21	217.64	211.35	206.08
18000	1600.85	848.90	599.47	475.66	402.10	353.66	319.55	294.40	275.22	260.20	248.20	238.46	230.44	223.78	218.20
19000	1689.79	896.06	632.77	502.09	424.44	373.30	337.30	310.76	290.51	274.65	261.99	251.70	243.25	236.22	230.32
20000	1778.73	943.22	666.07	528.51	446.78	392.95	355.06	327.11	305.80	289.11	275.77	264.95	256.05	248.65	242.44
21000	1867.66	990.38	699.38	554.94	469.12	412.60	372.81	343.47	321.09	303.56	289.56	278.20	268.85	261.08	254.56
22000	1956.60	1037.54	732.68	581.36	491.46	432.24	390.56	359.82	336.37	318.02	303.35	291.44	281.65	273.51	266.69
23000	2045.53	1084.70	765.98	607.79	513.80	451.89	408.31	376.18	351.66	332.47	317.14	304.69	294.46	285.95	278.81
24000	2134.47	1131.86	799.29	634.22	536.13	471.54	426.07	392.54	366.95	346.93	330.93	317.94	307.26	298.38	290.93
25000	2223.41	1179.02	832.59	660.64	558.47	491.19	443.82	408.89	382.24	361.38	344.72	331.19	320.06	310.81	303.05
26000	2312.34	1226.18	865.89	687.07	580.81	510.83	461.57	425.25	397.53	375.84	358.50	344.43	332.86	323.24	315.17
27000	2401.28	1273.34	899.20	713.49	603.15	530.48	479.32	441.60	412.82	390.29	372.29	357.68	345.66	335.67	327.30
28000	2490.21	1320.50	932.50	739.92	625.49	550.13	497.08	457.96	428.11	404.75	386.08	370.93	358.47	348.11	339.42
29000	2579.15	1367.66	965.80	766.34	647.83	569.78	514.83	474.31	443.40	419.20	399.87	384.18	371.27	360.54	351.54
30000	2668.09	1414.82	999.11	792.77	670.17	589.42	532.58	490.67	458.69	433.66	413.66	397.42	384.07	372.97	363.66
35000	3112.77	1650.62	1165.62	924.90	781.86	687.66	621.34	572.44	535.14	505.93	482.60	463.66	448.08	435.13	424.27
40000	3557.45	1886.43	1332.14	1057.02	893.55	785.90	710.11	654.22	611.59	578.21	551.54	529.90	512.09	497.29	484.88
45000	4002.13	2122.23	1498.66	1189.66	1005.25	884.13	798.87	736.00	688.03	650.48	620.48	596.13	576.10	559.45	545.49
50000	4446.81	2358.03	1665.18	1321.28	1116.94	982.37	887.63	817.78	764.48	722.76	689.43	662.37	640.11	621.61	606.10

MONTHLY PAYMENT
REQUIRED TO AMORTIZE A LOAN
12½ %

TERM AMOUNT	35 YEARS	30 YEARS	28 YEARS	27 YEARS	26 YEARS	25 YEARS	24 YEARS	23 YEARS	22 YEARS	21 YEARS	20 YEARS	19 YEARS	18 YEARS	17 YEARS	16 YEARS
$100	1.04	1.05	1.06	1.06	1.07	1.07	1.08	1.09	1.10	1.11	1.12	1.13	1.15	1.17	1.19
200	2.07	2.09	2.11	2.12	2.13	2.14	2.15	2.17	2.19	2.21	2.23	2.26	2.29	2.33	2.38
300	3.10	3.13	3.16	3.17	3.19	3.21	3.23	3.25	3.28	3.31	3.35	3.39	3.44	3.50	3.56
400	4.13	4.18	4.21	4.23	4.25	4.27	4.30	4.33	4.37	4.41	4.46	4.52	4.58	4.66	4.75
500	5.16	5.22	5.26	5.28	5.31	5.34	5.38	5.42	5.46	5.51	5.58	5.65	5.73	5.82	5.93
600	6.19	6.26	6.31	6.34	6.37	6.41	6.45	6.50	6.55	6.62	6.69	6.77	6.87	6.99	7.12
700	7.22	7.31	7.36	7.39	7.43	7.47	7.53	7.58	7.64	7.72	7.80	7.90	8.02	8.15	8.31
800	8.25	8.35	8.41	8.45	8.49	8.54	8.60	8.66	8.73	8.82	8.92	9.03	9.16	9.31	9.49
900	9.28	9.39	9.46	9.50	9.55	9.61	9.67	9.74	9.83	9.92	10.03	10.16	10.31	10.48	10.68
1000	10.31	10.44	10.51	10.56	10.61	10.68	10.75	10.83	10.92	11.02	11.15	11.29	11.45	11.64	11.86
2000	20.61	20.86	21.02	21.11	21.22	21.35	21.49	21.65	21.83	22.04	22.29	22.57	22.90	23.28	23.72
3000	30.91	31.29	31.53	31.67	31.83	32.02	32.23	32.47	32.74	33.06	33.43	33.85	34.34	34.91	35.58
4000	41.22	41.72	42.04	42.22	42.44	42.69	42.97	43.29	43.66	44.08	44.57	45.13	45.79	46.55	47.44
5000	51.52	52.15	52.54	52.78	53.05	53.36	53.71	54.11	54.57	55.10	55.71	56.42	57.23	58.18	59.30
6000	61.82	62.58	63.05	63.33	63.66	64.03	64.45	64.93	65.48	66.12	66.85	67.70	68.68	69.82	71.16
7000	72.13	73.01	73.56	73.89	74.27	74.70	75.19	75.75	76.39	77.14	77.99	78.98	80.13	81.46	83.02
8000	82.43	83.44	84.07	84.44	84.88	85.37	85.93	86.57	87.31	88.16	89.13	90.26	91.57	93.10	94.88
9000	92.73	93.87	94.57	95.00	95.48	96.04	96.67	97.39	98.22	99.18	100.27	101.55	103.02	104.73	106.74
10000	103.04	104.30	105.08	105.55	106.09	106.71	107.41	108.21	109.13	110.19	111.42	112.83	114.46	116.37	118.60
11000	113.34	114.73	115.59	116.10	116.70	117.38	118.15	119.03	120.05	121.21	122.56	124.11	125.91	128.01	130.46
12000	123.64	125.16	126.10	126.66	127.31	128.05	128.89	129.85	130.96	132.23	133.70	135.39	137.36	139.64	142.32
13000	133.95	135.59	136.61	137.21	137.92	138.72	139.62	140.68	141.87	143.25	144.84	146.67	148.80	151.28	154.18
14000	144.25	146.02	147.11	147.77	148.53	149.39	150.37	151.50	152.79	154.27	155.98	157.96	160.25	162.92	166.04
15000	154.55	156.45	157.62	158.33	159.14	160.06	161.11	162.32	163.70	165.29	167.12	169.24	171.69	174.55	177.90
16000	164.86	166.88	168.13	168.88	169.75	170.73	171.85	173.14	174.61	176.31	178.26	180.52	183.14	186.19	189.76
17000	175.16	177.31	178.64	179.44	180.35	181.40	182.59	183.96	185.53	187.33	189.40	191.80	194.59	197.83	201.62
18000	185.46	187.74	189.15	189.99	190.96	192.07	193.33	194.78	196.44	198.36	200.54	203.09	206.03	209.46	213.48
19000	195.77	198.17	199.65	200.55	201.57	202.74	204.06	205.60	207.35	209.38	211.69	214.37	217.48	221.10	225.34
20000	206.07	208.60	210.16	211.10	212.18	213.41	214.81	216.42	218.26	220.40	222.83	225.65	228.92	232.74	237.20
21000	216.37	219.03	220.67	221.66	222.79	224.08	225.55	227.24	229.18	231.42	233.97	236.93	240.37	244.37	249.06
22000	226.68	229.46	231.18	232.21	233.40	234.75	236.29	238.06	240.09	242.44	245.11	248.21	251.82	256.01	260.92
23000	236.98	239.89	241.68	242.77	244.01	245.42	247.03	248.88	251.00	253.46	256.25	259.50	263.26	267.65	272.78
24000	247.28	250.32	252.19	253.32	254.62	256.09	257.78	259.70	261.92	264.48	267.39	270.78	274.71	279.28	284.64
25000	257.59	260.75	262.70	263.88	265.23	266.76	268.52	270.52	272.83	275.50	278.53	282.06	286.15	290.92	296.50
26000	267.89	271.18	273.21	274.43	275.83	277.43	279.26	281.35	283.74	286.52	289.67	293.34	297.60	302.56	308.36
27000	278.19	281.61	283.71	284.99	286.44	288.10	290.00	292.17	294.66	297.54	300.81	304.63	309.05	314.19	320.21
28000	288.50	292.04	294.22	295.54	297.05	298.77	300.74	302.99	305.57	308.54	311.96	315.91	320.49	325.83	332.07
29000	298.80	302.47	304.73	306.10	307.66	309.44	311.48	313.81	316.48	319.55	323.10	327.19	331.94	337.47	343.93
30000	309.10	312.90	315.24	316.65	318.27	320.11	322.22	324.63	327.39	330.57	334.24	338.47	343.38	349.10	355.79
35000	360.62	365.05	367.78	369.43	371.31	373.46	375.92	378.73	381.96	385.67	389.94	394.88	400.61	407.29	415.09
40000	412.13	417.20	420.32	422.20	424.36	426.81	429.62	432.84	436.52	440.76	445.65	451.29	457.84	465.47	474.39
45000	463.65	469.35	472.85	474.98	477.40	480.17	483.32	486.94	491.09	495.86	501.35	507.71	515.07	523.65	533.69
50000	515.17	521.50	525.39	527.75	530.45	533.52	537.03	541.04	545.65	550.95	557.06	564.12	572.30	581.84	592.99

MONTHLY PAYMENT
12¾% REQUIRED TO AMORTIZE A LOAN

TERM AMOUNT	1 YEAR	2 YEARS	3 YEARS	4 YEARS	5 YEARS	6 YEARS	7 YEARS	8 YEARS	9 YEARS	10 YEARS	11 YEARS	12 YEARS	13 YEARS	14 YEARS	15 YEARS
$100	8.91	4.73	3.35	2.66	2.25	1.98	1.79	1.65	1.55	1.46	1.40	1.34	1.30	1.26	1.23
200	17.81	9.46	6.69	5.31	4.50	3.96	3.58	3.30	3.09	2.92	2.79	2.68	2.60	2.52	2.46
300	26.72	14.19	10.03	7.97	6.74	5.94	5.37	4.95	4.63	4.38	4.18	4.02	3.89	3.78	3.69
400	35.62	18.91	13.37	10.62	8.99	7.91	7.16	6.60	6.17	5.84	5.58	5.36	5.19	5.04	4.92
500	44.53	23.64	16.71	13.28	11.23	9.89	8.95	8.25	7.72	7.30	6.97	6.70	6.48	6.30	6.14
600	53.43	28.37	20.06	15.93	13.48	11.87	10.73	9.90	9.26	8.76	8.36	8.04	7.78	7.55	7.37
700	62.34	33.10	23.40	18.58	15.73	13.84	12.52	11.55	10.80	10.22	9.76	9.38	9.07	8.81	8.60
800	71.24	37.82	26.74	21.24	17.97	15.82	14.31	13.19	12.34	11.68	11.15	10.72	10.37	10.07	9.83
900	80.15	42.55	30.08	23.89	20.22	17.80	16.10	14.84	13.89	13.14	12.54	12.06	11.66	11.33	11.05
1000	89.05	47.28	33.42	26.55	22.46	19.78	17.89	16.49	15.43	14.60	13.93	13.40	12.96	12.59	12.28
2000	178.10	94.55	66.84	53.09	44.92	39.55	35.77	32.98	30.85	29.19	27.86	26.79	25.91	25.17	24.56
3000	267.15	141.82	100.26	79.63	67.38	59.32	53.65	49.47	46.28	43.78	41.79	40.18	38.86	37.75	36.83
4000	356.19	189.09	133.67	106.17	89.84	79.09	71.53	65.95	61.70	58.38	55.72	53.57	51.81	50.33	49.11
5000	445.24	236.36	167.09	132.72	112.30	98.86	89.41	82.44	77.13	72.97	69.65	66.97	64.76	62.92	61.38
6000	534.29	283.64	200.51	159.26	134.76	118.63	107.29	98.93	92.55	87.56	83.58	80.36	77.71	75.50	73.66
7000	623.34	330.91	233.93	185.80	157.22	138.41	125.17	115.41	107.97	102.16	97.51	93.75	90.66	88.09	85.94
8000	712.38	378.18	267.34	212.34	179.68	158.18	143.05	131.90	123.40	116.75	111.44	107.14	103.61	100.67	98.21
9000	801.43	425.45	300.76	238.89	202.14	177.95	160.93	148.39	138.82	131.34	125.37	120.53	116.56	113.25	110.49
10000	890.48	472.72	334.18	265.43	224.60	197.72	178.80	164.87	154.25	145.94	139.30	133.93	129.51	125.84	122.76
11000	979.52	519.99	367.59	291.97	247.06	217.49	196.69	181.36	169.67	160.53	153.23	147.32	142.46	138.42	135.04
12000	1068.57	567.27	401.01	318.51	269.52	237.26	214.57	197.85	185.10	175.12	167.16	160.71	155.41	151.00	147.31
13000	1157.62	614.54	434.43	345.06	291.98	257.03	232.45	214.33	200.52	189.72	181.09	174.10	168.36	163.59	159.59
14000	1246.67	661.81	467.85	371.60	314.43	276.80	250.33	230.82	215.94	204.31	195.02	187.49	181.31	176.17	171.87
15000	1335.71	709.08	501.26	398.14	336.89	296.58	268.20	247.31	231.37	218.90	208.95	200.89	194.26	188.75	184.14
16000	1424.76	756.35	534.68	424.68	359.35	316.35	286.09	263.79	246.79	233.50	222.88	214.28	207.21	201.34	196.42
17000	1513.81	803.62	568.10	451.23	381.81	336.12	303.97	280.28	262.22	248.09	236.81	227.67	220.16	213.92	208.69
18000	1602.86	850.90	601.51	477.77	404.27	355.89	321.85	296.77	277.64	262.68	250.74	241.06	233.11	226.50	220.97
19000	1691.90	898.17	634.93	504.31	426.73	375.66	339.73	313.25	293.07	277.28	264.67	254.45	246.06	239.09	233.24
20000	1780.95	945.44	668.35	530.85	449.19	395.43	357.61	329.74	308.49	291.87	278.60	267.85	259.01	251.67	245.52
21000	1870.00	992.71	701.77	557.40	471.65	415.20	375.49	346.23	323.91	306.46	292.53	281.24	271.96	264.25	257.80
22000	1959.04	1039.98	735.18	583.94	494.11	434.97	393.37	362.71	339.34	321.06	306.46	294.63	284.91	276.83	270.07
23000	2048.09	1087.25	768.60	610.48	516.57	454.75	411.25	379.20	354.76	335.65	320.39	308.02	297.86	289.42	282.35
24000	2137.14	1134.53	802.02	637.02	539.03	474.52	429.13	395.69	370.19	350.24	334.32	321.41	310.81	302.00	294.62
25000	2226.19	1181.80	835.43	663.57	561.49	494.29	447.01	412.17	385.61	364.84	348.25	334.81	323.76	314.58	306.90
26000	2315.23	1229.07	868.85	690.11	583.95	514.06	464.89	428.66	401.04	379.43	362.18	348.20	336.71	327.17	319.18
27000	2404.28	1276.34	902.27	716.65	606.41	533.83	482.77	445.15	416.46	394.02	376.11	361.59	349.66	339.75	331.45
28000	2493.33	1323.61	935.69	743.19	628.86	553.60	500.65	461.63	431.88	408.62	390.04	374.98	362.61	352.33	343.73
29000	2582.37	1370.88	969.10	769.74	651.32	573.37	518.53	478.12	447.31	423.21	403.97	388.37	375.56	364.92	356.00
30000	2671.42	1418.16	1002.52	796.28	673.78	593.15	536.41	494.61	462.73	437.80	417.90	401.77	388.51	377.50	368.28
35000	3116.66	1654.51	1169.61	928.99	786.08	692.00	625.81	577.04	539.85	510.77	487.55	468.73	453.26	440.42	429.66
40000	3561.89	1890.87	1336.69	1061.70	898.38	790.86	715.22	659.47	616.98	583.73	557.20	535.69	518.01	503.33	491.04
45000	4007.13	2127.13	1503.78	1194.42	1010.67	889.70	804.62	741.90	694.10	656.70	626.85	602.65	582.76	566.25	552.41
50000	4452.37	2363.59	1670.86	1327.13	1122.97	988.57	894.02	824.34	771.22	729.67	696.50	669.61	647.51	629.16	613.79

MONTHLY PAYMENT
REQUIRED TO AMORTIZE A LOAN

12¾ %

TERM AMOUNT	35 YEARS	30 YEARS	28 YEARS	27 YEARS	26 YEARS	25 YEARS	24 YEARS	23 YEARS	22 YEARS	21 YEARS	20 YEARS	19 YEARS	18 YEARS	17 YEARS	16 YEARS
$100	1.05	1.07	1.07	1.08	1.08	1.09	1.10	1.10	1.11	1.12	1.14	1.15	1.17	1.18	1.21
200	2.10	2.14	2.14	2.15	2.16	2.17	2.19	2.20	2.21	2.24	2.27	2.29	2.33	2.36	2.41
300	3.15	3.19	3.21	3.23	3.24	3.26	3.28	3.30	3.33	3.36	3.40	3.44	3.49	3.54	3.61
400	4.20	4.25	4.28	4.30	4.32	4.34	4.37	4.40	4.44	4.48	4.53	4.58	4.65	4.72	4.81
500	5.25	5.31	5.35	5.37	5.40	5.43	5.46	5.50	5.55	5.60	5.66	5.73	5.81	5.90	6.01
600	6.30	6.37	6.42	6.45	6.48	6.51	6.55	6.60	6.66	6.72	6.79	6.87	6.97	7.08	7.21
700	7.35	7.43	7.49	7.52	7.56	7.60	7.65	7.70	7.76	7.84	7.92	8.02	8.13	8.26	8.41
800	8.40	8.50	8.56	8.59	8.63	8.68	8.74	8.80	8.87	8.96	9.05	9.16	9.29	9.44	9.62
900	9.45	9.56	9.63	9.67	9.71	9.77	9.83	9.90	9.98	10.07	10.18	10.31	10.45	10.62	10.82
1000	10.50	10.62	10.69	10.74	10.79	10.85	10.92	11.00	11.08	11.19	11.31	11.45	11.61	11.80	12.02
2000	20.99	21.23	21.38	21.47	21.58	21.70	21.84	21.99	22.17	22.38	22.62	22.90	23.22	23.60	24.04
3000	31.48	31.85	32.07	32.21	32.37	32.55	32.75	32.98	33.26	33.57	33.93	34.35	34.83	35.39	36.05
4000	41.97	42.46	42.76	42.94	43.15	43.39	43.67	43.98	44.34	44.76	45.24	45.79	46.44	47.19	48.07
5000	52.46	53.07	53.45	53.68	53.94	54.24	54.58	54.97	55.43	55.94	56.54	57.24	58.04	58.99	60.09
6000	62.96	63.69	64.14	64.41	64.73	65.09	65.50	65.97	66.51	67.13	67.85	68.69	69.65	70.78	72.10
7000	73.45	74.30	74.83	75.15	75.51	75.93	76.41	76.96	77.59	78.32	79.16	80.13	81.26	82.58	84.12
8000	83.94	84.91	85.52	85.88	86.30	86.78	87.33	87.96	88.68	89.51	90.47	91.58	92.87	94.37	96.14
9000	94.43	95.53	96.21	96.62	97.09	97.63	98.24	98.95	99.76	100.70	101.78	103.03	104.48	106.17	108.15
10000	104.92	106.14	106.89	107.35	107.88	108.47	109.16	109.94	110.85	111.88	113.08	114.47	116.08	117.97	120.17
11000	115.42	116.75	117.58	118.09	118.66	119.32	120.07	120.94	121.93	123.07	124.39	125.92	127.69	129.76	132.18
12000	125.91	127.37	128.27	128.82	129.45	130.17	130.99	131.93	133.02	134.26	135.70	137.37	139.30	141.56	144.20
13000	136.40	137.98	138.96	139.56	140.24	141.01	141.90	142.92	144.11	145.45	147.01	148.81	150.91	153.35	156.22
14000	146.89	148.60	149.65	150.29	151.02	151.86	152.82	153.92	155.18	156.64	158.31	160.26	162.52	165.15	168.23
15000	157.38	159.21	160.34	161.03	161.81	162.71	163.74	164.91	166.26	167.84	169.62	171.71	174.12	176.95	180.25
16000	167.88	169.82	171.03	171.76	172.60	173.55	174.65	175.91	177.35	179.01	180.93	183.15	185.73	188.74	192.27
17000	178.37	180.44	181.72	182.50	183.38	184.40	185.57	186.90	188.43	190.20	192.24	194.60	197.34	200.54	204.28
18000	188.86	191.05	192.41	193.23	194.17	195.24	196.48	197.89	199.52	201.39	203.55	206.05	208.95	212.33	216.30
19000	199.35	201.66	203.10	203.97	204.96	206.09	207.40	208.89	210.60	212.58	214.85	217.49	220.56	224.13	228.32
20000	209.84	212.28	213.78	214.70	215.75	216.94	218.31	219.88	221.69	223.76	226.16	228.94	232.16	235.93	240.33
21000	220.34	222.89	224.47	225.43	226.53	227.79	229.23	230.87	232.77	234.95	237.47	240.39	243.77	247.72	252.35
22000	230.83	233.50	235.16	236.17	237.32	238.64	240.14	241.87	243.85	246.14	248.78	251.83	255.38	259.52	264.36
23000	241.32	244.12	245.85	246.90	248.11	249.48	251.06	252.86	254.94	257.33	260.09	263.28	266.99	271.31	276.38
24000	251.81	254.73	256.54	257.64	258.89	260.33	261.97	263.86	266.02	268.51	271.40	274.73	278.60	283.11	288.40
25000	262.30	265.35	267.23	268.37	269.68	271.18	272.89	274.85	277.11	279.70	282.70	286.17	290.20	294.91	300.41
26000	272.80	275.96	277.92	279.11	280.47	282.02	283.80	285.84	288.19	290.89	294.01	297.62	301.81	306.70	312.43
27000	283.29	286.57	288.61	289.84	291.26	292.87	294.72	296.84	299.28	302.08	305.32	309.07	313.42	318.50	324.45
28000	293.78	297.19	299.30	300.58	302.04	303.72	305.63	307.83	310.36	313.27	316.62	320.51	325.03	330.29	336.46
29000	304.27	307.80	309.99	311.31	312.83	314.56	316.54	318.82	321.45	324.46	327.93	331.96	336.64	342.09	348.48
30000	314.76	318.41	320.67	322.05	323.62	325.41	327.46	329.82	332.53	335.64	339.24	343.41	348.24	353.86	360.50
35000	367.22	371.48	374.12	375.72	377.55	379.64	382.04	384.79	387.95	391.58	395.78	400.64	406.28	412.87	420.58
40000	419.68	424.55	427.56	429.40	431.49	433.88	436.62	439.79	443.37	447.52	452.32	457.87	464.32	471.85	480.66
45000	472.14	477.62	481.01	483.07	485.42	488.11	491.19	494.73	498.79	503.46	508.86	515.11	522.36	530.83	540.74
50000	524.60	530.69	534.45	536.74	539.36	542.35	545.77	549.70	554.21	559.40	565.40	572.34	580.40	589.81	600.82

MONTHLY PAYMENT
13 % REQUIRED TO AMORTIZE A LOAN

TERM AMOUNT	1 YEAR	2 YEARS	3 YEARS	4 YEARS	5 YEARS	6 YEARS	7 YEARS	8 YEARS	9 YEARS	10 YEARS	11 YEARS	12 YEARS	13 YEARS	14 YEARS	15 YEARS
$100	8.92	4.74	3.36	2.67	2.26	1.99	1.81	1.67	1.56	1.48	1.41	1.36	1.31	1.28	1.25
200	17.84	9.48	6.71	5.34	4.52	3.98	3.61	3.33	3.12	2.95	2.82	2.71	2.62	2.55	2.49
300	26.75	14.22	10.06	8.00	6.78	5.97	5.41	4.99	4.67	4.42	4.23	4.07	3.93	3.83	3.73
400	35.67	18.96	13.42	10.67	9.04	7.96	7.21	6.65	6.23	5.90	5.63	5.42	5.24	5.10	4.98
500	44.58	23.70	16.77	13.33	11.30	9.95	9.01	8.31	7.78	7.37	7.04	6.77	6.55	6.37	6.22
600	53.50	28.43	20.12	16.00	13.55	11.94	10.81	9.98	9.34	8.84	8.45	8.13	7.86	7.65	7.46
700	62.42	33.17	23.48	18.67	15.81	13.93	12.61	11.64	10.90	10.32	9.86	9.48	9.17	8.92	8.71
800	71.33	37.91	26.83	21.33	18.07	15.92	14.41	13.30	12.45	11.79	11.26	10.83	10.48	10.19	9.95
900	80.25	42.65	30.18	24.00	20.33	17.91	16.21	14.96	14.01	13.26	12.67	12.19	11.79	11.47	11.19
1000	89.16	47.39	33.54	26.66	22.59	19.90	18.01	16.62	15.56	14.74	14.08	13.54	13.10	12.74	12.44
2000	178.32	94.77	67.07	53.32	45.17	39.80	36.02	33.24	31.12	29.47	28.15	27.08	26.20	25.47	24.87
3000	267.48	142.15	100.60	79.98	67.75	59.69	54.03	49.86	46.68	44.20	42.22	40.62	39.30	38.21	37.30
4000	356.64	189.54	134.13	106.64	90.33	79.59	72.04	66.48	62.24	58.93	56.29	54.15	52.40	50.94	49.73
5000	445.80	236.92	167.66	133.30	112.91	99.48	90.05	83.10	77.80	73.66	70.37	67.69	65.50	63.68	62.16
6000	534.96	284.30	201.19	159.96	135.49	119.38	108.05	99.72	93.36	88.40	84.44	81.23	78.60	76.41	74.59
7000	624.11	331.69	234.72	186.62	158.07	139.28	126.06	116.33	108.92	103.13	98.51	94.77	91.70	89.15	87.02
8000	713.27	379.07	268.25	213.28	180.65	159.17	144.07	132.95	124.48	117.86	112.58	108.30	104.79	101.88	99.45
9000	802.43	426.45	301.78	239.94	203.23	179.07	162.08	149.57	140.04	132.59	126.65	121.84	117.89	114.62	111.88
10000	891.59	473.83	335.32	266.60	225.80	198.96	180.09	166.19	155.60	147.32	140.73	135.38	130.99	127.35	124.31
11000	980.75	521.22	368.85	293.26	248.39	218.86	198.10	182.81	171.16	162.05	154.80	148.92	144.09	140.08	136.74
12000	1069.91	568.60	402.38	319.92	270.97	238.75	216.10	199.43	186.72	176.79	168.87	162.45	157.19	152.82	149.17
13000	1159.06	615.98	435.91	346.58	293.55	258.65	234.11	216.04	202.28	191.52	182.94	175.99	170.29	165.56	161.60
14000	1248.22	663.37	469.44	373.24	316.13	278.55	252.12	232.66	217.84	206.25	197.01	189.53	183.39	178.29	174.03
15000	1337.38	710.75	502.97	399.90	338.71	298.44	270.13	249.28	233.40	220.98	211.09	203.07	196.49	191.03	186.46
16000	1426.54	758.13	536.50	426.56	361.29	318.34	288.14	265.90	248.96	235.72	225.16	216.60	209.58	203.76	198.89
17000	1515.70	805.51	570.03	453.22	383.87	338.23	306.15	282.52	264.52	250.45	239.24	230.14	222.68	216.50	211.32
18000	1604.86	852.90	603.56	479.88	406.45	358.13	324.15	299.14	280.08	265.18	253.30	243.68	235.78	229.23	223.75
19000	1694.02	900.28	637.09	506.54	429.03	378.02	342.16	315.75	295.64	279.91	267.37	257.22	248.88	241.97	236.18
20000	1783.17	947.66	670.63	533.20	451.61	397.92	360.17	332.37	311.20	294.64	281.44	270.75	261.98	254.70	248.61
21000	1872.33	995.05	704.16	559.86	474.19	417.82	378.18	348.99	326.76	309.38	295.52	284.29	275.08	267.44	261.04
22000	1961.49	1042.43	737.69	586.52	496.77	437.71	396.19	365.61	342.31	324.11	309.59	297.83	288.18	280.17	273.47
23000	2050.65	1089.81	771.22	613.18	519.35	457.61	414.20	382.23	357.87	338.84	323.66	311.37	301.28	292.91	285.91
24000	2139.81	1137.19	804.75	639.84	541.93	477.50	432.20	398.85	373.43	353.57	337.73	324.90	314.37	305.64	298.33
25000	2228.97	1184.58	838.28	666.50	564.51	497.40	450.21	415.46	388.99	368.30	351.81	338.44	327.47	318.38	310.76
26000	2318.12	1231.96	871.81	693.16	587.09	517.30	468.22	432.08	404.55	383.04	365.88	351.98	340.57	331.11	323.19
27000	2407.28	1279.34	905.34	719.82	609.67	537.19	486.23	448.70	420.11	397.77	379.95	365.52	353.67	343.85	335.63
28000	2496.44	1326.73	938.87	746.48	632.25	557.09	504.24	465.32	435.67	412.50	394.02	379.05	366.77	356.58	348.06
29000	2585.60	1374.11	972.41	773.14	654.83	576.98	522.25	481.94	451.23	427.23	408.10	392.59	379.87	369.32	360.49
30000	2674.76	1421.49	1005.94	799.80	677.41	596.88	540.26	498.56	466.79	441.96	422.17	406.13	392.97	382.05	372.92
35000	3120.55	1658.43	1173.59	933.09	790.31	696.36	630.30	581.65	544.59	515.62	492.53	473.82	458.46	445.72	435.07
40000	3566.34	1895.32	1341.25	1066.39	903.21	795.84	720.34	664.74	622.39	589.28	562.89	541.50	523.95	509.40	497.22
45000	4012.13	2132.23	1508.90	1199.80	1016.11	895.32	810.38	747.83	700.18	662.94	633.25	609.19	589.45	573.07	559.37
50000	4457.93	2369.15	1676.56	1332.99	1129.01	994.79	900.42	830.92	777.98	736.60	703.61	676.88	654.94	636.75	621.52

MONTHLY PAYMENT
REQUIRED TO AMORTIZE A LOAN   13%

TERM AMOUNT	35 YEARS	30 YEARS	28 YEARS	27 YEARS	26 YEARS	25 YEARS	24 YEARS	23 YEARS	22 YEARS	21 YEARS	20 YEARS	19 YEARS	18 YEARS	17 YEARS	16 YEARS
$100	1.07	1.08	1.09	1.10	1.10	1.11	1.11	1.12	1.13	1.14	1.15	1.17	1.18	1.20	1.22
200	2.14	2.16	2.18	2.19	2.20	2.21	2.22	2.24	2.26	2.28	2.30	2.33	2.36	2.40	2.44
300	3.21	3.24	3.27	3.28	3.29	3.31	3.33	3.36	3.38	3.41	3.45	3.49	3.54	3.59	3.66
400	4.28	4.32	4.35	4.37	4.39	4.41	4.44	4.47	4.51	4.55	4.60	4.65	4.71	4.79	4.87
500	5.35	5.40	5.44	5.46	5.49	5.52	5.55	5.59	5.63	5.68	5.74	5.81	5.89	5.98	6.09
600	6.41	6.48	6.53	6.55	6.58	6.62	6.66	6.71	6.76	6.82	6.89	6.97	7.07	7.18	7.31
700	7.48	7.56	7.61	7.65	7.68	7.72	7.77	7.82	7.88	7.96	8.04	8.13	8.24	8.37	8.53
800	8.55	8.64	8.70	8.74	8.78	8.82	8.88	8.94	9.01	9.09	9.19	9.29	9.42	9.57	9.74
900	9.62	9.72	9.79	9.83	9.87	9.93	9.99	10.06	10.14	10.23	10.33	10.46	10.60	10.77	10.96
1000	10.69	10.80	10.88	10.92	10.97	11.03	11.10	11.17	11.26	11.36	11.48	11.62	11.78	11.96	12.18
2000	21.37	21.60	21.75	21.84	21.94	22.05	22.19	22.34	22.51	22.72	22.96	23.23	23.55	23.92	24.35
3000	32.05	32.40	32.62	32.75	32.90	33.08	33.28	33.51	33.77	34.08	34.43	34.84	35.32	35.87	36.53
4000	42.73	43.20	43.49	43.67	43.87	44.10	44.37	44.67	45.03	45.44	45.91	46.45	47.09	47.83	48.70
5000	53.41	53.99	54.36	54.58	54.83	55.13	55.46	55.84	56.28	56.80	57.38	58.06	58.86	59.79	60.87
6000	64.09	64.79	65.23	65.50	65.80	66.15	66.55	67.01	67.54	68.15	68.86	69.68	70.63	71.74	73.05
7000	74.77	75.59	76.10	76.41	76.77	77.17	77.64	78.18	78.80	79.51	80.33	81.29	82.40	83.70	85.22
8000	85.45	86.39	86.97	87.33	87.73	88.20	88.73	89.34	90.05	90.87	91.81	92.90	94.17	95.65	97.40
9000	96.14	97.19	97.84	98.24	98.70	99.22	99.82	100.51	101.31	102.22	103.28	104.51	105.94	107.61	109.57
10000	106.82	107.98	108.71	109.16	109.66	110.25	110.91	111.68	112.56	113.58	114.76	116.12	117.71	119.57	121.74
11000	117.50	118.78	119.58	120.07	120.63	121.27	122.00	122.85	123.82	124.94	126.23	127.74	129.48	131.52	133.92
12000	128.18	129.58	130.45	130.99	131.60	132.29	133.09	134.01	135.07	136.30	137.71	139.35	141.25	143.48	146.09
13000	138.86	140.38	141.32	141.90	142.56	143.32	144.19	145.18	146.33	147.65	149.18	150.96	153.02	155.44	158.26
14000	149.54	151.18	152.20	152.82	153.53	154.34	155.28	156.35	157.59	159.01	160.66	162.57	164.79	167.39	170.44
15000	160.22	161.97	163.07	163.73	164.49	165.37	166.37	167.52	168.84	170.37	172.13	174.18	176.57	179.35	182.61
16000	170.90	172.77	173.94	174.65	175.46	176.39	177.46	178.68	180.10	181.73	183.61	185.79	188.34	191.30	194.79
17000	181.58	183.57	184.81	185.56	186.43	187.41	188.55	189.85	191.35	193.08	195.09	197.41	200.11	203.26	206.96
18000	192.27	194.37	195.68	196.48	197.39	198.44	199.64	201.02	202.61	204.44	206.56	209.02	211.88	215.22	219.13
19000	202.95	205.16	206.55	207.39	208.36	209.46	210.73	212.19	213.86	215.80	218.04	220.63	223.65	227.17	231.31
20000	213.63	215.96	217.42	218.31	219.32	220.48	221.82	223.35	225.12	227.16	229.51	232.24	235.42	239.13	243.48
21000	224.31	226.76	228.29	229.22	230.29	231.51	232.91	234.52	236.38	238.51	240.99	243.85	247.19	251.08	255.65
22000	234.99	237.56	239.16	240.14	241.25	242.53	244.00	245.69	247.63	249.87	252.46	255.47	258.96	263.04	267.83
23000	245.67	248.36	250.03	251.05	252.22	253.56	255.09	256.86	258.89	261.23	263.94	267.08	270.73	275.00	280.00
24000	255.35	259.15	260.90	261.97	263.19	264.58	266.18	268.02	270.14	272.59	275.41	278.69	282.50	286.95	292.18
25000	267.03	269.95	271.77	272.88	274.15	275.61	277.27	279.19	281.40	283.94	286.89	290.30	294.27	298.91	304.35
26000	277.71	280.75	282.64	283.80	285.12	286.63	288.37	290.36	292.66	295.30	298.36	301.91	306.04	310.87	316.52
27000	288.40	291.55	293.51	294.71	296.08	297.66	299.46	301.53	303.91	306.66	309.84	313.52	317.81	322.82	328.70
28000	299.08	302.35	304.39	305.63	307.05	308.68	310.55	312.69	315.17	318.02	321.31	325.14	329.58	334.78	340.87
29000	309.76	313.14	315.26	316.54	318.02	319.70	321.64	323.86	326.42	329.37	332.79	336.75	341.35	346.73	353.04
30000	320.44	323.94	326.13	327.46	328.98	330.73	332.73	335.03	337.68	340.73	344.26	348.36	353.13	358.69	365.22
35000	373.84	377.93	380.48	382.03	383.81	385.85	388.18	390.87	393.96	397.52	401.64	406.42	411.98	418.47	426.09
40000	427.25	431.92	434.83	436.61	438.65	440.97	443.66	446.70	450.24	454.31	459.02	464.48	470.83	478.25	486.96
45000	480.66	485.91	489.19	491.19	493.47	496.09	499.09	502.54	506.51	511.10	516.39	522.54	529.69	538.03	547.82
50000	534.06	539.90	543.54	545.76	548.30	551.21	554.55	558.38	562.79	567.88	573.77	580.60	588.54	597.81	608.69

TERM AMOUNT	1 YEAR	2 YEARS	3 YEARS	4 YEARS	5 YEARS	6 YEARS	7 YEARS	8 YEARS	9 YEARS	10 YEARS	11 YEARS	12 YEARS	13 YEARS	14 YEARS	15 YEARS
$100	8.93	4.75	3.37	2.68	2.28	2.01	1.82	1.68	1.57	1.49	1.43	1.37	1.33	1.29	1.26
200	17.86	9.50	6.73	5.36	4.55	4.01	3.63	3.36	3.14	2.98	2.85	2.74	2.65	2.58	2.52
300	26.79	14.25	10.10	8.04	6.82	6.01	5.45	5.03	4.71	4.47	4.27	4.11	3.98	3.87	3.78
400	35.71	19.00	13.46	10.72	9.09	8.01	7.26	6.71	6.28	5.95	5.69	5.48	5.30	5.16	5.04
500	44.64	23.75	16.83	13.39	11.36	10.02	9.07	8.38	7.85	7.44	7.11	6.85	6.63	6.45	6.30
600	53.57	28.50	20.19	16.07	13.63	12.02	10.89	10.06	9.42	8.93	8.53	8.22	7.95	7.74	7.56
700	62.49	33.25	23.56	18.75	15.90	14.02	12.70	11.73	10.99	10.41	9.96	9.58	9.28	9.03	8.81
800	71.42	38.00	26.92	21.43	18.17	16.02	14.51	13.41	12.56	11.90	11.38	10.95	10.60	10.31	10.07
900	80.35	42.75	30.29	24.10	20.44	18.02	16.33	15.08	14.13	13.39	12.80	12.32	11.93	11.60	11.33
1000	89.27	47.50	33.65	26.78	22.71	20.03	18.14	16.76	15.70	14.88	14.22	13.69	13.25	12.89	12.59
2000	178.54	94.99	67.30	53.56	45.41	40.05	36.28	33.51	31.40	29.75	28.43	27.37	26.50	25.78	25.18
3000	267.81	142.49	100.94	80.34	68.11	60.09	54.42	50.26	47.09	44.62	42.65	41.06	39.75	38.67	37.76
4000	357.08	189.98	134.59	107.11	90.81	80.09	72.55	67.01	62.79	59.49	56.86	54.74	53.00	51.55	50.35
5000	446.35	237.48	168.23	133.89	113.51	100.11	90.69	83.76	78.48	74.36	71.08	68.42	66.24	64.44	62.93
6000	535.62	284.97	201.88	160.67	136.21	120.13	108.83	100.51	94.18	89.23	85.29	82.11	79.49	77.33	75.52
7000	624.89	332.46	235.52	187.44	158.91	140.15	126.96	117.26	109.87	104.10	99.51	95.79	92.74	90.21	88.10
8000	714.16	379.96	269.17	214.22	181.61	160.17	145.10	134.01	125.57	118.97	113.72	109.47	105.99	103.10	100.69
9000	803.43	427.45	302.81	241.00	204.31	180.19	163.24	150.76	141.26	133.85	127.94	123.16	119.23	115.99	113.28
10000	892.70	474.95	336.46	267.78	227.02	200.21	181.37	167.51	156.96	148.72	142.15	136.84	132.48	128.88	125.86
11000	981.97	522.44	370.10	294.55	249.72	220.23	199.51	184.26	172.65	163.59	156.37	150.52	145.73	141.76	138.45
12000	1071.24	569.93	403.75	321.33	272.42	240.25	217.65	201.01	188.35	178.46	170.58	164.21	158.98	154.65	151.03
13000	1160.51	617.43	437.39	348.11	295.12	260.27	235.78	217.76	204.04	193.33	184.80	177.89	172.23	167.54	163.62
14000	1249.78	664.92	471.04	374.88	317.82	280.29	253.92	234.51	219.74	208.20	199.01	191.57	185.48	180.42	176.20
15000	1339.05	712.42	504.68	401.66	340.52	300.31	272.06	251.26	235.43	223.07	213.23	205.26	198.72	193.31	188.79
16000	1428.32	759.91	538.33	428.44	363.22	320.33	290.19	268.01	251.13	237.94	227.44	218.94	211.97	206.20	201.38
17000	1517.59	807.40	571.97	455.22	385.92	340.35	308.33	284.76	266.82	252.82	241.66	232.62	225.22	219.09	213.96
18000	1606.86	854.90	605.62	481.99	408.62	360.39	326.47	301.51	282.52	267.69	255.87	246.31	238.47	231.97	226.55
19000	1696.13	902.39	639.26	508.77	431.33	380.39	344.60	318.26	298.21	282.56	270.09	259.99	251.72	244.86	239.13
20000	1785.40	949.89	672.91	535.55	454.03	400.44	362.74	335.01	313.91	297.43	284.30	273.67	264.96	257.75	251.72
21000	1874.67	997.38	706.55	562.32	476.73	420.44	380.87	351.76	329.61	312.30	298.51	287.36	278.21	270.63	264.30
22000	1963.94	1044.88	740.20	589.10	499.43	440.46	399.01	368.52	345.30	327.17	312.73	301.04	291.46	283.52	276.89
23000	2053.21	1092.37	773.84	615.88	522.13	460.48	417.15	385.27	361.00	342.04	326.94	314.72	304.71	296.41	289.47
24000	2142.48	1139.86	807.49	642.66	544.83	480.50	435.28	402.02	376.69	356.91	341.16	328.41	317.96	309.30	302.06
25000	2231.75	1187.36	841.13	669.43	567.53	500.52	453.42	418.77	392.39	371.79	355.37	342.09	331.20	322.18	314.65
26000	2321.01	1234.85	874.78	696.21	590.23	520.54	471.56	435.52	408.08	386.66	369.59	355.78	344.45	335.07	327.23
27000	2410.28	1282.35	908.42	722.99	612.93	540.56	489.69	452.27	423.78	401.53	383.80	369.46	357.70	347.96	339.82
28000	2499.55	1329.84	942.07	749.76	635.64	560.58	507.83	469.02	439.47	416.40	398.02	383.14	370.95	360.84	352.40
29000	2588.82	1377.33	975.71	776.54	658.34	580.60	525.97	485.77	455.17	431.27	412.23	396.83	384.19	373.73	364.99
30000	2678.09	1424.83	1009.36	803.32	681.04	600.60	544.11	502.52	470.86	446.14	426.45	410.51	397.44	386.62	377.57
35000	3124.44	1662.30	1177.58	937.20	794.54	700.72	634.79	586.27	549.34	520.50	497.52	478.93	463.68	451.05	440.50
40000	3570.79	1899.77	1345.81	1071.09	908.05	800.83	725.48	670.02	627.81	594.85	568.60	547.34	529.92	515.49	503.43
45000	4017.14	2137.14	1514.03	1204.97	1021.55	900.93	816.16	753.78	706.29	669.21	639.67	615.76	596.16	579.93	566.36
50000	4463.49	2374.71	1682.26	1338.86	1135.06	1001.03	906.84	837.53	784.77	743.57	710.74	684.18	662.40	644.36	629.29

MONTHLY PAYMENT
REQUIRED TO AMORTIZE A LOAN 13¼ %

TERM AMOUNT	35 YEARS	30 YEARS	28 YEARS	27 YEARS	26 YEARS	25 YEARS	24 YEARS	23 YEARS	22 YEARS	21 YEARS	20 YEARS	19 YEARS	18 YEARS	17 YEARS	16 YEARS
$100	1.09	1.10	1.11	1.11	1.12	1.13	1.13	1.14	1.15	1.16	1.17	1.18	1.20	1.22	1.24
200	2.18	2.20	2.22	2.23	2.23	2.24	2.25	2.27	2.29	2.31	2.33	2.36	2.39	2.42	2.47
300	3.27	3.30	3.32	3.33	3.34	3.36	3.38	3.40	3.43	3.46	3.49	3.53	3.58	3.64	3.70
400	4.35	4.40	4.43	4.44	4.46	4.48	4.51	4.54	4.57	4.61	4.66	4.71	4.77	4.85	4.94
500	5.44	5.50	5.53	5.55	5.57	5.60	5.63	5.67	5.71	5.76	5.82	5.89	5.97	6.06	6.17
600	6.53	6.59	6.64	6.66	6.69	6.72	6.76	6.81	6.86	6.92	6.99	7.07	7.16	7.27	7.40
700	7.61	7.69	7.74	7.77	7.80	7.84	7.89	7.94	8.00	8.07	8.15	8.24	8.35	8.48	8.64
800	8.70	8.79	8.85	8.88	8.92	8.96	9.01	9.07	9.14	9.22	9.31	9.42	9.55	9.69	9.87
900	9.79	9.89	9.95	9.99	10.03	10.08	10.14	10.21	10.29	10.38	10.48	10.60	10.74	10.91	11.10
1000	10.88	10.99	11.06	11.10	11.14	11.20	11.27	11.34	11.43	11.53	11.64	11.78	11.93	12.12	12.34
2000	21.75	21.97	22.11	22.19	22.29	22.40	22.53	22.68	22.86	23.06	23.29	23.56	23.87	24.23	24.67
3000	32.62	32.95	33.16	33.29	33.43	33.61	33.80	34.03	34.28	34.58	34.93	35.33	35.80	36.35	37.00
4000	43.49	43.94	44.22	44.38	44.58	44.81	45.07	45.37	45.71	46.11	46.57	47.11	47.74	48.47	49.33
5000	54.36	54.92	55.27	55.48	55.72	56.01	56.34	56.71	57.14	57.64	58.22	58.89	59.67	60.59	61.66
6000	65.23	65.90	66.32	66.58	66.87	67.21	67.60	68.05	68.57	69.17	69.86	70.67	71.61	72.70	74.00
7000	76.10	76.88	77.38	77.67	78.01	78.41	78.87	79.39	80.00	80.70	81.51	82.44	83.54	84.82	86.33
8000	86.97	87.87	88.43	88.77	89.16	89.62	90.14	90.74	91.43	92.22	93.15	94.22	95.47	96.94	98.66
9000	97.84	98.85	99.48	99.87	100.30	100.82	101.40	102.08	102.85	103.75	104.79	106.00	107.41	109.05	110.99
10000	108.71	109.83	110.54	110.96	111.45	112.02	112.67	113.42	114.28	115.28	116.44	117.78	119.34	121.17	123.32
11000	119.58	120.81	121.59	122.06	122.59	123.22	123.94	124.76	125.71	126.81	128.08	129.56	131.28	133.29	135.65
12000	130.45	131.80	132.64	133.15	133.74	134.42	135.20	136.10	137.14	138.34	139.72	141.33	143.21	145.40	147.98
13000	141.32	142.78	143.69	144.25	144.88	145.63	146.47	147.45	148.57	149.86	151.37	153.11	155.14	157.52	160.32
14000	152.19	153.76	154.75	155.35	156.03	156.83	157.74	158.79	160.00	161.39	163.01	164.89	167.08	169.64	172.65
15000	163.06	164.74	165.80	166.44	167.17	168.03	169.01	170.13	171.42	172.92	174.65	176.67	179.01	181.76	184.98
16000	173.93	175.73	176.85	177.54	178.32	179.23	180.27	181.47	182.85	184.45	186.30	188.44	190.95	193.87	197.31
17000	184.81	186.71	187.91	188.64	189.46	190.43	191.54	192.81	194.28	195.98	197.94	200.22	202.88	205.99	209.64
18000	195.68	197.69	198.96	199.73	200.61	201.64	202.81	204.16	205.71	207.50	209.58	212.00	214.82	218.11	221.98
19000	206.55	208.67	210.01	210.83	211.75	212.84	214.07	215.50	217.14	219.03	221.23	223.78	226.75	230.22	234.31
20000	217.42	219.66	221.07	221.92	222.90	224.04	225.34	226.84	228.56	230.56	232.87	235.56	238.68	242.34	246.64
21000	228.29	230.64	232.12	233.02	234.04	235.24	236.61	238.18	239.99	242.09	244.52	247.33	250.62	254.46	258.97
22000	239.16	241.62	243.17	244.12	245.19	246.44	247.87	249.52	251.42	253.62	256.16	259.11	262.55	266.57	271.30
23000	250.03	252.61	254.22	255.21	256.33	257.65	259.14	260.87	262.85	265.14	267.80	270.89	274.49	278.69	283.64
24000	260.90	263.59	265.28	266.31	267.48	268.85	270.41	272.21	274.28	276.67	279.45	282.67	286.42	290.81	295.97
25000	271.77	274.57	276.33	277.41	278.62	280.05	281.68	283.55	285.71	288.20	291.09	294.45	298.36	302.93	308.30
26000	282.64	285.55	287.38	288.50	289.76	291.25	292.94	294.89	297.13	299.73	302.73	306.22	310.29	315.04	320.63
27000	293.51	296.54	298.44	299.60	300.91	302.45	304.21	306.23	308.56	311.26	314.38	318.00	322.22	327.16	332.96
28000	304.38	307.52	309.49	310.69	312.05	313.66	315.48	317.58	319.99	322.78	326.02	329.78	334.16	339.28	345.30
29000	315.25	318.50	320.54	321.79	323.20	324.86	326.74	328.92	331.42	334.31	337.66	341.56	346.09	351.39	357.63
30000	326.12	329.48	331.60	332.89	334.34	336.06	338.01	340.26	342.85	345.84	349.31	353.33	358.03	363.51	369.96
35000	380.48	384.40	386.86	388.37	390.07	392.07	394.35	396.97	399.99	403.48	407.53	412.22	417.70	424.10	431.62
40000	434.83	439.31	442.13	443.85	445.79	448.08	450.68	453.68	457.13	461.12	465.74	471.11	477.37	484.68	493.28
45000	489.18	494.22	497.39	499.33	501.52	504.09	507.02	510.39	514.27	518.76	523.96	530.00	537.04	545.27	554.94
50000	543.53	549.14	552.66	554.81	557.24	560.10	563.35	567.10	571.41	576.40	582.18	588.89	596.71	605.85	616.60

MONTHLY PAYMENT
13½ % REQUIRED TO AMORTIZE A LOAN

TERM AMOUNT	1 YEAR	2 YEARS	3 YEARS	4 YEARS	5 YEARS	6 YEARS	7 YEARS	8 YEARS	9 YEARS	10 YEARS	11 YEARS	12 YEARS	13 YEARS	14 YEARS	15 YEARS
$100	8.94	4.77	3.38	2.69	2.29	2.02	1.83	1.69	1.59	1.51	1.44	1.39	1.34	1.31	1.28
200	17.88	9.53	6.76	5.38	4.57	4.03	3.66	3.38	3.17	3.01	2.88	2.77	2.68	2.61	2.55
300	26.82	14.29	10.13	8.07	6.85	6.05	5.48	5.07	4.75	4.51	4.31	4.15	4.02	3.92	3.83
400	35.76	19.05	13.51	10.76	9.13	8.06	7.31	6.76	6.34	6.01	5.75	5.54	5.36	5.22	5.10
500	44.70	23.81	16.88	13.45	11.42	10.08	9.14	8.45	7.92	7.51	7.18	6.92	6.70	6.53	6.38
600	53.63	28.57	20.26	16.14	13.70	12.09	10.96	10.13	9.50	9.01	8.62	8.30	8.04	7.83	7.65
700	62.57	33.33	23.64	18.83	15.98	14.11	12.79	11.82	11.09	10.51	10.06	9.69	9.38	9.13	8.92
800	71.51	38.09	27.01	21.52	18.26	16.12	14.62	13.51	12.67	12.01	11.49	11.07	10.72	10.44	10.20
900	80.45	42.85	30.39	24.20	20.55	18.15	16.44	15.20	14.25	13.51	12.93	12.45	12.06	11.74	11.47
1000	89.39	47.61	33.76	26.90	22.83	20.15	18.27	16.89	15.84	15.02	14.36	13.84	13.40	13.05	12.75
2000	178.77	95.22	67.52	53.79	45.65	40.30	36.54	33.77	31.67	30.03	28.72	27.67	26.80	26.09	25.49
3000	268.15	142.82	101.28	80.69	68.47	60.44	54.80	50.65	47.50	45.04	43.08	41.51	40.20	39.13	38.23
4000	357.53	190.43	135.04	107.58	91.29	80.59	73.07	67.54	63.33	60.05	57.44	55.33	53.60	52.17	50.97
5000	446.91	238.03	168.80	134.48	114.12	100.73	91.33	84.42	79.16	75.06	71.79	69.16	66.99	65.21	63.71
6000	536.29	285.64	202.56	161.37	136.94	120.88	109.60	101.30	94.99	90.07	86.15	82.99	80.39	78.25	76.45
7000	625.67	333.24	236.32	188.27	159.76	141.02	127.86	118.19	110.83	105.08	100.51	96.82	93.79	91.29	89.20
8000	715.05	380.85	270.08	215.16	182.58	161.17	146.13	135.07	126.66	120.09	114.87	110.65	107.19	104.33	101.94
9000	804.43	428.45	303.84	242.06	205.41	181.32	164.40	151.95	142.49	135.10	129.23	124.48	120.58	117.37	114.68
10000	893.81	476.06	337.60	268.95	228.23	201.46	182.66	168.84	158.32	150.11	143.58	138.31	133.98	130.41	127.42
11000	983.19	523.66	371.36	295.85	251.05	221.61	200.93	185.72	174.15	165.13	157.94	152.14	147.38	143.45	140.16
12000	1072.57	571.27	405.11	322.74	273.87	241.75	219.19	202.60	189.98	180.14	172.30	165.97	160.78	156.49	152.90
13000	1161.95	618.87	438.87	349.64	296.70	261.90	237.46	219.48	205.81	195.15	186.66	179.80	174.18	169.53	165.65
14000	1251.34	666.48	472.63	376.53	319.52	282.04	255.72	236.37	221.65	210.16	201.02	193.63	187.57	182.57	178.39
15000	1340.72	714.09	506.39	403.42	342.34	302.19	273.99	253.25	237.48	225.17	215.37	207.46	200.97	195.61	191.13
16000	1430.10	761.69	540.15	430.32	365.16	322.33	292.25	270.13	253.31	240.18	229.73	221.29	214.37	208.65	203.87
17000	1519.48	809.30	573.91	457.21	387.99	342.48	310.52	287.02	269.14	255.19	244.09	235.12	227.77	221.69	216.61
18000	1608.86	856.90	607.67	484.11	410.81	362.63	328.79	303.90	284.97	270.20	258.45	248.95	241.16	234.73	229.35
19000	1698.24	904.51	641.43	511.00	433.63	382.77	347.05	320.78	300.80	285.21	272.81	262.78	254.56	247.77	242.09
20000	1787.62	952.11	675.19	537.90	456.45	402.92	365.32	337.67	316.63	300.22	287.16	276.60	267.96	260.81	254.84
21000	1877.00	999.72	708.95	564.79	479.27	423.06	383.58	354.55	332.47	315.24	301.52	290.44	281.36	273.85	267.58
22000	1966.38	1047.32	742.71	591.69	502.10	443.21	401.85	371.43	348.30	330.25	315.88	304.27	294.76	286.89	280.32
23000	2055.76	1094.93	776.47	618.58	524.92	463.35	420.11	388.31	364.13	345.26	330.24	318.10	308.15	299.93	293.06
24000	2145.14	1142.53	810.22	645.48	547.74	483.50	438.38	405.20	379.96	360.27	344.60	331.93	321.55	312.97	305.80
25000	2234.52	1190.14	843.98	672.37	570.56	503.64	456.64	422.08	395.79	375.28	358.95	345.76	334.95	326.01	318.54
26000	2323.90	1237.74	877.74	699.27	593.39	523.79	474.91	438.96	411.62	390.29	373.31	359.59	348.35	339.05	331.29
27000	2413.29	1285.35	911.50	726.16	616.21	543.94	493.18	455.85	427.45	405.30	387.67	373.42	361.74	352.09	344.03
28000	2502.67	1332.96	945.26	753.06	639.03	564.08	511.44	472.73	443.29	420.31	402.03	387.25	375.14	365.13	356.77
29000	2592.05	1380.56	979.02	779.95	661.85	584.23	529.71	489.61	459.12	435.32	416.39	401.08	388.54	378.17	369.51
30000	2681.43	1428.17	1012.78	806.85	684.68	604.37	547.97	506.50	474.95	450.33	430.74	414.91	401.94	391.21	382.25
35000	3128.33	1666.20	1181.57	941.32	798.79	705.10	639.30	590.91	554.11	525.39	502.53	484.06	468.93	456.41	445.96
40000	3575.23	1904.22	1350.37	1075.77	912.90	805.83	730.63	675.33	633.26	600.44	574.32	553.21	535.90	521.61	509.67
45000	4022.14	2142.25	1519.17	1210.27	1027.01	906.56	821.96	759.74	712.42	675.50	646.11	622.36	602.90	586.81	573.37
50000	4469.04	2380.27	1687.96	1344.74	1141.12	1007.28	913.28	844.16	791.58	750.55	717.90	691.51	669.89	652.01	637.08

MONTHLY PAYMENT
REQUIRED TO AMORTIZE A LOAN — 13½ %

TERM AMOUNT	16 YEARS	17 YEARS	18 YEARS	19 YEARS	20 YEARS	21 YEARS	22 YEARS	23 YEARS	24 YEARS	25 YEARS	26 YEARS	27 YEARS	28 YEARS	30 YEARS	35 YEARS
$100	1.25	1.23	1.21	1.20	1.19	1.17	1.17	1.16	1.15	1.14	1.14	1.13	1.13	1.12	1.11
200	2.50	2.46	2.42	2.39	2.37	2.34	2.33	2.31	2.29	2.28	2.27	2.26	2.25	2.24	2.22
300	3.75	3.69	3.63	3.59	3.55	3.51	3.49	3.46	3.44	3.42	3.40	3.39	3.38	3.36	3.32
400	5.00	4.92	4.84	4.78	4.73	4.68	4.65	4.61	4.58	4.56	4.54	4.52	4.50	4.47	4.43
500	6.25	6.14	6.05	5.98	5.91	5.85	5.81	5.76	5.73	5.70	5.67	5.64	5.62	5.59	5.54
600	7.50	7.37	7.26	7.17	7.09	7.02	6.97	6.92	6.87	6.83	6.80	6.77	6.75	6.71	6.64
700	8.75	8.60	8.47	8.37	8.27	8.19	8.13	8.07	8.02	7.97	7.93	7.90	7.87	7.82	7.75
800	10.00	9.83	9.68	9.56	9.45	9.36	9.29	9.22	9.16	9.11	9.07	9.03	8.99	8.94	8.85
900	11.25	11.06	10.89	10.75	10.64	10.53	10.45	10.37	10.30	10.25	10.20	10.15	10.12	10.06	9.96
1000	12.50	12.28	12.10	11.95	11.82	11.70	11.61	11.52	11.45	11.39	11.33	11.28	11.24	11.17	11.07
2000	24.99	24.56	24.20	23.89	23.63	23.40	23.21	23.04	22.89	22.77	22.66	22.56	22.48	22.34	22.13
3000	37.48	36.84	36.30	35.84	35.45	35.10	34.81	34.56	34.34	34.15	33.98	33.84	33.71	33.51	33.19
4000	49.97	49.12	48.40	47.78	47.25	46.80	46.41	46.07	45.78	45.53	45.31	45.11	44.95	44.68	44.25
5000	62.46	61.40	60.50	59.73	59.07	58.50	58.01	57.59	57.22	56.91	56.63	56.39	56.18	55.84	55.31
6000	74.95	73.68	72.59	71.67	70.88	70.20	69.61	69.11	68.67	68.29	67.96	67.67	67.42	67.01	66.37
7000	87.44	85.95	84.69	83.61	82.69	81.90	81.21	80.62	80.11	79.67	79.28	78.95	78.66	78.18	77.43
8000	99.93	98.23	96.79	95.56	94.50	93.60	92.81	92.14	91.55	91.05	90.61	90.22	89.89	89.35	88.49
9000	112.42	110.51	108.89	107.50	106.32	105.29	104.42	103.66	103.00	102.43	101.93	101.50	101.13	100.52	99.55
10000	124.91	122.79	120.99	119.45	118.13	116.99	116.02	115.17	114.44	113.81	113.26	112.78	112.36	111.68	110.61
11000	137.40	135.07	133.08	131.39	129.94	128.69	127.62	126.69	125.89	125.19	124.58	124.06	123.60	122.85	121.67
12000	149.89	147.35	145.18	143.33	141.75	140.39	139.22	138.21	137.33	136.57	135.91	135.33	134.83	134.02	132.73
13000	162.38	159.62	157.28	155.28	153.56	152.09	150.82	149.72	148.77	147.95	147.23	146.61	146.07	145.19	143.79
14000	174.87	171.90	169.38	167.22	165.38	163.79	162.42	161.24	160.22	159.33	158.56	157.89	157.31	156.35	154.85
15000	187.36	184.18	181.48	179.16	177.19	175.49	174.02	172.76	171.66	170.71	169.88	169.17	168.54	167.52	165.91
16000	199.85	196.46	193.57	191.11	189.00	187.19	185.62	184.27	183.10	182.09	181.21	180.44	179.78	178.69	176.97
17000	212.35	208.74	205.67	203.06	200.81	198.89	197.22	195.79	194.55	193.47	192.54	191.72	191.01	189.86	188.03
18000	224.84	221.02	217.77	215.00	212.63	210.58	208.83	207.31	205.99	204.85	203.86	203.00	202.25	201.03	199.09
19000	237.33	233.30	229.87	226.94	224.44	222.28	220.43	218.82	217.43	216.23	215.19	214.28	213.48	212.19	210.15
20000	249.82	245.57	241.97	238.89	236.25	233.98	232.03	230.34	228.88	227.61	226.51	225.55	224.72	223.36	221.21
21000	262.31	257.85	254.07	250.83	248.06	245.68	243.63	241.86	240.32	238.99	237.84	236.83	235.96	234.53	232.27
22000	274.80	270.13	266.16	262.78	259.87	257.38	255.23	253.37	251.77	250.37	249.16	248.11	247.19	245.70	243.33
23000	287.29	282.41	278.26	274.72	271.69	269.08	266.83	264.89	263.21	261.75	260.49	259.39	258.43	256.86	254.39
24000	299.78	294.69	290.36	286.66	283.50	280.78	278.44	276.41	274.65	273.13	271.81	270.66	269.66	268.03	265.45
25000	312.27	306.97	302.46	298.61	295.31	292.48	290.03	287.92	286.10	284.51	283.14	281.94	280.90	279.20	276.51
26000	324.76	319.24	314.56	310.55	307.12	304.17	301.64	299.44	297.54	295.89	294.46	293.22	292.14	290.37	287.57
27000	337.26	331.52	326.65	322.50	318.94	315.87	313.24	310.96	308.98	307.27	305.79	304.50	303.37	301.54	298.63
28000	349.74	343.80	338.75	334.44	330.75	327.57	324.84	322.47	320.43	318.65	317.11	315.77	314.61	312.70	309.69
29000	362.23	356.08	350.85	346.39	342.56	339.27	336.44	333.99	331.87	330.03	328.44	327.05	325.84	323.87	320.75
30000	374.72	368.36	362.95	358.33	354.37	350.97	348.04	345.51	343.32	341.41	339.76	338.33	337.08	335.04	331.82
35000	437.18	429.75	423.44	418.05	413.43	409.47	406.05	403.09	400.53	398.32	396.39	394.72	393.26	390.88	387.12
40000	499.63	491.14	483.93	477.78	472.50	467.96	464.05	460.68	457.75	455.22	453.02	451.10	449.45	446.72	442.42
45000	562.08	552.54	544.42	537.49	531.56	526.46	522.06	518.26	514.97	512.12	509.64	507.49	505.62	502.56	497.72
50000	624.54	613.93	604.91	597.21	590.62	584.95	580.06	575.84	572.19	569.02	566.27	563.88	561.79	558.40	553.02

MONTHLY PAYMENT
13¾% REQUIRED TO AMORTIZE A LOAN

TERM AMOUNT	1 YEAR	2 YEARS	3 YEARS	4 YEARS	5 YEARS	6 YEARS	7 YEARS	8 YEARS	9 YEARS	10 YEARS	11 YEARS	12 YEARS	13 YEARS	14 YEARS	15 YEARS
$100	8.95	4.78	3.39	2.71	2.30	2.03	1.84	1.71	1.60	1.52	1.46	1.40	1.36	1.32	1.29
200	17.90	9.55	6.78	5.41	4.59	4.06	3.68	3.41	3.20	3.04	2.91	2.80	2.71	2.64	2.58
300	26.85	14.32	10.17	8.11	6.89	6.09	5.52	5.11	4.80	4.55	4.36	4.20	4.07	3.96	3.87
400	35.80	19.09	13.55	10.81	9.18	8.11	7.36	6.81	6.39	6.07	5.81	5.60	5.42	5.28	5.16
500	44.75	23.86	16.94	13.51	11.48	10.14	9.20	8.51	7.99	7.58	7.26	6.99	6.78	6.60	6.45
600	53.70	28.64	20.33	16.21	13.77	12.17	11.04	10.21	9.59	9.10	8.71	8.39	8.13	7.92	7.74
700	62.65	33.41	23.72	18.91	16.07	14.20	12.88	11.92	11.18	10.61	10.16	9.79	9.49	9.24	9.03
800	71.60	38.18	27.10	21.61	18.36	16.22	14.72	13.62	12.78	12.13	11.61	11.19	10.84	10.56	10.32
900	80.55	42.95	30.49	24.32	20.65	18.25	16.56	15.32	14.38	13.64	13.06	12.58	12.20	11.88	11.61
1000	89.50	47.72	33.88	27.02	22.95	20.28	18.40	17.02	15.97	15.16	14.51	13.98	13.55	13.20	12.90
2000	178.99	95.44	67.75	54.03	45.89	40.55	36.79	34.04	31.94	30.31	29.01	27.96	27.10	26.39	25.80
3000	268.48	143.16	101.63	81.04	68.84	60.82	55.19	51.05	47.91	45.46	43.51	41.94	40.65	39.59	38.70
4000	357.97	190.87	135.50	108.05	91.78	81.09	73.58	68.07	63.88	60.61	58.01	55.91	54.20	52.78	51.60
5000	447.46	238.59	169.37	135.07	114.72	101.36	91.98	85.08	79.85	75.76	72.51	69.89	67.75	65.97	64.50
6000	536.96	286.31	203.25	162.08	137.67	121.63	110.37	102.10	95.81	90.91	87.02	83.87	81.29	79.17	77.39
7000	626.45	334.02	237.12	189.09	160.61	141.90	128.77	119.12	111.78	106.06	101.52	97.85	94.84	92.36	90.29
8000	715.94	381.74	270.99	216.10	183.56	162.17	147.16	136.13	127.75	121.21	116.02	111.82	108.39	105.55	103.19
9000	805.43	429.46	304.87	243.12	206.50	182.44	165.56	153.15	143.72	136.37	130.52	125.80	121.94	118.75	116.09
10000	894.92	477.17	338.74	270.13	229.44	202.71	183.95	170.16	159.69	151.52	145.02	139.78	135.49	131.94	128.99
11000	984.42	524.89	372.61	297.14	252.39	222.99	202.35	187.18	175.65	166.67	159.52	153.75	149.03	145.13	141.88
12000	1073.91	572.61	406.49	324.15	275.33	243.26	220.74	204.20	191.62	181.82	174.03	167.73	162.58	158.33	154.78
13000	1163.40	620.32	440.36	351.17	298.28	263.53	239.14	221.21	207.59	196.97	188.53	181.71	176.13	171.52	167.68
14000	1252.89	668.04	474.23	378.18	321.22	283.80	257.53	238.23	223.56	212.12	203.03	195.69	189.68	184.72	180.58
15000	1342.38	715.76	508.11	405.19	344.16	304.04	275.93	255.24	239.53	227.27	217.53	209.66	203.23	197.91	193.48
16000	1431.87	763.47	541.98	432.20	367.11	324.34	294.32	272.26	255.49	242.42	232.03	223.64	216.78	211.10	206.37
17000	1521.37	811.19	575.85	459.22	390.05	344.61	312.72	289.28	271.46	257.58	246.53	237.62	230.32	224.30	219.27
18000	1610.86	858.91	609.73	486.23	413.00	364.88	331.11	306.29	287.43	272.73	261.04	251.60	243.87	237.49	232.17
19000	1700.35	906.62	643.60	513.24	435.94	385.15	349.51	323.31	303.40	287.88	275.54	265.57	257.42	250.68	245.07
20000	1789.84	954.34	677.47	540.25	458.88	405.42	367.90	340.32	319.37	303.03	290.04	279.55	270.97	263.88	257.97
21000	1879.33	1002.06	711.35	567.27	481.83	425.69	386.29	357.34	335.30	318.18	304.54	293.53	284.52	277.07	270.87
22000	1968.83	1049.77	745.22	594.28	504.77	445.97	404.69	374.36	351.30	333.33	319.04	307.50	298.06	290.26	283.76
23000	2058.32	1097.49	779.09	621.29	527.71	466.24	423.08	391.37	367.27	348.48	333.55	321.48	311.61	303.46	296.66
24000	2147.81	1145.21	812.97	648.30	550.66	486.51	441.48	408.39	383.24	363.63	348.05	335.46	325.16	316.65	309.56
25000	2237.30	1192.92	846.84	675.32	573.60	506.78	459.87	425.40	399.21	378.79	362.55	349.44	338.71	329.85	322.46
26000	2326.79	1240.64	880.71	702.33	596.55	527.05	478.27	442.42	415.18	393.94	377.05	363.41	352.26	343.04	335.36
27000	2416.28	1288.36	914.59	729.34	619.49	547.32	496.66	459.44	431.14	409.09	391.55	377.39	365.81	356.23	348.25
28000	2505.78	1336.07	948.46	756.35	642.43	567.59	515.06	476.45	447.11	424.24	406.05	391.37	379.35	369.43	361.15
29000	2595.27	1383.79	982.33	783.38	665.38	587.86	533.45	493.47	463.08	439.39	420.56	405.34	392.90	382.62	374.05
30000	2684.76	1431.51	1016.21	810.38	688.32	608.13	551.85	510.48	479.05	454.54	435.06	419.32	406.45	395.81	386.95
35000	3132.22	1670.09	1185.57	945.44	803.04	709.49	643.82	595.56	558.89	530.30	507.57	489.21	474.19	461.78	451.44
40000	3579.68	1908.67	1354.94	1080.50	917.76	810.84	735.80	680.64	638.73	606.05	580.08	559.09	541.93	527.75	515.93
45000	4027.14	2147.26	1524.31	1215.57	1032.48	912.20	827.77	765.72	718.57	681.81	652.58	628.98	609.67	593.72	580.42
50000	4474.60	2385.84	1693.67	1350.63	1147.20	1013.55	919.74	850.80	798.41	757.57	725.09	698.87	677.41	659.69	644.91

MONTHLY PAYMENT
REQUIRED TO AMORTIZE A LOAN   13¾ %

TERM AMOUNT	35 YEARS	30 YEARS	28 YEARS	27 YEARS	26 YEARS	25 YEARS	24 YEARS	23 YEARS	22 YEARS	21 YEARS	20 YEARS	19 YEARS	18 YEARS	17 YEARS	16 YEARS
$100	1.13	1.14	1.15	1.15	1.16	1.16	1.17	1.17	1.18	1.19	1.20	1.22	1.23	1.25	1.27
200	2.26	2.28	2.29	2.30	2.31	2.32	2.33	2.34	2.36	2.38	2.40	2.43	2.46	2.49	2.54
300	3.38	3.41	3.43	3.44	3.46	3.47	3.49	3.51	3.54	3.57	3.60	3.64	3.68	3.74	3.80
400	4.51	4.55	4.57	4.59	4.61	4.63	4.65	4.68	4.71	4.75	4.80	4.85	4.91	4.98	5.07
500	5.63	5.68	5.71	5.73	5.76	5.78	5.82	5.85	5.89	5.94	6.00	6.06	6.14	6.23	6.33
600	6.76	6.82	6.86	6.88	6.91	6.94	6.98	7.02	7.07	7.13	7.19	7.27	7.36	7.47	7.60
700	7.88	7.95	8.00	8.03	8.06	8.10	8.14	8.19	8.25	8.31	8.39	8.48	8.59	8.71	8.86
800	9.01	9.09	9.14	9.17	9.21	9.25	9.30	9.36	9.42	9.50	9.59	9.69	9.82	9.96	10.13
900	10.13	10.22	10.28	10.32	10.36	10.41	10.46	10.53	10.60	10.69	10.79	10.91	11.04	11.20	11.39
1000	11.26	11.36	11.42	11.46	11.51	11.56	11.63	11.70	11.78	11.88	11.99	12.12	12.27	12.45	12.66
2000	22.51	22.71	22.84	22.92	23.02	23.12	23.25	23.39	23.55	23.75	23.97	24.23	24.53	24.89	25.31
3000	33.76	34.07	34.26	34.38	34.52	34.68	34.87	35.08	35.33	35.62	35.95	36.34	36.79	37.33	37.96
4000	45.01	45.42	45.68	45.84	46.03	46.24	46.49	46.77	47.10	47.50	47.93	48.45	49.06	49.77	50.61
5000	56.26	56.77	57.10	57.30	57.53	57.80	58.11	58.47	58.88	59.36	59.91	60.56	61.32	62.21	63.26
6000	67.51	68.13	68.52	68.76	69.04	69.36	69.73	70.16	70.65	71.24	71.90	72.67	73.58	74.65	75.91
7000	78.76	79.48	79.94	80.22	80.55	80.92	81.35	81.85	82.43	83.11	83.88	84.78	85.84	87.09	88.56
8000	90.01	90.83	91.36	91.68	92.05	92.48	92.97	93.54	94.20	94.99	95.86	96.90	98.11	99.53	101.21
9000	101.26	102.19	102.78	103.14	103.56	104.04	104.59	105.24	105.98	106.86	107.84	109.01	110.37	111.97	113.86
10000	112.51	113.54	114.20	114.60	115.06	115.60	116.21	116.93	117.75	118.73	119.82	121.12	122.63	124.41	126.51
11000	123.76	124.89	125.61	126.06	126.57	127.16	127.84	128.62	129.53	130.60	131.80	133.23	134.90	136.85	139.16
12000	135.01	136.25	137.03	137.52	138.07	138.72	139.46	140.31	141.30	142.48	143.79	145.34	147.16	149.29	151.81
13000	146.26	147.60	148.45	148.98	149.58	150.28	151.08	152.00	153.08	154.35	155.77	157.45	159.42	161.73	164.46
14000	157.51	158.95	159.87	160.44	161.09	161.83	162.70	163.70	164.85	166.22	167.75	169.56	171.68	174.17	177.11
15000	168.76	170.31	171.29	171.90	172.59	173.39	174.32	175.39	176.63	178.09	179.73	181.67	183.95	186.61	189.76
16000	180.01	181.66	182.71	183.35	184.10	184.95	185.94	187.08	188.40	189.97	191.71	193.79	196.21	199.05	202.41
17000	191.26	193.01	194.13	194.81	195.60	196.51	197.56	198.77	200.18	201.84	203.69	205.90	208.47	211.50	215.06
18000	202.51	204.37	205.55	206.27	207.11	208.07	209.18	210.47	211.95	213.71	215.68	218.01	220.74	223.94	227.71
19000	213.76	215.72	216.97	217.73	218.62	219.63	220.80	222.16	223.73	225.58	227.66	230.12	233.00	236.38	240.36
20000	225.01	227.07	228.39	229.19	230.12	231.19	232.42	233.85	235.50	237.46	239.64	242.23	245.26	248.82	253.01
21000	236.26	238.43	239.80	240.65	241.63	242.75	244.05	245.54	247.28	249.33	251.62	254.34	257.52	261.26	265.66
22000	247.51	249.78	251.22	252.11	253.13	254.31	255.67	257.24	259.05	261.20	263.60	266.45	269.79	273.70	278.31
23000	258.76	261.13	262.64	263.57	264.64	265.87	267.29	268.93	270.83	273.07	275.58	278.56	282.05	286.14	290.96
24000	270.01	272.49	274.06	275.03	276.14	277.43	278.91	280.62	282.60	284.95	287.57	290.68	294.31	298.58	303.61
25000	281.26	283.84	285.48	286.49	287.65	288.99	290.53	292.31	294.37	296.82	299.55	302.79	306.58	311.02	316.26
26000	292.51	295.19	296.90	297.95	299.16	300.55	302.15	304.00	306.15	308.69	311.53	314.90	318.84	323.46	328.91
27000	303.76	306.55	308.32	309.41	310.66	312.11	313.77	315.70	317.92	320.56	323.51	327.01	331.10	335.90	341.56
28000	315.02	317.90	319.74	320.87	322.17	323.66	325.39	327.39	329.70	332.44	335.49	339.12	343.36	348.34	354.21
29000	326.27	329.25	331.16	332.33	333.67	335.22	337.01	339.08	341.47	344.31	347.47	351.23	355.63	360.78	366.86
30000	337.52	340.61	342.57	343.79	345.18	346.78	348.63	350.77	353.25	356.18	359.46	363.34	367.89	373.22	379.51
35000	393.77	397.37	399.67	401.08	402.71	404.58	406.74	409.23	412.12	415.54	419.36	423.90	429.20	435.42	442.76
40000	450.02	454.14	456.77	458.38	460.24	462.38	464.84	467.70	471.00	474.91	479.27	484.46	490.52	497.63	506.01
45000	506.27	510.91	513.86	515.68	517.77	520.17	522.95	526.16	529.87	534.27	539.18	545.01	551.83	559.83	569.26
50000	562.52	567.68	570.96	572.97	575.29	577.97	581.05	584.62	588.74	593.53	599.09	605.57	613.15	622.03	632.51

MONTHLY PAYMENT
14 % REQUIRED TO AMORTIZE A LOAN

TERM AMOUNT	1 YEAR	2 YEARS	3 YEARS	4 YEARS	5 YEARS	6 YEARS	7 YEARS	8 YEARS	9 YEARS	10 YEARS	11 YEARS	12 YEARS	13 YEARS	14 YEARS	15 YEARS
$100	8.97	4.79	3.40	2.72	2.31	2.04	1.86	1.72	1.62	1.53	1.47	1.42	1.37	1.34	1.31
200	17.93	9.57	6.80	5.43	4.62	4.08	3.71	3.43	3.23	3.06	2.93	2.83	2.74	2.67	2.62
300	26.89	14.35	10.20	8.14	6.92	6.12	5.56	5.15	4.84	4.59	4.40	4.24	4.11	4.01	3.92
400	35.85	19.14	13.60	10.86	9.23	8.16	7.41	6.86	6.46	6.12	5.86	5.65	5.48	5.34	5.23
500	44.81	23.92	17.00	13.57	11.54	10.20	9.27	8.58	8.06	7.65	7.33	7.07	6.85	6.68	6.53
600	53.77	28.70	20.40	16.28	13.84	12.24	11.12	10.29	9.67	9.18	8.79	8.48	8.22	8.01	7.84
700	62.73	33.48	23.80	19.00	16.15	14.28	12.97	12.01	11.28	10.71	10.26	9.89	9.59	9.35	9.14
800	71.69	38.27	27.20	21.71	18.46	16.32	14.82	13.72	12.89	12.24	11.72	11.30	10.96	10.68	10.45
900	80.65	43.05	30.59	24.42	20.76	18.36	16.68	15.44	14.50	13.77	13.19	12.72	12.33	12.02	11.75
1000	89.61	47.83	33.99	27.14	23.07	20.40	18.53	17.15	16.11	15.30	14.65	14.13	13.70	13.35	13.06
2000	179.21	95.66	67.98	54.27	46.14	40.80	37.05	34.30	32.22	30.59	29.30	28.25	27.40	26.70	26.12
3000	268.81	143.49	101.97	81.40	69.20	61.19	55.58	51.45	48.32	45.88	43.94	42.38	41.10	40.05	39.17
4000	358.42	191.32	135.96	108.53	92.27	81.59	74.10	68.60	64.43	61.17	58.59	56.50	54.80	53.40	52.23
5000	448.02	239.15	169.94	135.66	115.33	101.99	92.63	85.75	80.53	76.47	73.24	70.63	68.50	66.74	65.28
6000	537.62	286.97	203.93	162.79	138.40	122.38	111.15	102.90	96.64	91.76	87.88	84.75	82.20	80.09	78.34
7000	627.23	334.80	237.92	189.92	161.46	142.78	129.68	120.05	112.74	107.05	102.53	98.88	95.90	93.44	91.39
8000	716.83	382.63	271.91	217.05	184.53	163.18	148.20	137.20	128.85	122.34	117.17	113.00	109.60	106.79	104.45
9000	806.43	430.46	305.89	244.18	207.60	183.57	166.72	154.35	144.95	137.63	131.82	127.13	123.30	120.14	117.50
10000	896.04	478.29	339.88	271.31	230.66	203.97	185.25	171.50	161.06	152.93	146.47	141.25	137.00	133.48	130.56
11000	985.64	526.11	373.87	298.44	253.73	224.37	203.77	188.65	177.16	168.22	161.11	155.38	150.70	146.83	143.61
12000	1075.24	573.94	407.86	325.57	276.79	244.76	222.30	205.80	193.27	183.51	175.76	169.50	164.40	160.18	156.67
13000	1164.84	621.77	441.85	352.70	299.86	265.16	240.82	222.95	209.37	198.80	190.40	183.63	178.09	173.53	169.72
14000	1254.45	669.60	475.83	379.83	322.92	285.56	259.35	240.10	225.48	214.09	205.05	197.75	191.79	186.87	182.78
15000	1344.05	717.43	509.82	406.96	345.96	305.95	277.87	257.25	241.58	229.39	219.70	211.88	205.49	200.22	195.83
16000	1433.65	765.25	543.81	434.09	369.06	326.35	296.39	274.39	257.69	244.68	234.34	226.00	219.19	213.57	208.89
17000	1523.25	813.08	577.80	461.22	392.12	346.75	314.92	291.54	273.79	259.97	248.99	240.13	232.89	226.92	221.95
18000	1612.86	860.91	611.78	488.35	415.19	367.54	333.44	308.69	289.90	275.26	263.63	254.25	246.59	240.27	235.00
19000	1702.46	908.74	645.77	515.48	438.25	387.54	351.97	325.84	306.00	290.55	278.28	268.38	260.29	253.61	248.06
20000	1792.06	956.57	679.76	542.61	461.32	407.94	370.49	342.99	322.11	305.85	292.93	282.50	273.99	266.96	261.11
21000	1881.67	1004.39	713.75	569.74	484.38	428.33	389.01	360.14	338.21	321.14	307.57	296.63	287.69	280.31	274.17
22000	1971.27	1052.22	747.73	596.87	507.45	448.73	407.54	377.29	354.32	336.43	322.22	310.75	301.39	293.66	287.22
23000	2060.87	1100.05	781.72	624.00	530.52	469.13	426.06	394.44	370.42	351.72	336.86	324.88	315.09	307.00	300.28
24000	2150.48	1147.88	815.71	651.13	553.58	489.52	444.59	411.59	386.53	367.01	351.51	339.00	328.79	320.35	313.33
25000	2240.08	1195.71	849.70	678.26	576.65	509.92	463.11	428.74	402.64	382.31	366.16	353.13	342.49	333.70	326.39
26000	2329.68	1243.53	883.69	705.40	599.71	530.32	481.64	445.89	418.74	397.60	380.80	367.25	356.18	347.05	339.44
27000	2419.28	1291.36	917.67	732.53	622.78	550.71	500.16	463.04	434.85	412.89	395.45	381.38	369.88	360.40	352.50
28000	2508.89	1339.19	951.66	759.66	645.84	571.11	518.69	480.19	450.95	428.18	410.09	395.50	383.58	373.74	365.55
29000	2598.49	1387.02	985.65	786.79	668.91	591.51	537.21	497.34	467.06	443.47	424.74	409.63	397.28	387.09	378.61
30000	2688.09	1434.85	1019.64	813.92	691.98	611.89	555.73	514.48	483.16	458.77	439.39	423.75	410.98	400.44	391.66
35000	3136.11	1667.99	1189.57	949.57	807.30	713.89	648.36	600.23	563.69	535.23	512.62	494.38	479.48	467.18	456.94
40000	3584.12	1913.13	1359.51	1085.22	922.63	815.87	740.98	685.98	644.21	611.69	585.85	565.00	547.97	533.92	522.22
45000	4032.14	2152.27	1529.45	1220.87	1037.96	917.85	833.60	771.72	724.74	688.15	659.08	635.62	616.47	600.66	587.49
50000	4480.15	2391.41	1699.39	1356.52	1153.29	1019.83	926.22	857.47	805.27	764.61	732.31	706.25	684.97	667.39	652.77

MONTHLY PAYMENT
REQUIRED TO AMORTIZE A LOAN   14 %

TERM AMOUNT	35 YEARS	30 YEARS	28 YEARS	27 YEARS	26 YEARS	25 YEARS	24 YEARS	23 YEARS	22 YEARS	21 YEARS	20 YEARS	19 YEARS	18 YEARS	17 YEARS	16 YEARS
$100	1.15	1.16	1.17	1.17	1.17	1.18	1.18	1.19	1.20	1.21	1.22	1.23	1.25	1.27	1.29
200	2.29	2.31	2.33	2.33	2.34	2.35	2.36	2.38	2.39	2.41	2.44	2.46	2.49	2.53	2.57
300	3.44	3.47	3.49	3.50	3.51	3.53	3.54	3.57	3.59	3.62	3.65	3.69	3.73	3.79	3.85
400	4.58	4.62	4.65	4.66	4.68	4.70	4.72	4.75	4.78	4.82	4.87	4.92	4.98	5.05	5.13
500	5.73	5.77	5.81	5.83	5.85	5.87	5.90	5.94	5.98	6.03	6.08	6.14	6.22	6.31	6.41
600	6.87	6.93	6.97	6.99	7.02	7.05	7.08	7.13	7.17	7.23	7.30	7.37	7.46	7.57	7.69
700	8.01	8.08	8.13	8.15	8.19	8.22	8.26	8.31	8.37	8.43	8.51	8.60	8.70	8.83	8.97
800	9.16	9.24	9.29	9.32	9.35	9.40	9.44	9.50	9.56	9.64	9.73	9.83	9.95	10.09	10.25
900	10.30	10.39	10.45	10.48	10.52	10.57	10.62	10.69	10.76	10.84	10.94	11.06	11.19	11.35	11.53
1000	11.45	11.54	11.61	11.65	11.69	11.74	11.80	11.87	11.95	12.05	12.16	12.28	12.43	12.61	12.82
2000	22.89	23.08	23.21	23.29	23.38	23.48	23.60	23.74	23.90	24.09	24.31	24.56	24.86	25.21	25.63
3000	34.33	34.62	34.81	34.93	35.07	35.22	35.40	35.61	35.85	36.13	36.46	36.84	37.29	37.82	38.44
4000	45.77	46.16	46.42	46.57	46.75	46.96	47.20	47.48	47.80	48.18	48.61	49.12	49.72	50.42	51.25
5000	57.21	57.70	58.02	58.21	58.44	58.70	59.00	59.35	59.75	60.22	60.76	61.40	62.15	63.02	64.06
6000	68.65	69.24	69.62	69.86	70.13	70.44	70.80	71.22	71.70	72.26	72.92	73.68	74.57	75.63	76.87
7000	80.09	80.78	81.22	81.50	81.81	82.18	82.60	83.08	83.65	84.30	85.07	85.96	87.00	88.23	89.68
8000	91.53	92.32	92.83	93.14	93.50	93.92	94.40	94.95	95.60	96.35	97.22	98.24	99.43	100.83	102.49
9000	102.97	103.86	104.43	104.78	105.19	105.65	106.20	106.82	107.55	108.39	109.37	110.52	111.86	113.44	115.30
10000	114.41	115.40	116.03	116.42	116.87	117.39	117.99	118.69	119.50	120.43	121.52	122.80	124.29	126.04	128.11
11000	125.85	126.94	127.64	128.06	128.56	129.13	129.79	130.56	131.45	132.48	133.67	135.08	136.72	138.65	140.92
12000	137.29	138.48	139.24	139.71	140.25	140.87	141.59	142.43	143.39	144.52	145.83	147.36	149.14	151.25	153.73
13000	148.73	150.02	150.84	151.35	151.93	152.61	153.39	154.29	155.34	156.56	157.98	159.63	161.57	163.85	166.54
14000	160.17	161.56	162.44	162.99	163.62	164.35	165.19	166.16	167.29	168.60	170.13	171.91	174.00	176.46	179.35
15000	171.61	173.10	174.05	174.63	175.31	176.09	176.99	178.03	179.24	180.65	182.28	184.19	186.43	189.06	192.16
16000	183.06	184.64	185.65	186.27	186.99	187.83	188.79	189.90	191.19	192.69	194.43	196.47	198.86	201.66	204.97
17000	194.50	196.17	197.25	197.92	198.68	199.56	200.59	201.77	203.14	204.73	206.58	208.75	211.28	214.27	217.78
18000	205.94	207.71	208.86	209.56	210.37	211.30	212.39	213.64	215.09	216.78	218.74	221.03	223.71	226.87	230.59
19000	217.38	219.25	220.46	221.20	222.05	223.04	224.19	225.50	227.04	228.82	230.89	233.31	236.14	239.48	243.40
20000	228.82	230.79	232.06	232.84	233.74	234.78	235.98	237.37	238.99	240.86	243.04	245.59	248.57	252.08	256.21
21000	240.26	242.33	243.66	244.48	245.43	246.52	247.78	249.24	250.94	252.90	255.19	257.87	260.99	264.68	269.02
22000	251.70	253.87	255.27	256.12	257.11	258.26	259.58	261.11	262.89	264.95	267.34	270.15	273.43	277.29	281.83
23000	263.14	265.41	266.87	267.77	268.80	270.00	271.38	272.98	274.84	276.99	279.50	282.43	285.85	289.89	294.64
24000	274.58	276.95	278.47	279.41	280.49	281.74	283.18	284.85	286.79	289.03	291.65	294.71	298.28	302.49	307.45
25000	286.02	288.49	290.07	291.05	292.17	293.47	294.98	296.71	298.73	301.07	303.80	306.98	310.71	315.10	320.26
26000	297.46	300.03	301.68	302.69	303.86	305.21	306.78	308.58	310.68	313.12	315.95	319.26	323.14	327.70	333.07
27000	308.90	311.57	313.28	314.33	315.55	316.95	318.58	320.45	322.63	325.16	328.10	331.54	335.57	340.30	345.88
28000	320.34	323.11	324.88	325.97	327.24	328.69	330.38	332.32	334.58	337.20	340.26	343.82	347.99	352.91	358.69
29000	331.78	334.65	336.49	337.62	338.92	340.43	342.18	344.19	346.53	349.25	352.41	356.10	360.42	365.51	371.50
30000	343.22	346.19	348.09	349.26	350.61	352.17	353.97	356.06	358.48	361.29	364.56	368.38	372.85	378.12	384.31
35000	400.43	403.88	406.10	407.47	409.04	410.86	412.97	415.40	418.23	421.50	425.32	429.78	434.99	441.13	448.36
40000	457.63	461.58	464.12	465.68	467.48	469.56	471.96	474.74	477.97	481.72	486.08	491.17	497.13	504.15	512.41
45000	514.83	519.28	522.13	523.89	525.91	528.25	530.96	534.08	537.72	541.93	546.84	552.57	559.27	567.17	576.46
50000	572.04	576.97	580.14	582.09	584.34	586.94	589.95	593.42	597.46	602.14	607.59	613.96	621.41	630.19	640.51

MONTHLY PAYMENT
14¼ % REQUIRED TO AMORTIZE A LOAN

TERM AMOUNT	1 YEAR	2 YEARS	3 YEARS	4 YEARS	5 YEARS	6 YEARS	7 YEARS	8 YEARS	9 YEARS	10 YEARS	11 YEARS	12 YEARS	13 YEARS	14 YEARS	15 YEARS
$100	8.98	4.80	3.42	2.73	2.32	2.06	1.87	1.73	1.63	1.55	1.48	1.43	1.39	1.36	1.33
200	17.95	9.59	6.83	5.45	4.64	4.11	3.74	3.46	3.25	3.09	2.96	2.86	2.78	2.71	2.65
300	26.92	14.39	10.24	8.18	6.96	6.16	5.60	5.19	4.88	4.63	4.44	4.29	4.16	4.06	3.97
400	35.89	19.18	13.65	10.90	9.28	8.21	7.47	6.92	6.50	6.18	5.92	5.71	5.55	5.41	5.29
500	44.86	23.97	17.06	13.63	11.60	10.27	9.33	8.65	8.13	7.72	7.40	7.14	6.93	6.76	6.61
600	53.83	28.77	20.47	16.35	13.92	12.32	11.20	10.37	9.75	9.26	8.88	8.57	8.32	8.11	7.93
700	62.80	33.56	23.88	19.08	16.24	14.37	13.06	12.10	11.37	10.81	10.36	10.00	9.70	9.46	9.25
800	71.78	38.36	27.29	21.80	18.56	16.42	14.93	13.83	13.00	12.35	11.84	11.42	11.09	10.81	10.58
900	80.75	43.15	30.70	24.53	20.87	18.48	16.79	15.56	14.62	13.89	13.32	12.85	12.47	12.16	11.90
1000	89.72	47.94	34.11	27.25	23.19	20.53	18.66	17.29	16.25	15.44	14.80	14.28	13.86	13.51	13.22
2000	179.43	95.88	68.21	54.50	46.38	41.05	37.31	34.57	32.49	30.87	29.59	28.55	27.71	27.01	26.43
3000	269.15	143.82	102.31	81.75	69.57	61.57	55.97	51.85	48.73	46.30	44.38	42.82	41.56	40.51	39.64
4000	358.86	191.76	136.41	109.00	92.76	82.10	74.62	69.14	64.98	61.74	59.17	57.10	55.41	54.02	52.86
5000	448.57	239.70	170.52	136.25	115.94	102.62	93.28	86.42	81.22	77.17	73.96	71.37	69.26	67.52	66.07
6000	538.29	287.64	204.62	163.50	139.13	123.14	111.93	103.70	97.46	92.60	88.75	85.64	83.11	81.02	79.28
7000	628.00	335.58	238.72	190.74	162.32	143.66	130.58	120.99	113.70	108.04	103.54	99.92	96.96	94.53	92.50
8000	717.72	383.52	272.82	217.99	185.51	164.19	149.24	138.27	129.95	123.47	118.33	114.19	110.81	108.03	105.71
9000	807.43	431.46	306.92	245.24	208.69	184.71	167.89	155.55	146.19	138.90	133.12	128.46	124.66	121.53	118.92
10000	897.14	479.40	341.03	272.49	231.88	205.23	186.55	172.84	162.43	154.34	147.91	142.74	138.51	135.04	132.14
11000	986.86	527.34	375.13	299.74	255.07	225.75	205.20	190.12	178.68	169.77	162.71	157.01	152.36	148.53	145.35
12000	1076.57	575.28	409.23	326.99	278.26	246.28	223.86	207.40	194.92	185.20	177.50	171.28	166.21	162.04	158.56
13000	1166.29	623.22	443.33	354.24	301.45	266.80	242.51	224.69	211.16	200.64	192.29	185.56	180.07	175.54	171.78
14000	1256.00	671.16	477.44	381.48	324.63	287.32	261.16	241.97	227.40	216.07	207.08	199.83	193.92	189.04	184.99
15000	1345.71	719.10	511.54	408.73	347.82	307.84	279.82	259.25	243.65	231.50	221.87	214.10	207.77	202.54	198.20
16000	1435.43	767.04	545.64	435.98	371.01	328.37	298.47	276.53	259.89	246.94	236.66	228.38	221.62	216.05	211.41
17000	1525.14	814.98	579.74	463.23	394.20	348.89	317.13	293.82	276.13	262.37	251.45	242.65	235.47	229.55	224.63
18000	1614.86	862.92	613.84	490.48	417.39	369.41	335.78	311.10	292.38	277.80	266.24	256.92	249.32	243.05	237.84
19000	1704.57	910.85	647.95	517.73	440.57	389.93	354.44	328.38	308.62	293.24	281.03	271.20	263.17	256.55	251.05
20000	1794.28	958.79	682.05	544.98	463.76	410.46	373.09	345.67	324.86	308.67	295.82	285.47	277.02	270.06	264.27
21000	1884.00	1006.73	716.15	572.22	486.95	430.98	391.74	362.95	341.10	324.10	310.61	299.74	290.87	283.56	277.48
22000	1973.71	1054.67	750.25	599.47	510.13	451.50	410.40	380.23	357.35	339.54	325.41	314.02	304.72	297.06	290.69
23000	2063.43	1102.61	784.35	626.72	533.32	472.02	429.05	397.52	373.59	354.97	340.20	328.29	318.57	310.56	303.91
24000	2153.14	1150.55	818.46	653.97	556.51	492.55	447.70	414.80	389.83	370.40	354.99	342.56	332.42	324.07	317.12
25000	2242.85	1198.49	852.56	681.22	579.70	513.07	466.36	432.08	406.07	385.84	369.78	356.84	346.28	337.57	330.33
26000	2332.57	1246.43	886.66	708.47	602.89	533.59	485.01	449.37	422.32	401.27	384.57	371.11	360.13	351.07	343.55
27000	2422.28	1294.37	920.76	735.72	626.07	554.11	503.67	466.65	438.56	416.70	399.36	385.38	373.98	364.57	356.76
28000	2512.00	1342.31	954.87	762.96	649.26	574.64	522.32	483.93	454.80	432.14	414.15	399.66	387.83	378.08	369.97
29000	2601.71	1390.25	988.97	790.21	672.45	595.16	540.98	501.22	471.05	447.57	428.94	413.93	401.68	391.58	383.18
30000	2691.42	1438.19	1023.07	817.46	695.64	615.68	559.63	518.50	487.29	463.00	443.73	428.20	415.53	405.08	396.40
35000	3139.99	1677.89	1193.58	953.70	811.57	718.29	652.90	604.91	568.50	540.17	517.69	499.57	484.78	472.60	462.46
40000	3588.56	1917.59	1364.09	1089.95	927.51	820.91	746.17	691.33	649.67	617.34	591.64	570.93	554.04	540.11	528.53
45000	4037.13	2157.29	1534.60	1226.19	1043.45	923.52	839.44	777.75	730.93	694.50	665.60	642.30	623.29	607.62	594.59
50000	4485.70	2396.98	1705.11	1362.43	1159.39	1026.13	932.72	864.16	812.14	771.67	739.55	713.67	692.55	675.13	660.66

MONTHLY PAYMENT
REQUIRED TO AMORTIZE A LOAN — 14¼%

TERM AMOUNT	35 YEARS	30 YEARS	28 YEARS	27 YEARS	26 YEARS	25 YEARS	24 YEARS	23 YEARS	22 YEARS	21 YEARS	20 YEARS	19 YEARS	18 YEARS	17 YEARS	16 YEARS
$100	1.17	1.18	1.18	1.19	1.19	1.20	1.20	1.21	1.22	1.23	1.24	1.25	1.26	1.28	1.30
200	2.33	2.35	2.36	2.37	2.38	2.39	2.40	2.41	2.43	2.45	2.47	2.49	2.52	2.56	2.60
300	3.49	3.52	3.54	3.55	3.57	3.58	3.60	3.62	3.64	3.67	3.70	3.74	3.78	3.84	3.90
400	4.66	4.70	4.72	4.73	4.75	4.77	4.79	4.82	4.85	4.89	4.93	4.98	5.04	5.11	5.19
500	5.82	5.87	5.90	5.92	5.94	5.96	5.99	6.03	6.07	6.11	6.17	6.23	6.30	6.39	6.49
600	6.98	7.04	7.08	7.10	7.13	7.16	7.19	7.23	7.28	7.33	7.40	7.47	7.56	7.67	7.79
700	8.15	8.21	8.26	8.28	8.31	8.35	8.39	8.44	8.49	8.56	8.63	8.72	8.82	8.94	9.08
800	9.31	9.39	9.43	9.46	9.50	9.54	9.59	9.64	9.70	9.78	9.86	9.96	10.08	10.22	10.38
900	10.47	10.56	10.61	10.65	10.69	10.73	10.78	10.85	10.92	11.00	11.09	11.21	11.34	11.50	11.68
1000	11.64	11.73	11.79	11.83	11.87	11.92	11.98	12.05	12.13	12.22	12.33	12.45	12.60	12.77	12.98
2000	23.27	23.46	23.58	23.65	23.74	23.84	23.96	24.10	24.25	24.44	24.65	24.90	25.19	25.54	25.95
3000	34.90	35.18	35.37	35.48	35.61	35.76	35.94	36.14	36.38	36.65	36.97	37.35	37.79	38.31	38.92
4000	46.53	46.91	47.15	47.30	47.48	47.68	47.91	48.19	48.50	48.87	49.29	49.79	50.38	51.07	51.89
5000	58.16	58.63	58.94	59.13	59.35	59.60	59.89	60.23	60.62	61.08	61.62	62.24	62.98	63.84	64.86
6000	69.79	70.36	70.73	70.95	71.21	71.52	71.87	72.28	72.75	73.30	73.94	74.69	75.57	76.61	77.83
7000	81.42	82.09	82.51	82.78	83.08	83.44	83.85	84.32	84.87	85.51	86.26	87.14	88.16	89.37	90.80
8000	93.05	93.81	94.30	94.60	94.95	95.35	95.82	96.37	97.00	97.73	98.58	99.58	100.76	102.14	103.77
9000	104.68	105.54	106.09	106.43	106.82	107.27	107.80	108.41	109.12	109.94	110.91	112.03	113.35	114.91	116.74
10000	116.32	117.26	117.87	118.25	118.69	119.19	119.78	120.46	121.24	122.16	123.23	124.48	125.95	127.67	129.71
11000	127.95	128.99	129.66	130.08	130.56	131.11	131.75	132.50	133.37	134.38	135.55	136.93	138.54	140.44	142.68
12000	139.58	140.71	141.45	141.90	142.42	143.03	143.73	144.55	145.49	146.59	147.87	149.37	151.13	153.21	155.65
13000	151.21	152.44	153.23	153.72	154.29	154.95	155.71	156.59	157.61	158.81	160.20	161.82	163.73	165.97	168.63
14000	162.84	164.17	165.02	165.55	166.16	166.87	167.69	168.64	169.74	171.02	172.52	174.27	176.32	178.74	181.60
15000	174.47	175.89	176.81	177.37	178.03	178.79	179.66	180.68	181.86	183.24	184.84	186.72	188.92	191.51	194.57
16000	186.10	187.62	188.59	189.20	189.90	190.70	191.64	192.73	193.99	195.45	197.16	199.16	201.51	204.27	207.54
17000	197.73	199.34	200.38	201.02	201.77	202.62	203.62	204.77	206.11	207.67	209.49	211.61	214.11	217.04	220.51
18000	209.36	211.07	212.17	212.85	213.63	214.54	215.59	216.82	218.23	219.88	221.81	224.06	226.70	229.81	233.48
19000	221.00	222.79	223.95	224.67	225.50	226.46	227.57	228.86	230.36	232.10	234.13	236.51	239.29	242.57	246.45
20000	232.63	234.52	235.74	236.50	237.37	238.38	239.55	240.91	242.48	244.31	246.45	248.95	251.89	255.34	259.42
21000	244.26	246.25	247.53	248.32	249.24	250.30	251.53	252.95	254.61	256.53	258.78	261.40	264.48	268.11	272.39
22000	255.89	257.97	259.32	260.15	261.11	262.22	263.50	265.00	266.73	268.75	271.10	273.85	277.08	280.87	285.36
23000	267.52	269.70	271.10	271.97	272.97	274.14	275.48	277.04	278.85	280.96	283.42	286.30	289.67	293.64	298.33
24000	279.15	281.42	282.89	283.80	284.84	286.05	287.46	289.09	291.00	293.18	295.74	298.74	302.26	306.41	311.30
25000	290.78	293.15	294.68	295.62	296.71	297.97	299.44	301.13	303.10	305.39	308.07	311.19	314.86	319.17	324.27
26000	302.41	304.87	306.46	307.44	308.58	309.89	311.41	313.18	315.22	317.61	320.39	323.64	327.45	331.94	337.25
27000	314.04	316.60	318.25	319.27	320.45	321.81	323.39	325.22	327.35	329.82	332.71	336.09	340.05	344.71	350.22
28000	325.68	328.33	330.04	331.09	332.32	333.73	335.37	337.27	339.47	342.04	345.03	348.53	352.64	357.47	363.19
29000	337.31	340.05	341.82	342.92	344.18	345.65	347.34	349.31	351.60	354.25	357.36	360.98	365.23	370.24	376.16
30000	348.94	351.78	353.61	354.74	356.05	357.57	359.32	361.36	363.72	366.47	369.68	373.43	377.83	383.01	389.13
35000	407.09	410.41	412.54	413.87	415.39	417.16	419.21	421.58	424.34	427.55	431.29	435.67	440.80	446.84	453.98
40000	465.25	469.05	471.48	472.99	474.74	476.75	479.09	481.81	484.95	488.62	492.90	497.90	503.77	510.68	518.84
45000	523.40	527.66	530.41	532.11	534.08	536.35	538.98	542.03	545.58	549.70	554.51	560.14	566.74	574.51	583.69
50000	581.56	586.29	589.35	591.24	593.42	595.94	598.87	602.26	606.20	610.78	616.13	622.38	629.71	638.34	648.54

MONTHLY PAYMENT
14½ % REQUIRED TO AMORTIZE A LOAN

TERM AMOUNT	1 YEAR	2 YEARS	3 YEARS	4 YEARS	5 YEARS	6 YEARS	7 YEARS	8 YEARS	9 YEARS	10 YEARS	11 YEARS	12 YEARS	13 YEARS	14 YEARS	15 YEARS
$100	8.99	4.81	3.43	2.74	2.34	2.07	1.88	1.75	1.64	1.56	1.50	1.45	1.41	1.37	1.34
200	17.97	9.62	6.85	5.48	4.67	4.13	3.76	3.49	3.28	3.12	2.99	2.89	2.81	2.74	2.68
300	26.95	14.42	10.27	8.22	7.00	6.20	5.64	5.23	4.92	4.68	4.49	4.33	4.21	4.10	4.02
400	35.93	19.23	13.69	10.95	9.33	8.26	7.52	6.97	6.56	6.24	5.98	5.77	5.61	5.47	5.35
500	44.92	24.03	17.11	13.69	11.66	10.33	9.40	8.71	8.20	7.79	7.47	7.22	7.01	6.83	6.69
600	53.90	28.84	20.54	16.43	13.99	12.39	11.28	10.46	9.83	9.35	8.97	8.66	8.41	8.20	8.03
700	62.88	33.64	23.96	19.16	16.32	14.46	13.15	12.20	11.47	10.91	10.46	10.10	9.81	9.57	9.37
800	71.86	38.45	27.38	21.90	18.65	16.52	15.03	13.94	13.11	12.47	11.95	11.54	11.21	10.93	10.70
900	80.85	43.25	30.80	24.64	20.98	18.59	16.91	15.68	14.75	14.02	13.45	12.98	12.61	12.30	12.04
1000	89.83	48.06	34.22	27.37	23.31	20.65	18.79	17.42	16.39	15.58	14.94	14.43	14.01	13.66	13.38
2000	179.65	96.11	68.44	54.74	46.62	41.30	37.57	34.84	32.77	31.16	29.88	28.85	28.01	27.32	26.75
3000	269.48	144.16	102.66	82.11	69.93	61.95	56.36	52.26	49.15	46.73	44.81	43.27	42.01	40.98	40.12
4000	359.30	192.21	136.87	109.47	93.24	82.60	75.14	69.67	65.53	62.31	59.75	57.69	56.02	54.64	53.49
5000	449.13	240.26	171.09	136.84	116.55	103.25	93.93	87.07	81.91	77.88	74.69	72.12	70.02	68.29	66.86
6000	538.95	288.31	205.31	164.21	139.86	123.90	112.71	104.51	98.29	93.46	89.62	86.54	84.02	81.95	80.23
7000	628.78	336.36	239.52	191.57	163.17	144.55	131.50	121.93	114.67	109.03	104.56	100.96	98.03	95.61	93.61
8000	718.60	384.41	273.74	218.94	186.48	165.20	150.28	139.34	131.05	124.61	119.50	115.38	112.03	109.27	106.98
9000	808.43	432.46	307.96	246.31	209.79	185.84	169.07	156.76	147.43	140.18	134.43	129.80	126.03	122.93	120.35
10000	898.25	480.51	342.17	273.67	233.10	206.49	187.85	174.18	163.81	155.76	149.37	144.23	140.03	136.58	133.72
11000	988.08	528.56	376.39	301.04	256.41	227.14	206.63	191.60	180.19	171.33	164.30	158.65	154.04	150.24	147.09
12000	1077.90	576.60	410.61	328.41	279.72	247.79	225.42	209.01	196.57	186.91	179.24	173.07	168.04	163.90	160.46
13000	1167.73	624.67	444.82	355.77	303.03	268.44	244.20	226.43	212.96	202.48	194.18	187.49	182.05	177.56	173.83
14000	1257.55	672.72	479.04	383.14	326.34	289.09	262.99	243.85	229.34	218.06	209.11	201.91	196.05	191.22	187.21
15000	1347.38	720.77	513.26	410.51	349.65	309.74	281.77	261.27	245.72	233.63	224.05	216.34	210.05	204.87	200.58
16000	1437.20	768.82	547.47	437.87	372.96	330.39	300.56	278.68	262.10	249.21	238.99	230.76	224.05	218.53	213.95
17000	1527.03	816.87	581.69	465.24	396.27	351.04	319.34	296.10	278.48	264.78	253.82	245.18	238.06	232.19	227.32
18000	1616.85	864.92	615.91	492.61	419.58	371.68	338.13	313.52	294.86	280.36	268.86	259.60	252.06	245.85	240.69
19000	1706.68	912.97	650.12	519.98	442.89	392.33	356.91	330.93	311.24	295.93	283.79	274.02	266.06	259.51	254.06
20000	1796.50	961.02	684.34	547.34	466.20	412.98	375.70	348.35	327.62	311.51	298.73	288.45	280.06	273.16	267.44
21000	1886.33	1009.07	718.56	574.71	489.51	433.63	394.48	365.77	344.00	327.08	313.67	302.87	294.07	286.82	280.81
22000	1976.15	1057.12	752.77	602.08	512.82	454.28	413.26	383.19	360.38	342.66	328.60	317.29	308.07	300.48	294.18
23000	2065.98	1105.18	786.99	629.44	536.13	474.93	432.05	400.60	376.76	358.24	343.54	331.71	322.07	314.14	307.55
24000	2155.80	1153.23	821.21	656.81	559.44	495.58	450.83	418.02	393.14	373.81	358.48	346.14	336.08	327.80	320.92
25000	2245.63	1201.28	855.42	684.18	582.75	516.23	469.62	435.44	409.53	389.38	373.41	360.56	350.08	341.45	334.29
26000	2335.45	1249.33	889.64	711.54	606.06	536.87	488.40	452.86	425.91	404.96	388.35	374.98	364.08	355.11	347.66
27000	2425.28	1297.38	923.86	738.91	629.37	557.52	507.19	470.27	442.29	420.53	403.29	389.40	378.09	368.77	361.04
28000	2515.10	1345.43	958.07	766.28	652.68	578.17	525.97	487.69	458.67	436.11	418.22	403.82	392.09	382.43	374.41
29000	2604.93	1393.43	992.29	793.64	675.99	598.82	544.75	505.11	475.05	451.68	433.16	418.25	406.09	396.09	387.78
30000	2694.75	1441.53	1026.51	821.01	699.30	619.47	563.54	522.52	491.43	467.26	448.09	432.67	420.09	409.74	401.15
35000	3143.88	1681.79	1197.59	957.84	815.85	722.71	657.46	609.61	573.33	545.13	522.78	504.78	490.11	478.03	468.01
40000	3593.00	1922.04	1368.67	1094.68	932.40	825.96	751.38	696.70	655.24	623.00	597.46	576.89	560.12	546.32	534.87
45000	4042.13	2162.30	1539.76	1231.51	1048.95	929.20	845.31	783.78	737.14	700.88	672.14	649.00	630.14	614.61	601.72
50000	4491.25	2402.55	1710.84	1368.35	1165.50	1032.45	939.23	870.87	819.05	778.76	746.82	721.11	700.15	682.90	668.58

MONTHLY PAYMENT
REQUIRED TO AMORTIZE A LOAN   14½ %

TERM AMOUNT	16 YEARS	17 YEARS	18 YEARS	19 YEARS	20 YEARS	21 YEARS	22 YEARS	23 YEARS	24 YEARS	25 YEARS	26 YEARS	27 YEARS	28 YEARS	30 YEARS	35 YEARS
$100	1.32	1.30	1.28	1.27	1.25	1.24	1.23	1.23	1.22	1.21	1.21	1.21	1.20	1.20	1.19
200	2.63	2.59	2.56	2.53	2.50	2.48	2.46	2.45	2.44	2.42	2.42	2.41	2.40	2.39	2.37
300	3.94	3.88	3.83	3.79	3.75	3.72	3.69	3.67	3.65	3.63	3.62	3.61	3.60	3.58	3.55
400	5.26	5.18	5.11	5.05	5.00	4.96	4.92	4.89	4.87	4.84	4.83	4.81	4.79	4.77	4.73
500	6.57	6.47	6.39	6.31	6.25	6.20	6.15	6.12	6.08	6.05	6.03	6.01	5.99	5.96	5.92
600	7.88	7.76	7.66	7.57	7.50	7.44	7.38	7.34	7.30	7.26	7.24	7.21	7.19	7.15	7.10
700	9.20	9.06	8.94	8.84	8.75	8.68	8.61	8.56	8.51	8.47	8.44	8.41	8.38	8.34	8.28
800	10.51	10.35	10.22	10.10	10.00	9.92	9.84	9.78	9.73	9.68	9.65	9.61	9.58	9.53	9.46
900	11.82	11.64	11.49	11.36	11.25	11.15	11.07	11.00	10.94	10.89	10.85	10.81	10.78	10.73	10.64
1000	13.14	12.94	12.77	12.62	12.50	12.39	12.30	12.23	12.16	12.10	12.06	12.01	11.98	11.92	11.83
2000	26.27	25.87	25.53	25.24	24.99	24.78	24.60	24.45	24.32	24.20	24.11	24.02	23.95	23.83	23.65
3000	39.40	38.80	38.29	37.85	37.49	37.17	36.90	36.67	36.47	36.30	36.16	36.03	35.92	35.74	35.47
4000	52.53	51.73	51.05	50.47	49.98	49.56	49.20	48.89	48.63	48.40	48.21	48.04	47.89	47.65	47.29
5000	65.66	64.66	63.81	63.09	62.47	61.95	61.50	61.11	60.79	60.50	60.26	60.05	59.86	59.57	59.11
6000	78.80	77.59	76.57	75.70	74.97	74.34	73.80	73.34	72.94	72.60	72.31	72.05	71.83	71.48	70.94
7000	91.93	90.52	89.33	88.32	87.46	86.73	86.10	85.56	85.10	84.70	84.36	84.06	83.80	83.39	82.76
8000	105.06	103.45	102.09	100.94	99.95	99.12	98.40	97.78	97.25	96.80	96.41	96.07	95.78	95.30	94.58
9000	118.19	116.38	114.85	113.55	112.45	111.50	110.70	110.00	109.41	108.90	108.46	108.08	107.75	107.22	106.40
10000	131.33	129.31	127.61	126.17	124.94	123.89	123.00	122.23	121.57	121.00	120.51	120.08	119.72	119.13	118.22
11000	144.46	142.24	140.37	138.79	137.44	136.28	135.30	134.45	133.72	133.10	132.56	132.09	131.69	131.04	130.04
12000	157.59	155.17	153.13	151.40	149.93	148.67	147.59	146.67	145.88	145.20	144.61	144.10	143.66	142.95	141.87
13000	170.72	168.10	165.89	164.02	162.42	161.06	159.89	158.89	158.03	157.30	156.66	156.11	155.63	154.87	153.69
14000	183.85	181.03	178.65	176.64	174.92	173.45	172.19	171.12	170.19	169.39	168.71	168.12	167.60	166.78	165.51
15000	196.98	193.97	191.42	189.25	187.41	185.84	184.49	183.34	182.35	181.49	180.76	180.12	179.57	178.69	177.33
16000	210.12	206.90	204.18	201.87	199.90	198.23	196.79	195.56	194.50	193.59	192.81	192.13	191.55	190.60	189.15
17000	223.25	219.83	216.94	214.48	212.40	210.62	209.09	207.78	206.66	205.69	204.86	204.14	203.52	202.52	200.98
18000	236.38	232.76	229.70	227.10	224.89	223.00	221.39	220.00	218.81	217.79	216.91	216.15	215.49	214.43	212.80
19000	249.51	245.69	242.46	239.72	237.38	235.39	233.69	232.23	230.97	229.89	228.96	228.15	227.46	226.34	224.62
20000	262.65	258.62	255.22	252.33	249.88	247.78	245.99	244.45	243.13	241.99	241.01	240.16	239.43	238.25	236.44
21000	275.78	271.55	267.98	264.95	262.37	260.17	258.29	256.67	255.28	254.09	253.06	252.17	251.40	250.17	248.26
22000	288.91	284.48	280.74	277.57	274.87	272.56	270.58	268.89	267.44	266.19	265.11	264.18	263.37	262.08	260.08
23000	302.04	297.41	293.50	290.18	287.36	284.95	282.89	281.12	279.60	278.28	277.16	276.19	275.35	273.99	271.91
24000	315.17	310.34	306.26	302.80	299.85	297.34	295.18	293.34	291.75	290.39	289.21	288.19	287.32	285.90	283.73
25000	328.31	323.27	319.02	315.42	312.35	309.73	307.48	305.56	303.91	302.49	301.26	300.20	299.29	297.82	295.55
26000	341.44	336.20	331.78	328.03	324.84	322.12	319.78	317.78	316.06	314.58	313.31	312.21	311.26	309.73	307.37
27000	354.57	349.14	344.54	340.65	337.33	334.50	332.08	330.00	328.22	326.68	325.36	324.22	323.23	321.64	319.19
28000	367.70	362.07	357.30	353.27	349.83	346.89	344.38	342.23	340.38	338.78	337.41	336.23	335.20	333.55	331.01
29000	380.83	375.00	370.07	365.88	362.32	359.28	356.68	354.45	352.53	350.88	349.46	348.23	347.17	345.47	342.84
30000	393.97	387.93	382.83	378.50	374.82	371.67	368.98	366.67	364.69	362.98	361.51	360.24	359.14	357.38	354.66
35000	459.63	452.58	446.63	441.58	437.29	433.61	430.48	427.78	425.47	423.47	421.76	420.28	419.00	416.94	413.77
40000	525.29	517.24	510.43	504.66	499.75	495.56	491.97	488.89	486.25	483.97	482.01	480.32	478.86	476.50	472.88
45000	590.95	581.89	574.24	567.75	562.22	557.50	553.47	550.00	547.03	544.47	542.26	540.36	538.71	536.06	531.99
50000	656.61	646.54	638.04	630.83	624.69	619.45	614.96	611.12	607.81	604.97	602.51	600.40	598.57	595.63	591.09

MONTHLY PAYMENT
14¾ % REQUIRED TO AMORTIZE A LOAN

TERM AMOUNT	1 YEAR	2 YEARS	3 YEARS	4 YEARS	5 YEARS	6 YEARS	7 YEARS	8 YEARS	9 YEARS	10 YEARS	11 YEARS	12 YEARS	13 YEARS	14 YEARS	15 YEARS
$100	9.00	4.82	3.44	2.75	2.35	2.08	1.90	1.76	1.66	1.58	1.51	1.46	1.42	1.39	1.36
200	17.99	9.64	6.87	5.50	4.69	4.16	3.79	3.52	3.31	3.15	3.02	2.92	2.84	2.77	2.71
300	26.99	14.45	10.30	8.25	7.03	6.24	5.68	5.27	4.96	4.72	4.53	4.38	4.25	4.15	4.06
400	35.98	19.27	13.74	11.00	9.38	8.32	7.57	7.03	6.61	6.29	6.04	5.83	5.67	5.53	5.42
500	44.97	24.09	17.17	13.75	11.72	10.39	9.46	8.78	8.26	7.86	7.55	7.29	7.08	6.91	6.77
600	53.97	28.90	20.60	16.50	14.06	12.47	11.35	10.54	9.91	9.44	9.05	8.75	8.50	8.29	8.12
700	62.96	33.72	24.04	19.24	16.41	14.55	13.25	12.29	11.57	11.01	10.56	10.21	9.91	9.67	9.48
800	71.95	38.53	27.47	21.99	18.75	16.63	15.14	14.05	13.22	12.58	12.07	11.66	11.33	11.06	10.83
900	80.95	43.35	30.90	24.74	21.09	18.70	17.03	15.80	14.87	14.15	13.58	13.12	12.75	12.44	12.18
1000	89.94	48.17	34.34	27.49	23.44	20.78	18.92	17.56	16.52	15.72	15.09	14.58	14.16	13.82	13.54
2000	179.88	96.33	68.67	54.98	46.87	41.56	37.84	35.11	33.04	31.44	30.17	29.15	28.32	27.63	27.07
3000	269.81	144.49	103.00	82.46	70.30	62.33	56.75	52.66	49.56	47.16	45.25	43.72	42.47	41.45	40.60
4000	359.75	192.65	137.33	109.95	93.73	83.11	75.67	70.21	66.08	62.87	60.33	58.29	56.63	55.26	54.13
5000	449.68	240.82	171.66	137.43	117.17	103.88	94.58	87.76	82.60	78.59	75.42	72.86	70.78	69.07	67.66
6000	539.62	288.98	205.99	164.92	140.60	124.66	113.49	105.31	99.12	94.31	90.50	87.43	84.94	82.89	81.19
7000	629.56	337.14	240.32	192.40	164.03	145.43	132.41	122.87	115.64	110.03	105.58	102.01	99.01	96.70	94.72
8000	719.49	385.30	274.66	219.89	187.46	166.21	151.33	140.42	132.16	125.74	120.66	116.58	113.25	110.52	108.25
9000	809.43	433.47	308.99	247.37	210.90	186.98	170.24	157.97	148.68	141.46	135.74	131.15	127.41	124.33	121.78
10000	899.36	481.63	343.32	274.86	234.33	207.76	189.16	175.52	165.20	157.18	150.83	145.72	141.56	138.14	135.31
11000	989.30	529.79	377.65	302.34	257.76	228.53	208.07	193.08	181.72	172.90	165.91	160.29	155.72	151.96	148.84
12000	1079.24	577.95	411.98	329.83	281.19	249.31	226.99	210.63	198.24	188.61	180.99	174.86	169.87	165.77	162.37
13000	1169.17	626.12	446.31	357.31	304.63	270.09	245.90	228.18	214.76	204.33	196.07	189.43	184.03	179.59	175.90
14000	1259.11	674.28	480.64	384.80	328.06	290.86	264.82	245.73	231.28	220.05	211.16	204.01	198.18	193.40	189.43
15000	1349.04	722.44	514.98	412.28	351.49	311.64	283.73	263.28	247.79	235.76	226.24	218.58	212.34	207.21	202.96
16000	1438.98	770.60	549.31	439.77	374.92	332.41	302.65	280.84	264.31	251.48	241.32	233.15	226.50	221.03	216.49
17000	1528.92	818.77	583.64	467.26	398.36	353.19	321.56	298.39	280.83	267.20	256.40	247.72	240.65	234.84	230.02
18000	1618.85	866.93	617.97	494.74	421.79	373.96	340.48	315.94	297.35	282.92	271.48	262.29	254.81	248.66	243.55
19000	1708.79	915.09	652.30	522.23	445.22	394.74	359.39	333.49	313.87	298.63	286.57	276.86	268.96	262.47	257.08
20000	1798.72	963.25	686.63	549.71	468.65	415.51	378.31	351.04	330.39	314.35	301.65	291.43	283.12	276.28	270.61
21000	1888.66	1011.41	720.96	577.20	492.09	436.29	397.22	368.60	346.90	330.07	316.73	306.01	297.28	290.10	284.15
22000	1978.60	1059.58	755.30	604.68	515.52	457.06	416.14	386.15	363.43	345.79	331.81	320.58	311.43	303.91	297.68
23000	2068.53	1107.74	789.63	632.17	538.95	477.84	435.05	403.70	379.95	361.50	346.90	335.15	325.59	317.72	311.21
24000	2158.47	1155.90	823.96	659.65	562.38	498.61	453.97	421.25	396.47	377.22	361.98	349.72	339.74	331.54	324.74
25000	2248.40	1204.06	858.29	687.14	585.82	519.39	472.88	438.80	412.99	392.94	377.06	364.29	353.90	345.35	338.27
26000	2338.34	1252.22	892.62	714.62	609.25	540.16	491.80	456.35	429.51	408.65	392.14	378.86	368.05	359.17	351.80
27000	2428.28	1300.39	926.95	742.11	632.68	560.94	510.71	473.91	446.03	424.37	407.22	393.44	382.21	372.98	365.33
28000	2518.21	1348.55	961.28	769.59	656.11	581.72	529.63	491.46	462.55	440.09	422.31	408.01	396.37	386.79	378.86
29000	2608.15	1396.71	995.62	797.08	679.55	602.49	548.54	509.01	479.07	455.81	437.39	422.58	410.52	400.61	392.39
30000	2698.08	1444.88	1029.95	824.57	702.98	623.27	567.46	526.56	495.58	471.52	452.47	437.15	424.68	414.42	405.92
35000	3147.76	1685.69	1201.60	961.99	820.14	727.14	662.03	614.32	578.18	550.11	527.88	510.01	495.46	483.49	473.57
40000	3597.44	1926.50	1373.26	1099.42	937.30	831.02	756.61	702.08	660.77	628.70	603.29	582.86	566.24	552.56	541.22
45000	4047.12	2167.31	1544.92	1236.85	1054.47	934.90	851.18	789.84	743.37	707.28	678.70	655.72	637.01	621.63	608.88
50000	4496.80	2408.12	1716.57	1374.27	1171.63	1038.78	945.76	877.60	825.97	785.87	754.11	728.58	707.79	690.70	676.53

MONTHLY PAYMENT
REQUIRED TO AMORTIZE A LOAN — 14¾ %

TERM AMOUNT	35 YEARS	30 YEARS	28 YEARS	27 YEARS	26 YEARS	25 YEARS	24 YEARS	23 YEARS	22 YEARS	21 YEARS	20 YEARS	19 YEARS	18 YEARS	17 YEARS	16 YEARS
$100	1.24	1.24	1.25	1.25	1.26	1.26	1.27	1.27	1.28	1.29	1.30	1.31	1.32	1.34	1.36
200	2.47	2.49	2.50	2.51	2.51	2.52	2.53	2.55	2.56	2.58	2.60	2.62	2.65	2.68	2.72
300	3.71	3.73	3.75	3.76	3.77	3.78	3.80	3.82	3.84	3.87	3.90	3.93	3.97	4.02	4.08
400	4.95	4.98	5.00	5.01	5.03	5.05	5.07	5.09	5.12	5.15	5.19	5.24	5.29	5.36	5.44
500	6.18	6.22	6.25	6.27	6.28	6.31	6.33	6.36	6.40	6.44	6.49	6.55	6.62	6.70	6.80
600	7.42	7.47	7.50	7.52	7.54	7.57	7.60	7.64	7.68	7.73	7.79	7.86	7.94	8.04	8.16
700	8.66	8.71	8.75	8.77	8.80	8.83	8.87	8.91	8.96	9.02	9.09	9.17	9.27	9.38	9.52
800	9.89	9.96	10.00	10.02	10.06	10.09	10.13	10.18	10.24	10.31	10.39	10.48	10.59	10.72	10.87
900	11.13	11.20	11.25	11.28	11.31	11.35	11.40	11.46	11.52	11.60	11.69	11.79	11.91	12.06	12.23
1000	12.36	12.44	12.50	12.53	12.57	12.61	12.67	12.73	12.80	12.88	12.98	13.10	13.24	13.40	13.59
2000	24.73	24.89	25.00	25.06	25.14	25.23	25.33	25.46	25.60	25.77	25.97	26.20	26.47	26.80	27.19
3000	37.09	37.33	37.49	37.59	37.71	37.84	38.00	38.19	38.40	38.65	38.95	39.30	39.71	40.20	40.78
4000	49.46	49.78	49.99	50.12	50.28	50.46	50.67	50.91	51.20	51.54	51.93	52.40	52.95	53.60	54.37
5000	61.82	62.22	62.49	62.65	62.85	63.07	63.34	63.64	64.00	64.42	64.92	65.50	66.19	67.01	67.97
6000	74.19	74.67	74.99	75.19	75.42	75.69	76.00	76.37	76.80	77.31	77.90	78.60	79.42	80.41	81.56
7000	86.55	87.11	87.48	87.72	87.99	88.30	88.67	89.10	89.60	90.19	90.88	91.70	92.66	93.81	95.16
8000	98.92	99.56	99.98	100.25	100.56	100.92	101.34	101.83	102.40	103.08	103.87	104.80	105.90	107.21	108.75
9000	111.28	112.00	112.48	112.78	113.13	113.53	114.00	114.56	115.20	115.96	116.85	117.90	119.14	120.61	122.34
10000	123.65	124.45	124.98	125.31	125.70	126.15	126.67	127.29	128.00	128.85	129.84	131.00	132.37	134.01	135.94
11000	136.01	136.89	137.47	137.84	138.27	138.76	139.34	140.01	140.80	141.73	142.82	144.10	145.61	147.41	149.53
12000	148.38	149.34	149.97	150.37	150.84	151.37	152.01	152.74	153.61	154.62	155.80	157.20	158.85	160.81	163.12
13000	160.74	161.78	162.47	162.90	163.40	163.99	164.67	165.47	166.41	167.50	168.79	170.30	172.09	174.21	176.72
14000	173.11	174.23	174.97	175.43	175.97	176.60	177.34	178.20	179.21	180.39	181.77	183.40	185.32	187.61	190.31
15000	185.47	186.67	187.47	187.96	188.54	189.22	190.01	190.93	192.01	193.27	194.75	196.50	198.56	201.02	203.91
16000	197.84	199.12	199.96	200.49	201.11	201.83	202.67	203.66	204.81	206.16	207.74	209.60	211.80	214.42	217.50
17000	210.20	211.56	212.46	213.03	213.68	214.45	215.34	216.38	217.61	219.04	220.72	222.70	225.04	227.82	231.09
18000	222.57	224.01	224.96	225.56	226.25	227.06	228.01	229.11	230.41	231.92	233.70	235.80	238.27	241.22	244.69
19000	234.93	236.45	237.46	238.09	238.82	239.68	240.68	241.84	243.21	244.81	246.69	248.90	251.51	254.62	258.28
20000	247.30	248.90	249.95	250.62	251.39	252.29	253.34	254.57	256.01	257.69	259.67	262.00	264.75	268.02	271.87
21000	259.66	261.34	262.45	263.15	263.96	264.91	266.01	267.30	268.81	270.58	272.65	275.10	277.99	281.42	285.47
22000	272.03	273.79	274.95	275.68	276.53	277.52	278.68	280.03	281.61	283.46	285.64	288.20	291.22	294.82	299.06
23000	284.39	286.23	287.45	288.21	289.10	290.13	291.34	292.76	294.41	296.35	298.62	301.30	304.46	308.22	312.66
24000	296.75	298.68	299.95	300.74	301.67	302.75	304.01	305.48	307.21	309.23	311.60	314.40	317.70	321.62	326.25
25000	309.12	311.12	312.44	313.27	314.24	315.36	316.68	318.21	320.01	322.12	324.59	327.50	330.94	335.03	339.84
26000	321.48	323.57	324.94	325.80	326.81	327.98	329.35	330.94	332.81	335.00	337.57	340.60	344.17	348.43	353.44
27000	333.85	336.01	337.44	338.33	339.38	340.59	342.01	343.67	345.61	347.89	350.55	353.70	357.41	361.83	367.03
28000	346.21	348.46	349.94	350.86	351.95	353.21	354.68	356.40	358.41	360.77	363.54	366.80	370.65	375.23	380.62
29000	358.58	360.90	362.43	363.40	364.52	365.82	367.35	369.13	371.21	373.66	376.52	379.90	383.88	388.63	394.22
30000	370.94	373.35	374.93	375.93	377.09	378.44	380.01	381.86	384.01	386.54	389.51	393.00	397.12	402.03	407.81
35000	432.77	435.57	437.42	438.58	439.94	441.51	443.35	445.50	448.02	450.96	454.42	458.50	463.31	469.04	475.78
40000	494.59	497.80	499.91	501.24	502.78	504.58	506.69	509.14	512.02	515.39	519.34	524.00	529.50	536.04	543.75
45000	556.42	560.02	562.40	563.89	565.63	567.66	570.02	572.78	576.02	579.81	584.26	589.50	595.68	603.05	611.72
50000	618.24	622.25	624.89	626.54	628.48	630.73	633.36	636.43	640.02	644.24	649.18	655.01	661.87	670.05	679.69

MONTHLY PAYMENT
15% REQUIRED TO AMORTIZE A LOAN

TERM AMOUNT	1 YEAR	2 YEARS	3 YEARS	4 YEARS	5 YEARS	6 YEARS	7 YEARS	8 YEARS	9 YEARS	10 YEARS	11 YEARS	12 YEARS	13 YEARS	14 YEARS	15 YEARS
$100	9.01	4.83	3.45	2.77	2.36	2.10	1.91	1.77	1.67	1.59	1.53	1.48	1.44	1.40	1.37
200	18.01	9.66	6.89	5.53	4.72	4.19	3.81	3.54	3.33	3.18	3.05	2.95	2.87	2.79	2.74
300	27.02	14.49	10.34	8.29	7.07	6.28	5.72	5.31	5.00	4.76	4.57	4.42	4.30	4.19	4.11
400	36.02	19.31	13.78	11.05	9.43	8.37	7.62	7.08	6.67	6.35	6.10	5.89	5.73	5.59	5.48
500	45.03	24.14	17.23	13.81	11.78	10.46	9.53	8.85	8.33	7.94	7.62	7.37	7.16	6.99	6.85
600	54.03	28.97	20.67	16.57	14.14	12.55	11.43	10.62	10.00	9.52	9.14	8.84	8.59	8.38	8.22
700	63.04	33.80	24.12	19.33	16.49	14.63	13.34	12.39	11.67	11.11	10.67	10.31	10.02	9.78	9.59
800	72.04	38.62	27.56	22.09	18.85	16.73	15.24	14.15	13.33	12.69	12.19	11.78	11.45	11.18	10.96
900	81.05	43.45	31.01	24.85	21.20	18.82	17.15	15.92	15.00	14.28	13.71	13.25	12.88	12.57	12.33
1000	90.05	48.28	34.45	27.61	23.56	20.91	19.05	17.69	16.66	15.87	15.23	14.73	14.31	13.97	13.70
2000	180.10	96.55	68.90	55.21	47.12	41.81	38.09	35.38	33.32	31.73	30.46	29.45	28.62	27.95	27.39
3000	270.15	144.83	103.34	82.82	70.67	62.71	57.14	53.07	49.98	47.59	45.69	44.17	42.93	41.92	41.08
4000	360.19	193.10	137.79	110.42	94.23	83.61	76.18	70.75	66.63	63.45	60.92	58.89	57.24	55.89	54.77
5000	450.24	241.37	172.24	138.03	117.78	104.52	95.23	88.44	83.29	79.31	76.15	73.61	71.55	69.86	68.46
6000	540.29	289.65	206.68	165.63	141.34	125.42	114.28	106.13	99.95	95.17	91.38	88.33	85.86	83.83	82.15
7000	630.33	337.92	241.13	193.23	164.89	146.32	133.33	123.81	116.61	111.03	106.61	103.06	100.17	97.80	95.84
8000	720.38	386.20	275.57	220.84	188.45	167.22	152.37	141.50	133.27	126.89	121.83	117.78	114.48	111.77	109.53
9000	810.43	434.47	310.02	248.44	212.00	188.13	171.42	159.18	149.93	142.75	137.06	132.50	128.79	125.74	123.22
10000	900.47	482.74	344.47	276.05	235.56	209.03	190.47	176.87	166.59	158.61	152.29	147.22	143.10	139.71	136.91
11000	990.52	531.02	378.91	303.65	259.11	229.93	209.51	194.56	183.25	174.47	167.52	161.94	157.40	153.68	150.60
12000	1080.57	579.29	413.36	331.25	282.67	250.83	228.56	212.24	199.90	190.32	182.75	176.66	171.71	167.65	164.29
13000	1170.61	627.57	447.81	358.86	306.22	271.73	247.60	229.93	216.56	206.19	197.98	191.38	186.02	181.62	177.98
14000	1260.66	675.84	482.25	386.46	329.78	292.64	266.65	247.62	233.22	222.05	213.20	206.10	200.33	195.59	191.67
15000	1350.71	724.11	516.70	414.07	353.33	313.54	285.70	265.31	249.88	237.90	228.43	220.83	214.64	209.56	205.36
16000	1440.76	772.39	551.14	441.67	376.89	334.44	304.74	282.99	266.53	253.77	243.66	235.55	228.95	223.53	219.05
17000	1530.80	820.66	585.59	469.27	400.44	355.34	323.79	300.68	283.19	269.63	258.89	250.27	243.26	237.50	232.74
18000	1620.85	868.94	620.04	496.88	424.00	376.25	342.83	318.37	299.85	285.48	274.12	264.99	257.57	251.47	246.43
19000	1710.90	917.21	654.48	524.48	447.55	397.15	361.88	336.05	316.51	301.35	289.35	279.71	271.88	265.44	260.12
20000	1800.94	965.48	688.93	552.09	471.11	418.05	380.92	353.74	333.17	317.20	304.58	294.43	286.19	279.41	273.81
21000	1890.99	1013.76	723.37	579.69	494.66	438.95	399.97	371.43	349.83	333.07	319.81	309.16	300.50	293.38	287.50
22000	1981.04	1062.03	757.82	607.29	518.22	459.86	419.02	389.11	366.48	348.93	335.03	323.88	314.80	307.35	301.19
23000	2071.08	1110.30	792.27	634.90	541.78	480.76	438.06	406.80	383.14	364.79	350.26	338.60	329.11	321.32	314.88
24000	2161.13	1158.58	826.71	662.50	565.33	501.66	457.11	424.49	399.80	380.64	365.49	353.32	343.42	335.30	328.57
25000	2251.18	1206.85	861.16	690.11	588.89	522.56	476.16	442.18	416.46	396.51	380.72	368.04	357.73	349.27	342.26
26000	2341.22	1255.13	895.61	717.71	612.44	543.46	495.20	459.86	433.12	412.37	395.95	382.76	372.04	363.24	355.95
27000	2431.27	1303.40	930.05	745.31	636.00	564.37	514.25	477.55	449.78	428.23	411.18	397.48	386.35	377.21	369.64
28000	2521.32	1351.67	964.50	772.92	659.55	585.27	533.30	495.24	466.44	444.09	426.41	412.21	400.66	391.18	383.33
29000	2611.36	1399.95	998.94	800.52	683.11	606.17	552.34	512.92	483.09	459.95	441.63	426.93	414.97	405.15	397.02
30000	2701.41	1448.22	1033.39	828.13	706.66	627.07	571.39	530.61	499.75	475.81	456.86	441.65	429.28	419.12	410.71
35000	3151.65	1689.59	1205.62	966.15	824.44	731.59	666.62	619.05	583.04	555.11	533.01	515.26	500.82	488.97	479.16
40000	3601.88	1930.96	1377.85	1104.17	942.21	836.10	761.85	707.48	666.34	634.41	609.15	588.86	572.37	558.82	547.61
45000	4052.11	2172.33	1550.08	1242.19	1059.99	940.61	857.08	795.92	749.63	713.71	685.29	662.47	643.91	628.68	616.06
50000	4502.35	2413.70	1722.31	1380.21	1177.77	1045.12	952.31	884.35	832.92	793.01	761.44	736.08	715.46	698.53	684.51

MONTHLY PAYMENT
REQUIRED TO AMORTIZE A LOAN 15%

TERM AMOUNT	35 YEARS	30 YEARS	28 YEARS	27 YEARS	26 YEARS	25 YEARS	24 YEARS	23 YEARS	22 YEARS	21 YEARS	20 YEARS	19 YEARS	18 YEARS	17 YEARS	16 YEARS
$100	1.23	1.23	1.24	1.24	1.25	1.25	1.26	1.26	1.27	1.28	1.29	1.30	1.31	1.33	1.35
200	2.45	2.46	2.47	2.48	2.49	2.50	2.51	2.52	2.54	2.55	2.57	2.60	2.62	2.66	2.70
300	3.67	3.69	3.71	3.72	3.73	3.74	3.76	3.78	3.80	3.83	3.86	3.89	3.93	3.98	4.04
400	4.89	4.92	4.94	4.96	4.97	4.99	5.01	5.04	5.07	5.10	5.14	5.19	5.24	5.31	5.39
500	6.11	6.15	6.18	6.19	6.21	6.24	6.26	6.29	6.33	6.37	6.42	6.48	6.55	6.64	6.73
600	7.33	7.38	7.41	7.43	7.45	7.48	7.51	7.55	7.60	7.65	7.71	7.78	7.86	7.96	8.08
700	8.55	8.61	8.64	8.67	8.70	8.73	8.77	8.81	8.86	8.92	8.99	9.07	9.17	9.29	9.42
800	9.77	9.83	9.88	9.91	9.94	9.97	10.02	10.07	10.13	10.19	10.28	10.37	10.48	10.61	10.77
900	10.99	11.06	11.11	11.14	11.18	11.22	11.27	11.33	11.39	11.47	11.56	11.67	11.79	11.94	12.12
1000	12.21	12.29	12.35	12.38	12.42	12.47	12.52	12.59	12.66	12.74	12.84	12.96	13.10	13.27	13.46
2000	24.41	24.58	24.69	24.76	24.84	24.93	25.04	25.16	25.31	25.48	25.68	25.92	26.20	26.53	26.92
3000	36.62	36.87	37.03	37.13	37.25	37.39	37.55	37.74	37.96	38.22	38.52	38.88	39.29	39.79	40.37
4000	48.82	49.15	49.37	49.51	49.67	49.85	50.07	50.32	50.61	50.95	51.36	51.83	52.39	53.05	53.83
5000	61.02	61.44	61.71	61.88	62.08	62.31	62.58	62.90	63.26	63.69	64.19	64.79	65.48	66.31	67.29
6000	73.23	73.73	74.06	74.26	74.50	74.77	75.10	75.47	75.91	76.43	77.03	77.74	78.58	79.57	80.74
7000	85.43	86.01	86.39	86.63	86.91	87.24	87.61	88.05	88.56	89.17	89.87	90.70	91.67	92.83	94.20
8000	97.63	98.30	98.74	99.01	99.33	99.70	100.13	100.63	101.22	101.90	102.71	103.65	104.77	106.09	107.66
9000	109.84	110.59	111.08	111.39	111.74	112.16	112.64	113.21	113.87	114.64	115.55	116.61	117.87	119.35	121.11
10000	122.04	122.87	123.42	123.76	124.16	124.62	125.16	125.79	126.52	127.38	128.38	129.57	130.96	132.61	134.57
11000	134.24	135.16	135.76	136.14	136.57	137.08	137.67	138.36	139.17	140.11	141.22	142.52	144.06	145.87	148.03
12000	146.45	147.45	148.10	148.51	148.99	149.54	150.19	150.94	151.82	152.85	154.06	155.48	157.15	159.13	161.48
13000	158.65	159.73	160.44	160.89	161.40	162.00	162.70	163.52	164.47	165.59	166.90	168.43	170.25	172.39	174.94
14000	170.86	172.02	172.78	173.26	173.82	174.47	175.22	176.10	177.12	178.33	179.73	181.39	183.34	185.65	188.39
15000	183.06	184.31	185.13	185.64	186.23	186.93	187.73	188.68	189.78	191.06	192.57	194.35	196.44	198.91	201.85
16000	195.26	196.59	197.47	198.01	198.65	199.39	200.25	201.25	202.43	203.80	205.41	207.30	209.53	212.17	215.31
17000	207.47	208.88	209.81	210.39	211.06	211.85	212.76	213.83	215.08	216.54	218.25	220.26	222.63	225.43	228.76
18000	219.67	221.17	222.15	222.76	223.48	224.31	225.28	226.41	227.73	229.27	231.09	233.22	235.73	238.69	242.22
19000	231.87	233.45	234.49	235.14	235.89	236.77	237.80	238.99	240.38	242.01	243.92	246.17	248.82	251.96	255.68
20000	244.08	245.74	246.83	247.52	248.31	249.23	250.31	251.57	253.03	254.75	256.76	259.13	261.92	265.22	269.13
21000	256.28	258.03	259.17	259.89	260.73	261.70	262.83	264.14	265.68	267.49	269.60	272.08	275.01	278.48	282.59
22000	268.48	270.31	271.52	272.27	273.14	274.16	275.34	276.72	278.34	280.22	282.44	285.04	288.11	291.74	296.05
23000	280.69	282.60	283.86	284.64	285.56	286.62	287.86	289.30	290.99	292.96	295.28	298.00	301.20	305.00	309.50
24000	292.89	294.89	296.20	297.02	297.97	299.08	300.37	301.88	303.64	305.70	308.11	310.95	314.30	318.26	322.96
25000	305.10	307.17	308.54	309.39	310.39	311.54	312.89	314.46	316.29	318.44	320.95	323.91	327.39	331.52	336.41
26000	317.30	319.46	320.88	321.77	322.80	324.00	325.40	327.03	328.94	331.17	333.79	336.86	340.49	344.78	349.87
27000	329.50	331.75	333.22	334.15	335.22	336.46	337.92	339.61	341.59	343.91	346.63	349.82	353.59	358.04	363.33
28000	341.71	344.03	345.56	346.52	347.63	348.93	350.43	352.19	354.24	356.65	359.46	362.78	366.68	371.30	376.78
29000	353.91	356.32	357.91	358.90	360.05	361.39	362.95	364.77	366.90	369.38	372.30	375.73	379.78	384.56	390.24
30000	366.11	368.61	370.25	371.27	372.46	373.85	375.46	377.35	379.55	382.12	385.14	388.69	392.87	397.82	403.70
35000	427.13	430.04	431.95	433.15	434.54	436.16	438.04	440.24	442.80	445.81	449.33	453.47	458.35	464.12	470.98
40000	488.15	491.47	493.66	495.03	496.62	498.46	500.62	503.13	506.06	509.49	513.52	518.25	523.83	530.43	538.26
45000	549.17	552.90	555.37	556.90	558.69	560.77	563.19	566.02	569.32	573.16	577.71	583.03	589.31	596.73	605.54
50000	610.19	614.34	617.08	618.78	620.77	623.08	625.77	628.91	632.57	636.87	641.90	647.81	654.78	663.03	672.82

Map of a section of land showing area and distances

A section of land contains 1 sq mile or 640 acres.

20 chains (80 rods)	20 chains (80 rods)	40 chains (160 rods)			
W.$\frac{1}{2}$, N.W.$\frac{1}{4}$ 80 acres	E.$\frac{1}{2}$, N.W.$\frac{1}{4}$ 80 acres	N.E. $\frac{1}{4}$ 160 acres			
1,320 ft	1,320 ft	2,640 ft			
N.W.$\frac{1}{4}$, S.W.$\frac{1}{4}$ 40 acres	N.E.$\frac{1}{4}$, S.W.$\frac{1}{4}$ 40 acres	N.$\frac{1}{2}$, N.W.$\frac{1}{4}$, S.E.$\frac{1}{4}$ 20 acres	W.$\frac{1}{2}$ N.E.$\frac{1}{4}$ S.E.$\frac{1}{4}$ 20 acres	E.$\frac{1}{2}$ N.E.$\frac{1}{4}$ S.E.$\frac{1}{4}$ 20 acres	
		S.$\frac{1}{2}$, N.W.$\frac{1}{4}$, S.E.$\frac{1}{4}$ 20 acres			
		20 chains	10 chains	10 chains	
S.W.$\frac{1}{4}$, S.W.$\frac{1}{4}$ 40 acres	S.E.$\frac{1}{4}$, S.W.$\frac{1}{4}$ 40 acres	N.W.$\frac{1}{4}$ S.W.$\frac{1}{4}$ S.E.$\frac{1}{4}$ 10 acres	N.E. $\frac{1}{4}$ S.W. $\frac{1}{4}$ S.E. $\frac{1}{4}$ 10 acres	5 acres	5 acres, 5 acre
				5 acres 1 furlong	5 chains, 20 r
		S.W.$\frac{1}{4}$ S.W.$\frac{1}{4}$ S.E.$\frac{1}{4}$ 10 acres	S.E.$\frac{1}{4}$ S.W.$\frac{1}{4}$ S.E.$\frac{1}{4}$ 10 acres	$2\frac{1}{2}$ acres $2\frac{1}{2}$ acres	10 acres m be divided into about
				$2\frac{1}{2}$ acres $2\frac{1}{2}$ acres	80 lots eac 30 X 125 f
80 rods	440 yards	660 ft	660 ft		

← —————————— 1 mile–320 rods–80 chains – 5,280 ft —————————— →

1 link is 7.92 in.

1 foot is 12 in.

1 yard is 3 ft or 36 in.

1 rod is $16\frac{1}{2}$ ft, $5\frac{1}{2}$ yds, or 25 links.

1 chain is 66 ft, 4 rods, or 100 links.

1 furlong is 660 ft or 40 rods.

1 mile is 8 furlongs, 320 rods, 80 chains, or 5,280 ft

1 square rod is $272\frac{1}{4}$ sq ft or $30\frac{1}{4}$ sq yd.

1 acre contains 43,560 sq ft.

1 acre contains 160 sq rods.

1 acre is about 8 X 20 rods, or any two numbers (of rods) whose product is 160.

1 acre may be divided into about 8 lots each 30 X 125 ft.

Widths times Depths Equaling 1 Acre

1 acre equals		1 acre equals		1 acre equals	
Length, ft.	Width, ft.	Length, ft.	Width, ft.	Length, ft.	Width, ft.
16.5	2,640	66	660	132	330
33	1,320	75	580.8	150	290.4
50	871.2	100	435.6	208.71	208.71

Price per Acre Produced by Certain Prices per Square Foot

Cents per sq. ft.	Dollars per acre	Cents per sq. ft.	Dollars per acre	Cents per sq. ft.	Dollars per acre	Cents per sq. ft.	Dollars per acre
1	435.60	9	3,920.40	30	13,068	70	30,492
2	871.20	10	4,356.00	35	15,246	75	32,670
3	1,306.80	12	5,227.20	40	17,424	80	34,848
4	1,742.40	14	6,098.40	45	19,602	85	37,026
5	2,178.00	16	6,969.60	50	21,780	90	39,204
6	2,613.60	18	7,840.80	55	23,958	95	41,382
7	3,049.20	20	8,712.00	60	26,136	100	43,560
8	3,484.80	25	10,890.00	65	28,314		

Computing Square Feet

Sq. ft.	Acres	Sq. ft.	Acres	Sq. ft.	Acres	Sq. ft.	Acres
1,742,400	40	217,800	5	26,136	0.6	3,049.2	0.07
1,306,800	30	174,240	4	21,780	0.5	2,613.6	0.06
871,200	20	130,680	3	17,424	0.4	2,178	0.05
435,600	10	87,120	2	13,068	0.3	1,742.4	0.04
392,040	9	43,560	1	8,712	0.2	1,306.8	0.03
348,480	8	39,204	0.9	4,356	0.1	871.2	0.02
304,920	7	34,848	0.8	3,920.4	0.09	435.6	0.01
261,360	6	30,492	0.7	3,484.8	0.08		

Days of the Year

January		February		March		May		June		July	
1	1	11	42	24	83	2	122	12	163	23	204
2	2	12	43	25	84	3	123	13	164	24	205
3	3	13	44	26	85	4	124	14	165	25	206
4	4	14	45	27	86	5	125	15	166	26	207
5	5	15	46	28	87	6	126	16	167	27	208
6	6	16	47	29	88	7	127	17	168	28	209
7	7	17	48	30	89	8	128	18	169	29	210
8	8	18	49	31	90	9	129	19	170	30	211
9	9	19	50	**April**		10	130	20	171	31	212
10	10	20	51	1	91	11	131	21	172	**August**	
11	11	21	52	2	92	12	132	22	173	1	213
12	12	22	53	3	93	13	133	23	174	2	214
13	13	23	54	4	94	14	134	24	175	3	215
14	14	24	55	5	95	15	135	25	176	4	216
15	15	25	56	6	96	16	136	26	177	5	217
16	16	26	57	7	97	17	137	27	178	6	218
17	17	27	58	8	98	18	138	28	179	7	219
18	18	28	59	9	99	19	139	29	180	8	220
19	19	**March**		10	100	20	140	30	181	9	221
20	20	1	60	11	101	21	141	**July**		10	222
21	21	2	61	12	102	22	142	1	182	11	223
22	22	3	62	13	103	23	143	2	183	12	224
23	23	4	63	14	104	24	144	3	184	13	225
24	24	5	64	15	105	25	145	4	185	14	226
25	25	6	65	16	106	26	146	5	186	15	227
26	26	7	66	17	107	27	147	6	187	16	228
27	27	8	67	18	108	28	148	7	188	17	229
28	28	9	68	19	109	29	149	8	189	18	230
29	29	10	69	20	110	30	150	9	190	19	231
30	30	11	70	21	111	31	151	10	191	20	232
31	31	12	71	22	112	**June**		11	192	21	233
February		13	72	23	113	1	152	12	193	22	234
1	32	14	73	24	114	2	153	13	194	23	235
2	33	15	74	25	115	3	154	14	195	24	236
3	34	16	75	26	116	4	155	15	196	25	237
4	35	17	76	27	117	5	156	16	197	26	238
5	36	18	77	28	118	6	157	17	198	27	239
6	37	19	78	29	119	7	158	18	199	28	240
7	38	20	79	30	120	8	159	19	200	29	241
8	39	21	80	**May**		9	160	20	201	30	242
9	40	22	81	1	121	10	161	21	202	31	243
10	41	23	82			11	162	22	203		

Days of the Year (Cont.)

September		September		October		November		November		December	
1	244	22	265	11	284	1	305	22	326	11	345
2	245	23	266	12	285	2	306	23	327	12	346
3	246	24	267	13	286	3	307	24	328	13	347
4	247	25	268	14	287	4	308	25	329	14	348
5	248	26	269	15	288	5	309	26	330	15	349
6	249	27	270	16	289	6	310	27	331	16	350
7	250	28	271	17	290	7	311	28	332	17	351
8	251	29	272	18	291	8	312	29	333	18	352
9	252	30	273	19	292	9	313	30	334	19	353
10	253			20	293	10	314			20	354
11	254	October		21	294	11	315	December		21	355
12	255	1	274	22	295	12	316	1	335	22	356
13	256	2	275	23	296	13	317	2	336	23	357
14	257	3	276	24	297	14	318	3	337	24	358
15	258	4	277	25	298	15	319	4	338	25	359
16	259	5	278	26	299	16	320	5	339	26	360
17	260	6	279	27	300	17	321	6	340	27	361
18	261	7	280	28	301	18	322	7	341	28	362
19	262	8	281	29	302	19	323	8	342	29	363
20	263	9	282	30	303	20	324	9	343	30	364
21	264	10	283	31	304	21	325	10	344	31	365

Leap years contain one additional day (February 29) above the standard 365-day year. When using the above chart during a leap year, February 29 becomes the sixtieth day of the year. Each date then following will require the addition of one day to determine its respective day of the year.

Income Converter

Hour	Day	Week	Month	Year
$ 2.00	$16.00	$ 80	$ 347	$ 4,160
2.20	17.60	88	379	4,576
2.40	19.20	96	416	4,992
2.50	20.00	100	433	5,200
2.60	20.80	104	451	5,408
2.80	22.40	112	485	5,824
3.00	24.00	120	520	6,240
3.20	25.60	128	555	6,656
3.40	27.20	136	589	7,072
3.50	28.00	140	607	7,280
3.60	28.80	144	624	7,488
3.80	30.40	152	659	7,904

Income Converter (Cont.)

Hour	Day	Week	Month	Year
4.00	32.00	160	693	8,320
4.20	33.60	168	728	8,736
4.40	35.20	176	763	9,152
4.50	36.00	180	780	9,360
4.60	36.80	184	797	9,568
4.80	38.40	192	832	9,984
5.00	40.00	200	867	10,400
5.20	41.60	208	901	10,816
5.40	43.20	216	936	11,232
5.50	44.00	220	953	11,440
5.60	44.80	224	971	11,648
5.80	46.60	232	1,005	12,064
6.00	48.00	240	1,040	12,480
6.20	49.60	248	1,075	12,896
6.40	51.20	256	1,109	13,312
6.50	52.00	260	1,127	13,520
6.60	52.80	264	1,144	13,728
6.80	54.40	272	1,179	14,144
7.00	56.00	280	1,213	14,560
7.20	57.60	288	1,248	14,976
7.40	59.20	296	1,283	15,392
7.50	60.00	300	1,300	15,600
7.60	60.80	304	1,317	15,808
7.80	62.40	312	1,352	16,224
8.00	64.00	320	1,387	16,640
8.20	65.60	328	1,421	17,056
8.40	67.20	336	1,456	17,472
8.50	68.00	340	1,473	17,680
8.60	68.80	344	1,491	17,888
8.80	70.40	352	1,525	18,304
9.00	72.00	360	1,560	18,720
9.20	73.60	368	1,595	19,136
9.40	75.20	376	1,629	19,552
9.50	76.00	380	1,647	19,760
9.60	76.80	384	1,668	19,968
9.80	78.40	392	1,699	20,364
10.00	80.00	400	1,733	20,800

Prorating Table for Rents, Taxes, and Insurance

No. of years, mos., and days	RENTS One month Days to month 30	RENTS One month Days to month 31	TAXES & INS. One year Mos.	TAXES & INS. One year Days	INSURANCE Three years Years	INSURANCE Three years Mos.	INSURANCE Three years Days	INSURANCE Five years Years	INSURANCE Five years Mos.	INSURANCE Five years Days	No. of years, mos., and days
1	0.0333	0.0323	0.0833	0.0028	0.3333	0.0278	0.0009	0.2000	0.0167	0.0006	1
2	0.0667	0.0645	0.1667	0.0056	0.6667	0.0556	0.0019	0.4000	0.0333	0.0011	2
3	0.1000	0.0968	0.2500	0.0083	1.0000	0.0833	0.0028	0.6000	0.0500	0.0017	3
4	0.1333	0.1290	0.3333	0.0111		0.1111	0.0037	0.8000	0.0667	0.0022	4
5	0.1667	0.1613	0.4167	0.0139		0.1389	0.0046	1.0000	0.0833	0.0028	5
6	0.2000	0.1935	0.5000	0.0167		0.1667	0.0056		0.1000	0.0033	6
7	0.2333	0.2258	0.5833	0.0194		0.1944	0.0065		0.1167	0.0039	7
8	0.2667	0.2581	0.6667	0.0222		0.2222	0.0074		0.1333	0.0044	8
9	0.3000	0.2903	0.7500	0.0250		0.2500	0.0083		0.1500	0.0050	9
10	0.3333	0.3226	0.8333	0.0278		0.2778	0.0093		0.1667	0.0056	10
11	0.3667	0.3548	0.9167	0.0306		0.3056	0.0102		0.1833	0.0061	11
12	0.4000	0.3871	1.0000	0.0333		0.3333	0.0111		0.2000	0.0067	12
13	0.4333	0.4194		0.0361			0.0120			0.0072	13
14	0.4667	0.4516		0.0389			0.0130			0.0078	14
15	0.5000	0.4839		0.0417			0.0139			0.0083	15
16	0.5333	0.5161		0.0444			0.0148			0.0089	16
17	0.5667	0.5484		0.0472			0.0157			0.0094	17
18	0.6000	0.5806		0.0500			0.0167			0.0100	18
19	0.6333	0.6129		0.0528			0.0176			0.0106	19
20	0.6667	0.6452		0.0556			0.0185			0.0111	20
21	0.7000	0.6774		0.0583			0.0194			0.0117	21
22	0.7333	0.7097		0.0611			0.0204			0.0122	22
23	0.7667	0.7419		0.0639			0.0213			0.0128	23
24	0.8000	0.7742		0.0667			0.0222			0.0133	24
25	0.8333	0.8065		0.0694			0.0231			0.0139	25
26	0.8667	0.8387		0.0722			0.0241			0.0144	26
27	0.9000	0.8710		0.0750			0.0250			0.0150	27
28	0.9333	0.9032		0.0778			0.0259			0.0156	28
29	0.9667	0.9355		0.0806			0.0269			0.0161	29
30	1.0000	0.9577		0.0833			0.0278			0.0167	30
31		1.0000									31

EXAMPLE
Rent $150 per month. To find the value of 24 days of a 31-day month:
From table: 24 days = 0.7742.   0.7742 × $150 = $116.13

EXAMPLE
Taxes = $1,000. To find the value of 8 months and 20 days:
From table: 8 months = 0.6667
              20 days   = 0.0556
              8 months, 20 days = 0.7223
              0.7223 × $1,000 = $722.30

EXAMPLE
3-year policy premium = $60. To find the value of 1 year, 6 months, 12 days:
From table: 1 year   0.3333
              6 months 0.1667
              12 days   0.0111
              1 year, 6 months, 12 days = 0.5111
              0.5111 × $60 = $30.66

EXAMPLE
5-year policy premium = $315. To find the value of 3 years, 6 months, 15 days:
From table: 3 years   0.6000
              6 months 0.1000
              15 days   0.0083
              3 years, 6 months, 15 days = 0.7083
              0.7083 × $315 = $223.11

Glossary

Before you attempt to negotiate the sale of your property, you should become familiar with certain real estate terminology.

The following list of definitions is not meant to be a definitive glossary; rather, it contains those terms which I feel will be most helpful to you. Some of the terms have a meaning other than the real estate definition, but I have for the most part provided only the real estate meaning. You do not necessarily have to be a seller to find this list useful.

Abstract of title. A history of the title to land, listing any conveyances and legal proceedings and including a description of the land and agreements set out to indicate the continuity of ownership.

Accretion. The adding of land by natural causes, such as when a river deposits soil on a location downstream.

Acre. A quantity of land consisting of 43,560 square feet or 160 square rods.

Ad valorem. According to value. An ad valorem property tax is a tax or duty based on the value of the property.

Adverse possession. The acquiring of title by possession. The occupancy of real estate in an open and notorious manner, to the exclusion of others, for a statutory period.

Air right. A right to use the space above the ground within vertical planes which correspond with the perimeter of the real estate described.

Allotment. A portion of land that has been divided into parts. A share or portion; that which is allotted; a division.

Amenity. A feature of real estate that the owner or occupant finds pleasant and desirable.

Amortization. The reduction of a debt by partial payments at stated times for a definite period, at the expiration of which the entire indebtedness will be extinguished.

Annuity. A sum of money paid yearly for life or a period of years.

Appraisal. A valuation or an estimation of the value of property.

Appreciation in value. An unearned increase in value, not including the added value created by additions or extensions.

Appurtenance. Something that is appended to a property or annexed to another thing, such as a barn, garden, or orchard. Employed in a lease to include any easements or servitudes used or enjoyed with the demised premises.

Assemblage. The act of collecting several parcels of land together under one ownership.

Assessed value. A value placed upon real property by governmental assessors for the purpose of assessing taxes.

Assessment. The valuation of property for taxation purposes. Also, the value so assigned. A nonrecurring charge levied against property to meet some specific purpose.

Assessor. An official chosen to appraise, value, or assess property.

Assets. Generally, any property which can be made available to pay debts.

Assignment. A transfer over to another of the interest in real estate or personal property.

Assumption of mortgage. The undertaking of a debt resting primarily upon another, as when the purchaser of real estate "assumes" a mortgage resting upon it, in which case he accepts the mortgage debt as his own and becomes liable for its payment.

Auction. A public sale of land or personalty, at public outcry, to the highest bidder.

Basis. The original cost of real estate plus the cost of added improvements made by the seller, less the depreciation taken by the seller.

Bill of sale. An agreement in writing by which one person assigns or transfers his right to, or interest in, personal property.

Blanket mortgage. A mortgage that contains more than one piece of real estate as security for the debt.

Book depreciation. The amount entered on the books of account to accommodate the retirement or replacement of an asset.

Broker. An agent employed, for a compensation, to negotiate and act as intermediary between a seller and buyer.

Building restrictions. Limitations on the use of land through covenants in a deed or legislation.

Built-in feature. Any feature attached to a house, such as appliances installed into kitchen cabinets.

Capital. Wealth acquired or held for profit or investment.

Carrying charges. The expenses necessary to hold property that is idle and not generating income, such as taxes or interest expense.

Chain of title. Successive conveyances from a starting point to the time the present holder of real property derives his title.

Chain store. A store that is part of a group of stores which are under the same ownership, with central management, and which follow a uniform procedure.

Chattel. An article of personal property; any property not amounting to real estate.

Chattel, personal. Movable things.

Chattel, real. Estates such as a leasehold estate, annexed to, or concerned with, real estate.

Closing statement. A recapitulation of the debits and credits for the buyer and seller in a real estate transaction for the financial conclusion of that transaction.

Commercial property. A building used as a hotel or used for stores, offices, or service businesses.

Commission. Reward or payment of an agent, factor, broker, or bailee when the payment is calculated as a percentage of the amount of his transaction.

Common property. Real estate owned jointly by several persons.

Compound interest. Interest upon interest. Compound interest is earned when the interest on a sum of money is added to the principal and then bears interest.

Condemnation. The process by which the property of a private owner is taken for public use without his consent, but upon the award of just compensation.

Condominium. A form of ownership of real property under which each unit is owned individually and each owner also receives an undivided interest in the land or other parts of the structure in common with other owners.

Consideration. The inducement to a contract. The price or impelling influence which motivates a contracting party to enter into a contract.

Construction loan. A loan to finance the improvement of real estate.

Contiguous. Neighboring; adjoining; near; touching.

Contingency. The possibility that an event may occur.

Contract. An agreement entered into by two or more parties by the terms of which one or more of the parties, for a consideration, undertakes to do or to refrain from doing something in accordance with the wishes of the other party.

Conveyance. An instrument in writing transferring the legal title to land or an interest in real estate.

Cooperative apartment. An apartment building owned by a corporation or trust; each individual owner purchases stock to the extent of the value of his apartment, title being evidenced by a proprietary lease.

Cost of reproduction. The present-day cost of exactly duplicating a building using similar materials.

Dedication. A gift of land given voluntarily by an owner for some public use and accepted for such use by or on behalf of the public.

Deed. A conveyance of realty; a written document signed by the grantor, whereby title to realty is transferred from one to another.

Default. Omission; neglect or failure of a party to take a step required by him in the progress of a cause, such as when a mortgagor fails to pay interest or principal on his mortgage when due.

Deferred maintenance. Repairs and rehabilitation yet to be done.

Deferred payments. Money payments to be made at some future time.

Demise. A conveyance of an estate to another for life, for a number of years, or at will.

Deposit. To commit to custody consideration placed in connection with an offer to purchase an interest in real estate.

Depreciation. A fall in value; a reduction of worth. Deterioration, or the loss of value, resulting from age, use, and obsolescence.

Devise. A gift of real property by last will and testament of the donor.

Documentary stamp. A revenue stamp issued for the payment of a tax on documents, such as deeds or wills.

Dower. A provision of the law which passes a portion of, or an interest in, the real estate of a deceased husband to his widow for life.

Easement. A right of the owner of one parcel of land, by reason of such ownership, to use the land of another for a special purpose not inconsistent with the other property owner's rights. A privilege which the owner of one parcel of land may have in the lands of another.

Encroachment. A fixture, such as a wall or fence, which illegally intrudes into or invades a street or another's property, diminishing its width or area.

Encumbrance. Any right to, or interest in, the real property of another which may diminish its value.

Endorsement. The signature on the back of a check, bill, note, or any other negotiable instrument that assigns and transfers property to another.

Equity. The remaining interest belonging to one who has pledged or mortgaged his property.

Erosion. The gradual eating away of the soil by the operation of currents or tides.

Escheat. The reversion of property to the state due to the lack of an heir.

Escrow. A deed which is conditionally held by a third party pending a condition.

Estate. The degree, quantity, nature, and extent of interest which a person has in real property.

Exchange. The mutual grant of equal interests in real property, the one in consideration of the other.

Exclusive listing. A contract with a real estate agency under which the owner will not sell property through any other agency.

Executor's deed. A deed given by an executor.

Existing mortgage. The present balance of an original mortgage amount.

Fair value. Present market value; a price agreed upon by buyer and seller.

Federal Deposit Insurance Corporation (FDIC). An agency of the federal government that insures deposits at commercial banks and savings banks.

Federal Housing Administration (FHA). An agency of the federal government that insures mortgage loans and administers other programs of housing assistance.

Federal Savings and Loan Insurance Corporation (FSLIC). An agency of the federal government that insures savers' accounts at savings and loan associations.

Fee simple absolute. An estate in which the owner is entitled to the entire property, with unconditional power of disposition during his life, and which descends to his heirs and legal representatives upon his death intestate (without having made a will).

Fiduciary. A person charged with the duty of acting for the benefit of another.

Fiduciary relationship. A relationship that exists whenever one person trusts and relies upon another.

First mortgage. A mortgage which has priority over all other mortgages.

Fixture. A chattel attached to realty usually in such manner that it cannot be independently moved without damage to itself or the house.

Forced sale. Usually, a sale at the direction of the court at public auction.

Foreclosure. A legal procedure under which all future rights existing in a mortgagor to redeem his estate are lost and his interest in the estate becomes the property of the mortgagee.

Front foot. A measure, 1 foot in length, of the width of lots applied at their frontage upon a street.

GI loan. A mortgage loan for which a veteran is eligible and which is insured by the Veterans Administration; a VA loan.

Grade. The degree of inclination of a hill, street, or other surface. Grading is the process of moving earth to effect the desired contour and drainage.

Grantee. One to whom a grant is made; one who receives a transfer of real property by deed.

Grantor. The person by whom a grant is made; one who transfers real property by deed.

Gross profit. Excess of price received over price paid for property before deductions are made for expenses or cost of operation.

Gross sales price. Total sales price received for property before deductions are made for expenses and other costs.

Guarantee. To agree to answer for the payments of another's debts or the performance of another's duty, liability, or obligation. Also, a contract for some particular thing to be done exactly as it is agreed to be done.

Highest and best use. The use of a site which will produce the maximum net land returns over a period of years; the optimum use for a site.

Hypothecate. To pledge property without delivering the possession of it to the pledgee; to pledge property as security for mortgage purposes.

Improvement on land. A structure built on a site, such as a house or a fence.

Improvements to land. Curbs, sidewalks, street lights, sewers, etc.

Income. The return, usually measured in money, from one's real estate, business, labor, or capital invested; gains or profits.

Industrial park. A controlled development, designed to accommodate specific types of industry and providing such amenities as public utilities, streets, railroad sidings, water, and sewer facilities.

Interest rate. The percentage of the principal sum of a loan charged for its use.

Joint tenancy. Tenancy in which two or more people share in the ownership of property with the right of survivorship.

Judgment. The official decision of a court of justice upon the rights and claims of the parties to an action or suit submitted to the court for a determination.

Land. Generally, any ground, soil, or earth whatsoever; minerals and trees are considered part of the land.

Land contract. Sometimes referred to as "contract for deed"; a contract given to a purchaser of real estate who pays a down payment when the contract is signed but who agrees to pay additional sums, at intervals and in amounts stated in the contract, until the total purchase price is paid and the seller gives a deed.

Lease. Any agreement which gives rise to a landlord-tenant relationship; a transfer of possession and the right to use property by a tenant for a specific period, during which the tenant pays rent to the owner.

Legal description. The identification of land according to a system set up by law or approved by law.

Lessee. One to whom a lease is made; one who possesses the right to occupy property under a lease.

Lessor. One who grants a lease; one who holds title to and conveys the right to use and occupy property under a lease agreement.

Lien. A charge or encumbrance upon property.

Listing. A record of property for sale by a real estate broker who has been authorized by the owner to sell. Also, the property so listed.

Mechanic's lien. A claim created by law for the purpose of securing priority of payment of the price or value of work performed and materials furnished in constructing or repairing a building.

Mortgage. A conditional conveyance of property contingent upon the failure of specific performance such as the payment of a debt; the instrument making such conveyance.

Mortgagee. One who takes or receives a mortgage; the source of the funds for a mortgage loan; the lender.

Mortgagor. One who, having all or some part of the title to property, by a written document, pledges that property for some specific purpose such as security for a debt; the borrower.

Net profit. What remains afer deducting all expenses and charges against gross profits.

Nonconforming use. A use permitted by zoning ordinances despite the fact that similar uses are not permitted in the area.

Note. A written document containing a promise by one party to pay to a specified person or bearer a definite sum of money at a specific time.

Option. A continuing contract granting one an exclusive right during a specific period of time, without creating any obligation to purchase, sell, or otherwise direct or contract the use of property, whether it be real estate or personal property.

Party wall. A wall dividing two separate properties to which the owners of the respective parcels have common usage rights.

Personalty. Property which can be moved—tables, chairs, refrigerators, etc. All property is personalty, realty, or a combination.

Plat (plot). A map, or representation on paper, of a piece of land subdivided into lots, with streets, alleys, etc., usually drawn to scale.

Point. A fee or charge expressed as a percentage of the principal sum of the loan. A point is 1 percent of the loan amount.

Prefabricated house (prefab). A house that is manufactured in a factory, and sometimes partly assembled, before delivery to the site.

Principal. The original amount of a loan payable at a certain time or times. Also, a party to a transaction, as opposed to an agent, middleman, or broker.

Prorate. To share, distribute, or divide proportionately; to apportion or assess on a pro rata basis.

Public Housing Administration. A unit of the U.S. Department of Housing and Urban Development which administers legislation providing for loans and subsidies to local housing authorities to encourage the creation of low-rental dwelling units. Now, the Housing Assistance Administration.

Purchase-money mortgage. A mortgage that is executed by the purchaser as a part of the purchase price.

Quitclaim deed. A deed of conveyance operating by way of release; intended to pass any title, interest, or claim which the grantor may have in the property, but not professing that such title is valid.

Realtor. A real estate broker who is an active member of a local board having membership in the National Association of Real Estate Boards.

Realty. A brief term for "real estate."

Rent. The income derived from property.

Rent schedule. A list of tenants' names by apartment number specifying the amount of rent to be paid each month and the term of the lease.

Riparian. Pertaining to the banks of a river, stream, waterway, etc.

Row houses. A series of individual dwelling units having architectural unity and a common wall between each unit.

Second mortgage. A mortgage which takes rank immediately after the first mortgage on the same property without any other indebtedness or lien intervening. The second mortgage is entitled to be paid out of the proceeds of the property next after the first mortgage.

Septic tank. An underground tank in which sewage from the house is reduced to liquid by bacterial action and drainage.

Setback. The distance a house or other structure must be set back from the street or property line in accordance with local zoning rules.

Site. A plot of ground suitable or set apart for some specific use; land made suitable for building purposes by dividing it into lots.

Special assessment. A charge against real estate by a public authority to help defray the cost of making public improvements from which the real estate site presumably benefits.

Sublease. An agreement conveying the right of use and occupancy of a property in which the original lessee becomes the lessor.

Survey. The process by which a parcel of land is measured and its contents ascertained with designated boundaries.

Tax. To enact or declare that a pecuniary contribution shall be made by the persons liable, for the support of government.

Tax abatement. A deduction or decrease in tax.

Taxable value. The total amount of base upon which taxes are computed under a predetermined tax rate.

Tax sale. A sale of property, usually at public auction, for nonpayment of taxes assessed against it.

Tenancy. The holding of real estate under a lease.

Term. A fixed period or prescribed amount of time.

Title. The means whereby the owner of real property has the just possession of his property; the elements which make up the verification of ownership.

Title company. A corporation organized for the purpose of insuring title to real estate.

Title guarantee policy. Title insurance furnished by the owner, provided as an alternative for an abstract of title. Sometimes called "Torrens certificate of title."

Topography. The contour of the land—its elevation and surface variations and the location of physical features.

Torrens certificate. A document, issued by the proper public authority, who is called a "registrar" and acts under the provisions of the Torrens Law, indicating the party in whom title resides. This system is not in effect in all states.

Trust deed. In some states, a trust deed or deed of trust is a security resembling a mortgage, being a conveyance of lands to trustees to secure the payment of a debt.

Trustee. One who holds title to property for the benefit of another.

Urban renewal. The controlled process of redevelopment within urban areas.

Value. The ability to command goods, including money; the utility of an object in satisfying the needs of human beings; purchasing power.

Warranty deed. A deed which contains a covenant of warranty; the title is guaranteed by the grantor.

Working drawing. A final blueprint in such detail as to be a guide to construction workmen in erecting a structure.

Zoning. The governmental regulation of land use, having to do with designs of buildings and with regulations prescribing the use to which buildings may be put.

Index